AF480640

THE GREAT AWAKENING

SELECTED SERMONS BY GEORGE WHITEFIELD

Compiled By Tom Flores

LIFE PUBLISHING HOUSE

George Whitefield The Great Awakening

George Whitefield (1714–1770) was one of the founders of Methodism and one of the most influential preachers of the eighteenth century. He played a major role in the spread of the First Great Awakening throughout Britain and the British North American colonies. Whitefield believed in preaching without notes so he could allow room for the Holy Spirit to guide his speaking. He became widely known for his dramatic and powerful preaching style that stirred thousands of listeners.

Whitefield studied at Oxford University, where he met Charles Wesley and John Wesley. The Wesley brothers were part of a group known as the "Holy Club," which Whitefield later joined and was greatly influenced by, eventually becoming its president. In 1738, Whitefield traveled to America for the first of seven trips across the Atlantic Ocean. During that first visit, he founded the Bethesda Orphan House near Savannah.

Throughout his life, Whitefield traveled extensively through New England, England, Scotland, and Wales, preaching to crowds that sometimes reached tens of thousands of people at a time. His ministry greatly influenced both the Great Awakening and the early Methodist movement. His voice became legendary. Without any amplification or microphones, Whitefield could reportedly be heard from nearly two miles away. Benjamin Franklin once attempted to calculate how many people could hear Whitefield preach and estimated that crowds of up to twenty thousand people could hear him clearly at one time. Many considered his voice almost supernatural because of its strength, clarity, and emotional power.

George Whitefield was born on December 16, 1714, in Gloucester, England. His father owned an inn called the Bell Inn, but after his father died, the family struggled financially. As a child, Whitefield showed a natural ability for speaking and drama. Those early communication skills later became one of the defining marks of his ministry.

Although Whitefield was deeply religious as a young man, he later testified that he did not truly understand salvation until he personally experienced conversion through faith in Jesus Christ. After reading *The Life of God in the Soul of Man* by Henry Scougal, Whitefield realized that Christianity was not merely outward religion or moral behavior. It was an inward transformation through the new birth. This message became the central focus of his preaching for the rest of his life.

At that time, many churches in England and the American colonies had become spiritually dry and formal. Religion had become routine for many people, and sermons often focused more on intellectual ideas than heartfelt repentance and salvation. Many attended church out of tradition, but few experienced a personal relationship with God.

Into this spiritual atmosphere came the First Great Awakening, a powerful revival movement that swept through England and the American colonies during the 1730s and 1740s. The revival emphasized personal conversion, repentance from sin, salvation through faith in Jesus Christ, and the necessity of being born again.

Whitefield quickly became one of the leading voices of the movement. Ordained into the Church of England in 1736, he soon began attracting massive crowds wherever he preached. Unlike many ministers of his day, Whitefield preached with passion, urgency, vivid imagery, and emotional intensity.

As churches began closing their pulpits to him because of the controversy surrounding his preaching, Whitefield took his message outdoors. He preached in open fields, parks, marketplaces, and public gathering places. Thousands gathered to hear him. In one well-known account, coal miners listening to his sermon wept openly, leaving clean streaks running down their coal-covered faces.

Whitefield's preaching tours throughout the American colonies became one of the driving forces behind the Great Awakening. People traveled long distances to hear him preach because of the powerful effect his sermons had on listeners.

Another major figure of the Great Awakening was Jonathan Edwards. Edwards preached powerful sermons about sin, judgment, and salvation, including his famous message *Sinners in the Hands of an Angry God*. While Edwards spoke with theological depth and seriousness, Whitefield stirred listeners through emotional and dramatic preaching. Together, these men became central leaders of the revival movement.

The Great Awakening produced strong emotional responses throughout the colonies. People openly confessed sins, wept during sermons, cried out for mercy, and testified to dramatic spiritual conversions. Prayer meetings, Bible studies, and evangelistic gatherings increased rapidly. Entire communities were affected by renewed spiritual interest.

One of the most important teachings of the revival was that salvation was personal. The movement challenged the belief that church membership or religious tradition alone could save a person. Revival preachers taught that every individual needed a genuine relationship with Christ and a transformed heart.

The Great Awakening also had a major impact on American society. For the first time, large numbers of people throughout the colonies shared a common spiritual experience that crossed denominational and regional lines. Historians believe the revival helped create a sense of unity among the colonies before the American Revolution.

The revival also influenced education and ministry training. Schools such as Princeton University and Brown University were connected to the movement and helped train future ministers and Christian leaders.

Not everyone supported the Great Awakening. Some ministers believed the emotional preaching had gone too far and accused revival leaders of creating disorder and fanaticism. Churches were often divided between supporters of the revival, known as "New Lights," and opponents called "Old Lights."

Whitefield's life also included serious flaws and controversy. Like many historical figures of his era, he supported slavery in Georgia, a painful and deeply criticized part of his legacy that cannot be ignored.

Despite declining health, Whitefield continued preaching tirelessly throughout his life. He often preached multiple times a day even while suffering from asthma and physical exhaustion. He famously declared, "I would rather wear out than rust out," a statement that reflected his passion for ministry.

On September 30, 1770, while still actively preaching in the American colonies, Whitefield died in Newburyport at the age of fifty-five.

The influence of George Whitefield and the First Great Awakening continued long after his death. The revival reshaped Christianity in England and America and helped lay the foundation for future revival movements and evangelical preaching. More than anything, the Great Awakening reminded a generation that Christianity was not merely tradition or ceremony, but a transformed life through a personal relationship with Jesus Christ.

Introduction

This book is a collection of sermons preached by George Whitefield during the Great Awakening between approximately 1738 and 1770. Whitefield is estimated to have preached more than 18,000 sermons during his lifetime to audiences throughout England, Scotland, Wales, and the American colonies. This book is a small collection of some of his most well-known and influential sermons. These sermons have been rewritten in easy-to-read modern English. The purpose is not to change what Whitefield preached, but to make his words easier for today's reader to understand. Because Whitefield preached in a style common to his time, his sermons often included long sentences, older words, and expressions that can be difficult for modern readers. In this edition, the language has been simplified while preserving the original message, biblical doctrine, and spiritual emphasis.

The purpose of this book is to preserve and share the powerful gospel preaching of George Whitefield with a new generation of readers. Many people have heard of Whitefield and the Great Awakening, yet few have taken the time to read his sermons because of the older style of language. This collection seeks to remove that barrier by presenting his messages in clear, understandable English while remaining faithful to what he originally preached. It is meant to help readers not only understand Whitefield's sermons, but also personally experience the biblical truths he proclaimed with such passion and urgency.

Whitefield's preaching was centered on Jesus Christ. He did not preach religion as outward duty alone. He preached the necessity of a changed heart. He warned against trusting in self-righteousness, religious formality, and empty profession. He called sinners to come to Christ by faith and urged believers to follow Him with sincerity, humility, and self-denial.

These sermons still speak because the needs of the human heart have not changed. People still need forgiveness, grace, the new birth, and a living faith in Christ as Savior, Lord, righteousness, strength, and hope. Whitefield's message was urgent because eternity was real to him. Heaven was real. Judgment was real. The cross was real. The love of Christ was real.

As you read these sermons, do not read them only as religious history. Read them as messages meant to search the heart. Let them challenge you, comfort you, awaken you, and draw you closer to Jesus Christ. Some sermons speak strongly about sin, judgment, and repentance. Others lift your eyes to the mercy of God, the beauty of Christ, and the hope of eternal life. Both are needed.

The goal of this collection is simple: to place these powerful gospel messages into the hands of modern readers in a form that is clear, faithful, and easy to follow. May these sermons stir your heart, strengthen your faith, and lead you to a deeper walk with God.

May the same Christ whom Whitefield preached be seen, loved, trusted, and followed today.

These sermons are based on public domain works by George Whitefield. The original sermon texts are in the public domain. This edition has been rewritten and adapted into easy to read modern English while seeking to preserve the original message, biblical doctrine, and spiritual emphasis.

Published by LIFE PUBLISHING HOUSE

Printed in the United States of America.

Contents

Chapter One

Walking With God

Genesis 5:24 *"And Enoch walked with God: and he was not; for God took him."*

There are many excuses people make for not obeying God. Some say His commands are too difficult. Others say His ways are not realistic in a world like ours. Some believe that living for God goes against human nature so strongly that it cannot truly be done. Deep down, they see God's commands as too demanding, as though He asks more from us than we are able to give.

But the Bible gives us a different picture. God has not only given us His commands, He has also given us examples of men and women who walked with Him by faith. They were not perfect people, but they were surrendered people. They lived in difficult times, faced real temptations, endured hardship, and still chose to follow God. Hebrews chapter 11 gives us a great cloud of witnesses, people who trusted God and obeyed Him even when it cost them something.

Among those faithful witnesses is a man named Enoch. We are not told a great deal about his life, but what we are told is powerful. The Bible says, **Genesis 5:24**, *"And Enoch walked with God: and he was not; for God took him."* That one sentence gives us both the story of his life and the testimony of his faith. Enoch walked with God, and then God took him. He did not die in the ordinary way. Hebrews tells us, **Hebrews 11:5**, *"By faith Enoch was translated that he should not see death; and was not found, because God had translated him."*

Before God took Enoch, the Bible says he had this testimony, that he pleased God. What a powerful thing to have said about a person's life. Not that he was famous. Not that he was wealthy. Not that he was admired by the world. The testimony of Enoch was that he pleased God. If, when our life is over, it can truly be said that we walked with God, then we will have no reason to feel that our life was wasted.

To walk with God means more than simply believing that God exists. It means living in fellowship with Him. It means walking in agreement with Him, depending on Him, obeying Him, and growing closer to Him day by day. Walking with God is not merely attending church, reading a verse, or saying a prayer from time to time. It is a life that is turned toward God. It is the direction of the heart, the surrender of the will, and the daily desire to please Him.

Before a person can truly walk with God, the ruling power of sin must be broken in the heart. The Bible teaches that the natural heart resists God. Apart from the work of the Holy Spirit, man does not naturally run toward God. He hides from Him. That is what happened in the garden of Eden. When Adam sinned, he did not come running to God with an open heart. He hid among the trees. When God questioned him, Adam shifted the blame. He said that the woman God had given him caused him to sin. In that moment, sin did not only break man's obedience. It broke his fellowship.

That same sinful nature has passed down through mankind. It is why people avoid prayer, resist correction, excuse sin, and struggle against the commands of God. The problem is deeper than behavior. The real problem is the heart. Before a person can walk with God, the Holy Spirit must deal with the heart. He must break the ruling power of sin and turn the soul toward God.

This does not mean the believer will never be tempted again. Even the apostle Paul spoke of the struggle within him. He said that when he desired to do good, evil was present with him. The difference is that sin no longer has to rule. The believer may struggle, but he is not a slave. The old nature may resist, but the Spirit of God gives power to obey. Walking with God begins when the power of sin is broken and the heart is made alive toward Him.

Walking with God also means being reconciled to God through Jesus Christ. Two people cannot walk together unless they are in agreement. The prophet Amos asked, **Amos 3:3**, *"Can two walk together, except they be agreed?"* Before we can walk with God, we must first be brought into peace with God. That peace does not come through human effort, religious activity, or good intentions. It comes only through Jesus Christ.

Jesus is our peace. Through His death on the cross and His resurrection from the dead, He made the way for sinners to be forgiven and brought back to the Father. When we place our faith in Christ, we are justified before God. The guilt of sin is removed. The separation is dealt with. The sinner becomes a child of God. Only then can the walk truly begin.

A person cannot walk with God while remaining separated from Him. Walking with God begins at the cross. It begins when we stop trusting ourselves and come to Jesus by faith. It begins when we receive the grace of God and are reconciled to Him.

Walking with God also means living in ongoing fellowship with Him. It is not a one-time religious experience. It is a daily relationship. The Holy Spirit does not come into the life of a believer like a visitor who stays for a short time and then leaves. He comes to dwell within us. He leads, teaches, corrects, strengthens, and comforts the people of God.

When the Bible says Enoch walked with God, it means he lived in steady fellowship with God. His life had a Godward direction. His heart was turned toward the Lord. He depended on God's strength, trusted God's promises, honored God's Word, and lived for God's glory. Walking with God means that our lives are no longer centered on ourselves. We begin to seek what pleases Him. We begin to care about His will. We begin to desire His presence more than the approval of people.

To walk with God also means to make progress in the spiritual life. Walking implies movement. A person who walks does not remain in the same place. He moves forward. In the same way, the Christian life is meant to grow. We are called to grow in grace, to become stronger in faith, deeper in love, and more like Christ in character.

Peter wrote, **2 Peter 3:18**, *"But grow in grace, and in the knowledge of our Lord and Saviour Jesus Christ."* A believer is fully a child of God from the moment he is born again, but that child is still called to mature. There are babes in Christ, young men in Christ, and fathers in Christ. This shows us that there are stages of growth in the life of faith.

No believer should be content to remain spiritually stagnant. God calls us forward. He calls us to deeper surrender, stronger obedience, greater faith, and closer fellowship. Walking with God means we are being shaped more and more into the image of Christ.

One of the primary ways we maintain our walk with God is through His Word. The Word of God is light for the path. The psalmist said, **Psalm 119:105**, *"Thy word is a lamp unto my feet, and a light unto my path."* If we want to walk with God, we must walk in the light of what He has spoken.

The Bible teaches us who God is. It reveals Jesus Christ to us. It corrects our thinking, exposes our sin, strengthens our faith, and guides our decisions. Without the Word of God, we are easily led by feelings, opinions, emotions, and deception. But when the Word is hidden in the heart, it becomes a lamp in dark places.

Even Jesus, when He was tempted by the devil, answered with the written Word. Again and again He said, "It is written." If the Son of God used the Scriptures as His weapon, how much more do we need them? The Word of God is called the sword of the Spirit. There is no weapon like it and no guide like it.

If we neglect the Bible, our walk with God will weaken. But when we read it, meditate on it, believe it, and obey it, our souls are strengthened. The Word becomes food for the heart. It becomes counsel for the mind. It becomes strength for the journey.

Another way we maintain our walk with God is through secret prayer. Prayer is the breath of the Christian life. Where there is spiritual life, there will be prayer. The same Spirit who gives new birth also teaches us to call upon God.

Secret prayer keeps the heart close to God. It is in the quiet place that burdens are poured out, strength is renewed, sins are confessed, and fellowship is deepened. Jesus said, **Matthew 26:41**, *"Watch and pray, that ye enter not into temptation."* Paul also wrote, **1 Thessalonians 5:17**, *"Pray without ceasing."*

This does not mean that we spend every moment on our knees. It means that our hearts remain in a prayerful posture before God. There should be set times when we get alone with Him, but there should also be prayers lifted throughout the day. Short prayers of faith, whispered in the middle of ordinary responsibilities, reach the heart of God.

Prayer lifts the soul toward God and brings the help of God into the soul. It keeps the fire alive. It strengthens us against temptation. It reminds us that we are not walking alone. If we desire to walk closely with God, we must be people of prayer.

Meditation is also necessary for a close walk with God. Meditation is when we slow down and think deeply about God, His Word, His promises, His works, His mercy, and especially the work of Christ. Reading brings truth into the mind, but meditation helps that truth settle into the heart.

David said, **Psalm 39:3**, *"While I was musing the fire burned."* There is something powerful that happens when the believer sits with the truth of God. The heart begins to warm again. Faith begins to rise. Love for God is stirred. Conviction becomes clearer. Gratitude becomes stronger.

Meditation is to the soul what digestion is to the body. It is not enough to receive truth quickly and move on. We must give the truth time to work within us. We must think on the goodness of God, the cross of Christ, the promises of Scripture, and the hope of glory. A hurried soul will struggle to walk closely with God. But a meditating soul learns to hear, receive, and respond.

Those who walk with God also learn to recognize His providence in their lives. God is not absent from the details. Jesus said that even the hairs of our head are numbered and that not even a sparrow falls to the ground apart from the Father's knowledge. If God sees the sparrow, then surely He sees His children.

Every season has something to teach us. Every blessing has a message. Every trial has a purpose. Every closed door, every open door, every delay, every correction, and every provision can become part of God's work in us. When affliction comes, God may be calling us to surrender an idol. When blessing comes, God may be calling us to give Him our heart more fully.

Walking with God means we do not see life as random. We learn to ask, "Lord, what are You teaching me? What are You showing me? Where are You leading me?" Faith pays attention to the hand of God. Faith watches for His direction. Faith trusts that even when we cannot see the whole picture, God is still working.

The believer must also learn to follow the leading of the Holy Spirit in agreement with the Word of God. Paul wrote, **Romans 8:14**, *"For as many as are led by the Spirit of God, they are the sons of God."* The children of God are led by the Spirit, but the Spirit will never lead contrary to Scripture.

This is important because some people claim to be led by the Spirit while ignoring the Word. That is dangerous. Others claim to honor the Word, but they live with no sensitivity to the Spirit. That is also dangerous. The believer must walk in both. We need the written Word of God, and we need the active leading of the Spirit of God.

Every impression, desire, direction, or thought must be tested by Scripture. If it agrees with the Word, we can prayerfully follow. If it contradicts the Word, we must reject it. The Holy Spirit and the holy Scriptures never disagree.

Walking with God also includes faithfulness to worship and the gathering of God's people. God never intended His people to walk alone. The ordinances of God, the preaching of the Word, prayer, communion, baptism, and the fellowship of believers are gifts to strengthen us.

David said, **Psalm 122:1**, *"I was glad when they said unto me, Let us go into the house of the Lord."* A person who walks with God will love the house of God, the worship of God, and the people of God. Gathering with believers is not just a religious habit. It is part of how God keeps our hearts alive.

We also maintain our walk with God by keeping company with others who are walking with Him. The people around us affect us more than we often realize. Fellowship can strengthen the soul, but the wrong company can pull the heart away from God.

The Bible says, **Proverbs 27:17**, *"Iron sharpeneth iron; so a man sharpeneth the countenance of his friend."* Godly friends sharpen us. They encourage us when we are weary. They correct us when we are drifting. They remind us of truth when our emotions are loud. It is hard to stay spiritually warm alone.

That is why Hebrews tells us not to forsake the assembling of ourselves together. **Hebrews 10:25** says, *"Not forsaking the assembling of ourselves together, as the manner of some is."* The Christian life was never meant to be lived in isolation. If we want to walk closely with God, we should walk with people who are also walking closely with Him.

Walking with God is one of the most honorable things a person can do. People often desire honor from the world. They want to be known, respected, included, and admired. But what honor could be greater than walking with the King of kings? What privilege could be higher than being called a friend of God?

Jesus said, **John 15:15**, *"Henceforth I call you not servants... but I have called you friends."* To be close to an earthly ruler may be considered a great honor, but to walk with God is far greater. The Lord shares His presence with those who fear Him. He allows His people to know His heart, receive His counsel, and enjoy His fellowship.

David understood this. He said he would rather be a doorkeeper in the house of God than dwell in the tents of wickedness. He knew that one moment in the presence of God was better than all the pleasures sin could offer.

Walking with God is not only honorable. It is also pleasant. The world often thinks that obedience to God is heavy, joyless, or restrictive. But those who truly walk with God know that His ways are full of peace. The Bible says, **Proverbs 3:17**, *"Her ways are ways of pleasantness, and all her paths are peace."*

There is a joy in God that sin can never provide. There is a sweetness in His Word, a peace in His presence, a comfort in prayer, and a freedom in obedience. The yoke of Christ is easy, and His burden is light. His service is not bondage. His service is true freedom.

This does not mean believers will never suffer. Those who walk with God may be misunderstood, rejected, tempted, afflicted, and spoken against. But even in suffering, God gives joy. Paul and Silas sang praises in prison. Stephen's face shone like the face of an angel while he was being persecuted. The early believers rejoiced that they were counted worthy to suffer for the name of Jesus.

The world may despise the people of God, but God comforts them. Afflictions may abound, but His consolations abound even more. Some of the sweetest moments with God are often found in the hardest seasons of life.

But the greatest reason to walk with God is this: there is heaven at the end of the walk. Enoch walked with God on earth, and then God took him. We may not be taken in the same way Enoch was. Most of us will face death in the ordinary way. But for those who walk with God, death is not the end. It is the doorway into His presence.

The spirit of the believer returns to God, and one day the body will be raised in glory. Those who walk with God now will dwell with God forever. They will see Christ. They will be made like Him. They will be free from sin, sorrow, temptation, pain, and death. They will be filled with joy in the presence of the Lord.

The path may be narrow, but it leads to life. The road may be difficult, but it ends in glory. If even a small taste of God's presence is precious now, what will the fullness of His presence be like then? If the firstfruits are glorious, what will the harvest be?

If you are not walking with God, the invitation is clear. Come to Him now. Do not continue walking in sin. Do not keep following the desires of the flesh, the pride of life, and the empty promises of this world. The way that seems right to man ends in death, but the way of Christ leads to life.

Turn from sin and come to Jesus. Be reconciled to God through His blood. Say farewell to the old way of life. Say farewell to the lust of the flesh, the lust of the eyes, and the pride of life. Say farewell to anything that keeps you from God. And say, "Welcome, Jesus. Welcome, Your Word. Welcome, Your Spirit. Welcome, Your people. From this day forward, I want to walk with God."

God receives the humble and contrite heart. He will not reject the one who comes to Him through Jesus Christ. The blood of Jesus is able to cleanse every sin, break every chain, and bring the sinner into fellowship with God.

And to those who already belong to Christ, the call is to walk closer. Do not follow Jesus from a distance. Do not become cold, careless, formal, or indifferent. Do not neglect prayer. Do not neglect the Word. Do not forsake the gathering of believers. Do not lose your first love.

Think often of the love of Jesus. Let His love draw you nearer. The closer you walk with God, the more you will enjoy His presence. The more you enjoy His presence, the more prepared you will be for eternity.

Walk with Him in His Word. Walk with Him in prayer. Walk with Him in obedience. Walk with Him in worship. Walk with Him in fellowship. Walk with Him through trials. Walk with Him when life is joyful, and walk with Him when life is painful. Keep walking with Him until your earthly journey is finished.

And when your walk on earth is over, you will be with Him forever.

To God the Father, to the Lord Jesus Christ, and to the eternal Spirit be all honor and glory, now and forever.

Amen.

Chapter Two

The Lord Our Righteousness

Jeremiah 23:6 NKJV "Now this is His name by which He will be called: THE LORD OUR RIGHTEOUSNESS."

Anyone who understands human nature, or who honestly knows his own heart, must admit that self-righteousness is one of the hardest idols to remove. Because we are born with a works-based way of thinking, we naturally try to approach God by our own efforts. We want to believe that we have done something to earn God's favor. Even if we do not say it plainly, something in fallen man wants at least part of the credit for salvation.

We may speak against false religion, pride, and man-made righteousness, and we should. But by nature, all of us are tempted to trust in ourselves. We may be ashamed to say that we deserve anything from God, but we still try to establish a righteousness of our own. Like the Pharisees, we struggle to fully submit to the righteousness that comes from God through Jesus Christ.

This is one of the greatest and most common spiritual dangers. It is especially dangerous when the doctrine of Christ's complete righteousness is rarely preached or only lightly mentioned. When people stop hearing that Jesus Christ is the sinner's only righteousness, their love often grows cold. The truth that Christ is our righteousness is not a small doctrine. It is central to the gospel.

The righteousness of Jesus Christ is one of the great mysteries angels desire to look into. It was one of the first gospel lessons God taught after the fall. When Adam and Eve sinned, they tried to cover themselves with fig leaves. But God made them coats of skin. Those coats pointed forward to the covering sinners need through the righteousness of Christ. The animals were likely slain in sacrifice, pointing to the greater sacrifice that would one day be made by the Lamb of God.

This is also what Scripture means when it says Abraham believed God, and it was accounted to him for righteousness. Abraham was not accepted because of his own goodness. He was accepted because he believed God, and righteousness was counted to him. This truth is found throughout the law and the prophets, and Jeremiah says it clearly in this great name: "The Lord our righteousness."

The Lord spoken of in this verse is Jesus Christ. Jeremiah says that God would raise up to David a righteous Branch, a King who would reign and prosper and execute judgment and righteousness in the earth. In His days Judah would be saved and Israel would dwell safely. Then Jeremiah says this King would be called "The Lord our righteousness."

This righteous Branch is Christ. He is the Lord. The word translated "Lord" is the covenant name of God. This means Jesus is not merely a good man, a prophet, or a created being. He is truly God. He is Jehovah. He is very God of very God. He is worthy of the same honor as the Father.

Those who deny the divinity of Christ should seriously consider this. If Jesus is called the Lord, and if the name Lord belongs to God Himself, then Christ must be divine. If Christ were only a man, then trusting Him for salvation would be trusting in human strength. But Scripture says cursed is the man who trusts in man and makes flesh his strength. Christ is not merely an arm of flesh. He is God blessed forever.

So when Jeremiah says, "The Lord our righteousness," he is speaking of Jesus Christ, the eternal Son of God, who became man for our salvation.

Now we must ask: How is the Lord our righteousness?

The answer is by imputation. That means Christ's righteousness is counted to the believer. It is credited to us, not because we earned it, but because God gives it to us through faith.

God made man in His image. In the beginning, God made a covenant with man. If man had obeyed perfectly, he would have lived. But Adam and Eve broke that covenant by sinning against God. Once they sinned, they needed a righteousness better than their own. They were still responsible to obey God perfectly, but now they were guilty and without strength. They not only owed perfect obedience from that moment forward, but they also owed satisfaction for the sin they had already committed.

This is where the love of God is displayed. What man could not do, Jesus Christ came to do for him. Though He was in the form of God, He took the form of a servant and became man. In our human nature, He obeyed the law perfectly. He fulfilled every command of God. Then He died on the cross and bore the curse for those the Father had given Him.

As man, Christ obeyed and suffered. As God, His obedience and suffering had infinite worth. Being God and man in one Person, He worked out a full, perfect, and sufficient righteousness for His people.

When we speak of the righteousness of Christ, we must include both His active obedience and His passive obedience. His active obedience refers to His perfect life. He obeyed the law of God completely. His passive obedience refers to His suffering and death on the cross. He bore the punishment sinners deserved.

Many people speak only of Christ's death, but His life of obedience is also necessary. We need more than forgiveness. We need righteousness. Christ did not only die for sinners. He also lived for sinners. He obeyed in our place and suffered in our place. Together, His life and death make up the complete righteousness that is counted to the believer.

This is what Paul means in Romans 5 when he compares Adam and Christ. Adam's disobedience was counted to us, and through Adam sin and death came upon the human race. But Christ, the second Adam, obeyed perfectly, and His righteousness is counted to those who believe in Him. This is what it means that we are made the righteousness of God in Him.

This is also why Jeremiah later says that the church herself will be called "The Lord our righteousness." The righteousness of Christ is counted to His people. They stand before God, not in their own merit, but in the righteousness of their Savior.

Many people object to this doctrine because the proud human heart does not like it. One common objection is that the doctrine of imputed righteousness will destroy good works and lead people to live carelessly. People say, "If you tell sinners they are justified by Christ's righteousness alone, they will think they can live however they want."

But this is a false accusation. The doctrine of Christ's righteousness does not destroy good works. It puts good works in their proper place. Good works are not the cause of our justification before God. They are the evidence that we have truly been justified. They do not earn our acceptance with God, but they show that grace has changed our hearts.

The doctrine may be abused by those who only talk about grace but never truly experience it. Some may speak of justification by faith and Christ's righteousness while continuing in sin. But that does not make the doctrine false. It only proves that they do not truly know the power of it. Every doctrine of grace can be abused by corrupt hearts, but the abuse of truth does not make truth dangerous.

Paul faced this same objection in Romans. Some accused the gospel of grace of encouraging sin. But Paul answered strongly, "Certainly not!" No one who has truly received Christ's righteousness will use it as an excuse to live in rebellion. The same grace that justifies also sanctifies. The same Christ who is our righteousness also becomes our holiness.

Another objection is that Jesus did not preach this doctrine, and that in the Sermon on the Mount He only taught morality. But this misunderstands the Sermon on the Mount. Jesus did teach holiness, morality, and obedience. Every faithful minister should do the same. But before Jesus spoke of outward obedience, He spoke of inward spiritual condition. He spoke of being poor in spirit, meek, pure in heart, merciful, and hungering and thirsting for righteousness.

Then He said, **Matthew 5:16 NKJV**, *"Let your light so shine before men, that they may see your good works and glorify your Father in heaven."* Good works are the light shining outwardly from a changed heart. They are evidence of grace, not the root of justification.

Jesus also said He did not come to destroy the Law, but to fulfill it. He fulfilled the Law in its deepest and fullest sense. He showed that the Law reaches not only outward actions, but also inward thoughts and desires. This only proves how much we need His righteousness. If the Law demands purity of heart as well as outward obedience, then none of us can stand before God in our own righteousness.

Another objection comes from the story of the rich young ruler. He came running to Jesus and asked, "Good Teacher, what shall I do that I may inherit eternal life?" Jesus pointed him to the commandments. Some say this proves that works are part of the cause of justification.

But Jesus was not teaching the young man that he could earn eternal life by keeping the commandments. He was using the Law to expose the young man's need. The young man thought he had kept the commandments from his youth. But if he had truly understood the Law, he would have known that he had broken it. Even if he had not committed adultery outwardly, had he never lusted in his heart? Even if he had not murdered, had he never been angry without cause? Even one sin makes a person guilty before God.

Jesus was showing him that he needed a righteousness greater than his own. The Law was meant to be his tutor, leading him to Christ. The young man went away sorrowful because he still trusted in himself and loved his possessions too much. His story does not disprove the need for Christ's righteousness. It proves it.

Some also point to Matthew 25, where Jesus speaks of the final judgment and says to the righteous that they fed the hungry, gave drink to the thirsty, welcomed the stranger, clothed the naked, visited the sick, and came to those in prison. Some say this proves people are saved by their works.

But that is not what the passage teaches. Good works follow justification as fruit follows the root. They are rewarded by grace, not because they earn salvation, but because they show real faith. When Jesus mentions their works, He is pointing to the evidence of their love for Him.

Notice that the righteous are surprised. They ask, "Lord, when did we see You hungry and feed You, or thirsty and give You drink?" This is not the language of people trusting in their own works. They are not boasting. They are humbled that the Lord would even mention their acts of love.

On the other hand, those who are condemned are condemned for their lack of love and obedience. God may justly condemn a person for failing to do what His Law requires. But that does not mean anyone earns heaven by doing good works. Even the holiest believer must confess, "We are unprofitable servants." Our works cannot justify us before God. Christ alone can.

If we deny the doctrine of Christ's imputed righteousness, serious consequences follow. First, we undermine the teaching of Scripture. The Bible says we are saved by grace, not by works, lest anyone should boast. It says salvation is the gift of God. It says the one who glories must glory in the Lord. But if any part of my acceptance with God depends on my own works, then I have something to boast in. That would contradict the gospel.

The doctrine of imputed righteousness is not a small part of Scripture. It is at the heart of the whole Bible. If we deny it, we may as well deny divine revelation itself. Christ our righteousness is the beginning and end of the gospel.

Second, if we deny this doctrine, we fall into a form of man-made religion. If someone told us we must ask saints to intercede for us because Christ's intercession is not enough, we would rightly reject it. If someone told us that Christ's death is not enough unless our death is added to it, we would reject that too. Why then would we say that Christ's obedience is not enough unless our obedience is added to it?

If it is wrong to add the intercession of saints to Christ's intercession, and wrong to add our suffering to Christ's suffering, then it is also wrong to add our righteousness to Christ's righteousness as the ground of our acceptance with God. Christ is sufficient. His obedience is sufficient. His death is sufficient. His righteousness is sufficient.

Third, if we deny this doctrine, we put ourselves in great danger. If there were no such thing as imputed righteousness, those who trust in Christ and bring forth fruit in holiness would still be safe. But if there is such a thing, and there certainly is, what will become of those who deny it and stand before God in their own works? Their works will be weighed in the balance and found wanting. Outside of Christ, God will be a consuming fire.

It is far safer to appear before God in the righteousness of Christ than to lean on the broken reed of our own righteousness. Why stand on something that cannot hold you when the Rock of Ages is offered to you?

Now we must bring this truth close to the heart. It is not enough to understand the doctrine in the mind. Can you truly say, "The Lord our righteousness"? Can you say He is your righteousness? To know the words without receiving Christ by living faith will only increase your guilt. An unapplied Christ is no Christ to you.

Can you say with Thomas, "My Lord and my God"? Is Christ your sanctification as well as your righteousness? For the Lord never separates justification from sanctification. If you are justified by His blood, you are also being sanctified by His Spirit. God never gives Christ as righteousness to a person while leaving that person unchanged in sin.

Have you ever been brought to see and hate your sin? Have you ever been made to see that even your own righteousness is like filthy rags? Have you ever seen the all-sufficiency of Christ's righteousness and hungered and thirsted for it? Has your heart ever cried, "Give me Christ, and I am satisfied. Nothing but Christ. Nothing but the righteousness of Christ can save me"?

Have you ever reached out by faith and embraced Jesus as your Savior? Have you ever been able to say, "My beloved is mine, and I am His"? If so, take comfort. The Lord Jesus Christ, the everlasting God, is your righteousness. If Christ has justified you, who can condemn you? Christ died for you, rose again, and ever lives to make intercession for you.

Being justified by grace, you have peace with God. One day you will be with Jesus in glory and enjoy the everlasting fruit of His salvation in body and soul. There is no condemnation for those who are truly in Christ Jesus.

If the Lord is your righteousness, speak often of His righteousness. Talk of it when you lie down and when you rise up, when you go out and when you come in. Recommend the righteousness of Christ to others. Let your life show that you are waiting for your Lord from heaven.

Be holy, because the One who called you and washed you in His blood is holy. Do not let the righteousness of Christ be spoken evil of because of your life. Do not wound Jesus in the house of His friends. Grow in grace and in the knowledge of the Lord Jesus Christ.

Think often of His dying love. Let that love constrain you to obedience. Since you have been forgiven much, love much. Ask continually, "What can I do to show gratitude to the Lord for giving me His righteousness?" And let this humble question remain in your heart: "Why me, Lord? Why was I chosen? Why was I shown mercy? Why has the Lord become my righteousness when I deserved condemnation?"

Now let the invitation go out to every person who does not yet know Christ. Many precious souls are always standing on the edge of eternity. If God required your soul today, could you honestly say, "The Lord is my righteousness"?

Do you think you can stand in the day of judgment without Christ's righteousness? You cannot. Christ's righteousness is the wedding garment you must wear. If death finds you spiritually naked, where will you hide? Your own righteousness will be like the fig leaves Adam used, unable to cover your shame before God.

Think of death. Think of judgment. Soon time will be no more. What will become of you if the Lord is not your righteousness? If you do not belong to Christ, Christ Himself will pronounce judgment. Can you bear the thought of hearing Jesus say, **Matthew 25:41 NKJV**, *"Depart from Me, you cursed, into the everlasting fire prepared for the devil and his angels"*?

Can you bear eternal separation from Christ? Ask those believers who have ever felt the sorrow of God's felt presence being withdrawn for a short time. Ask them how painful it is to walk in darkness and feel far from the Lord. If losing the comfort of Christ's presence for a short season is so painful, what must it be to be banished from Him forever?

If Christ is not your righteousness, God's justice must still be satisfied. Either Christ's righteousness must be counted to you now, or you must bear the punishment of sin yourself forever. Knowing the terror of the Lord, I urge you to come to Christ and do not rest until you can say, "The Lord our righteousness."

Ask God to give you faith. If He gives you faith, you will receive Christ, His righteousness, and all His benefits. Do not be afraid because your sins are many. Are you a sinner? So am I. Are you the chief of sinners? So am I. Are you a backslider? So am I. Yet by rich, free, sovereign grace, the Lord is my righteousness.

Young men, come home to Christ. Do not keep playing the prodigal. Do not keep wandering far from your Father's house. Leave the pigpen of sin. Stop feeding on the husks of sensual pleasure. Arise and come home. The Father calls you. The best robe is ready, even the righteousness of His dear Son. See how costly that robe was. It was purchased by the blood of Christ. Without it, you are lost and undone forever. Come home, guilty prodigals. Heaven will rejoice, and so will the people of God.

Young women, consider your souls. Many are careful to adorn the body, but what about the soul? Can you say, "The Lord is my righteousness"? Have you sought the robe of Christ's righteousness, without which outward beauty is nothing before God? Do not forget your greatest ornament. Seek the Lord as your righteousness, or earthly beauty will soon fade and judgment will come.

Those in the middle years of life, busy with business, work, money, family, and responsibility, consider this carefully. What profit is all your labor if you do not have Christ? What good are all your gains if you miss the one thing needful? Stop laboring only for the food that perishes. Seek the righteousness that leads to everlasting life.

Older sinners, do not delay. Your gray hairs should be a crown of wisdom, but if you do not know Christ, they stand as a warning. You are close to eternity. Your life is nearly spent. Your sun is going down. If the Lord is not your righteousness, it will set in eternal darkness. But do not despair. With God all things are possible. Even at the eleventh hour, Christ will not cast out the one who comes to Him. Ask Him to teach you what it means to be born again, even when you are old.

And children, come to Christ. You are not too young to be converted. Jesus loved little children and said that of such is the kingdom of heaven. Some children younger than you have known the Lord as their righteousness. Do not wait for your parents if they will not come. You come to Christ. Perhaps your faith may even lead them. Jesus is willing to receive young hearts. May God make you willing early to take the Lord as your righteousness.

And to the poor, the forgotten, and those society may look down upon, Christ died for you too. In Jesus Christ there is neither male nor female, slave nor free, rich nor poor. Every person who believes in Him may become a child of God. The Ethiopian eunuch believed and was saved. The same Christ who saved him can save you. Believe in Jesus, and you shall be saved. He is the same yesterday, today, and forever. He can wash you in His blood and clothe you in His righteousness.

So turn this text into a prayer. Say, "Lord, be my righteousness." Come, Lord Jesus, come quickly into our souls. Be our righteousness, our salvation, our sanctification, and our eternal hope.

Amen.

Chapter Three

The Power of Christ's Resurrection

Philippians 3:10 NKJV *"That I may know Him and the power of His resurrection."*

In the verses before this text, the apostle Paul warned the Philippians to beware of false teachers who were trying to turn them away from the simplicity of the gospel. These teachers insisted that Christians still needed to keep circumcision and the ordinances of Moses. Paul did not speak against them because he was ignorant of the Jewish religion. He knew it very well. If anyone could have trusted in outward religious privileges, Paul could have trusted in them more.

He said that he was circumcised the eighth day. He was of the stock of Israel, not a Gentile convert, but a natural Israelite. He was of the tribe of Benjamin, the tribe that remained with Judah when others turned away. He was a Hebrew of the Hebrews, a Jew on both his father's and mother's side. Concerning the law, he was a Pharisee, which was the strictest sect among the Jews.

Paul was not careless in religion. His zeal, though misguided at the time, was so strong that he persecuted the church of Christ. Concerning the righteousness of the law, as the Pharisees understood it, he was blameless. He had kept it from his youth.

But when it pleased God, who had separated him from his mother's womb, to reveal His Son in him, everything changed. Paul said in **Philippians 3:7 NKJV**, *"But what things were gain to me, these I have counted loss for Christ."* The very privileges he once boasted in and depended on for righteousness, he now counted as loss.

And Paul did not regret that decision. He was more convinced of it than ever. He said in **Philippians 3:8 NKJV**, *"Yet indeed I also count all things loss for the excellence of the knowledge of Christ Jesus my Lord."* He had proven the sincerity of these words because he had suffered the loss of all things for Christ. Yet he was still willing to lose more. He counted all things as rubbish, so that he might gain Christ and be found in Him.

Paul did not want to stand before God with his own righteousness, which came from the law. He did not want to depend on being a child of Abraham, or on any works of righteousness he had done, either to atone for his sins or to balance out his evil deeds. He wanted the righteousness that comes through faith in Christ, the righteousness of God by faith. This righteousness is appointed by God and imputed to the believer.

Then Paul says that his great desire was **Philippians 3:10 NKJV**, *"That I may know Him and the power of His resurrection."* He wanted to know Christ, not merely by information, but by experience. He wanted to know the power and effectiveness of Christ's resurrection by feeling the influence of His blessed Spirit upon his soul.

These words imply two important truths. First, Jesus Christ truly rose from the dead. Second, it deeply concerns us to know the power of His resurrection.

First, Christ is truly risen from the dead.

It was absolutely necessary that Jesus rise from the dead.

First, it was necessary on His own account. Jesus had often appealed to His resurrection as the final and most convincing proof that He was the Messiah. He said in **Matthew 12:39 NKJV**, *"No sign will be given to it except the sign of the prophet Jonah."* He also said in **John 2:19 NKJV**, *"Destroy this temple, and in three days I will raise it up."*

His enemies remembered these words. They used them as a reason to ask Pilate for a guard at the tomb, so that His body would not be stolen. They said in **Matthew 27:63 NKJV**, *"Sir, we remember, while He was still alive, how that deceiver said, 'After three days I will rise.'"* If Jesus had not risen, they could have rightly said that He was an impostor. His own claim would have failed.

Second, it was necessary for our sake. Paul says in **Romans 4:25 NKJV**, *"Who was delivered up because of our offenses, and was raised because of our justification."* Christ rose again so that we might be assured that the debt we owed God for our sins had been fully paid.

God the Father, forever praised for His infinite love and free grace, was pleased to wound His only Son for our transgressions. Jesus was arrested, condemned, crucified, and laid in the prison of the grave as our Surety. He bore the guilt we had earned by breaking God's commandments.

If Christ had remained forever in the grave, we would have had no assurance that our sins had been fully satisfied for. A debtor cannot be sure the debt is settled while his surety remains in prison. But because Christ was released from the power of death, we are assured that God was pleased with His sacrifice, that the atonement was finished on the cross, and that He made a full, perfect, and sufficient sacrifice, offering, and satisfaction for the sins of the world.

Third, it was necessary that Jesus rise from the dead to assure us of the future resurrection of our own bodies.

The Gentile world largely rejected the doctrine of the resurrection. When Paul preached Jesus and the resurrection in Athens, some mocked him and called him a babbler and a preacher of strange things. Many Jews believed in the resurrection, but not all. The Sadducees denied it altogether.

But the resurrection of Jesus Christ puts this truth beyond dispute. He acted as our representative. If our Head is risen, then we who are His members must rise also. As in the first Adam all die, so in Christ, the second Adam, all will be made alive in this sense.

It was necessary for Christ to rise, and it is also clear beyond contradiction that He did rise.

No historical fact has been better witnessed. Every precaution was taken to prevent deception. Jesus was buried in a tomb cut out of rock, so no one could dig underneath and carry Him away. It was a new tomb, where no one had ever been laid before, so if anyone rose from that tomb, it had to be Jesus of Nazareth. The tomb was sealed.

A great stone was rolled in front of it. A guard of soldiers, not His friends but His enemies, was placed there to watch it.

The idea that the disciples came by night and stole His body is unreasonable. Not long before, they had all forsaken Him. They were slow to believe in His resurrection themselves. And even if the soldiers had fallen asleep, they would have had to be in a very deep sleep not to wake up while such a large stone was being rolled away.

After His resurrection, Jesus appeared many times and in many ways to His disciples. He appeared to them when they were gathered together. He appeared to two disciples on the road to Emmaus. He appeared to them while they were fishing. He showed them His hands and His feet. He even appeared to more than five hundred believers at one time. All of this places the truth of His resurrection beyond doubt.

Someone may object that the books recording these facts were written by His disciples. But who was better qualified to write them than those who were eyewitnesses and who ate and drank with Him after His resurrection?

Some may say they were uneducated and ordinary men. But that made them no less able to testify to a plain fact. In fact, it made them less likely to invent a clever lie. They sealed their testimony with their own lives. Men may sometimes lie to gain advantage, as Jacob once lied to receive his father's blessing. But it has never been known that a whole group of men would willingly die as martyrs for something they knew was false, especially when they gained no earthly advantage from it.

This proves that they were true Israelites, in whom there was no deceit. The success God gave to their ministry afterward confirms it even more. Three thousand people were converted through one sermon. Twelve poor fishermen were made more than conquerors over all the opposition of men and devils. This was as clear a demonstration that Christ was risen as the falling walls of Jericho were a demonstration of divine power.

But what need do we have of more witnesses? Do you believe the resurrection of our blessed Lord? I believe you do. Your gathering on the first day of the week in the Lord's house testifies to it.

But the more important question is this: Have you experimentally known the power of His resurrection? Have you received the Holy Spirit? Have you, by His powerful work in your heart, been raised from the death of sin to a life of righteousness and true holiness?

This is what Paul most desired to know. He already believed that Christ's body had risen. But he knew that Christ's bodily resurrection would not profit him unless he experienced its power in the raising of his own dead soul.

One great purpose of Christ's resurrection was that He might enter heaven as our representative and send down the Holy Spirit to apply to our hearts the redemption He finished on the cross. He applies that redemption by working a complete change within us.

Without this inward work, Christ would have died in vain for us. It would not benefit us to have His outward righteousness imputed to us if no inward righteousness were worked in us. Because we are conceived and born in sin, we are unfit for communion with an infinitely pure and holy God. We cannot be made fit to see or enjoy Him until our hearts are thoroughly renewed.

Without this, we leave the Holy Spirit out of the great work of redemption. As we were made by the joint counsel and work of the blessed Trinity, and as we were baptized in the name of the Father, Son, and Holy Spirit, so all three Persons must be involved in our salvation. The Father created us. The Son redeemed us. The Holy Spirit must sanctify and seal us, or else we have believed in vain.

This is what Paul means by the power of Christ's resurrection. This is what we are just as concerned to know by experience as we are to believe that Christ rose at all.

Without this, we may be moral people. We may be civilized, kind, and respectable. But we are not true Christians. A true Christian is not merely one outwardly. We are not true believers simply because we profess every day that Christ rose again the third day from the dead. A true Christian is one inwardly. We are truly believers only when we not only profess belief in Christ's resurrection, but have felt its power by being made alive and raised by His Spirit from death in trespasses and sins to newness of heart and life.

Even the devils believe the doctrine of the resurrection, and they tremble. Yet they remain devils because the benefits of Christ's resurrection have not been applied to them, nor have they received its renewing power to change their nature. In the same way, unless we not only profess that Christ is risen, but also feel that He is risen indeed by being born again from above, our faith will be as ineffective as the faith of devils.

Nothing has done more harm to Christianity than the vain idea that religion is mainly something outside of us. We must understand that everything Christ did outwardly must, in a spiritual way, be done within our souls. Otherwise, believing that a divine Person once lived on earth, conquered hell and the grave, and rose again will profit us no more than believing there was once a great conqueror named Alexander.

As Christ was born of the Virgin Mary, so Christ must be spiritually formed in our hearts. As Christ died for sin, we must die to sin. As Christ rose from the dead, we must rise to a divine life.

Only those who follow Him in this regeneration, or new birth, will sit with Him in glory when He comes in majesty to judge the world.

It is true that the outward work of redemption was completed once for all on the cross. But the application of that redemption to hearts will continue until the end of the world. As long as there is one elect person breathing on earth, naturally descended from the first Adam, the quickening Spirit, purchased through the resurrection of the second Adam, must breathe upon that soul.

Though we may exist by Christ as creatures, we cannot be said to exist in Christ as believers until we are united to Him by one Spirit and brought into a new state of life, just as He entered a new state of life when He rose from the dead.

We may crowd around Christ and call Him, "Lord, Lord," when we come to worship. But we have not truly touched Him until, by living faith in His resurrection, we perceive divine virtue coming from Him to renew and purify our souls.

How greatly mistaken are those who rest in a bare historical faith in the resurrection and look only for outward proofs of it. Even if we were the greatest scholars in the world and could defend the certainty of Christ's resurrection with the tongues of men and angels, yet without the inward testimony of it in our hearts, we might convince others but never be saved by it ourselves.

By nature, we are dead. We are like corpses wrapped in grave clothes until the same Jesus who called Lazarus from the tomb, and by whose resurrection many who slept also arose, raises us by His quickening Spirit from our natural death into a holy and heavenly life.

We might think ourselves blessed if we had seen the risen Jesus with our own eyes and handled the Lord of life with our own hands. But more blessed are those who have not seen and yet believe because they have felt the power of His resurrection. Many saw Jesus after He rose and were still not saved by Him. But whoever has truly felt the power of His resurrection has the earnest of his inheritance in his heart. He has passed from death to life and shall never come into final condemnation.

I know this sounds foolish to the natural man. Many similar truths seemed foolish even to Christ's own disciples when their faith was weak before He rose again. But when natural men feel the power of His resurrection, they will confess that this doctrine is from God. Like the Samaritans, they will say that they believe not merely because someone told them, but because they have experienced it for themselves.

O that all unbelievers and all learned religious teachers who now treat the doctrine of the new birth and the power of Christ's resurrection as an idle tale, and who condemn its preachers as madmen, would feel this power in their own souls. They would no longer ask, "How can these things be?" They would be as convinced as Thomas was when he saw the risen Christ. They would cry out with him in holy confession, **John 20:28 NKJV**, *"My Lord and my God!"*

But how can an unbeliever or a formal Christian come to know Christ and the power of His resurrection? God, who cannot lie, has told us. Jesus said in **John 11:25 NKJV**, *"I am the resurrection and the life. He who believes in Me, though he may die, he shall live."* The apostle also says in **Ephesians 2:8 NKJV**, *"For by grace you have been saved through faith, and that not of yourselves; it is the gift of God."*

This is the way. Walk in it. Believe, and you shall live in Christ, and Christ in you. You shall be one with Christ, and Christ one with you. Without this, your outward goodness and religious profession will profit you nothing.

But by faith, we do not mean a dead, speculative faith in the head. We mean a living principle worked in the heart by the powerful operation of the Holy Spirit. This faith enables us to overcome the world and forsake all in affection for Jesus Christ. Our Lord said in **Luke 14:33 NKJV**, *"So likewise, whoever of you does not forsake all that he has cannot be My disciple."*

Paul, right after the text, speaks of being made conformable to Christ's death. This means that we cannot know the power of Christ's resurrection unless we are also made like Him in His death.

If we can reconcile light and darkness, heaven and hell, then perhaps we can know the power of Christ's resurrection without dying to self and the world. But until that can happen, it is foolish to imagine that Christ will have fellowship with Belial.

There is such a great opposition between the spirit of this world and the Spirit of Jesus Christ that whoever is friends with one must be an enemy of the other. Jesus said in **Matthew 6:24 NKJV**, *"You cannot serve God and mammon."*

This may sound hard, and many, like the rich young ruler, may be tempted to go away sorrowful. But why should this offend anyone? What is all that is in the world, the lust of the eyes, the lust of the flesh, and the pride of life, except vanity and vexation of spirit?

God is love. If our own wills or the world could have made us truly happy, God would never have sent His dear Son, Jesus Christ, to die and rise again to deliver us from their power. But because they torment and cannot satisfy, God commands us to renounce them.

If someone had persuaded Esau not to sell his birthright for one bowl of red stew, would we not say that person was Esau's friend? That is how God deals with us. Through the death and resurrection of Jesus Christ, we are born again to a heavenly inheritance among those who are sanctified. But our corrupt wills tempt us to sell this glorious birthright for the passing vanities of the world. Like Esau's stew, those vanities may please us for a short time, but they will soon be taken away.

God knows this. Therefore, He lovingly commands us to renounce them for a season rather than lose the glorious birthright that belongs to those who know the power of the resurrection of Jesus Christ.

O the depth of the riches and excellence of Christianity. No wonder Paul counted all things as rubbish for the excellence of the knowledge of Christ Jesus his Lord. No wonder he so deeply desired to know Jesus and the power of His resurrection. Even on this side of eternity, this power raises us above the world and makes us sit in heavenly places in Christ Jesus.

No wonder the great company of saints recorded in Scripture, supported by a deep sense of their heavenly calling, despised the pleasures and profits of this life. They wandered in sheepskins and goatskins, in dens and caves of the earth, being destitute, afflicted, and tormented.

O that we were all of the same mind. O that we felt the power of Christ's resurrection as they did. Then we would count all things as rubbish for the excellence of the knowledge of Christ Jesus our Lord. Then we would recover our original dignity, trample the earth under our feet, and have souls continually longing after God.

What prevents us from being so minded? Has Jesus Christ, our great High Priest, changed? No. **Hebrews 13:8 NKJV** says, *"Jesus Christ is the same yesterday, today, and forever."* Though He is exalted to the right hand of God, He is not ashamed to call us brethren. The power of His resurrection is as great now as it was before. The Holy Spirit, assured to us by His resurrection, is as ready and able to make alive those who are dead in trespasses and sins as He was for any saint who ever lived.

Let us cry out to Him immediately, for He is mighty to save. Let us sincerely and truly renounce ourselves and the world, without secretly holding back any part. Then we shall be Christians indeed. Though the world may cast us out and separate from our company, Jesus Christ will walk with us and dwell in us.

And at the general resurrection on the last day, when the voice of the archangel and the trumpet of God command the sea and the graves to give up their dead, and all nations appear before Christ, then He will confess us before His Father and before the holy angels. Then we will receive the invitation He will give to all who love and fear Him: **Matthew 25:34 NKJV**, *"Come, you blessed of My Father, inherit the kingdom prepared for you from the foundation of the world."*

Grant this, O Father, for the sake of Your dear Son, Jesus Christ our Lord. To Him, with You and the Holy Spirit, be all glory, honor, and praise forever.

Amen.

Chapter Four

The Faith of Abraham

Genesis 22:12 *"And he said, Lay not thine hand upon the lad, neither do thou any thing unto him, for now I know that thou fearest God, seeing thou hast not withheld thy Son, thine only Son from me."*

The apostle Paul tells us that the things written in Scripture were written for our learning, so that through patience and the comfort of the Scriptures we might have hope. That means the stories of the Old Testament are not just ancient history. They were written to teach us, strengthen us, warn us, and encourage us in our walk with God.

Faith has always been necessary to please God. No one can come to God without faith. No one can truly obey God without faith. No one can endure the testing of life without faith. This is why Hebrews chapter 11 gives us such a powerful list of men and women who trusted God. They subdued kingdoms, worked righteousness, stopped the mouths of lions, endured suffering, and held on to the promises of God.

Among all these people of faith, Abraham shines brightly. He is called the friend of God and the father of the faithful. Those who believe in Christ are called the children of Abraham, because Abraham's life shows us what real faith looks like. His faith was not merely something he said he had. His faith was proven through obedience.

God tested Abraham many times. God first called him to leave his country, his family, and everything familiar, and go to a land that He would show him. Abraham obeyed. He followed God without knowing every detail of the journey. But the greatest test of Abraham's faith came later, when God asked him to offer up his son Isaac.

The story begins with these words: "And it came to pass after these things, that God did tempt Abraham." This does not mean God tempted Abraham to sin. The Bible clearly teaches that God does not tempt anyone with evil. But God does test His people. He allows circumstances that reveal what is in the heart. He tests faith, obedience, love, and surrender.

Abraham had already gone through many trials. He was now older, and perhaps he thought the hardest tests of life were behind him. But after all those things, God tested Abraham again. This reminds us that as long as we live, our faith may still be tested. We cannot say that all trials are finished until our earthly life is over. Some of the greatest tests may come after we have already walked with God for many years.

God called Abraham by name, and Abraham answered, "Here I am." There is something beautiful about that response. Abraham knew the voice of God. He was not hiding like Adam hid in the garden after he sinned. Abraham was ready to answer. He lived in fellowship with God, and when God spoke, Abraham listened.

Then God gave Abraham a command that must have pierced his heart. God said, "Take now thy son, thine only son Isaac, whom thou lovest, and get thee into the land of Moriah, and offer him there for a burnt offering upon one of the mountains which I shall tell thee of."

Every word made the command heavier. God did not simply say, "Take a sacrifice." He said, "Take your son." Then He said, "Your only son Isaac." Then He added, "Whom you love." Isaac was the son of promise. Isaac was the child Abraham and Sarah had waited for. Isaac was the miracle son of their old age. Isaac was the one through whom God had promised to build a great nation.

If God had asked Abraham to offer an animal from his flock, it would have been much easier. But God asked for Isaac. He asked for the one Abraham loved deeply. He asked for the one connected to the promise. He asked for the treasure of Abraham's heart.

Abraham could have argued with God. He could have said, "Lord, this does not make sense. You promised that through Isaac my descendants would come. How can Your promise be fulfilled if Isaac dies?" He could have said, "This goes against the love of a father. This goes against everything I feel." He could have worried about what Sarah would say or what the surrounding nations would think.

But Abraham did not argue. He did not delay. He did not try to escape the command. The Bible says he rose early in the morning, saddled his donkey, took two young men with him, took Isaac his son, split the wood for the burnt offering, and went to the place God had told him.

This is the obedience of faith. Abraham did not understand everything, but he trusted the God who had spoken. Hebrews tells us that Abraham believed God was able to raise Isaac from the dead. In Abraham's mind, God's promise could not fail. If Isaac had to die, then God could raise him up again.

This teaches us something powerful about faith. Faith does not always understand how God will do what He promised. Faith simply trusts that God is faithful. Faith believes God even when the command is difficult. Faith obeys even when the outcome is hidden.

Abraham's journey to Moriah took three days. That means this was not a quick emotional decision. He had time to think. He had time to feel the weight of what God had commanded. He had time to look at Isaac, to remember the promise, and to wrestle quietly with the cost of obedience.

We can only imagine what Abraham felt during those three days. He walked beside the son he loved. He saw Isaac alive, young, and full of promise. Perhaps his heart broke again and again. Perhaps there were moments when he had to turn aside and pour out his soul before God. Yet he kept walking.

On the third day, Abraham lifted his eyes and saw the place from afar. He told the young men to stay behind with the donkey. Then he said something remarkable: "I and the lad will go yonder and worship, and come again to you." Abraham said, "We will come again." This shows the confidence of his faith. He believed that somehow, some way, God would still keep His promise.

Then Abraham took the wood for the burnt offering and laid it on Isaac. He took the fire and the knife, and the two of them went together. Isaac carried the wood on which he was to be offered. This picture points us forward to Christ, who would one day carry the cross on which He would die.

As they walked together, Isaac noticed something was missing. He said, "My father." Abraham answered, "Here I am, my son." Isaac said, "Behold the fire and the wood: but where is the lamb for a burnt offering?"

That question must have gone straight to Abraham's heart. Isaac knew enough about worship to know that a sacrifice was needed. He saw the fire. He saw the wood. But he did not see the lamb.

Abraham answered, "My son, God will provide himself a lamb for a burnt offering." Those words carry deep meaning. Abraham may have been speaking by faith more than he realized. God would indeed provide a lamb. He would provide a substitute for Isaac. And in the greater sense, God would provide His own Son, Jesus Christ, the Lamb of God who takes away the sin of the world.

At some point, Isaac must have understood what was happening. Yet the Bible gives no record of Isaac fighting, running, or resisting. Abraham was old, and Isaac was strong enough to carry the wood. If Isaac had wanted to resist, he likely could have. But he submitted. Father and son went together in obedience to God.

When they arrived at the place God had shown him, Abraham built an altar. He laid the wood in order. He bound Isaac his son and laid him on the altar upon the wood. This is one of the most moving scenes in all of Scripture. The father stood over the son he loved. The promise seemed to be lying on the altar. Everything Abraham had waited for, hoped for, and loved was now surrendered to God.

We should pause and feel the weight of this moment. Abraham was not a cold man without affection. He loved Isaac. God Himself had said, "whom thou lovest." This obedience cost him something. Real faith often does. True surrender is not giving God what we do not care about. True surrender is trusting God with what is most precious to us.

Then Abraham stretched out his hand and took the knife to slay his son. He had gone all the way in his heart. Isaac had already been surrendered. Abraham had obeyed to the point of no return.

But at that very moment, the angel of the Lord called to him from heaven and said, "Abraham, Abraham." Abraham answered, "Here I am." Then the Lord said, "Lay not thine hand upon the lad, neither do thou any thing unto him, for now I know that thou fearest God, seeing thou hast not withheld thy son, thine only son from me."

God stopped Abraham before Isaac was slain. Abraham had proven his faith. He had shown that he feared God. He had shown that he would not withhold even his beloved son from the Lord.

Then Abraham lifted his eyes and saw a ram caught in a thicket by its horns. God had provided a substitute. Abraham took the ram and offered it instead of his son. Isaac was spared because another sacrifice was provided in his place.

Abraham called the name of that place Jehovah-jireh, meaning, "The Lord will provide." On that mountain, Abraham learned that God sees, God knows, and God provides.

This story teaches us many things, but above all, it points us to the love of God in giving His Son, Jesus Christ. If our hearts are moved when we see Abraham willing to offer Isaac, how much more should we be moved by the Father who truly gave His only begotten Son for us?

Abraham was stopped before the knife fell. But at Calvary, the Father did not spare His own Son. Isaac was released from the altar, but Jesus went all the way to the cross. A ram took Isaac's place, but no one took the place of Jesus. He became the substitute for sinners.

The Bible says God so loved the world that He gave His only begotten Son. We should never read Genesis 22 without seeing the shadow of Calvary. Isaac carried the wood up the mountain, and Jesus carried His cross to Golgotha. Isaac submitted to his father, and Jesus submitted perfectly to the will of the Father. Isaac was laid on the wood, but Jesus was nailed to the cross. Isaac was spared because a substitute was provided, but Jesus became the Substitute so that we could be spared.

When we think of Abraham's pain, we should think even more deeply about the love of God. Abraham was the servant of God, but God is the Creator of all. Abraham owed God everything, but God owed us nothing. We were not His friends by nature. We were sinners. Yet while we were still sinners, Christ died for us.

This is love beyond understanding. God gave His Son for those who had sinned against Him. Jesus bore our sins. He carried our guilt. He suffered in our place. The Father laid on Him the iniquity of us all.

If we are moved by Isaac on the altar, we should be even more moved by Jesus on the cross. There He was crowned with thorns, mocked, pierced, and crucified. There He shed His blood for sinners. There He cried out and gave up His life. Isaac lived because God provided a sacrifice. We live because God provided His Son.

This story also teaches us the nature of true faith. We are not saved by our works. Salvation is the free gift of God. We are justified by faith in Jesus Christ, not by any righteousness of our own. The righteousness that saves us is the righteousness of Christ. His obedience, His sacrifice, His blood, and His finished work are the basis of our acceptance before God.

Abraham was justified by faith. He believed God, and it was counted to him for righteousness. That happened before he offered Isaac. His obedience did not earn his salvation. His obedience revealed the reality of his faith.

This is important. Good works do not save us, but true faith produces obedience. Faith that never changes the heart, never moves the will, and never leads to surrender is not living faith. Even demons believe certain truths about God, but they do not love Him, obey Him, or trust Him.

Abraham's faith was more than words. His faith worked by love. His faith obeyed. His faith surrendered Isaac. That is why God said, "Now I know that thou fearest God." God already knew Abraham's heart, but Abraham's obedience displayed the reality of his faith.

We should examine ourselves in light of this. It is easy to say, "I believe." It is easy to speak about grace, salvation, and the promises of God. But has our faith changed us? Has it moved our hearts toward

God? Has it made us willing to obey? Has it loosened our grip on the things of this world? Has it enabled us to surrender our Isaac?

Everyone has an Isaac. For Abraham, Isaac was his beloved son, the child of promise. For us, Isaac may be a relationship, a dream, a comfort, a possession, a plan, a pleasure, a position, or something deeply loved. It may even be something good that has become too central in the heart.

The question is not whether we love Isaac. Abraham truly loved Isaac. The question is whether we love God more. True faith does not mean we have no affection for earthly blessings. It means we hold every blessing with surrendered hands.

God does not always take away what He asks us to surrender. Sometimes He gives it back, as He did with Isaac. But He tests the heart to see whether the gift has taken the place of the Giver.

We must learn to sit loosely to the comforts of this world. Our children, our families, our friendships, our ministries, our possessions, our plans, and our dreams all belong to God. They are gifts, not gods. We may enjoy them, but we must not worship them. We may love them, but we must not love them more than the Lord.

This does not make obedience easy. Abraham's obedience was not easy. Surrender often comes with tears. But faith trusts the character of God even when the command is painful. Faith says, "Lord, You gave this to me, and I give it back to You. I trust You with what I love."

Those who have been tested in deep ways can find comfort in Abraham's story. God saw Abraham. God knew the cost. God provided what was needed. And God proved Himself faithful.

The same God sees you. He knows what obedience has cost you. He knows the things you have laid on the altar. He knows the tears behind your surrender. And He is faithful.

There is coming a day when every surrendered thing will make sense in the presence of God. Abraham now sees clearly what he could only trust then. One day, we too will understand more fully. We will see how God led us, tested us, strengthened us, and provided for us. We will praise Him not only for the blessings He gave, but also for the trials He used to deepen our faith.

Until then, we are called to trust. We are called to obey. We are called to surrender. We are called to believe that the God who provided a ram for Isaac and gave His Son for sinners will always be faithful to His people.

So let Abraham's faith speak to us. Let Isaac on the altar remind us to surrender what we love. Let the ram in the thicket remind us that God provides. And let the cross of Jesus Christ remind us that the greatest provision has already been given.

God did not withhold His Son, His only Son, from us. Therefore, we can trust Him with everything.

Amen.

Chapter Five

The Great Duty of Family Religion

Joshua 24:15 *"As for me and my house, we will serve the Lord."*

These words give us the strong and holy decision of Joshua. He had just reminded the people of Israel of all the great things God had done for them. He spoke to them with love, urgency, and conviction. He reminded them how gracious God had been, how faithfully God had led them, and how powerfully God had delivered them. Then Joshua called them to respond the only right way they could respond. Since God had been so good to them, they should give themselves fully to Him.

Joshua told them to fear the Lord and serve Him in sincerity and truth. He told them to put away the false gods their fathers had served and choose the Lord. Later, the prophet Samuel would give the people a similar command when he said, **1 Samuel 12:24**, *"Only fear the Lord, and serve him in truth with all your heart: for consider how great things he hath done for you."* The goodness of God should move us to serve Him. When we remember His mercy, His provision, His forgiveness, and His faithfulness, our hearts should respond with surrender.

But Joshua did not only tell the people what they should do. He also told them what he was going to do. He did not place a burden on others that he himself was unwilling to carry. He did not preach one thing and live another. He stood before the people and said, **Joshua 24:15**, *"As for me and my house, we will serve the Lord."*

That was not only a personal decision. It was a household decision. Joshua understood that his responsibility before God did not end with his own private devotion. He was responsible to lead his household in the service of the Lord. He knew that his family was not to be spiritually neglected. His home was to be a place where God was honored, worshiped, obeyed, and served.

This same resolution is needed today. Every person entrusted with the care of a family should be able to say, "As for me and my house, we will serve the Lord." If there was ever a time when family religion needed to be preached, practiced, and restored, it is now. Many homes may carry the name Christian, but the daily life of the home often shows little evidence that Christ is truly honored there.

People may still attend church and maintain some outward form of religion, but in many homes the spiritual life is weak or missing altogether. There may be church on Sunday, but no prayer in the home. There may be a Bible on the shelf, but no reading of the

Word together. There may be Christian language, but little spiritual instruction, little worship, and little intentional leadership.

If angels were to observe the spiritual condition of many homes, would they be able to say, “Surely the fear of God is in this place”? Or would they see homes full of activity, noise, entertainment, and earthly concern, but little evidence that the Lord is being served?

This was not the pattern of the early Christians. They did not believe religion belonged only in public worship. Their faith entered their homes. Their households became places of prayer, teaching, fellowship, and devotion. In the New Testament, Paul often referred to the church that met in someone’s house. Their homes were not spiritually empty. Their homes were places where Christ was honored.

If we want to see a true revival of godliness, we must also desire a revival of family religion. Churches will be stronger when homes are stronger. Children will be better grounded when parents are faithful. Servants, family members, and everyone under our care will be better helped when the home is ordered under the Lordship of Christ.

Every person who governs or leads a household has a responsibility before God. That person is not only called to serve God personally, but also to care for the spiritual welfare of those entrusted to them. A home is, in a sense, a small congregation. A parent or household leader has a duty to instruct, pray, guide, protect, correct, and provide spiritual leadership.

Many people are careful to provide for the physical needs of their household. They make sure there is food, clothing, shelter, safety, education, and opportunity. These things are important, and it would be wrong to neglect them. But how much more serious is it to neglect the soul? If it is wrong not to provide for the body, how much more wrong is it to ignore the eternal condition of those God has placed under our care?

A minister who refused to teach or watch over the people entrusted to him would be considered unfaithful. In a similar way, a parent or household leader who gives no thought to the spiritual condition of the home is neglecting a sacred responsibility. Every home is a small field of ministry. Every family is a flock of souls. If those souls are ignored, the leader of the home will one day answer to God.

The Bible gives us examples of faithful household leadership. Job cared deeply about the spiritual condition of his children. After his children feasted, Job offered sacrifices for them because he thought, "It may be that my sons have sinned." He did this continually. Job did not only care about his own soul. He cared about the souls of his children.

Joshua also cared for his household. He did not say, "I will serve the Lord, and everyone else can do what they want." He said, "As for me and my house, we will serve the Lord." Cornelius is another example. The Bible says he feared God with all his house. His faith had influence in his home.

If Christians today had the spirit of Job, Joshua, and Cornelius, our homes would look different. There would be prayer. There would be Scripture. There would be instruction. There would be a clear spiritual direction. The family would know that the Lord is honored in that house.

But what about those who not only fail to lead their household to God, but actually discourage those in their home who want to serve Him? Some mock faith. Some make prayer difficult. Some ridicule those who want to follow Christ. Such people do great harm. They do not enter the kingdom themselves, and they hinder others who desire to enter.

God may allow such opposition as a test of faith for His children, but those who become stumbling blocks in their own homes carry a serious guilt. It is a fearful thing to use influence, authority, or position to pull others away from God.

A household that serves the Lord must first give attention to the Word of God. Scripture is not only for the church building. It belongs in the home. Jesus said, **John 5:39**, *"Search the scriptures; for in them ye think ye have eternal life: and they are they which testify of me."* This command is for every believer, but it especially applies to those who lead a home.

God commanded Israel to teach His words diligently to their children. **Deuteronomy 6:6–7** says, *"And these words, which I command thee this day, shall be in thine heart: and thou shalt teach them diligently unto thy children."* The Word was to be spoken of in the house, on the road, in daily life, and through ordinary conversation.

This shows us that spiritual instruction should not be rare or forced. It should be part of the rhythm of the home. Children and family members should hear the Word of God. They should learn what God says, who God is, what Christ has done, and how they are called to live.

The reason many parents do not speak the Word diligently to their children is often because the Word is not deeply rooted in their own hearts. What fills the heart will eventually come out of the mouth. If the Word of God is treasured in the heart, it will naturally become part of the life and language of the home.

Children, young people, and even adults in the household often need instruction. Many do not know the Scriptures well. Many are strangers to the basic truths of the faith. How will they know unless someone teaches them? And who is better placed to teach them than those who live with them, love them, and are responsible for them?

The Word of God is able to make people wise unto salvation. It gives understanding. It corrects false ideas. It shows the way of life. Therefore, every Christian home should have some regular place for the reading and teaching of Scripture.

A home that neglects the Word of God is spiritually poor, even if it has everything else. It may have food on the table, money in the bank, and comfort in every room, but if there is no Word, the soul is unfed. This should not be so among the people of God.

Along with the reading of Scripture, family prayer must also have a place in the home. Reading prepares the heart for prayer, and prayer helps the Word become fruitful in the heart. A household that serves the Lord should be a household that calls upon His name.

Prayer is one of the clearest signs that a family depends on God. When a family prays together, they acknowledge that they need God's mercy, guidance, protection, forgiveness, and strength. They thank Him for shared blessings. They bring shared burdens before

Him. They confess shared failures. They ask Him to rule over the home.

Jesus prayed with His disciples. They were, in a sense, His little household during His earthly ministry. He also promised a special blessing where two or three are gathered in His name. Family prayer may be simple, but it is powerful. It does not need to be long or impressive. It needs to be sincere.

Every family has reasons to pray. There are blessings to thank God for. There are needs to bring before Him. There are temptations to ask Him for strength against. There are sins to confess. There are decisions that require wisdom. There are children who need grace. There are marriages that need protection. There are homes that need peace.

How can a family say it serves the Lord if it never calls upon Him together? A prayerless home is in a dangerous place. It may have Christian decoration and religious language, but if there is no prayer, something vital is missing.

Many households would be greatly changed if morning and evening prayer became part of their life. The home would be reminded daily that God is first. Children would grow up seeing that prayer is not only for emergencies or church services. They would learn that God is near, that He hears, and that He is worthy to be sought.

The third duty of family religion is instruction. Parents and household leaders must teach, train, and guide those under their care in the ways of the Lord. This includes teaching children the truths of Scripture, helping them understand the gospel, correcting them with wisdom, and bringing them up in the nurture and admonition of the Lord.

God commended Abraham for this very thing. He said, **Genesis 18:19**, *"For I know him, that he will command his children and his household after him, and they shall keep the way of the Lord."* Abraham's faith was not private only. It shaped his leadership. He taught his household to keep the way of the Lord.

The New Testament gives the same instruction. Parents are told to bring up their children in the nurture and admonition of the Lord. This means Christian parents must not leave the spiritual formation of their children to chance. They must not assume that children will somehow learn the faith without guidance. They must teach them.

If children were instructed in the ceremonies and commandments of the Old Testament, how much more should they be taught the truths of the gospel? We live in a world full of confusion, false teaching, temptation, and unbelief. Many voices are trying to shape the minds and hearts of the next generation. If parents and household leaders do not teach the truth, someone else will teach something else.

Some may object that family religion takes too much time. They may say there is too much work to do, too many responsibilities, and too many demands. But has God given us time for everything else and no time for Him? We find time for meals, work, errands, entertainment, conversations, and personal interests. Surely we can give some time each day to the worship and instruction of the Lord.

God is the One who gives us the ability to work, earn, provide, and succeed. Jesus told us to seek first the kingdom of God and His righteousness, and all needed things would be added to us. When we put God first, we are not losing what matters. We are placing everything else under the right authority.

Abraham was a man with many responsibilities, yet he found time to command his household after him. David was a king with the affairs of a nation on his shoulders, yet he said he would walk within his house with a perfect heart. Joshua was a leader responsible for Israel, yet he declared that his household would serve the Lord. If these men found time to honor God in their homes, then we should not say we are too busy.

One strong reason to practice family religion is gratitude to God. Every household leader has received blessings from the Lord. The ability to have a home, family, provision, influence, and authority is a trust from God. These gifts should not be used only for personal comfort or earthly success. They should be used for His glory.

Parents and leaders often use their authority in many areas. They tell children what to do. They direct the affairs of the home. They make decisions about schedules, work, money, discipline, and daily responsibilities. But if authority is used for everything except the things of God, something is deeply wrong.

Joshua used his authority rightly. He said, "As for me and my house, we will serve the Lord." He was not ashamed to lead spiritually. He was not passive. He did not wait for everyone else to decide the spiritual direction of the home. He took responsibility.

Love for our children should also move us to family religion. Most parents love their children deeply. They sacrifice for them, feed them, clothe them, protect them, educate them, and work hard to give them a better life. But the greatest need of a child is not merely physical, educational, or financial. The greatest need of a child is spiritual.

What good is it to prepare a child for success in this world but leave him unprepared for eternity? What good is it to care for the body and neglect the soul? A parent may provide a child with many opportunities, but if that child is not taught to know and fear the Lord, the most important responsibility has been neglected.

True love cares about the soul. True love teaches children the Word of God. True love prays for them and with them. True love shows them the way of salvation. True love does not leave them to wander without spiritual guidance.

Justice toward those in our care should also move us. If servants, employees, or household members give their time and strength to serve in a home, those who lead that home should care for more than their labor. They should care for their souls. It is not enough to provide material wages while ignoring spiritual welfare.

Every person under our roof is made in the image of God. Every person has an eternal soul. Those who lead a household should desire the spiritual good of everyone entrusted to them.

Even self-interest should move us to family religion. Every parent desires faithful children. Every household leader desires peace, honesty, order, and blessing in the home. But how can we expect godly fruit if we never plant spiritual seed? If children and family members are never taught the Word, never led in prayer, and never shown the fear of God, should we be surprised when their hearts drift?

Christianity does not make children worse sons and daughters. It does not make servants worse servants. It does not make family members less faithful. True Christianity teaches people to honor authority, walk in love, tell the truth, work honestly, forgive freely, and live humbly. The more a person truly knows God, the better he will fulfill his responsibilities toward others.

Therefore, family religion is not against the good of the home. It is one of the greatest blessings a home can have.

Finally, the seriousness of judgment should move us. One day we will all stand before the judgment seat of Christ. We will give an account not only for what we believed in public, but how we lived in private. Parents and household leaders will give an account for the influence they had in their homes.

What a sorrow it would be to see children, servants, or family members rise up as witnesses against those who neglected their souls. What grief to hear them say, "You cared for many things, but you did not lead me to God. You provided for my body, but you ignored my soul. You taught me the ways of the world, but not the ways of Christ."

This is a serious thought. Our own sins are enough to humble us. We should not add to them the guilt of neglecting those entrusted to our care.

But the purpose of this message is not merely to condemn. It is to awaken. God calls families to return to Him. He calls parents and household leaders to take up the holy resolution of Joshua and say, "As for me and my house, we will serve the Lord."

This begins with remembering the value of the soul. Your own soul is precious, and so are the souls of those in your home. Christ shed His blood for souls. He came to seek and save the lost. He died so sinners could be forgiven, born again, restored to God, and made ready for eternal life.

When the love of God fills the heart, it will not be content to care only for itself. Grace makes us concerned for others, especially those nearest to us. If God has saved us, how can we not desire the salvation of our household? If Christ has shown mercy to us, how can we not pray that mercy would reach our children, family members, and all under our care?

After all our efforts, some may still resist. Some may continue unchanged. Some may reject the instruction, prayer, and love given to them. But even then, the faithful leader of the home will have this comfort: "I did what I could. I prayed. I taught. I led. I pointed them to Christ."

Let every Christian home become a place where God is honored. Let the Bible be opened. Let prayer be heard. Let children be instructed. Let worship be sincere. Let authority be used for the glory of God. Let love care for the soul and not only the body.

The home does not need to be perfect, but it should be surrendered. The prayers do not need to be eloquent, but they should be sincere. The teaching does not need to be complicated, but it should be faithful. The leader does not need to know everything, but he must be willing to lead.

Joshua's words are still needed. They should be written not only on signs and walls, but on the heart of every believer entrusted with a household.

As for me and my house, we will serve the Lord.

Amen.

Chapter Six

The Benefits of Early Godliness

Ecclesiastes 12:1 *"Remember now thy Creator in the days of thy youth."*

There is something beautiful about a life that begins walking with God early. True religion is not a burden that ruins life. It is a gift that gives life its proper direction. It blesses the person who embraces it, and it also blesses the people around them. Even those who do not fully follow God often recognize, in their more serious moments, that there is something admirable about a righteous life. Many may not want to live like the godly, but they would like to die like them.

The question for many people is not whether they should seek God at all. Most people know, at least deep down, that the soul matters and that eternity must be faced. The greater question is when they should begin. Many are convinced that religion is necessary, but they want to delay it. They know that following God will require repentance, self-denial, surrender, and change, so they put it off.

The young person chasing pleasure says, "Let me enjoy myself a little longer, and then I will get serious with God." The person consumed with money says, "Let me build my life, gather wealth, and secure my future, and then I will seek heaven." Others wait for a more convenient season, like Felix, who trembled under conviction but postponed obedience.

But Scripture does not tell us to remember our Creator later. It says, "Remember now thy Creator in the days of thy youth." The word remember does not mean merely to think about God once in a while. It means to live in obedience to Him. In Scripture, to forget God means to neglect Him, disobey Him, and live as though He does not matter. To remember God means to honor Him, obey Him, worship Him, and live with Him at the center of life.

So when Solomon says, "Remember now thy Creator in the days of thy youth," he is saying, "Begin serving God while you are young. Do not wait until later. Give God your heart, your strength, your mind, your gifts, and your future now."

True religion is not merely an outward profession. It is not simply saying the name of Christ, attending church, being baptized, receiving communion, or being known as a religious person. These things may have their place, but by themselves they do not make a person truly godly. Jesus said that many would one day say, "Lord, Lord," and yet be rejected because they never truly knew Him.

True religion is an inward work of grace. It is a real change of heart produced by the Holy Spirit. It is being born again. It is the renewing of a corrupted nature. It is the turning of the soul from darkness to light. It is putting off the old man and putting on the new. It is the image of God being restored in the heart. This inward change then shows itself outwardly through a changed life and the fruit of the Spirit.

This work is not something man can accomplish by his own strength. Nicodemus, though he was a teacher in Israel, did not understand it when Jesus told him that he must be born again. The new birth is a work of God. Only the Holy Spirit can give spiritual life. Only God can change the heart, subdue corrupt desires, and make a sinner new.

Yet though salvation is the work of God, it is not a small or shallow thing. It involves the death of pride, the denial of self, the forsaking of sin, and the surrender of the whole life to Christ. The spiritual birth has its pains, just as natural birth does. The way of wisdom becomes pleasant, but the soul must first be humbled, corrected, and trained by grace.

For this reason, youth is a fitting season to begin. In youth, the body is strong, the mind is active, and the heart is not yet as hardened by years of sinful habits. If there are difficulties in following Christ, then why not begin when strength is fresh? People understand this in ordinary life. They train children early. They send young people into study, labor, and responsibility because they know youth is a season for formation. Why should we not think the same way about the soul?

If true religion involves the renewing of the heart, then it is not only difficult, it also takes time to mature. Growth in grace is not completed in a moment. A believer must learn to pray, trust, obey, forgive, resist temptation, love the Word, endure hardship, and walk by faith. These things deepen over time. The earlier a person begins walking with God, the longer he has to grow strong in the ways of God.

Life is short. We do not have endless years to waste. Jesus said that the night is coming when no man can work. If a person had a long and important journey to take, and he wasted the whole day before beginning, we would call that foolish. Yet many do this with eternity. They have a journey before them that matters more than anything else, but they delay until sickness, age, or death begins to overtake them.

Some may be saved late in life. God is merciful, and He can call a sinner even at the eleventh hour. But no one should presume upon that mercy. It is dangerous to delay obedience to God. The proper time to seek Him is now.

One of the great benefits of early godliness is that it brings honor to God. The whole purpose of our lives is to glorify Him. We were created for His glory, and we were redeemed by the blood of Jesus Christ so that we might live for Him.

When a young person follows Christ, it beautifully displays the worth of God. Many people say God's commands are too hard, that holiness is unreasonable, and that self-denial is impossible. But when young people choose Christ over the pleasures of sin, they show that God is worthy. When they resist the lust of the flesh, the lust of the eyes, and the pride of life, they prove that the grace of God is powerful. They show that the yoke of Christ is easy and His burden is light.

It honors God when the strength of youth is given to Him. It honors God when a young person says, "I will not wait until I am old and weak to serve the Lord. I will give Him my best years."

Early godliness also brings honor to the person who lives it. God honors those who honor Him. Scripture remembers Obadiah because he feared the Lord from his youth. Samuel is remembered because he stood before the Lord as a child. Timothy is remembered because from childhood he knew the Holy Scriptures. John is remembered as the beloved disciple, and even our Lord Jesus, at twelve years old, was found in the temple listening, asking questions, and being about His Father's business.

There is a special beauty in early devotion. It is beautiful to see a young heart set on God, a young mind filled with Scripture, and youthful strength used for the kingdom. The world may mock it, but heaven honors it.

Early godliness also brings comfort. One of the great sorrows of delayed repentance is uncertainty. A person who waits until the end of life may be troubled by many fears. He may wonder whether his sorrow is true repentance or only fear of punishment. He may wonder whether he is turning to God because he loves Him or because death is near and earthly pleasures can no longer be enjoyed.

But the one who serves God in youth does not carry that same burden. He did not come to God only because the world was fading. He did not leave sin only because he could no longer enjoy it. He took up the cross when the world was still offering him pleasure. He followed Christ when he still had strength to go another way. That brings a deep assurance of sincerity.

Early godliness also makes obedience more natural over time. The person who begins walking with God young forms holy habits. Prayer becomes familiar. The Word becomes loved. Fellowship becomes desirable. Self-denial becomes less strange. Obedience becomes part of the pattern of life.

This does not mean the young believer never struggles. But it does mean that grace, over time, trains the heart. Duties that once seemed hard can become sweet. The person who practices prayer learns the comfort of prayer. The person who practices Scripture reading learns the strength of Scripture. The person who practices obedience learns the joy of walking in God's ways.

There is also great comfort in early godliness when old age comes. Solomon says to remember the Creator in the days of youth before the evil days come, when a person says, "I have no pleasure in them." Old age brings weakness. The body changes. The hands tremble. The legs grow weak. The eyes dim. The teeth fail. Strength declines. Many pleasures that once seemed so important fade away.

In those days, what comfort can compare with the memory of a life spent walking with God? When a person reaches old age and can look back, not with pride but with gratitude, and say, "By God's grace, I have sought to follow Him from my youth," there is a comfort the world cannot give. Even with many failures and shortcomings, there is peace in knowing that the Lord has been the guide of one's life.

Early godliness also prepares a person for death. Since the fall, death is a debt every person must pay. Death often comes with fear, uncertainty, and trembling. But the believer who has walked with God does not have to face death as the king of terrors. He can see death as a messenger that brings him home.

The godly person has spent life preparing for eternity. He has waited for the great change. He has trusted Christ, followed Christ, and looked for the coming of Christ. When death comes, he may say with faith that he is going to be with the Lord.

Beyond death, early godliness gives confidence for the day of judgment. The one who belongs to Christ does not stand in his own righteousness. He stands in the righteousness of Jesus. But a life of sincere faith gives evidence that his profession was real. He can look to Christ as his Savior and enter his Master's joy.

So why should anyone delay? Why should a young person give the best strength of life to sin and then offer God only the weakness of later years? Did Jesus shed His blood so that we could spend our youth serving the very sins He came to destroy? Did He die to deliver us from bondage so that we could willingly remain enslaved?

No one has ever truly regretted coming to Christ too early. But many have regretted waiting too long. Samuel does not regret serving God from childhood. Timothy does not regret knowing the Scriptures from his youth. Every saint in glory rejoices that grace reached them when it did.

To the young, the call is clear. Remember your Creator now. Do not wait for a more convenient season. Do not wait until sin has hardened you. Do not wait until habits are deeply rooted. Do not wait until your heart is cold, your conscience dull, and your strength spent. Give God your life now.

But this message is not only a warning against delay. It is also an encouragement to those young people who already desire to follow Christ. It is a blessed thing to see young believers gathering together, encouraging one another, praying, worshiping, studying the Word, serving others, and seeking the things of God. Such faith brings joy to the church and honor to Christ.

When young people form godly friendships and spiritual communities, they can strengthen one another in the Lord. They can help one another resist temptation, grow in knowledge, serve the church, and remain faithful. There is great value in young believers walking together with their faces set toward heaven.

But young believers must also be careful. Religious activity can sometimes lead to pride. A person may begin to think highly of himself because he attends meetings, serves in ministry, knows Scripture, or is part of a spiritual group. That is dangerous. The more we gather, serve, and learn, the more humble we should become. Spiritual privileges should not make us proud. They should make us watchful.

Young believers should never look down on others. They should not think themselves righteous and despise those who are weaker, slower, or still wandering. Instead, they should fear the Lord, examine their own hearts, and pray that their lives match their profession. It is possible to help others and still neglect one's own soul. Therefore, every believer must remain humble before God.

Another danger for young believers is worldliness. This has ruined many who once appeared to follow Christ. Some begin well. They attend church, love the Word, and show spiritual promise. But when they gain freedom, success, money, or independence, their hearts are drawn back into the world. Their first love grows cold. They become entangled again in the very things they once escaped.

This is why young believers must remind one another to stay free from the spirit of the world. There is nothing wrong with honest work, responsibility, provision, or building a life. But these things must never replace the kingdom of God. Jesus said to seek first the kingdom of God and His righteousness, and the needed things will be added.

The Christian must work, but not worship work. He must provide, but not live for possessions. He must be responsible, but not become worldly. He must live in this world while remembering that he belongs to another.

Young believers must be diligent. Scripture says to make your calling and election sure. It says to beware lest you fall from your own steadfastness. It says, "Let him that thinketh he standeth take heed lest he fall." These warnings are not meant to destroy assurance, but to keep us humble and alert.

The Christian life has real enemies. There is the devil, who is subtle and persistent. There is the world, which is attractive and deceptive. There is the flesh, which still pulls against the Spirit. There is also the treachery of our own hearts. The gate is narrow, and the way is difficult.

But believers should not be afraid. The One who is with us is greater than all who are against us. The same God who has already helped us overcome past temptations can help us overcome future ones. The God who delivered David from the lion and the bear also gave him victory over Goliath. The God who begins the work of grace is able to carry it on.

Therefore, be steadfast. Do not be ashamed of the gospel of Christ. Do not fear the opinions of people. Do not be moved by ridicule, rejection, or pressure. If you suffer for a short time now, you will share in glory with Christ forever.

The world may offer pleasure, but it cannot offer peace with God. Sin may promise freedom, but it brings bondage. Christ calls us to take up the cross, but He also gives life, joy, strength, and eternal reward.

Remember your Creator now. Serve Him while your heart is young, your strength is fresh, and your life is before you. Let your youth be an offering to God. Let your gifts be used for His glory. Let your habits be formed in His Word. Let your friendships draw you closer to Him. Let your life begin early in the path that leads to eternal joy.

And may God give us grace that we would not be among those who draw back, but among those who believe, endure, and are saved through Jesus Christ our Lord.

Amen.

Chapter Seven

The Potter and the Clay

Jeremiah 18:1–6 NKJV *"The word which came to Jeremiah from the Lord, saying: 'Arise and go down to the potter's house, and there I will cause you to hear My words.' Then I went down to the potter's house, and there he was, making something at the wheel. And the vessel that he made of clay was marred in the hand of the potter; so he made it again into another vessel, as it seemed good to the potter to make. Then the word of the Lord came to me, saying: 'O house of Israel, can I not do with you as this potter?' says the Lord. 'Look, as the clay is in the potter's hand, so are you in My hand, O house of Israel!'"*

In many different ways and at many different times, God spoke to His people through the prophets before He spoke to us fully through His Son. To Elijah, He revealed Himself in a still small voice. To Jacob, He spoke through a dream. To Moses, He spoke face to face. Sometimes God sent a prophet on a special errand, and while that prophet was obeying, God gave him a message to deliver to the people.

One powerful example of this is found in the passage from Jeremiah. The Bible tells us that the word of the Lord came to Jeremiah. We are not told exactly when this happened or what Jeremiah was doing at the time. Perhaps he was praying for people who would not pray for themselves. Perhaps it was early in the morning while he was thinking deeply on his bed. But the word came to him, saying, "Arise."

God told Jeremiah to go down to the potter's house, and there God would cause him to hear His words. Jeremiah did not argue with God. He did not say it was too early, too cold, too dark, or too inconvenient. He did not ask God to give him the message where he was. He simply obeyed. He went down to the potter's house.

When Jeremiah arrived, he saw the potter working at the wheel. At first, that may not seem unusual. A potter working with clay is exactly what you would expect to see in a potter's house. But Jeremiah was not there by accident. God had sent him there to teach him something. So Jeremiah watched carefully.

The potter was shaping a vessel out of clay. But while the vessel was in the potter's hands, it became marred. It did not turn out as intended. It was spoiled, damaged, and unfit for the purpose the potter first had in mind. The potter could have thrown it away. He could have pushed it aside and started with a new piece of clay. No one would have accused him of being unjust. It was his clay. He had the right to do with it as he pleased.

But that is not what the potter did. Instead, he made it again into another vessel. He reshaped it as it seemed good to him. He did not ask the clay what it wanted to become. He did not gather the household and ask for advice. He did what seemed right to him as the potter.

Then the word of the Lord came to Jeremiah. God said, "O house of Israel, can I not do with you as this potter?" In other words, God was saying, "Am I not allowed to do with My people what this potter does with his clay? Are you not in My hand?"

God had formed Israel into a people. He had blessed them above the nations. But by their backsliding, they had marred themselves. They had turned from Him and ruined what He had called them to be. Just as the potter could have thrown away the marred clay, God could have rejected Israel. He could have removed their place as a people. He could have judged them completely.

But God was also showing mercy. He was saying that just as the potter could remake the clay into another vessel, He could also restore His people. He could heal their backsliding. He could revive His work among them. He could remake what had been damaged. Israel was in His hand. He could judge, and He could restore. He could tear down, and He could rebuild. He could reject, and He could renew. No one could say to Him, "What are You doing?"

This message was first given to the house of Israel, but it also speaks to every person. What God said of Israel is true of every one of us. By nature, because of sin, every person born from Adam is like a piece of marred clay in the sight of God. And because we are marred by sin, we must be renewed by the power of God.

Man was not originally created this way. When God first made man, he was not broken, sinful, rebellious, and corrupt. God made man upright. The Bible says that God created man in His own image. There is great dignity in that truth. God did not make man as an accident or as a meaningless creature. God formed him with purpose, value, and honor.

When God created the world, He spoke and things came into existence. But when He created man, the language is different. God said, "Let Us make man in Our image, according to Our likeness." Man was made to reflect God. He was made with understanding, righteousness, holiness, and the ability to know and enjoy fellowship with God.

But man did not remain in that blessed condition. He fell. Sin entered. The image of God was defaced. It was not destroyed completely, because man still bears the mark of his Creator. But the glory of that image was marred. Like an old coin whose original stamp can still faintly be seen, man still shows traces of what he once was, but sin has deeply damaged him.

We can see this first in the understanding of man. Before the fall, Adam's understanding was clear. He knew God rightly. He knew himself rightly. He understood the creation around him. He had a mind filled with light. He was made a little lower than the angels and was excellent in knowledge.

But now our understanding is darkened. Even in natural things, we know very little compared with what could be known. Whatever knowledge we gain comes with effort, labor, study, and weariness. People may gain a little education and begin to think highly of themselves. They may learn a few languages, grasp some science, or acquire some knowledge and then imagine themselves wiser than others.

But truly wise people know how much they do not know. The more a person honestly learns, the more he sees how vast the unknown still is. Socrates, when asked why he was called wise, said in effect that perhaps it was because he knew how ignorant he was. Many who call themselves Christians have not even learned that much humility. They boast about their understanding, but their boasting often proves how little they truly understand.

If our understanding is dark in natural things, it is even darker in spiritual things. Apart from the grace of God, the natural person cannot rightly understand the things of the Spirit. Paul says in **1 Corinthians 2:14 NKJV**, *"But the natural man does not receive the things of the Spirit of God, for they are foolishness to him."* Spiritual truth must be spiritually understood.

This is why Nicodemus, though he was a teacher in Israel, was confused when Jesus told him he must be born again. He asked how a man could be born when he was old. He wondered whether he could enter a second time into his mother's womb. This shows how blind even a religious and educated man can be when it comes to spiritual truth.

So in our understanding, man is marred clay.

We also see this in the will of man. Before the fall, man's will was in harmony with God's will. There was no rebellion, no resistance, no inward war against God. Adam's will and God's will were in agreement.

But now the human will is bent away from God. Scripture says the carnal mind is enmity against God. It is not subject to the law of God, nor can it be. People often speak strongly against outward forms of antichrist, false religion, and spiritual corruption. But there is a dangerous antichrist within the human heart, and that is self-will. Self-will sits in the heart and says of Christ, "We will not have this Man to reign over us."

Even the people of God feel this inward struggle. When they are under affliction, temptation, or spiritual darkness, they sometimes feel something within them rise up against the wise dealings of God. Something inside wants to question God and say, "Why are You dealing with me this way?" This is why Paul cried out in **Romans 7:24 NKJV**, *"O wretched man that I am! Who will deliver me from this body of death?"*

The renewed believer groans under this burden. But the natural person, who has not been awakened by grace, does not feel this struggle in the same way. Self-will reigns in him. He may not see it or confess it, but it is there. So in the will, man is marred clay.

We also see this in the affections of man. Before the fall, man's affections were ordered rightly. He loved what he should love. He hated what he should hate. His desires flowed toward God like rivers flowing into the sea. His heart was fixed on the right object.

But now our affections are disordered. We often love what we should hate and hate what we should love. We fear what we should hope for and hope for what we should fear. Our desires can become so strong that even when our judgment tells us something is wrong, we still choose it. We know the better way, but we follow the worse.

Some people are offended when fallen mankind is compared to beasts or devils. We do not mean that people are physically beasts or literally devils. We mean that morally, sin has made man beastlike and devilish in his desires and passions. David said in **Psalm 73:22 NKJV**, *"I was so foolish and ignorant; I was like a beast before You."* Jesus said to some in **John 8:44 NKJV**, *"You are of your father the devil."*

Our stupidity toward spiritual things, our obsession with earthly things, and our desire to gratify the flesh show something beastlike in us. Our anger, hatred, envy, malice, and pride show something devilish in us. These are strong words, but Scripture itself uses strong language because sin is a serious disease. So in our affections, man is marred clay.

We also see this in the conscience. In the beginning, conscience was like the lamp of the Lord in man's soul. It helped him clearly see right and wrong. Even now, some remains of conscience are left. People still have some sense of good and evil. But conscience has been dimmed by sin. It can be ignored, silenced, corrupted, hardened, and even seared.

We do not have to look far to see this. Our own experience proves it. We have all sinned against conscience. We have all made excuses for what we knew was wrong. We have all tried to quiet the inward voice that warned us. This shows again that man is marred clay.

Human reason also proves this. Reason itself is not evil. God gave reason. Christ is even called the Logos, the Word, or divine Reason. True reason agrees with Christ. The service of God is called reasonable service. But reason, apart from God's light, is fallen and unable to lead us into salvation.

The wisest thinkers of the ancient world made terrible mistakes about God, worship, morality, and eternity. Even modern people who boast in reason often use it to reason themselves away from faith, away from Scripture, and away from salvation. Fallen reason does not lead man to peace with God. It must be enlightened by divine revelation.

So in our reason, man is marred clay.

We also see this in the body. In the most literal sense, man was made from clay, from the dust of the earth. No matter what earthly family or background a person comes from, all people share the same beginning. We were formed from the dust. God built the body of man with wisdom, beauty, and purpose. Though God Himself has no body, the human body was fearfully and wonderfully made.

Some have believed that man originally had a visible glory about him. Whether or not that is true, we can safely say that Adam's body, before sin, was not subject to sickness, pain, corruption, and death as ours is now. But after the fall, even the body became marred. It is now subject to weakness, disease, suffering, misuse, decay, and death.

Paul called the body in its present state a lowly body. That is not because the body has no value, but because sin has brought it into humiliation and decay. Dust we are, and to dust we shall return. This may be part of why Jesus wept at the grave of Lazarus. He saw what sin had done to human nature. He saw death laying low what God had made.

When we consider man's understanding, will, affections, conscience, reason, and body, we must admit that mankind is marred by sin. How far we have fallen from what God created us to be. God made man in His image, in righteousness and true holiness, but sin has ruined the beauty of that original condition.

We only know these things clearly because God has revealed them in His Word. Scripture tells us what we were, what we are, and what we must become. The Bible is like a mirror that shows us our true condition. It tells us where evil came from, why the world is broken, why the human heart is corrupt, and why we need redemption.

Some deny the truth of divine revelation, but their denial only further proves the disorder of the human heart. The Bible carries both outward and inward evidence that it is from God. It has been preserved, tested, attacked, examined, criticized, hated, and persecuted through the ages, yet it still stands. It has convicted, converted, comforted, and transformed millions of souls.

Revelation itself is built upon the truth of the fall. If man had remained upright, the law of God would still be written clearly on the heart, and we would not need revelation in the same way. But because we have fallen, we should be thankful that God has given us His Word. In a few lines of Scripture, God reveals more truth about man's condition than all the philosophers of the world could have discovered on their own.

Some who claim to believe the Bible still reject the doctrine of man's universal corruption. They try to say that the Scriptures only speak of certain bad people or only of the heathen world. But this is a mistake. By nature, there is no difference between Jew and Gentile,

Greek and barbarian, slave and free. All have sinned and fall short of the glory of God. All are marred clay.

There are questions we cannot fully answer. How did God permit man to fall? How long did man stand before he fell? How exactly is the corruption of the fall passed down to every person? These are deep questions, and we should not spend our time trying to satisfy sinful curiosity. It is far more important to face the practical truth: fallen human nature must be renewed.

If man is marred clay, then he must be remade.

Most people hope to go to heaven when they die. My prayer is that every person would have a place prepared there. But we must understand this clearly: heaven would not be heaven to an unrenewed soul. If the heavens opened right now, and Jesus Himself invited an unconverted person to enter, that person would not be happy there unless his heart had first been changed.

What fellowship can light have with darkness? What communion can an unrenewed heart have with a holy Christ? Heaven is not merely a place of beauty, music, and rest. Heaven is a state of holiness, love, worship, purity, and fellowship with God. If a person does not love holiness now, he would not enjoy heaven then.

Many people imagine heaven in earthly terms. They picture comfort, pleasure, and rest, but they do not think deeply about holiness. Heaven is more than a place. It is the full enjoyment of God. Grace is glory begun, and glory is grace completed. Holiness, happiness, and heaven belong together.

One dying believer once said, "I am changing my place, but not my company." He had walked with God on earth, and now he was going to continue that fellowship in heaven, only in a fuller and purer way. That is what heaven is for the believer.

To enjoy that heavenly company, our marred nature must be changed. Our understanding must be enlightened. Our will must be renewed. Our conscience must be cleansed. Our reason must be guided by truth. Our affections must be lifted from earthly things and fixed on things above. And because flesh and blood cannot inherit the kingdom of God, even this mortal body must one day put on immortality.

This change is called by different names. Some call it repentance. Some call it conversion. Some call it regeneration. Scripture calls it holiness, sanctification, the new creation, and the new birth. Jesus called it being born again, or born from above.

These are not empty phrases. They do not simply describe an outward religious label. They do not merely mean baptism or church membership. They describe a real change of heart and life, a true work of God in the soul. Unless a person experiences this change, all his learning, religion, and outward respectability cannot save him.

Jesus said in **John 3:3 NKJV**, *"Most assuredly, I say to you, unless one is born again, he cannot see the kingdom of God."* This applies to everyone. Learned or unlearned, rich or poor, religious or irreligious, moral or immoral, every person must be born again.

But who can bring about this change? Who is the Potter who can remake the marred clay?

This change is not produced merely by moral persuasion. Preaching, reasoning, and urging people to turn to God have their proper place. God Himself says in **Isaiah 1:18 NKJV**, *"Come now, and* *let us reason together."* Paul reasoned with Felix about righteousness, self-control, and the judgment to come, and Felix trembled. A preacher should use truth, reason, warning, persuasion, and appeal when calling sinners to be reconciled to God.

But reasoning alone cannot raise the spiritually dead. A preacher might as well walk into a graveyard and command dead bodies to rise if he does not depend on a higher power to make the Word effective. Without the power of God, preaching is only sound. It cannot save.

This change is also not produced by the power of human free will. Fallen man cannot turn himself into a new creature. Jesus said in **John 6:44 NKJV**, *"No one can come to Me unless the Father who sent Me draws him."* Human will may restrain some outward sins. It may put a person near the means of grace. But it cannot renew the heart. Since the fall, man has no power in himself to turn fully to God.

We cannot control our own unruly wills and affections by our own strength any more than we can stop the tide or calm a stormy sea. The work required is too deep for human power.

The heavenly Potter is the Holy Spirit. He is the third Person of the blessed Trinity, one with the Father and the Son. He is the Spirit who moved upon the face of the waters at creation. He is the Spirit who overshadowed Mary before Christ was born. And He is the same Spirit who must move upon the chaos of our souls if we are to become children of God.

John the Baptist called this being baptized with the Holy Spirit. Without this work, outward baptism, whether as an infant or an adult, cannot profit the soul. We need the fire of the Spirit in the heart. We need Him to awaken, convict, renew, sanctify, and transform us.

The extraordinary gifts of the Spirit, such as miracles and speaking in different tongues, had their particular time and purpose. But the miracle of miracles still continues: the turning of the soul to God by the ordinary working of the Holy Spirit. This work will continue until time is no more.

True believers are born from above. They are born not of blood, nor of the will of the flesh, nor of the will of man, but of God. Their second creation, like the first, is divine. The new man is created after God in righteousness and true holiness.

This is the great truth the world mocks. But this is why Christ came. To bring about this new creation, Jesus left the glory of His Father. For this He lived a life of suffering and rejection. For this He died a shameful and cursed death. For this He rose again. For this He now sits at the right hand of the Father.

All the commands of the gospel, all the ordinances, all the providences of God, whether painful or pleasant, and all divine revelation from beginning to end have this purpose: to show us how far we have fallen and to bring about a glorious change in our souls.

This is a purpose worthy of the Son of God. To deliver souls from sin, to restore what was ruined, to remake what was marred, and to bring sinners into a condition even more glorious than what was lost in Adam, this is worthy of the blood of Christ.

What other religion offers anything like this? What system of human thought can compare with the gospel? The gospel is noble, reasonable, powerful, and divine. It does not merely tell man to improve himself. It tells man that God can make him new.

So why should anyone remain distant from this blessed restoration? Why continue to argue against God? Why resist His grace? Bring your clay to the heavenly Potter and pray from the heart, "Turn us, O Lord, and we shall be turned." Who knows but that this very day, this very hour, the heavenly Potter may take you in His hands and make you a vessel of honor fit for the Master's use?

Others who were once as far from God as you have been changed by grace. Mary Magdalene was once possessed by seven demons, yet Jesus delivered her. After His resurrection, He appeared to her first, and she became a witness to the apostles. Zacchaeus was a greedy and dishonest tax collector, yet when Jesus came to his house, his heart was changed, and he became willing to give generously and make restitution. Paul was once a blasphemer, persecutor, and violent man. He breathed threats against the disciples of the Lord and attacked the church. Yet on the road to Damascus, Christ met him, changed him, and made him a preacher of the gospel.

Why were these stories given to us? So that others would believe that the same grace can reach them. Therefore, believe the gospel. Repent. Come to Christ. These are glad tidings of great joy.

When you experience this grace, you will no longer argue against the truth of original sin. You will no longer accuse God foolishly for allowing the fall. You will no longer mock the new birth or call those who preach it fools. Once you feel the truth in your own soul, you will believe it. Once you believe it, you will speak of it. Instead of being vessels of wrath, hardened like clay in a furnace, you will become vessels of honor, prepared by Christ and presented to the Father as monuments of rich, free, sovereign grace forever.

To those who have already experienced the quickening work of the Spirit, let this message move you to pity and prayer for those who are still dead in sin. Pray for them. But do not only pray for them. Pray also for yourselves.

You know how much is still lacking in your faith. You know how far you still are from having the full mind of Christ. You know the body of sin and death you still carry. You know that God must continue working in you before you are fully delivered.

But take comfort. You are in safe hands. The One who began the work will finish it. He who is the Author of your faith will also be the Finisher. One day, like Christ, you will be able to say, "It is finished." Until then, you must patiently submit to the Potter's hand.

So let this be our prayer:

O Almighty Father, help us to possess our souls with patience. We are the clay, and You are the Potter. Do not let us, as the thing formed, argue against the One who formed us. Whatever Your will may be concerning us, teach us not to say, "Why are You dealing with us this way?" We place ourselves in Your hands. Deal with us as seems good in Your sight.

Let every cross, every affliction, every trial, and every temptation be used by You to stamp Your image more deeply on our hearts. Lead us from glory to glory by the power of Your blessed Spirit. Make us more and more ready for the full, perfect, endless, and uninterrupted enjoyment of glory with You.

To You, O Father, O Son, and O Holy Spirit, three Persons and one God, be all honor, power, might, majesty, and dominion, now and forever.

Amen.

Chapter Eight

The Eternity of Hell-Torments

Matthew 25:46 *"And these will go away into everlasting punishment, but the righteous into eternal life."*

One of the clearest teachings found throughout Scripture is that eternity is real. Every person who has ever lived will spend eternity somewhere. The gospel speaks not only of heaven and eternal life, but also of judgment and everlasting punishment. The promises of heaven reveal the goodness and mercy of God, while the warnings of hell reveal His holiness and justice. Together they remind us that the decisions we make in this life carry eternal consequences.

Most people gladly accept the idea of heaven. The thought of peace, joy, and eternal life with God is comforting to the human heart. But many struggle with the reality of eternal punishment. Some try to avoid the subject entirely, while others attempt to explain it away. Yet the same Bible that promises eternal life to believers also warns of everlasting judgment for those who reject God.

Jesus Himself spoke clearly about this truth.

Matthew 25:46

"And these will go away into everlasting punishment, but the righteous into eternal life."

If eternal life for the believer is real and unending, then the punishment Jesus warned about must also be real and unending. The same word used to describe the duration of heaven is used to describe the duration of judgment. Scripture never treats eternity as temporary.

The prophet Daniel also wrote about this future resurrection and judgment.

Daniel 12:2

"And many of those who sleep in the dust of the earth shall awake, Some to everlasting life, Some to shame and everlasting contempt."

The Bible consistently presents two eternal destinations. One leads to everlasting life in the presence of God. The other leads to everlasting separation and judgment.

The prophet Isaiah described the seriousness of eternal judgment with sobering words.

Isaiah 66:24

"For their worm does not die, and their fire is not quenched."

Jesus repeated this warning Himself in the Gospel of Mark.

Mark 9:43–44

"It is better for you to enter into life maimed, rather than having two hands, to go to hell, into the fire that shall never be quenched—where 'Their worm does not die and the fire is not quenched.'"

Again and again Scripture reminds us that eternity never ends.

Many people question how eternal punishment can exist. Yet instead of questioning the justice of God, we should first recognize the seriousness of sin. Sin is not merely breaking rules. Sin is rebellion against a holy and eternal God. The Bible says:

Romans 3:23

"For all have sinned and fall short of the glory of God."

Every one of us stands guilty before God apart from His mercy. Yet in His love, God made a way of salvation through Jesus Christ.

John 3:16

"For God so loved the world that He gave His only begotten Son, that whoever believes in Him should not perish but have everlasting life."

Notice the contrast in this verse. Without Christ, people perish. Through Christ, people receive everlasting life.

God does not delight in judgment. Scripture says:

2 Peter 3:9

"The Lord is not slack concerning His promise, as some count slackness, but is longsuffering toward us, not willing that any should perish but that all should come to repentance."

God warns people because He desires repentance. He calls sinners to turn to Him while there is still time. The cross itself is proof of God's mercy. Jesus Christ came into the world to save sinners.

Romans 5:8

"But God demonstrates His own love toward us, in that while we were still sinners, Christ died for us."

Jesus bore the punishment for sin so we could be forgiven. Through His death and resurrection, salvation is freely offered to all who believe.

Yet Scripture also makes clear that those who reject Christ remain under judgment.

John 3:36

"He who believes in the Son has everlasting life; and he who does not believe the Son shall not see life, but the wrath of God abides on him."

This life is the only opportunity we have to respond to the gospel. The Bible never promises another chance after death.

Hebrews 9:27

"And as it is appointed for men to die once, but after this the judgment."

Because of this, eternity should never be treated casually. Every heartbeat moves us closer to standing before God.

The Bible also teaches that the devil and his angels will face eternal punishment.

Matthew 25:41

"Depart from Me, you cursed, into the everlasting fire prepared for the devil and his angels."

If God judged the fallen angels who rebelled against Him, then humanity should not assume it can reject God without consequence. Yet mankind has received something the fallen angels never received: the offer of redemption through Jesus Christ.

This should cause us to marvel at the mercy of God. None of us deserve salvation, yet God offers grace freely through His Son.

Still, many continue living carelessly. Some openly reject God, while others trust in outward religion without true surrender. They assume there will always be more time. But Jesus repeatedly warned that eternity comes suddenly and unexpectedly.

Matthew 24:44

"Therefore you also be ready, for the Son of Man is coming at an hour you do not expect."

What temporary pleasure is worth losing your soul forever? Sin may satisfy for a moment, but eternity never ends.

Hebrews 11:25 speaks of the *"passing pleasures of sin."* Sin only offers temporary pleasure, but its consequences are eternal.

Imagine the regret of a soul separated from God forever, fully realizing too late what was lost. Imagine remembering every warning ignored, every opportunity rejected, and every call to repentance pushed aside. Jesus described hell as a place of sorrow, darkness, and anguish.

But for the believer, there is glorious hope.

Jesus did not come merely to warn us about judgment. He came to rescue us from it.

Romans 8:1

"There is therefore now no condemnation to those who are in Christ Jesus."

Those who trust in Christ are forgiven completely. Heaven is not wishful thinking. It is the promise of God.

John 14:2–3

"In My Father's house are many mansions... I go to prepare a place for

you. And if I go and prepare a place for you, I will come again and receive you to Myself; that where I am, there you may be also."

For believers, eternity means everlasting joy in the presence of God.

Revelation 21:4

"And God will wipe away every tear from their eyes; there shall be no more death, nor sorrow, nor crying. There shall be no more pain, for the former things have passed away."

This is why the gospel is such good news. No matter how broken or sinful a person may be, forgiveness is available through Jesus Christ.

But the invitation must be received.

A person cannot continue rejecting God forever and expect no consequence. Eternity is too serious to ignore.

2 Corinthians 6:2

"Behold, now is the accepted time; behold, now is the day of salvation."

Do not harden your heart toward God.

Do not settle for empty religion without true surrender.

Do not assume you have endless time.

Come to Jesus while the door of mercy is still open.

Trust fully in Him.

Walk in holiness.

Live with eternity in view.

And may the reality of eternity awaken within us a deeper gratitude for the mercy, grace, and salvation freely offered through Jesus Christ our Lord.

Chapter Nine

The Temptation of Christ

Matthew 4:1–11 NKJV *"Then Jesus was led up by the Spirit into the wilderness to be tempted by the devil. And when He had fasted forty days and forty nights, afterward He was hungry. Now when the tempter came to Him, he said, 'If You are the Son of God, command that these stones become bread.' But He answered and said, 'It is written, "Man shall not live by bread alone, but by every word that proceeds from the mouth of God."' Then the devil took Him up into the holy city, set Him on the pinnacle of the temple, and said to Him, 'If You are the Son of God, throw Yourself down. For it is written: "He shall give His angels charge over you," and, "In their hands they shall bear you up, lest you dash your foot against a stone."' Jesus said to him, 'It is written again, "You shall* *not tempt the Lord your God.'" Again, the devil took Him up on an exceedingly high mountain, and showed Him all the kingdoms of the world and their glory. And he said to Him, 'All these things I will give You if You will fall down and worship me.' Then Jesus said to him, 'Away with you, Satan! For it is written, "You shall worship the Lord your God, and Him only you shall serve."' Then the devil left Him, and behold, angels came and ministered to Him."*

Today we are invited to walk with Jesus into the wilderness. We are invited to look closely at our Savior as He is tempted, to feel the seriousness of the battle, and to receive instruction and comfort from His victory. In this conflict, Jesus proves Himself to be the beloved Son of God. The Father had already declared His pleasure in Him, and now Jesus demonstrates His perfect obedience.

Matthew gives us the details of this great battle. He shows us when it happened, where it happened, how it happened, and how Jesus overcame the devil. This was not a small event. This was a direct confrontation between the Son of God and the enemy of our souls.

Just before this, Jesus had been baptized. The heavens opened, the Spirit of God descended upon Him like a dove, and a voice from heaven said, **Matthew 3:17 NKJV**, *"This is My beloved Son, in whom I am well pleased."* Then, immediately after this powerful moment, Jesus was led by the Spirit into the wilderness to be tempted by the devil.

This is important. Jesus was not led into the wilderness because He had done something wrong. He was led there by the Spirit of

God. He was full of the Holy Spirit, and yet He was led into a place of testing. This teaches us that being filled with the Spirit does not mean we will never be tempted. Sometimes, after the greatest spiritual moments, the fiercest battles follow.

Jesus was led into a lonely wilderness. It was likely a wild and desolate place, away from people and comfort. Mark tells us He was with the wild beasts. There, Jesus was alone. No disciple was with Him. No friend stood beside Him. In this battle, as in His agony before the cross, He stood alone.

Before the temptation reached its height, Jesus fasted forty days and forty nights. Moses and Elijah had also fasted forty days in earlier times. These fasts were miraculous and should not be imitated carelessly or proudly. But they do teach us that fasting has a place in the life of God's people. Jesus prepared for the battle with prayer, fasting, and communion with the Father.

During those forty days, it seems Jesus did not feel ordinary hunger in the way we do. Fellowship with the Father was His strength. But afterward, He was hungry. His body was weak. He had a real human nature, and He truly felt hunger.

That is when the tempter came.

The devil often waits for moments of weakness. He comes when the body is tired, the mind is worn, the emotions are strained, and the soul feels pressed. He came to Jesus when He was hungry, and he began with these words: "If You are the Son of God."

This was a direct attack on the Father's word. The Father had just said, "This is My beloved Son." Satan now says, "If You are the Son of God." He wanted Jesus to question what the Father had declared.

He wanted Him to doubt His identity. He wanted Him to think, "If I am truly the beloved Son, why am I hungry? Why am I alone? Why am I in this wilderness? Why has the Father allowed this?"

This is still one of Satan's common weapons. He tries to make God's children doubt what God has said. He whispers, "If God loved you, would you be in this situation? If you were really His child, would you suffer like this? If God were pleased with you, would He allow you to feel so alone?"

Satan used a similar method with Adam and Eve. He suggested that God was withholding something good from them. He tried to make them think hard thoughts of their Creator. Now he tries to do the same with Christ.

Then Satan said, "Command that these stones become bread." This temptation was subtle. Jesus was hungry. He had the power to turn stones into bread. Satan was saying, "Prove who You are. Use Your power to meet Your own need. Do not wait on the Father. Take matters into Your own hands."

But Jesus saw through the temptation. He would not distrust His Father. He would not perform a miracle merely to satisfy Satan. He would not step outside the Father's will to relieve His hunger.

Jesus answered with Scripture. He said, **Matthew 4:4 NKJV**, *"It is written, 'Man shall not live by bread alone, but by every word that proceeds from the mouth of God.'"*

Jesus quoted from Deuteronomy, where God reminded Israel that He fed them with manna in the wilderness so they would learn that man does not live by bread alone. Israel was called God's son and was tested in the wilderness. Now Jesus, the true Son, is also in the wilderness. But where Israel failed, Jesus obeyed.

Jesus was saying, "My life does not depend on bread alone. My life depends on My Father. If He wants to feed Me, He can provide. If He wants to sustain Me without bread, He can do that too. I will not distrust Him. I will live by His Word."

In the first temptation, Satan was defeated. But he did not stop. Since he could not make Jesus distrust the Father, he tried to make Him presume upon the Father.

The devil took Jesus into the holy city and set Him on the pinnacle of the temple. This was a high place, possibly overlooking the courts of the temple below. It may have been during a time when many people were gathered for worship. Then Satan said, "If You are the Son of God, throw Yourself down."

Again, Satan used the same phrase: "If You are the Son of God." But this time, he added Scripture. He quoted from Psalm 91, saying that God would give His angels charge over Him and that they would bear Him up, lest He dash His foot against a stone.

This teaches us something serious. The devil can quote Scripture. He can use the Bible wrongly. He can take a true verse and twist it into a false application. He can leave out important parts and use religious language to lead people into sin.

In Psalm 91, God promises to keep His people in all their ways. But Satan left out the phrase "in all your ways." God promises protection when we walk in His will. He does not promise protection when we act proudly, foolishly, or presumptuously. If Jesus had thrown

Himself down just to prove something, He would not have been walking in the Father's way. He would have been testing God.

Jesus answered again with Scripture. He said, **Matthew 4:7 NKJV**, *"It is written again, 'You shall not tempt the Lord your God.'"*

Jesus would not use one Scripture in a way that contradicted another Scripture. He compared Scripture with Scripture. He refused to turn faith into presumption. He would not jump from the temple to force the Father to rescue Him. True faith trusts God. False faith tries to force God to prove Himself.

The second temptation failed.

Then Satan tried one more time. He took Jesus up on an exceedingly high mountain and showed Him all the kingdoms of the world and their glory. Luke says he showed them to Him in a moment of time. This may not have been a literal viewing of every kingdom at once, but a powerful presentation placed before the imagination of Christ. Satan showed the glory, not the grief. He showed the crowns, not the thorns. He showed the wealth, the palaces, the power, the honor, the beauty, and the greatness of the world.

That is how temptation works. Satan shows the shine, not the slavery. He shows the pleasure, not the pain. He shows the crown, not the thorns. He shows the glory of sin, but hides its chains.

Then Satan said, "All these things I will give You if You will fall down and worship me."

Here Satan finally reveals what he has wanted all along. He wants worship. He wants the heart. He says, in effect, "You do not need to suffer. You do not need the cross. Take the kingdoms now. Take the glory now. Just bow to me."

This was a direct temptation for Jesus to avoid the path of obedience and suffering. Satan was offering a kingdom without the cross. But Jesus came to do the Father's will. He would not receive anything from Satan's hand. He would not divide His worship. He would not turn away from the Father.

Jesus answered with holy authority: **Matthew 4:10 NKJV**, *"Away with you, Satan! For it is written, 'You shall worship the Lord your God, and Him only you shall serve.'"*

Jesus would not worship Satan. He would not worship the world. He would not worship power, comfort, fame, or ease. He would worship and serve the Father only.

Then the devil left Him. The battle was over. Jesus had conquered. Satan had used the lust of the flesh in the first temptation, the pride of life in the second, and the lust of the eyes in the third. But Jesus overcame them all.

The first Adam was tempted in a garden and fell. The second Adam was tempted in a wilderness and stood. Adam had food all around him and sinned. Jesus had no food and obeyed. Adam was surrounded by beauty and failed. Jesus was surrounded by wilderness and conquered. Adam listened to the serpent. Jesus silenced him with the Word of God.

After the devil left, angels came and ministered to Jesus. Heaven had watched. The Father had not abandoned His Son. The angels who had not interfered during the battle now came to serve Him. The Father provided for Him in the Father's time.

This victory of Christ should bring great comfort to believers. Jesus did not fight this battle only as a private person. He stood as our representative. He overcame the devil for His people. Because He conquered, we have hope that we too will conquer through Him.

Jesus is also our compassionate High Priest. He was tempted in all points as we are, yet without sin. He knows what temptation feels like. He knows what it means to be hungry, lonely, attacked, and pressured. He knows what it means to be tempted to doubt, to presume, and to take an easier path. Because He was tempted, He is able to help those who are tempted.

This should comfort those who are troubled by strong and frightening temptations. Some believers are tempted with thoughts of despair, self-harm, blasphemy, unbelief, or other terrible things. They may think God has cast them off because such temptations come against them. But temptation itself is not proof that God has rejected you. Jesus Himself was tempted by the devil. The servant is not greater than his Master.

It should not surprise us when temptation comes in waves. It should not surprise us when Satan follows us even into holy places. He followed Jesus from baptism into the wilderness and even took Him to the temple. If Satan tempted Christ after the Father's voice had declared Him beloved, then he may also tempt believers after seasons of great communion with God.

There are several lessons we should learn from this passage.

First, solitude and retirement can be useful, but too much isolation can become dangerous. There are times when we need to be alone with God. Jesus often withdrew to pray. But it is not good for a person to live always alone. A tree standing by itself is more exposed to the wind than trees standing together in a forest. A believer who isolates himself can become more vulnerable to temptation because he has no one to encourage, correct, or help him when he falls.

Jesus was led into the wilderness by the Spirit for a special purpose. We should not lead ourselves into unnecessary isolation and temptation. We should pray, "Lord, keep us from leading ourselves into temptation, and support us when Your providence brings us into seasons of testing."

Second, those who desire to minister to others must be prepared through prayer, fasting, and even temptation. Jesus prepared for public ministry through this wilderness battle. Those who preach, teach, counsel, or lead others spiritually must understand more than books. They must understand the devices of Satan and the struggles of the soul.

A minister who does not understand temptation may give terrible counsel to wounded people. He may mistake conviction for madness. He may tell a broken sinner to distract himself with entertainment when he should be pointing him to the blood of Christ. He may fail to comfort those who are under spiritual attack because he has never learned how the enemy works.

Those who would be useful in binding up the brokenhearted must be prepared by God. Prayer, meditation, Scripture, and temptation help make a faithful minister. If God allows young ministers or believers to experience spiritual conflict, they should not be discouraged. It may be part of how God prepares them to help others.

Paul said that if he was afflicted, it was for the comfort and salvation of others. God often uses our trials to make us more compassionate, wise, and useful. Those who have been tempted can better help others who are tempted.

Third, we learn that poverty and need can be seasons of temptation. Satan came to Jesus when He was hungry. Those who are brought low financially or physically should be on guard. Poverty can tempt people to doubt God's love, question their sonship, murmur against providence, or seek relief in unlawful ways.

Agur prayed not to be poor, lest he steal and profane the name of God. This is a real danger. But poverty and temptation are not signs that God has rejected you. Jesus was hungry. Jesus was tempted. Yet He remained the beloved Son.

If you are poor, hungry, or in need, learn from Christ. Do not distrust your Father. Do not take sinful shortcuts. Make your need known to God. He cares for you. The same Father who sent angels to minister to Christ can send help to you. Your extremity can become the Redeemer's opportunity. God can spread a table in the wilderness. Man does not live by bread alone, but by every word that proceeds from the mouth of God.

Fourth, those who are lifted high in life must also be watchful. Satan placed Jesus on the pinnacle of the temple. High places are dangerous places. Wealth, influence, honor, position, and spiritual prominence can make even strong people dizzy.

We should pray not only in times of trouble, but also in times of prosperity. Wealth has its own temptations. Agur prayed not only against poverty, but also against riches, lest he become full and say, "Who is the Lord?" Those who are rich or honored must watch and pray.

This is especially true for those in visible spiritual positions. If Satan can make a leader fall, others are often wounded by that fall. No one falls alone when others are watching and following. Pride, vanity, love of praise, and love of the world are dangerous temptations for those who stand in high places.

Satan does not care how high he lifts someone if he can gain that person's heart. He may offer success, recognition, opportunity, or influence if only the heart will bow to him. Therefore, we must learn from Christ and say, "Away with you, Satan. I will worship the Lord my God, and Him only will I serve."

Fifth, we must learn to fight temptation with the Word of God. Jesus had the Spirit without measure, yet He answered every temptation with Scripture. If He used the sword of the Spirit, how much more must we?

There is no weapon like the Word of God. But we must use it rightly. Satan also quoted Scripture, but he twisted it. Therefore, we must compare Scripture with Scripture. We must not take verses out of context or use them to justify pride, presumption, sin, or foolishness.

Many errors, false impressions, and strange ideas would be stopped if believers held closely to the written Word. When Satan misuses Scripture, we must not throw Scripture away. We must use it more carefully, more humbly, and more faithfully. The Word is still a lamp to our feet and a light to our path.

We should also remember that temptation may return. Luke says Satan left Jesus for a season. He would come again, especially near the time of Christ's suffering and death. In the same way, believers should not think the battle is over forever because one season of temptation has passed.

Our strongest temptations may still be ahead. We do not yet know all the corruption that remains in our hearts. We do not know which weak places Satan may attack. Therefore, we should not boast as though the battle were finished. But neither should we be afraid. Satan may tempt, but he cannot force. He may sift, but Christ prays. He who helped us before will help us to the end.

Jesus conquered for us in the wilderness, and He will make His people more than conquerors. One day the battle will be over. We now sow in tears, but soon we will reap with joy. We now pass through a wilderness, but one day angels will not merely minister to us in the wilderness; they will carry us home to the heavenly Canaan. Then the accuser, the tempter, the world, the flesh, and every enemy will trouble us no more.

But there is a warning here also.

Woe to those who laugh now in careless sin, for they will mourn later. Woe to those who do not believe there is a devil and have never felt the danger of his temptations. Woe to those who are at ease in Zion, living in idleness and self-indulgence, making continual provision for the flesh. Woe to those who not only sin themselves but tempt others to sin. Woe to those who deny God's Word or use it only to serve their own purposes. Woe to those who sell their conscience and pawn their souls for a little wealth, honor, or pleasure.

Woe to those who climb to high places by corruption, bribery, flattery, compromise, and bowing down to the sins of those who can advance them. Whether they admit it or not, they are doing the works of their father the devil. How will they escape the judgment of hell unless they repent?

But this message is especially meant to comfort those who know what it is to be tempted. If you have felt Satan's fiery darts, then you know there is a devil. But you must also know there is a Savior. Jesus was tempted, yet He triumphed. He is merciful. He is compassionate. He is able to help you.

May the Lord comfort His afflicted people. May the tempted Savior strengthen His tempted saints. May He bless this word to support those under attack and help them stand.

The Lord bless you and keep you. The Lord lift up the light of His countenance upon you. May He establish you, strengthen you, settle you, and bring you safely into His eternal kingdom.

Amen.

Chapter Ten

The Serious Sin of Profane Cursing and Swearing

Matthew 5:34 NKJV *"But I say to you, do not swear at all."*

Among the many sins that have become common in our world, one of the most serious and yet one of the most accepted is the sin of profane cursing and swearing. It is sad to hear how often people take the name of God lightly. In everyday conversation, in anger, in joking, in frustration, and even among children, the holy name of God is used without reverence.

This should grieve every sincere follower of Jesus Christ. The name of God is not ordinary. It is holy. It belongs to the One who created us, sustains us, saves us, and will one day judge us. To use His name carelessly or wickedly is no small thing.

A faithful minister of Christ cannot look at such a growing evil and remain silent. When sin becomes common, people often stop feeling how serious it is. Public correction is often neglected, and private correction is often rejected. Many people are so hardened by sin that when someone warns them, they become angry instead of thankful. It can feel like casting pearls before swine, because they turn and attack the one who tries to help them.

But the servant of God must still speak. Whether people listen or refuse to listen, the watchman must warn. The ambassador of Christ must show people their sin and call them to repentance. For that reason, we must consider the words of Jesus carefully: **Matthew 5:34 NKJV**, *"But I say to you, do not swear at all."*

Before we go further, we should understand what Jesus means. Some have taken this command to mean that all oaths are forbidden, even in a court of law or before a lawful authority. But that is not what Jesus is teaching here. Scripture shows that solemn oaths on proper occasions are not always sinful. Paul himself sometimes used serious statements such as, "God is my witness," or "God is my judge," when speaking solemnly before others.

Jesus is not forbidding lawful and serious testimony before proper authority. He is correcting the misuse of oaths in ordinary conversation. In His day, the Pharisees had twisted the law. God had commanded His people not to take His name in vain and not to swear falsely by His name. But the Pharisees taught that people could swear by other things, such as heaven, earth, Jerusalem, or their own head, as long as they did not directly use the name of God.

Jesus corrected this. He said not to swear by heaven because it is God's throne. Do not swear by the earth because it is His footstool. Do not swear by Jerusalem because it is the city of the great King. Do not swear by your head because you cannot make one hair white or black. Then He said in **Matthew 5:37 NKJV**, *"But let your 'Yes' be 'Yes,' and your 'No,' 'No.' For whatever is more than these is from the evil one."*

So Jesus is teaching that our normal speech should be plain, truthful, and reverent. We should not need careless oaths to make people believe us. Our words should be honest enough that a simple yes or no is enough.

This should also warn us against common expressions that may seem harmless but are really careless forms of swearing. People may say things like, "On my life," "As I live," "By heaven," "By my faith," or other phrases meant to strengthen their words. Many may not think anything of these expressions, but Jesus warns against this kind of careless speech. If our words go beyond simple truthfulness and begin calling on sacred things in ordinary conversation, we should take heed.

The sin Jesus is addressing is profane swearing in common conversation. It is the careless, irreverent, or wicked use of God's name or sacred things. This sin is serious for several reasons.

First, profane swearing is serious because there is no real temptation in it and no true pleasure from it. Many sins appeal to some desire in the fallen heart. A drunkard may say strong drink gives him pleasure. A greedy person may say dishonesty helps him gain money. A lustful person may say he is drawn by sinful desire. These excuses do not make sin right, but they show that some sins have an obvious temptation attached to them.

But what does the common swearer gain? What pleasure does he receive? What benefit comes from using God's name in vain? There is no lasting pleasure, no profit, no satisfaction, and no true advantage. It is a sin committed for nothing.

This makes the sin even more foolish. The swearer does not even sell his soul for some great earthly gain. He gives it away cheaply. He risks eternal judgment for words that bring him no good at all.

Second, profane swearing is serious because it can be repeated so often. Some sins take time to commit and repeat. A drunkard must recover before returning again to drunkenness. A person may profane the Lord's Day only when that day comes. But the swearer can sin again almost immediately. He can take God's name in vain many times in a single conversation.

Some people pour out oaths and curses so quickly that one follows another before the first is even finished. Their speech becomes filled with blasphemy. If God has said He will not hold guiltless the one who takes His name in vain, what a great weight of guilt lies on the person who does it again and again without repentance.

If such a person could see all his careless and wicked words gathered together before God, he would be terrified. What kind of hardened conscience must a person have to carry such guilt and not feel its weight?

Third, profane swearing is serious because it hardens unbelievers against the Christian faith. Christians are called to live in a way that honors God before the world. Jesus said in **Matthew 5:16 NKJV**, *"Let your light so shine before men, that they may see your good works and glorify your Father in heaven."* Paul also told believers to walk wisely toward those who are outside.

But when people who claim to be Christians use God's name carelessly, unbelievers are hardened. How can we expect unbelievers to honor God when those who profess to know Him dishonor His name? How can people be drawn to Christ when Christians treat His commands lightly?

Because of sins like this, Christianity is mocked. The name of God is blasphemed among those who do not believe. People look at careless Christians and say, "If they really believed in God, would they speak of Him that way?" This becomes a stumbling block to others.

Jesus gave serious warnings about causing others to stumble. It would be better for a man to have a millstone hung around his neck and be thrown into the sea than to cause one of Christ's little ones to stumble. How much more serious is it when someone causes unbelievers to mock God and sincere believers to grieve?

Profane swearing does not only harden unbelievers. It also wounds faithful Christians. David once cried out because he had to dwell among wicked and profane people. Lot's righteous soul was troubled day by day by the ungodly behavior around him. In the same way, true believers are grieved when they hear God's holy name used carelessly.

The name that angels adore is treated like a common word. The name we are not worthy to speak except with reverence in prayer is thrown around in anger and foolishness. This should pierce the heart of anyone who loves God.

The careless swearer may not care, but God cares. He sees the grief of His people. He hears the blasphemy of the wicked. He will not forget the ungodly words spoken against Him.

Fourth, profane swearing is serious because it resembles the language of hell. Those who are lost and without hope may rage and blaspheme in their misery because they know they are under judgment. But for people who are still living under God's daily mercy, still receiving breath, food, protection, and countless undeserved blessings, to use their mouths against God is a terrible evil.

Every morning, God's mercies are renewed. Every moment, people live because He sustains them. Yet many take the breath He gives and use it to dishonor His name. This is a height of sin that should make us tremble.

After considering these things, the words of Jesus should come to us with great force: **Matthew 5:34 NKJV**, *"But I say to you, do not swear at all."* Do not use God's name in a careless or profane way. Do not curse. Do not make light of sacred things. Do not speak as though the name of the Lord is common.

This sin is especially foolish when people think it makes them look bold, strong, fashionable, or impressive. Some imagine that swearing makes them appear powerful among their friends. But in truth, it reveals great foolishness and hardness of heart.

What could be more shameful than pretending to honor God in public worship and then blaspheming His name in ordinary conversation? If someone denied the existence of God, we might at least understand why he spoke so wickedly, though he would still be guilty. But for someone to say he believes in God, to confess that God is holy, powerful, and just, and then to use His name carelessly, is both foolish and fearful.

People would not dare insult a general while standing before his army. They would not provoke a lion while within reach of its paw. Yet they provoke Almighty God, the everlasting King, who can consume them in a moment and cast them into hell. Do they think God is the only One who can be offended without consequence?

God is patient, but He will not be mocked forever. The day will come when He will defend His holy name. Those who now use His name carelessly may one day cry for the rocks and mountains to fall on them and hide them from the wrath of the Lamb. They once used careless words calling for judgment, but if they do not repent, they may find that judgment has come indeed.

The psalmist says that the one who loved cursing would have it come upon him. He clothed himself with cursing like a garment, and it would enter his body like water and his bones like oil. That is a frightening picture. The words a person loves may one day return upon him in judgment.

Because this sin is so serious and so common, every person should do what he can to discourage and stop it. Love for God and love for neighbor both require this. Love for God calls us to defend the honor of His name. Love for neighbor calls us to warn people before they bring ruin on themselves.

If someone slandered our name or the name of a loved one, we would want to defend that reputation. How much more should we care when the great and holy name of God is dishonored? He is our Creator, King, Father, and best Friend. Shall His name be blasphemed constantly, and no one speak?

Those in authority have a special responsibility. Their office is meant, in part, to restrain evil. Many people are more affected by authority and consequence than by sermons or personal warnings. Therefore, those who have lawful authority should use it wisely and courageously to discourage profane cursing and swearing.

This may require courage. It may not be popular. But it is done for God. The Lord will support those who seek to honor Him faithfully and reward them in His time.

Now let every person take this seriously. If you have been guilty of this sin, do not wait until someone has to punish you or warn you again. Watch the door of your lips. Ask God for help, because without His grace all your efforts will fail. Pray that He would cleanse your speech, soften your heart, and make your mouth pleasing to Him.

Consider carefully what has been said. If you care about your soul, if you care about your witness as a Christian, if you do not want to be a grief to believers or a stumbling block to unbelievers, then take heed. Do not be like those who use their tongues as instruments of hell while living under the mercy of heaven.

In the name of the Lord Jesus Christ, hear His command: "Do not swear at all."

Let your yes be yes. Let your no be no. Let your speech be truthful, clean, reverent, and honoring to God.

Amen.

Chapter Eleven

The Folly and Danger of Not Being Righteous Enough

Ecclesiastes 7:16 NKJV *"Do not be overly righteous, nor be overly wise: Why should you destroy yourself?"*

It often happens that when people live in sin and follow the ways of the world, no one is very bothered by it. Their friends do not correct them. Their family does not warn them. Their companions do not think anything is wrong. As long as they live like everyone else, they are accepted.

But when a person begins to turn toward God, everything changes. When someone starts taking the things of God seriously, when they begin to pray, repent, read the Word, and desire a real relationship with Christ, people often begin to resist them. Sometimes the greatest opposition does not come from strangers. It comes from those closest to them.

Jesus told us this would happen. Those who desire to live godly will suffer persecution. Jesus also said He did not come to bring peace, but a sword. He did not mean that He delights in division. He meant that true faith in Him will often divide those who want God from those who are content with shallow religion.

Many people are fine with religion as long as it does not go too far. They do not want their loved ones to live wickedly. They do not want them to become immoral, reckless, or openly rebellious. They are happy if they attend church, say a prayer, read the Bible once in a while, and keep up the outward forms of Christianity.

But when a person goes beyond outward religion and begins to seek Christ with the whole heart, people begin to say, "Do not be too serious. Do not go too far. Do not become extreme. Spare yourself."

That is how many people misuse the words of Ecclesiastes 7:16. They say, "Do not be overly righteous," as if God is warning people not to be too holy or too committed. But the danger for most people is not that they are too righteous. The greater danger is that they are not righteous enough. They have the form of godliness, but not the power of God in the heart.

It is not being too righteous to say that we must have the Spirit of God. It is not extreme to say that the same Holy Spirit who worked in the first believers must also work in us. This does not mean every Christian will perform the same outward miracles the apostles did. We are not saying every believer must raise the dead, heal the sick, open blind eyes, or speak with miraculous tongues. Those signs had a special purpose in the early church.

But we are saying this: every true Christian must have the Holy Spirit working in the heart. A person may have gifts and still not have grace. A person may speak well, serve publicly, or do impressive religious works and still not be truly changed. Gifts alone do not save the soul. What we need is the sanctifying work of the Holy Spirit.

Jesus said in **John 3:3 NKJV**, *"Most assuredly, I say to you, unless one is born again, he cannot see the kingdom of God."* That is not religious exaggeration. That is the clear word of Christ. By nature, we are born in sin. Our hearts are far from God. We cannot fix ourselves. We must be made new by the Holy Spirit.

The Holy Spirit is not merely a feeling, an idea, or a good conscience. He is the third Person of the Trinity, equal with the Father and the Son. He must come and change us. He must renew us. He must give spiritual life. We are not true Christians merely because we were baptized, attend church, or use Christian language. We are true Christians when the Spirit of God has made us new.

Some people mock the idea that a believer can feel or know the work of the Spirit in the soul. But if a person cannot in any way know the Spirit's work, then how can he know he has been born again? Jesus compared the work of the Spirit to the wind. In **John 3:8 NKJV**, He said, *"The wind blows where it wishes, and you hear the sound of it, but cannot tell where it comes from and where it goes. So is everyone who is born of the Spirit."*

You cannot see the wind, but you can feel its effects. In the same way, we do not see the Holy Spirit with our physical eyes, but His work is known in the heart. He convicts of sin. He gives faith. He changes desires. He brings love for Christ. He gives power to obey. Religion that never reaches the heart is only a name. A person may have a name that he is alive, while spiritually he is dead.

Some ask for proof of the Spirit's work. They want signs and wonders. They ask, "Do you raise the dead? Do you heal lepers? Do you open blind eyes?" But there is a greater work than these. When a person dead in sin is made alive in Christ, that is the power of God. When a sinner is cleansed from guilt, that is the power of God. When someone who once had no desire for God now runs in the way of His commandments, that is the power of God. When ears that were once deaf to truth are opened to hear the Word of God, that is the power of God.

To reduce the Holy Spirit to nothing more than a good conscience is to reduce Christianity to human morality. Even unbelieving philosophers can talk about conscience, virtue, and doing good. Christianity is far greater than that. Christianity is the life of God in the soul. It is not built on common sense alone. It is built on the revelation of God and the power of the Holy Spirit.

So it is not being overly righteous to say we must have the Spirit of God. That is basic Christianity.

It is also not being overly righteous to gather often with the people of God. Some people think Sunday church, a few prayers, and occasional Bible reading are enough. They think anything beyond that is too much. But Christians need fellowship. Wicked people gather together to strengthen one another in sin. Should the people of God not gather to strengthen one another in Christ?

The early Christians loved fellowship. They gathered together, prayed together, worshiped together, broke bread together, and encouraged one another. We should follow their example. Until Christian fellowship becomes precious to us, we should not expect the gospel to flourish as it should.

It is also not being overly righteous to avoid the sinful entertainments and pleasures of the world. Scripture says in **1 Thessalonians 5:22 NKJV**, *"Abstain from every form of evil."* It also says in **1 Corinthians 10:31 NKJV**, *"Therefore, whether you eat or drink, or whatever you do, do all to the glory of God."*

The question is not whether a Christian may enjoy simple pleasures. The question is whether those pleasures honor God or pull the heart away from Him. If something does not violate your commitment to Christ, does not feed sin, does not harden the heart, and can truly be done for the glory of God, then enjoy it with a clear conscience. But if something keeps sinners from Christ, wastes precious time, hardens the heart, stirs sinful desires, and is something you would not want to be doing when Christ calls you into eternity, then stay away from it.

Many of the popular entertainments of the world do not help the soul. They do not stir love for God. They do not lead to holiness. They do not prepare people for death or judgment. They often fill the mind with vanity, pride, sensuality, foolishness, and forgetfulness of God.

Some may ask, "What harm is there in it?" But the Christian must ask more than that. The Christian must ask, "Does this glorify God? Does this strengthen my walk with Christ? Would I be glad to meet

Jesus while doing this? Does this feed my spirit, or does it feed my flesh?"

Many things the world calls harmless are spiritually dangerous. They are not safe simply because respectable people enjoy them. They are not right simply because society approves them. The world often celebrates what weakens the soul.

It is especially dangerous when ministers and spiritual leaders approve worldly living by their example. If ministers live like the world, attend worldly entertainments, and show little separation from sin, people will assume there is no danger. But ministers are called to be examples to the flock. If they place stumbling blocks before weaker believers, they will answer to God.

People who do not know the joy of God will search for joy in lesser things. Because they do not know the sweetness of Christ, they run to the world for pleasure. But when a person tastes the love of God and feels His power in the soul, old pleasures lose their grip. The Bible becomes food. Prayer becomes a delight. Fellowship with God becomes sweeter than the amusements of sin.

This does not mean Christians must always be on their knees, praying and reading every moment. The issue is not whether we ever rest or enjoy life. The issue is what our hearts love. People who love worldly hobbies never get tired of talking about them. In the same way, when a person is renewed by the Spirit, it becomes a joy to walk with God, talk about God, and tell others what Christ has done. Jesus said in **Matthew 12:34 NKJV**, *"For out of the abundance of the heart the mouth speaks."*

Now, while most people are not in danger of being too righteous, there is a wrong kind of "over-righteousness" that must be avoided. This does not mean loving Christ too much or obeying God too deeply. No one can be too holy, too humble, too loving, or too devoted to Jesus. But a person can become extreme in the wrong spirit.

A person is overly righteous in the wrong way when he confines the Spirit of God to only one church, group, or denomination and refuses fellowship with true believers who love Christ simply because they are not part of his group. That is not holiness. That is pride and narrowness.

The Holy Spirit is the true center of Christian unity. Wherever I see the image of Christ, I should show love. If a person sincerely loves the Lord Jesus Christ, he is my brother or sister, even if we differ on lesser things. The spirit of Christianity is not hateful, proud, or divisive. It is humble, loving, and centered on Christ.

Some people are so attached to their own party, opinion, or denomination that they cannot bear to be around believers who think differently. That spirit is not from God. If that kind of attitude entered heaven, heaven itself would feel like hell to such a person, because heaven is full of love, humility, unity, and worship.

Christianity will flourish when believers are united in Christ. Division, jealousy, and persecution will not advance the gospel. Truth, love, humility, holiness, and the power of the Spirit will.

This does not mean doctrine is unimportant. Doctrine matters. The church matters. Truth matters. But the Spirit of God must not be limited to church walls or religious systems. Christ can meet His people in a field as surely as in a church building. He is present wherever His people gather in sincerity and truth.

The spirit of persecution is always wrong. Some may not have the power to imprison, silence, or kill those who preach Christ, but the desire to do so may still be in their hearts. That is not the Spirit of Christ. The gospel is the gospel of peace.

The true servant of God does not preach from envy, jealousy, or rivalry. If others preach Christ faithfully and God gives them more success, we should rejoice. Paul said in **Philippians 1:18 NKJV**, *"Christ is preached; and in this I rejoice, yes, and will rejoice."* The kingdom is not advanced by jealousy. It is advanced when Jesus is exalted.

A person may also be overly righteous in the wrong way when he spends so much time in religious meetings that he neglects his family, work, and proper responsibilities. Christ does not give anyone permission to be lazy. From the beginning, God gave mankind work to do. Adam was placed in the garden to tend it. Abel kept sheep. Cain worked the ground. Jesus Himself was known as the carpenter's son. Paul worked as a tentmaker.

Work is part of our duty in this life. Every person should be useful in the place God has assigned him. We must seek first the kingdom of God, but seeking God first does not mean neglecting our God-given responsibilities. It means putting every responsibility under the Lordship of Christ.

There is a danger in working so much for earthly things that we forget the soul. But there is also a danger in pretending to be spiritual while neglecting ordinary duties. A Christian has responsibilities before God and responsibilities in daily life. He must care for his soul, and he must also fulfill his calling in the world.

The rich should work as well as the poor. Idleness often leads to vanity, luxury, and sin. Many waste their mornings in laziness and their evenings in entertainment while their souls are dying. That kind of life causes spiritual numbness.

But the answer is not laziness in the name of religion. The answer is faithful order. Work honestly. Provide responsibly. Be useful. But do not be so consumed with the cares of life that you neglect your soul. Seek oil for your lamp. Seek grace in your heart. Seek Christ above all.

A person may also be overly righteous in the wrong way when he fasts or disciplines his body so severely that he becomes unfit to serve God. Fasting is biblical. Jesus taught about fasting. It is right to discipline the body and bring it under control. But fasting must be done with wisdom. The purpose of fasting is to help us serve God, not to harm the body or make us useless.

Some people, when first awakened to their sin, may go too far in outward severity. They may think harming the body proves sincerity. But true Christian discipline is not about punishing the body for its own sake. It is about bringing the whole person into obedience to Christ.

There is also great danger in using the life of Christ to justify loose living. Some appeal to the wedding at Cana, where Jesus turned water into wine, as if He were encouraging excess. But that is a wrong and careless use of the miracle. Jesus never encouraged drunkenness. He never supported sin.

The miracle at Cana shows the glory, power, and goodness of Christ. When the wine ran out, Jesus provided what was needed. The empty waterpots can remind us of the empty human heart without grace. When Christ speaks, emptiness is filled. The waterpots filled to the brim can remind us that Christ fills His people with the Holy Spirit. The best wine being saved until the end can remind us that the believer's greatest comforts are still to come. Christ's best joys are often the last and greatest.

It is inconsistent to accuse serious believers of being too strict and then also accuse them of being too loose. Some say that preaching the new birth puts heavy burdens on people. Then they turn around and say the same preachers teach that people can live like devils as long as they claim to believe in Christ. Both accusations cannot be true. The gospel teaches neither legalism nor lawlessness.

The true gospel is this: salvation is the free gift of God. We are not saved by works, so no one can boast. Jesus Christ justifies the ungodly. He passes by sinners polluted in their own blood and says, "Live." Salvation is not earned by our righteousness. It is received by faith in Christ.

Faith does not save because it is a work that earns salvation. Faith is the instrument by which we receive Christ. The obedience, death, and resurrection of Jesus must be applied to us. Jesus fulfilled the law. Jesus satisfied the justice of the Father. His work is complete. God will not demand payment again from those whose debt Christ has already paid.

Jesus said in **John 14:6 NKJV**, *"I am the way, the truth, and the life. No one comes to the Father except through Me."* Christ must be our wisdom. Christ must be our righteousness. Christ must be our sanctification. Christ must be our redemption. If Christ is not everything to us, then we do not truly understand the gospel.

Our own righteousness cannot save us. Our best works, if we trust in them for acceptance with God, are like filthy rags. We are not justified by our past works, present works, or future works. We are justified by faith in Jesus Christ.

This offends proud people. It offends those who believe they are good enough. It offends those who want to bring their own righteousness to Christ. But man must be brought low so that God may be lifted high. The righteousness of Christ credited to the believer is one of the most comforting truths in all the Bible.

If a sinner asks, "What must I do to be saved?" it would be cruel to send him to his works. What if he has never done one truly good work in his whole life? What if his heart has been far from God? To tell him to save himself by works would drive him into despair. The gospel answer is found in **Acts 16:31 NKJV**, *"Believe on the Lord Jesus Christ, and you will be saved."*

No sinner needs to leave without hope. Come to Christ by faith, and He will receive you. You have no righteousness of your own to depend on. If you are saved, it will be through the righteousness of Christ, His atonement, and His sacrifice for sin.

By nature, there is no saving difference between the respectable sinner and the worst criminal. Any difference between one sinner and another is because of the restraining grace of God. Salvation is all of grace. It is free, rich, and undeserved. This humbles the proud, but it comforts the broken.

Do not come to Christ like a Pharisee, listing your religious achievements. Do not come saying, "I went to church. I prayed. I fasted. I received communion. I lived decently." Come as a poor, lost, guilty sinner who needs mercy. Come empty. Come helpless. Come to Christ, and He will receive you.

Do not flatter yourself that you are righteous enough because you live a decent life, do no harm, attend church, and use the outward means of grace. You may do all of that and still be far from a saving knowledge of Jesus Christ. You must know the power of God in your heart. You must know the reality of true religion now, or you will face the wrath of God hereafter.

This is not a message of despair. There is hope for every sinner who comes to Christ. If God had mercy on one who was running toward destruction, He can have mercy on you. Jesus Christ passes by sinners in their sin and says, "Live." Every saved person is a monument of free grace. Therefore, no sinner should despair if he is willing to come to Christ.

Christ is offered freely. He is offered to the curious, the careless, the religious, the poor, the rich, those who are serious, and those who are only listening to criticize. The place does not matter. Christ is not confined to church walls. Wherever His people gather in sincerity and truth, He is present. He can meet sinners in a field just as surely as in a sanctuary.

Can you think of a bleeding, suffering, dying Jesus offering Himself for sinners and still refuse Him? Can you hear that Christ died for the ungodly and still harden your heart against Him? Do not resist His mercy. Do not oppose His call. Do not delay.

The heart of the preacher is full of love for souls. He longs for sinners to come to Christ. He would speak until he had no strength left if only some might be saved. Time is short. We may not all meet again in this life. But we will all meet again at the judgment seat of Christ.

Therefore, pray. Pray for those who preach the gospel, that they would not only begin in the Spirit but continue in the Spirit. Pray that they would not fall away. Pray that they would not preach to others and become castaways themselves. Believers should carry one another before the throne of grace.

The work of God will always face opposition. When Christ's kingdom advances, the devil rages. As soon as the serpent's head begins to be bruised, he tries to bruise the heel. The enemy will not let his kingdom fall without a fight. He will oppose ministers, trouble believers, stir up critics, and try to stop the gospel.

But believers must not fear. David was only a young shepherd when he faced Goliath, but God gave him victory. If we pray and trust the Lord, He will give strength against every spiritual enemy. We must show our faith by our works. We must press forward. We must not stop, linger, or turn back.

Fight the good fight of faith. Strive to enter through the narrow gate. Seek the mercy of God in Christ. Press toward the goal. One day the people of God will meet at the right hand of the Father. There will be no scoffers there, no sin there, no sorrow there, and no enemy there. We will see Jesus, who died for us, and we will live with Him forever.

May God, in His infinite mercy, grant this through Jesus Christ our Lord. To Him, with the Father and the Holy Spirit, three Persons and one God, be all honor, praise, might, majesty, and dominion, now and forever.

Amen.

Chapter Twelve

The Seed of the Woman and the Seed of the Serpent

Genesis 3:15 *"And I will put enmity between thee and the woman, and between thy seed and her seed, it shall bruise thy head, and thou shalt bruise his heel."*

These words contain the first promise of a Savior given to fallen mankind. They were spoken in the garden after Adam and Eve sinned, after innocence was lost, after shame entered the human heart, and after sin brought separation between man and God. Yet in the middle of judgment, God gave a promise. Before Adam and Eve ever asked for mercy, God revealed mercy. Before they knew how to seek a Savior, God announced that a Savior would come.

When we read Genesis 3:15, we are reading the beginning of the gospel message. Many people think of Christ only when they come to the New Testament, but the promise of Christ begins much earlier. From the very beginning, God was revealing His plan of redemption. The light was not as full and clear in Genesis as it would later become in the Gospels, but the promise was there. God began with this first word of hope, then revealed more through Abraham, Moses, the prophets, and finally through the coming of Jesus Christ in the flesh.

Adam and Eve did not have the fullness of revelation that we now have. They did not see the cross as clearly as we do. They did not know all the details of the incarnation, the crucifixion, the resurrection, and the triumph of Christ. But they had enough to place their hope in the promise of God. Though the promise may have seemed dim to them, it was still the Word of God. By faith, they could look to the coming seed of the woman who would one day crush the serpent's head.

To understand the greatness of this promise, we must first understand why it was needed. Genesis tells us that God created man in His own image. Man was not created sinful, broken, ashamed, or separated from God. He was made upright. He was made to know God, walk with God, reflect God, and enjoy fellowship with God. God formed man from the dust of the ground and breathed into him the breath of life. Man became a living soul.

There was great dignity in the creation of man. God said, "Let us make man in our image, after our likeness." This means mankind was created with spiritual capacity, moral responsibility, and relational fellowship with God. Man was not an accident. He was not merely another creature among creatures. He was made by God and for God.

But man did not remain in that condition for long. The Bible does not tell us exactly how long Adam and Eve remained innocent before they fell. We should not speak where Scripture is silent. What we do know is that man fell from his original state, and the effects of that fall are seen everywhere. The corruption of sin runs through the human race. Even those who deny the fall prove it by their own pride, rebellion, and brokenness.

Before God revealed the truth, mankind could see the effects of sin but could not fully understand the cause. The world could see evil, suffering, shame, corruption, and death. But Genesis shows us where it all began. It traces the stream of sin back to its source.

The fall began with the serpent. The serpent was more subtle than any beast of the field, but the voice speaking through the serpent was the voice of Satan. The devil hated the happiness of man. He saw man made in the image of God, living in fellowship with God, and placed in the garden under God's blessing. Satan wanted to destroy what God had made good.

Satan did not first come with open violence. He came with deception. He did not force Adam and Eve to sin. He persuaded, twisted, questioned, and tempted. This is often how temptation works. The enemy rarely begins by showing the full ugliness of sin. He begins by planting a question.

He came to the woman and said, "Has God really said that you shall not eat of every tree of the garden?" This question was designed to make Eve doubt the goodness of God. Satan wanted her to think

God was withholding something good from her. He wanted her to believe that God's command was restrictive, unfair, and unreasonable.

This remains one of Satan's common strategies. He tries to make people think God is against them. He suggests that obedience to God will rob them of joy. He whispers that God is keeping them from something they need. He makes sin look like freedom and obedience look like bondage.

Eve answered the serpent by saying that they were allowed to eat from the trees of the garden, but not from the tree in the midst of the garden. God had warned them that if they ate from it, they would die. But even in Eve's answer, there seems to be a weakening of the command. God had said, "You shall surely die," but Eve said, "lest you die." The certainty of God's warning was softened.

This is dangerous. Whenever we begin to lessen the seriousness of God's Word, we are already moving toward sin. If Satan can convince us that God will not really do what He said, he has gained ground in the heart. Many people continue in sin because they believe the same lie Eve heard: "You shall not surely die." They think judgment is not real, hell is not eternal, and God's warnings are not certain. But God is true to His Word. What He promises, He fulfills. What He warns, He will not ignore.

Then Satan directly contradicted God. He told Eve that she would not surely die. He said that God knew that in the day she ate, her eyes would be opened and she would be like God, knowing good and evil. Satan accused God of holding back something desirable. He made disobedience appear to be the path to wisdom, freedom, and greatness.

This is how sin deceives. It promises elevation but brings ruin. It promises wisdom but brings darkness. It promises pleasure but brings shame. It promises life but brings death.

Eve looked at the tree and saw that it was good for food, pleasant to the eyes, and desirable to make one wise. The temptation entered through the eyes and moved into the heart. This reminds us how important it is to guard what we look at, what we dwell on, and what we desire. Sin often begins when the eye lingers where the heart should not go.

Eve took the fruit and ate. Then she gave it to her husband, and he ate also. The tragedy did not stop with one person. As soon as Eve sinned, she became an influence toward sin. Adam followed her into disobedience. This shows us that sin is never isolated. Our choices affect others. When we walk in righteousness, we encourage others toward righteousness. When we walk in rebellion, we can become instruments of temptation to those closest to us.

The sin of Adam and Eve was not a small thing. It was unbelief, ingratitude, pride, disobedience, and rebellion all in one act. God had given them a garden full of provision, fellowship, beauty, and blessing. They lacked nothing good. Yet they believed the serpent over God. They desired to be like God rather than trust God. They chose the creature's voice over the Creator's command.

Immediately their eyes were opened, but not in the way Satan had promised. They did not become glorious. They became ashamed.

They knew they were naked. The glory was gone. The innocence was lost. They were now exposed, guilty, and afraid.

Their first response was not repentance. It was self-covering. They sewed fig leaves together and made coverings for themselves. This is a picture of fallen humanity. Man knows he is naked before God, but instead of coming to God for mercy, he tries to cover himself. He tries to make his own righteousness. He tries to hide behind religion, good works, excuses, comparison, or self-improvement.

But fig leaves cannot cover guilt. Human righteousness cannot make a sinner acceptable before a holy God. Our best efforts cannot undo sin. Our own coverings will never stand before divine judgment. We need a covering God Himself provides.

Then Adam and Eve heard the voice of the Lord God walking in the garden in the cool of the day. Before sin, that sound would have brought joy. They would have welcomed the presence of God. But now they hid among the trees. Sin had changed their relationship with God. The presence that once gave comfort now brought fear.

This is what sin does. It makes man afraid of God. It causes people to hide from the One who made them. They hide behind excuses, busyness, religion, blame, and self-deception. But no one can truly hide from God.

God called to Adam and said, "Where are you?" God was not asking because He lacked knowledge. He knew exactly where Adam was. The question was meant to awaken Adam to his condition. It was as though God was saying, "Adam, look at what has happened. Look at where sin has brought you. Look at the condition of your soul."

This is often the first work of grace in a sinner's life. God makes a person see where they are. He exposes the soul's true condition. He shows us that we are lost, guilty, naked, helpless, and in need of mercy. Until we know where we are, we will not understand why we need a Savior.

Adam answered that he heard God's voice and was afraid because he was naked. God then asked, "Who told you that you were naked? Have you eaten of the tree that I commanded you not to eat?" Again, God knew the answer. But He drew Adam into confession. God often brings us to speak honestly about our sin, not because He needs information, but because we need humility.

But Adam did not truly repent. He blamed Eve, and in a deeper way, he blamed God. He said, "The woman whom You gave to be with me, she gave me of the tree, and I did eat." Instead of saying, "Lord, I have sinned," Adam said, in effect, "The woman You gave me caused this."

Sin had already corrupted his heart. He was unwilling to take responsibility. He blamed his wife. He implied fault in God. This is the nature of an unbroken heart. It shifts blame. It excuses itself. It accuses others. It would rather find fault with God than confess its own guilt.

Then God turned to Eve and asked, "What is this that you have done?" Eve also shifted blame. She said, "The serpent beguiled me, and I did eat." She did not fully own her sin either. She pointed to the serpent.

This scene shows us the helpless condition of fallen man. Adam and Eve were guilty, ashamed, afraid, hiding, and self-justifying. They did not come asking for grace. They did not plead for mercy. They did not offer true repentance. If salvation were to come, it would have to begin with God.

And that is exactly what happened.

God first pronounced judgment upon the serpent. Then He gave the promise of redemption. In Genesis 3:15, God said, *"And I will put enmity between thee and the woman, and between thy seed and her seed, it shall bruise thy head, and thou shalt bruise his heel."*

This promise was not spoken as a bargain between God and Adam. Adam was not standing there as a strong man able to fulfill conditions. He was guilty and fallen. This was not man reaching up to God. This was God revealing grace to man. This was the announcement of salvation through the coming seed of the woman.

The seed of the woman ultimately refers to Jesus Christ. He would be born of a woman. He would take on human flesh. He would come into the world to undo the works of the devil. He would obey where Adam disobeyed. He would suffer, die, and rise again to redeem fallen sinners.

The serpent would bruise His heel. This points to the suffering of Christ. Satan attacked Christ through temptation in the wilderness. He stirred opposition against Him throughout His ministry. He worked through betrayal, false accusation, mockery, scourging, and crucifixion. At the cross, it seemed as though the serpent had won.

But the bruising of the heel was not the end of the story. Christ would bruise the serpent's head. That means He would destroy Satan's power and break his dominion. Through His death, Jesus defeated the one who had the power of death. Through His resurrection, He triumphed over sin, Satan, death, and hell.

The cross looked like defeat, but it was victory. Satan bruised the heel of Christ, but Christ crushed the head of the serpent.

This promise was not only fulfilled in Christ personally. It is also seen in the people of God throughout history. From the beginning, there has been enmity between the seed of the woman and the seed of the serpent. Those who belong to God and those who belong to the world have always been in conflict.

This began almost immediately with Cain and Abel. Cain hated Abel because Abel's works were righteous. From that time forward, the people of God have often been opposed, mocked, persecuted, and hated by those who reject God.

This conflict continued through the Old Testament. It continued in the life of Christ. It continued in the early church. It continues today. The flesh persecutes the spirit. Darkness resists light. The world hates those who truly belong to Christ.

Yet persecution never defeats the church. The more the people of God are opposed, the more God displays His power through them. Israel multiplied in Egypt under oppression. The apostles continued preaching under persecution. The early church grew even when believers suffered. The blood of martyrs became seed for the spread of the gospel.

Satan often uses persecution to try to destroy the work of God, but God turns it for His glory. What the enemy means for evil, God uses for good. The serpent may bruise the heel, but he cannot stop the promise. Christ will crush his head.

This promise is also fulfilled in the life of every believer. Inside the Christian there is a conflict between the flesh and the Spirit. The old nature and the new nature struggle against one another. The believer knows what it is to desire holiness and yet feel the pull of sin. He knows what it is to love God and still battle temptation.

This struggle can be discouraging. Some believers feel the strength of remaining sin so deeply that they fear they will one day fall completely. They wonder why sinful desires still rise in the heart. They grieve over thoughts, attitudes, weaknesses, and temptations that continue to trouble them.

But Genesis 3:15 gives hope. The serpent may bruise the heel, but he will not win. Sin may trouble the believer, but it will not have the final victory. Christ has already secured the triumph. Grace will overcome nature. The Spirit will overcome the flesh. The believer may be wounded in the battle, but he will not be destroyed.

Jesus will finish what He began. He died not only to forgive sin, but to destroy sin's power. One day He will remove even the presence of sin from His people. At death, the believer will be freed from the inward corruption that now causes grief. At the resurrection, body and soul will be made completely whole.

The promise will be fully and finally completed at the last judgment. Then Christ will present His people without spot or wrinkle. Satan, the accuser of the brethren, will be cast down forever. The enemies of God will no longer trouble the people of God. The righteous will shine in the kingdom of their Father.

Until that day, believers must not grow weary. The battle is real, but the outcome is certain. The seed of the woman will bruise the serpent's head. Christ has conquered, and all who belong to Christ will share in His victory.

Therefore, do not be overcome by fear. Do not be terrified by opposition. Do not be too discouraged by the deceitfulness of your own heart. Do not think Satan has more power than Christ. The enemy is dangerous, but he is defeated. He may rage, but he is chained by the sovereign hand of God. He may tempt, accuse, and trouble, but he cannot overthrow those who are kept by Christ.

Believers should plead this promise in prayer. When temptation rises, remember that Christ has crushed the serpent's head. When persecution comes, remember that Christ has already triumphed. When sin feels strong, remember that grace is stronger. When the church appears weak, remember that the gates of hell will not prevail against it.

This promise should also warn the enemies of God. No one can fight against Christ and win. The serpent's head will be crushed. Those who remain in rebellion against God are on the losing side of history and eternity. Christ reigns now. He sits at the right hand of the Father. He rules over all things for the good of His people and the glory of His name.

Those who oppose His people, mock His gospel, and reject His grace should repent while mercy is still offered. The same Christ who crushes the serpent is also the Savior who receives sinners. The promise of Genesis 3:15 is a warning to the enemy, but it is also good news for the guilty. It tells us that God has provided a Redeemer.

Adam and Eve had sinned. They had hidden. They had blamed. They had no way to restore themselves. But God came with a promise. That promise has been fulfilled in Jesus Christ. He is the seed of the woman. He is the Lamb of God. He is the second Adam. He is the Savior of sinners. He is the conqueror of Satan.

The first Adam fell in a garden and brought sin and death. The second Adam suffered in a garden, went to a cross, and brought righteousness and life. The first Adam hid from God in shame. The second Adam cried out to God in obedience. The first Adam brought a curse. Christ bore the curse. The first Adam opened the door to death. Christ opened the way to eternal life.

Let every believer take courage. The promise still stands. Christ has bruised the serpent's head, and one day the victory will be seen in full. The battle will end. Sin will be gone. Satan will be cast down. Death will be destroyed. The people of God will be made perfect in His presence.

Until then, we fight in hope. We endure in faith. We pray with confidence. We follow Christ with courage. We do not trust in ourselves, but in the One who was promised from the beginning and revealed in the fullness of time.

The seed of the woman has come. Jesus Christ has conquered. And because He lives, all who belong to Him will overcome.

To God the Father, God the Son, and God the Holy Spirit be all honor, power, glory, majesty, and dominion, now and forever.

Amen.

Chapter Thirteen

Christ the Support of the Tempted

Matthew 6:13 NKJV *"And do not lead us into temptation, but deliver us from the evil one."*

One of the great duties of every Christian is to guard against evil. We must not only avoid open sin, but also watch against the first movement of sin in the heart. We must watch our actions, our words, our thoughts, and our desires, so that we do not fall into sin or even give the appearance of evil.

The devil is always trying to tempt us. Our own sinful hearts are also ready to join with him. Satan wants us to fall so that he may gain power over us. He wants people to become his subjects, his servants, and his slaves. And in the end, the wages he pays are death, both spiritual and eternal.

The Lord Jesus knew how His people would be tempted. He knew the great enemy of their souls would look for every opportunity to keep poor sinners from coming to Him. Satan will try to drive people into great sins. If he cannot succeed with great sins, he will try smaller ones. If that does not work, he will change his methods again and again. Sometimes he even transforms himself into an angel of light, using religious language, false comfort, or twisted truth to make the soul fall into sin.

Because Jesus knew how weak His disciples would be against temptation, He taught them to pray, **Matthew 6:13 NKJV**, *"And do not lead us into temptation, but deliver us from the evil one."* This is a prayer every believer needs. Satan is too subtle and too powerful for us to fight in our own strength. If the Lord is not on our side, we will fall. If we are left to ourselves, every temptation will be too strong for us.

These words are part of the prayer Christ gave to His disciples. Since they come from the mouth of Jesus, we must receive them as true and necessary. We need to know who tempts us, why he tempts us, how he works, and how earnestly we must seek Christ to preserve us.

The one who tempts us is Satan. He is the prince of the power of the air. He is the spirit who now works in the children of disobedience. He is an enemy of God, an enemy of goodness, and an enemy of truth. He showed his nature in the garden of Eden when he slandered God and said to Eve, "You will not surely die." He is full of malice, envy, and revenge.

Satan is also subtle. Because God has not given him unlimited power, he watches for opportunities. He looks for weak places. He waits for moments when we are careless, tired, proud, lonely, fearful, or discouraged. He does not always come openly. In the garden, he used the serpent. In our lives, he may use thoughts, desires, people, circumstances, false teaching, or even religious appearances to deceive us.

But when we speak of Satan's character, we should also examine our own hearts. Many of the tempter's qualities can be seen in fallen man. Do we not sometimes love a lie? Do people not often justify dishonesty in business, conversation, or personal gain? They may say, "It is just how business is done," or, "Everyone does it," but sin does not become innocent because it is common.

Man was created noble and good when he first came from the hand of God. But through the fall, man became corrupt. There is nothing in fallen man that can save himself. The human heart is polluted by sin and uncleanness. Yet many modern teachers speak as though man is naturally good and only needs a little help from God. They say that if we do our best, Christ will make up what is lacking.

But that makes Christ only half a Savior. It makes man the other half. That is not the gospel. Christ must be our whole righteousness, our whole wisdom, our whole sanctification, and our whole redemption. He does not come merely to complete our efforts. He comes to save sinners who cannot save themselves.

Many pulpits speak only of being decent, doing no one harm, living honestly, loving your neighbor, and doing what you can. These things may sound respectable, but if they are preached without the new birth, without the cross, without the righteousness of Christ, and without the power of the Holy Spirit, they are not enough. They leave people spiritually blind.

Some describe the Spirit of God as nothing more than a good conscience. But even the heathen philosophers could speak that way. The Holy Spirit is not simply the feeling that we have done well. The Holy Spirit is the One who brings the comforts of God, changes the heart, gives life, and produces a truly good conscience.

No matter how beautifully people try to paint fallen man, Scripture tells us the truth. Man by nature is full of pride, deceit, malice, envy, revenge, lust, and selfishness. These are the tempers of the devil and the beast. Fallen man is not merely weak. He is sinful. He needs more than improvement. He needs a Savior.

This is why Satan is pleased when people stay in outward religion but never come to Christ. He does not mind if a person attends church, takes the sacrament, reads, prays, or meditates, as long as that person trusts in himself and never truly comes to Jesus. If these things are done in our own strength and never lead us to Christ, they may only become a smoother road to hell.

Why does Satan tempt us? He tempts us because he envies us and hates the Lord Jesus Christ. He wants to keep sinners from closing with Christ by faith. If he can keep a person from laying hold of Jesus, he knows that person remains in danger.

When people are under temptation, their minds often become troubled and confused. Their thoughts are unsettled. Their affections are disturbed. Then Satan whispers that they should not come to Christ in such a condition. He says, "You are too confused. You are too sinful. You are too unworthy. Christ will not receive you like this." But that is one of his devices. He wants people to think low and dishonorable thoughts of Jesus.

Satan's goal is to make people careless and indifferent about Christ. He wants them ruined forever. He knows Jesus died for sinners, but he works to keep sinners from running to Christ, the true city of refuge. He wants to keep them from the balm of Gilead.

Satan rules in the hearts of scoffers and Pharisees. He blinds the eyes of those who mock the gospel, and he also blinds those who trust in their own righteousness. As long as he can keep people comfortable without a changed heart, he is content. If he can keep them careless, religiously proud, or hardened in sin, he has gained his purpose.

We must not give the devil an opportunity. If people willingly go to places of sin, worldly entertainment, drunkenness, lust, and vanity, they should not be surprised when temptation grows stronger. How can a person pray in the morning, "Lead us not into temptation," while planning to run into temptation that night?

When people pray with their lips but their hearts are far from God, they offer the sacrifice of fools. They may think that saying prayers is enough and that God and they have settled accounts. But God is not mocked. A person who prays against temptation while choosing temptation is deceiving himself.

Satan uses many methods to draw people away from Christ. One way is by making sin look small. He says, "It is not so serious. There is no need to be too strict. Do not be too righteous. Do not harm yourself by taking God too seriously." He shows the bait but hides the hook. He shows the pleasure, profit, or advantage of the world, but he hides the sorrow, bondage, guilt, and judgment that come with sin.

When Satan cannot draw people by flattery, he tries fear. He stirs up others to mock, criticize, slander, and hate believers. He causes people to point at them and say, "There goes one of those followers." He uses ridicule and pressure to make believers ashamed of Christ.

If mockery does not work, Satan throws doubts and discouragement into the mind. He asks, "Are you sure this is the right way? Do you really think Christ will save you? He did not die for you. You have been too great a sinner. You have sinned too long. You have committed sins Christ will never forgive." In this way, he tries to push poor sinners toward despair.

Sometimes, when the people of God gather to worship, Satan sends scoffers to disturb them. He stirs up opposition against the truth. But the Lord is able to protect His work. We should pray for those who persecute the truth, asking Jesus to forgive them and show them that they are fighting against Him. It is hard for them to kick against the goads.

These are some of the ways Satan tempts people and tries to keep them from Christ. There are many more, but these are enough to remind us that we must be watchful.

Because Satan is so subtle and powerful, we must be earnest with Christ. We must ask Him either to keep us from temptation or to preserve us under it. Go to Jesus and tell Him how the evil one attacks your soul. Tell Him that you are not able to defeat Satan in your own strength. Ask for His help.

Jesus is ready to help. He is ready to be your Guide, Comforter, Savior, and All. He will give strength to resist the fiery darts of the devil. There is no one more able to help the tempted than Jesus Christ. He knows what it is to be tempted. He was tempted by Satan in the wilderness, yet without sin. He can give the help of His Spirit so that the evil one must flee.

In Christ, we have the strength we need. The devil is strong, but he is not stronger than Jesus. The enemy may rage, threaten, and attack, but he can go no farther than Christ allows. Satan and his agents may breathe out threats and hatred, but Jesus holds them in His power.

If Satan and wicked men could do all they wanted, many of God's people would not live another day. But blessed be God, we can commit ourselves to His protection. He has protected us before, and He will protect us still.

Therefore, earnestly ask the Lord to support you under temptation. Satan is powerful and cunning. He would be too strong for us if Christ did not strengthen us. So look to Jesus. Ask Him to send His Spirit into your heart and keep you from falling.

And now we must ask: how do things stand between God and your soul? Is Jesus beautiful to you? Is He precious to you? If you have not turned away from Christ, be assured that He has not turned away from you. He will root out the cursed things of this world and dwell in your heart.

If you are a candidate for heaven, why set your heart on earth? What are all the pleasures of the earth without an interest in Jesus Christ? One smile from Him is more valuable than rubies, yes, more valuable than the whole world.

Those who have found Christ supporting them under the temptations of life should never forsake Him. Has He not been a gracious Master? Is He not the chief among ten thousand and altogether lovely? Once you see beauty in Christ that you never saw before, you will wish you had known Him sooner and loved Him more.

The love of Jesus is condescending love. It is amazing love. It is forgiving love. It is dying love. It is exalted and interceding love. It is glorified love. He loved us before we loved Him. He saw us polluted in our sin, full of spiritual disease, enslaved to sin, death, and hell, running toward destruction. Then He passed by and said, "Live." He snatched us like brands from the burning.

It is love that saves. It is all the free grace of God. Even a small experience of this love should fill us with wonder. How could Jesus have mercy on such sinners? How could He show such condescension and kindness? The kingdom of God within the soul fills the heart with love, gratitude, and longing for Christ. The believer would not return to his natural state for millions of worlds.

The soul that has tasted Christ longs to be with Him. It longs to live forever with the Lamb who was slain and to sing praises to Him. Eternity itself will not be long enough to fully declare the love of Jesus Christ.

If there are any who are still strangers to this love, do not despair. Come to Christ, and He will have mercy on you. He will pardon your sins. He will heal your backslidings. He will love you freely and take you to Himself. Come, guilty sinners, to Jesus, and you will find rest for your souls.

You do not need to fear or despair. If God has had mercy on others, He can have mercy on you. If you come to Him by faith, He will save you.

Why do you delay? Do you say you are poor and ashamed to come? Christ does not reject people because of poverty. Come in your rags. Come in your pollution. Come in your guilt. He will save you. Do not depend on anything but the blood of Jesus Christ. Do not wait another hour. Give your heart to Christ now.

Give Him what He asks for: your heart. When Jesus works an inward principle of grace in you, then you will know the sweetness of communion with God. Consider the love of Christ in dying for you. Will you despise such dying love? Your sins brought Christ from heaven. Do not let those sins send you to hell.

What words will make you leave your sins and come to Christ? If it were within human power to give grace, no one who hears this call would leave unchanged. Even the greatest scoffer would be brought from spiritual death to spiritual life. Then we would rejoice together. But grace belongs to God. You must ask Jesus for it.

Jesus said, **Matthew 7:7 NKJV**, *"Ask, and it will be given to you; seek, and you will find; knock, and it will be opened to you."* Ask Him. If you feel repulsed again and again, keep asking. Be like the Syrophoenician woman who came to Christ for her daughter and would not go away. If she was so earnest for her child's body, how much more earnest should we be for our souls? If you seek Him by faith, He will answer you with mercy.

Do not stop seeking the Lord. Do not neglect opportunities for the salvation of your soul. Do not forsake gathering with believers. Come together to strengthen the weak, build up faith, and call sinners to feel the power of God in their hearts until they cry, "What must we do to be saved?"

The devil and his followers have their gatherings for sin. They are not ashamed to be seen doing the works of their master. Surely the people of Christ should not be ashamed of Jesus, who died that they might live and who will confess them before His Father and the holy angels.

Dare to be different for God. Do not fear the face of man. Do not let threats or ridicule move you. What is the loss of earthly pleasure, reputation, or greatness compared to the loss of heaven, Christ, and your soul?

When the world reviles you, do not revile back. Do not answer insult with insult. Let love, kindness, meekness, patience, and long-suffering be found in you, just as they were found in Jesus. Keep gathering together and telling one another what great things Christ has done for your souls.

This does not mean you should neglect your lawful work or family responsibilities. God has given you both a general calling and a particular calling. You must care for your family and fulfill the work God has placed before you. If you neglect your family under the excuse of going to church or attending religious meetings, you are outside the path of duty.

But be careful that the business of this life does not keep you from preparing for the life to come. Do not let work, responsibility, or worldly care make you forget your soul. In all your ordinary actions and daily business, do everything with a view to the glory of God and the salvation of your soul.

As this message draws to a close, let every person hear this appeal. To the Pharisee, the self-righteous person, the one who will not come to Christ because he trusts in himself, hear this warning. You may think that because you live a decent, honest, moral life, all will be well in the end. But unless you come to Christ, you are still in danger.

Do not flatter yourself that you are on the way to heaven if you are still on the broad road to destruction. If you throw away your own righteousness and come to Christ, letting Him do everything for you and in you, He is willing to be your Savior. But if you bring your good works as the basis of your acceptance, you may seek justification forever and never find it.

Only the blood of Jesus Christ cleanses us from sin. Good works cannot justify us before God. Once we are justified, good works will follow as fruit. But we cannot do truly good works until we are cleansed and sanctified by the Spirit of God.

To the scoffer, come and see this Jesus, the Lord of glory whom you have despised. If you come to Christ, He is willing to receive you, even after all your mocking and opposition against His people. But if you remain stubborn, remember that salvation was offered to you. Christ and free grace were proclaimed to you. If you refuse Him, your blood will be on your own hands.

Even if you despise the preacher or the ministry, the warning must still be given. Your danger must be shown, and the remedy must be offered. The prayer is that God would show you your error and bring you into His fold, so that ravenous lions may become peaceful lambs.

To those who desire to choose Christ as Lord and experience His power in the soul, keep seeking Him. Even if you do not yet feel your prayers answered, continue. Christ will reveal Himself to you in a way the world does not know. You will see and feel His love in your soul. You will have a witness within that you belong to the Lord. Do not fear. Jesus will gather His elect when He comes on the great day of account, when every person will be judged according to the deeds done in the body.

May the thought of giving account to God make us more careful about our lives and our souls.

Now to all, high and low, rich and poor, one with another: accept mercy while it is offered. **2 Corinthians 6:2 NKJV** says, *"Behold, now is the accepted time; behold, now is the day of salvation."* Will you refuse salvation now that it is offered to you? Do not wait another moment. Come and receive Jesus Christ in His own way.

Then, at the last day, you will be taken up to be with Him forever. Let this make you long to be with Jesus, who has done so much for you, who now intercedes for you, and who is preparing a place for His people.

May we all arrive there and sit down with Jesus for all eternity.

Amen.

Chapter Fourteen

Worldly Business Is No Excuse for Neglecting God

Matthew 8:22 NKJV *"But Jesus said to him, 'Follow Me, and let the dead bury their own dead.'"*

When the apostle Paul preached in Athens, he told the people that as he passed through their city and observed their objects of worship, he perceived that they were very religious. But if Paul were to rise today and walk through many of our crowded cities, he may not say the same thing. Instead, he might say, "I perceive that in all things you are too worldly-minded."

Many people today are not too concerned about religion. They are too consumed with the business of life. They are busy working, buying, selling, building, planning, providing, and pursuing success.

Some of these things are lawful and necessary in their proper place. But many people are so taken up with the concerns of this life that they either completely neglect the one thing needful or give it only careless attention.

There is no greater kindness we can show people than to warn them of the danger of living only for this world. It is dangerous to spend all our strength chasing things that will pass away while giving little thought to the soul that will live forever. It is dangerous to be careful about earthly business and careless about eternal life.

Worldliness is especially dangerous because it can appear respectable. A person may not be living in open sin. He may not be drunk, immoral, violent, or dishonest. He may simply be busy. He may say he is providing for his family, fulfilling his responsibilities, and taking care of necessary business. But under that respectable appearance, his heart may be slipping into spiritual sleep. He may be laboring for the food that perishes while neglecting the food that endures to everlasting life.

This is why the words of Jesus are so important. In **Matthew 8:22 NKJV**, Jesus said, *"Follow Me, and let the dead bury their own dead."* At first, these words may sound difficult, but when we understand the setting, they carry a serious warning. Jesus had called a man to follow Him. The man answered, in effect, "Lord, let me first go and bury my father." Many have understood this to mean, "Let me first go and finish some important family or worldly business." But Jesus answered, "Follow Me, and let the dead bury their own dead."

In other words, Jesus was saying, "Do not let worldly business keep you from following Me. Leave the affairs of this world to those who are spiritually dead, if those affairs would keep you from obedience. Nothing is more important than following Christ."

Whether that man obeyed, we are not told. But we do know this: Christ has often spoken the same thing to many hearts by His Spirit. He has called people to draw their affections away from the things of this life, take up their cross, and follow Him. Yet many have answered, "Lord, first let me take care of my business. First let me handle my affairs. First let me settle my plans." To all such people, the message of Christ still stands: "Let the dead bury their own dead. Follow Me."

No worldly business, no matter how important it seems, can excuse a person from neglecting true religion.

By true religion, I do not mean a few moral virtues, partial self-improvement, or formal attendance to outward duties. True religion is deeper than that. It is the righteousness of Christ applied to the heart by faith. It is a real change of nature worked in us by the power of the Holy Spirit. It is preserved and nourished through the means of grace. It is shown by a changed life and by the fruit of the Spirit.

This is true and undefiled religion. This is why the eternal Son of God came into the world and shed His precious blood. This is why we were created and sent into the world. We were not made merely to earn money, build houses, raise families, run businesses, and then die. We were made for God. We were made to be born again from above, restored to the image of God through Jesus Christ, and prepared for the kingdom of heaven.

If we judged by the behavior of many people, we might think man was sent into the world only to work, worry, buy, sell, and gather possessions. But Scripture teaches us that we were born for higher things. We were born to know God, be renewed by His Spirit, and be made ready for eternity.

Some people think religion belongs mainly to ministers and clergy. They imagine that holiness is for those who serve at the altar, while ordinary people can be excused because they are busy with daily life. But this is a serious mistake. Every person is called to inward holiness. Every person is born with a corrupt nature and must be renewed and sanctified by God.

It is true that ministers have a special responsibility to be examples in faith, zeal, love, and holiness. But all Christians have been baptized into the death of Christ and are called to live in covenant faithfulness before God. Scripture shows only one entrance into the kingdom of Christ: the narrow gate of true conversion. Whether a person is a minister or not, if he does not enter by that door, he cannot enter at all.

To think that religion belongs only to ministers shows ignorance both of true religion and of true happiness. What does Christ require when He calls us to be religious? He calls us to subdue corrupt passions, root out sinful habits, receive the graces of the Holy Spirit, and be filled with the fullness of God.

Is that only for ministers? Is happiness only for ministers? Does the businessman not need his heart changed? Does the worker not need his passions brought under the rule of Christ? Does the wealthy person not need holiness? Does the poor person not need grace? Do people in business find their sinful nature so pleasant that they do not care whether it is changed?

If all people desire the same end, which is eternal life with God, then all must use the same means. No one should imagine that God will admit him into heaven in his natural state simply because he was busy with worldly concerns. God will not set aside the necessity of the new birth because a person had many responsibilities. Search the Scriptures. They give no room for such false hope.

Some people act as if temporal business is so important that it may excuse spiritual neglect. A covetous person who spends his life chasing wealth may think he is being wise and responsible. He may even look down on a prodigal who wastes his life in sinful pleasure. But soon both will discover that losing the soul through chasing riches is just as tragic as losing the soul through chasing pleasure.

Business may look more serious than sinful entertainment, but when it is weighed against the value of the immortal soul, it becomes very small. Jesus asked in **Mark 8:36–37 NKJV**, *"For what will it profit a man if he gains the whole world, and loses his own soul? Or what will a man give in exchange for his soul?"*

That question should settle the matter. What good is it to gain everything and lose your soul? What profit is there in success if the soul is lost? What will money, property, business, reputation, and achievement do for a person when he stands before God?

Because the heart is so easily deceived by riches and worldly care, we need to hear this warning again and again. In Luke 14, Jesus gave a parable about a man who prepared a great supper and invited many guests. When the servant came to call them, they all began to make excuses.

One said, "I have bought a piece of ground, and I must go and see it." Another said, "I have bought five yoke of oxen, and I am going to test them." Another said, "I have married a wife, and therefore I cannot come." These were not openly wicked activities. Buying land, testing oxen, and marriage are not sinful in themselves. But they became sinful when they were used as excuses to refuse the invitation.

The master did not accept their excuses. He was angry and said that none of those who were invited would taste his supper. This teaches us that even lawful callings become unlawful when they keep us from Christ. The marriage supper represents the gospel. The master is Christ. The servants are His ministers, who call people to come. Those who refuse because of worldly concerns show that their hearts love the world more than the kingdom of God.

There is nothing wrong with honest work, lawful business, family responsibilities, and daily duties. But if these things keep a person from working out his salvation with fear and trembling, they become a snare. Our particular calling, whether business, trade, profession, or household duty, must never interfere with our higher calling as Christians.

Christianity does not command us to abandon the world entirely or neglect ordinary responsibilities. Scripture gives examples of believers in many stations of life. There was a godly centurion. Cornelius was devout. There were believers even in Caesar's household. Jesus did not rebuke Martha for serving, but for being worried and troubled about many things.

We may work. We must work. We should labor in obedience to God for the food that perishes. But we must never let that labor cause us to neglect the food that endures to everlasting life.

Therefore, I plead with you by the mercies of God in Christ Jesus: do not let concern for earthly things cost you eternal things. Do not trade your soul for business. Do not trade heaven for money. Do not trade Christ for success. Remember again the words of Jesus, **Mark 8:36–37 NKJV**, *"For what will it profit a man if he gains the whole world, and loses his own soul? Or what will a man give in exchange for his soul?"*

If we were going to live in this world forever, worldly wisdom might be our highest wisdom. But we have no lasting city here. We are only passing through. We were sent into this world so our nature might be changed and we might be prepared for the world to come. To neglect that work for a little worldly gain is like Esau selling his birthright for a bowl of stew.

How unlike Christianity many Christians are. Jesus commands us in **Matthew 6:33 NKJV**, *"But seek first the kingdom of God and His righteousness, and all these things shall be added to you."* Yet many fear that if they seek God first, everything else will be taken from them. They are forbidden to be anxious about tomorrow, yet they spend day and night gathering riches for years to come, even though they do not know who will possess them after they die.

Is this how pilgrims and strangers should live? Is this keeping our baptismal vow? Or is it turning away from the service of Christ and joining ourselves to the service of mammon?

What hope will worldly people have when God takes away their souls? What if God says to them what He said to the rich fool: **Luke 12:20 NKJV**, *"Fool! This night your soul will be required of you; then whose will those things be which you have provided?"*

What will all your possessions do for you then? What will your plans mean then? What will your barns, accounts, houses, titles, and achievements matter then?

If eternal life could be purchased with money, there might be some excuse for chasing wealth so intensely. If people could carry their riches beyond the grave and buy oil for their lamps after death, perhaps they could justify their obsession. But money perishes. We brought nothing into this world, and it is certain we can carry nothing out.

Once the lamp of natural life goes out, there is no more opportunity to buy oil. There is no more opportunity to obtain grace. Would it not be wiser to seek grace now while it may be found? Would it not be better to secure the true riches instead of spending all your strength on things that will soon belong to someone else?

Think about the rich fool. Do you suppose he was grieved, after his soul entered eternity, that he did not get to finish building bigger barns? Do you think he still cared about his crops and storage? Surely all earthly things seemed very small to him then. His regret was not that he had failed to increase his wealth. His regret was that he had failed to become rich toward God.

So it will be with everyone who spends life chasing worldly gain while neglecting the soul. For a while, such people may appear wise, disciplined, and successful. Others may admire their business sense and careful planning. But when death opens their eyes, they will see how small all earthly cares really were. They will wonder how they could have been so blind to eternity while being praised for wisdom in this world.

They will grieve that they were so careful with temporal accounts and so careless with their account before God. Like the unjust steward, they may have been wise in earthly dealings, calling debtors and managing business carefully, yet they never seriously asked how much they owed their great Lord and Master.

What more can be said? Only the god of this world and the love of earthly things could so blind a conscience that a person would not feel the force of these truths.

Now let me speak especially to the rich and to those who are free from many of the burdens of daily labor. It may seem bold for a young preacher to address those in high stations, but Paul commanded Timothy, though young, to charge those who are rich. So I speak humbly, but seriously.

If people who are busy with ordinary work must still work out their salvation with fear and trembling, how much more should those do so who have more leisure, more comfort, and more opportunity? If the poor and busy must seek God, surely the rich and free must not neglect Him.

But is this what we see? Too often, those whom God has lifted above others, those who have comfort, wealth, food, clothing, and ease, abuse His bounty. They act as though their position places them above religion. They leave spiritual seriousness to the poor, while they themselves live for luxury, pleasure, and ease.

But woe to such rich people if they continue that way. They have received their consolation. If the careless tradesman cannot be saved while neglecting God, where will the luxurious and ungodly rich appear?

Therefore, let every person, high and low, rich and poor, make the renewal of the fallen nature the main business of life. Let no worldly profit and no worldly pleasure turn you aside from it. Let this cry always sound in your ears: "Behold, the Bridegroom is coming." Live as one who may at any moment be called away by death to judgment.

Remember that this life is a point between two eternities. After these few days are over, there remains no more sacrifice for sin. Ask yourself often, "How will I wish I had lived when I leave this world?" Then live now in such a way that you will not be afraid to die.

If we live, let us live to the Lord. If we die, let us die to the Lord. Whether living or dying, let us belong to the Lord.

To that end, let us pray to God, the protector of all who trust in Him. Without Him, nothing is strong and nothing is holy. May He increase His mercy upon us. May He be our ruler and guide. And may we pass through the things that are temporary in such a way that we do not lose the things that are eternal, through Jesus Christ our Lord.

Amen.

Chapter Fifteen

Christ the Only Rest for the Weary and Heavy-Laden

Matthew 11:28 "Come unto me, all ye that are weary and heavy laden, and I will give you rest."

Nothing is more generally known than our duties which belong to Christianity; and yet, how amazing is it, nothing is less practiced? There is much of it in name and show, but little of it in the heart and conversation; indeed, if going to church, and to the sacrament, or, if our being called after the name of Christ, and being baptized into that name; if that will make us Christians, I believe all of us would have a claim thereto: but if it consists in the heart, that there must be an inward principle wrought in us by faith; that there must be a change of the whole nature, a putting off the old man with his deeds, a turning from sin unto God, a cleaving only unto the Son of Righteousness; and that there must be a new birth, and we experience the pangs thereof; and that you must feel yourselves weary and heavy laden with your sins, before you will seek for deliverance from them; if this is to be the case, if there is so much in being children of God, alas! how many who please themselves with an outside show, a name to live whilst they are dead; and how few that have any share in this spiritual state, in this true and living name? How few are they who are weary and heavy laden with their sins, and seek to Christ for rest? They say, in a formal customary manner, we are sinners, and there is no health in us; but how few feel themselves sinners, and are so oppressed in their own spirits, that they have no quiet nor rest in them, because of the burden of their sins, and the weight that is fallen and lays on their minds?

Under these burdens, these heavy burdens, they are at a loss what to do whereby they may obtain rest; they fly to their works, they go to a minister, and he tells them to read, to pray, and meditate, and take the sacrament: thus they go away, and read, and pray, and meditate almost without ceasing, and never neglect the sacrament whenever there is an opportunity for the taking of it. Well, when the poor soul has done all this, it still finds no ease, there is yet no relief. Well, what must you do then? To lie still under the burden they cannot, and to get rid of it then cannot. O what must the burdened soul do! Why, goes to the clergyman again, and tells him the case, and what it has done, and that it is no better. Well, he asks, have you given alms to the poor? Why no. Then go and do that, and you will find rest. Thus the poor sinner is hurried from duty to duty, and still finds no rest: all things are uneasy and disquiet within, and there remains no rest in the soul. And if it was to go through all the duties of religion, and read over a thousand manuals of prayers, none would ever give the soul any rest; nothing will, until it goes to the Lord Jesus Christ, for there is the only true rest; that is the rest which abideth, and will continue for ever. It is not in your own works, nor in your endeavors: no; when Christ comes into your souls, he pardons you, without any respect to your works, either past, present, or to come.

From the words, my brethren, I have now read, I shall

I. Show you who are the weary and heavy laden.

II. Inquire what is meant by coming to Christ. And,

III. Conclude with exhorting you to accept of the invitation which the Lord Jesus Christ gives unto you to come unto him, with the assurance of finding rest.

First, I am to show you, who are the weary and heavy-laden.

And here it will be necessary to consider who are not; and then, to consider who they are that are really so.

1. Those who think themselves good enough, and are pleased that they are not so bad as others, these are not weary or heavy laden.

No, these Pharisees are not thus troubled; they laugh and jest at those who talk of feeling their sins, and think there is no occasion to make so much ado about religion: it is to be righteous over-much, and the means to destroy yourselves. They think if they do but mean well, and say their prayers, as they call them, it is sufficient: though they may say a prayer, yea, thousands of prayers, and all the while be only offering up the sacrifice of fools. They may call God, Father, every day, when it is only mocking of God, and offering up false fire unto him; and it would be just for him to serve them, as he did Nadab and Abihu, destroy them, cut them off from the face of the earth: but he is waiting to be gracious, and willing to try a little longer, whether you will bring forth any thing more than the leaven of an outward profession, which is not all that the Lord requires; no, he wants the heart; and unless you honor him with that, he does not regard your mouths, when the other is far from him. You may say over your prayers all your lives, and yet you may never pray over one: therefore, while you flatter yourselves you are good enough, and that you are in a state of salvation, you are only deceiving you own souls, and hastening on your own destruction. Come unto him, not as being good enough, but as vile sinners, as poor, and blind, and naked, and miserable, and then Jesus will have compassion.

O ye Pharisees, what fruits do ye bring forth? Why, you are moral, polite creatures; you do your endeavors, you do what you can, and so Jesus is to make up the rest. You esteem yourselves fine, rational, and polite beings, and think it is too unfashionable to pray; it is not polite enough: perhaps you have read some prayers, but knew not how to pray from your hearts; no, by no means: that was being righteous over-much indeed.

But when once you are sensible of your being lost, damned creatures, and see hell gaping ready to receive you: if God was but to cut the thread of life, O then, then you would cry earnestly unto the Lord to receive you, to open the door of mercy unto you; your bones would then be changed, you would no more flatter yourselves with your abilities and good wishes; no, you would see how unable you were, how incapable to save yourselves; that there is no fitness, no free will in you; no fitness, but for eternal damnation, no free will but that of doing evil; and that when you would do good, evil is present with you, and the thing that ye would not, that do ye. He knows the secret intent of every heart; and this is a pleasure to you, my dear brethren, who come on purpose to meet with him, though it be a field. And, however some may esteem me a mountebank, and an enthusiast, one that is only going to make you methodically mad; they may breathe out their invectives against me, yet Christ knows all; he takes notice of it, and I shall leave it to him to plead my cause, for he is a gracious Master: I have already found him so, and am sure he will continue so. Vengeance is his, and he will repay it. Let them revile me; let them cast me out of their synagogues, and have my name in reproach, I shall not answer them by reviling again, or in speaking evil against them: no, that is not the Spirit of Christ, but meekness, patience, long-suffering, kindness, &c.

Ye Pharisees, who are going about to establish your own righteousness; you, who are too polite to follow the Lord Jesus Christ in sincerity and truth; you, who are all for a little show, a little outside work; who lead moral, civil, decent lives, Christ will not know you at the great day, but will say unto you, O ye Pharisees, was there any place for me in your love? Alas! you are full of anger and malice, and self-will; yet you pretended to love and serve me, and to be my people: but, however, I despise you; I, who am God, and knoweth the secret of all hearts; I, who am truth itself, the faithful and true witness, say unto you, "Depart from me, ye workers of iniquity, into that place of torment, prepared for the devil and his angels." Good God! And must these discreet polite creatures, who never did any one harm, but led such civil, decent lives, must they suffer the vengeance of eternal fire? Cannot their righteous souls be saved? Where then must the sinner and the ungodly appear? Where wilt thou, O Sabbath-breaker, appear, thou, who canst take thy pleasure, thy recreation, on the Lord's-day, who refuseth to hear the word of God, who wilt not come to church to be instructed in the ways of the Lord? Where will you, O ye adulterers, fornicators, and such-like of this generation appear? Whoremongers and adulterers God will judge, and them he will condemn. Then you will not call these tricks of youth: no, but you will call on the rocks and the mountains to fall on you, to hide you from the fury and anger of the Lord. Where wilt thou, O man, appear, that takes pleasure in making a mock of sin, who despiseth all reproof, who throws about thy jests as a madman does fire, and asks whether thou art not in sport? Where wilt thou, O man, appear, that makes it thy business to preach against the children of the Most High; thou, who art inventing methods in order to stop the progress of the gospel, and using thy utmost power to quash [squash] the preaching thereof; who art raising of evil reports against the disciple of Christ, and esteemest them madmen, fools, schismatics, and a parcel of rabble? Thou, O man, with all thy letter-learning, wilt surely see the judgment seat of Christ, though, perhaps, sorely against your will; to be cast by him into eternal fire, a place prepared for the devil and his angels. There is a burning tophet kindled by the fury of an avenging God, which will never, never be quenched. The devil longs to embrace you in his hellish arms, whenever the sentence is past, where you must for ever bear the weight of your sin: there is no redemption then; the day of grace is past; the door of hope is shut;

mercy will be no more offered, but you must be shut out from God for ever. O who can dwell with everlasting burnings!

However you may think of hell, indeed it is not a painted fire; it is not an imagination to keep people in awe: then, then you will feel the power of the almighty arm. If you will not lay hold on his golden scepter, he will break you with his iron rod. O ye Pharisees, who are now so good, so much better than others, how will ye stand before Christ, when dressed in his glory as judge? You Arians, may now despise his divinity; then you shall have a proof of it; he will show, that he has all power, and that he was no subordinate God; he will show you that he has all power in heaven and earth; that he was King of kings, and Lord of lords; that he was the mighty God, the everlasting Father; and this power that he has, he will exercise in preserving you to no other end, but to punish you forever. Thus you, who please yourselves with being good enough now, who are not weary and heavy laden with a sense of your sins here, will be weary and heavy laden with a sense of your punishment hereafter.

2. Those, my brethren, are not weary and heavy laden with a sense of their sins, who can delight themselves in the polite entertainments of the age, and follow the sinful diversion of life.

Now they can go to balls and assemblies, play-houses and horse-racing; they have no thought of their sins; they know not what it is to weep for sin, or humble themselves under the mighty hand of God; they can laugh away their sorrows, and sing away their cares, and drive away these melancholy thoughts: they are too polite to entertain any sad thoughts; the talk of death and judgment is irksome to them, because it damps their mirth; they could not endure to think of their sin and danger; they could not go to a play, and think of hell; they could not go quietly to a masquerade, and think of their danger; they could not go to a ball or an assembly in peace, if they thought of their sins.

And so it is proved, even to a demonstration, that these are not weary and heavy laden: for if they are not thoughtful about their sins, they will never be weary and heavy laden of them. But at the day of judgment all will be over; they shall lose all their carnal mirth, all their pleasure, all their delight will be gone forever.

They will say then of their laughter, it is mad; and of mirth, What dost thou? Their merry conceits, and witty jests against the poor despised people of God, are then over. Their mirth was but as the crackling of thorns under a pot; it made a great blaze and unseemly noise for a while, but it was presently gone, and will return no more.

They think now, that if they were to fast or to pray, and meditate and mourn, they should be righteous over-much, and destroy themselves; their lives would be a continual trouble, and it would make them run mad. Alas, my brethren, what misery must that life be, where there is no more pleasant days, no more balls or plays, no cards or dice, those wasters of precious time, no horse-racing and cock-fighting, from whence no good ever came, unless abusing God Almighty's creatures, and putting them to that use which he never designed them, can be called so. How miserable will your life be, when all your joys are over, when your pleasures are all past, and no more mirth or pastime? Do you think there is one merry heart in hell? One pleasing countenance? Or jesting, scoffing, swearing tongue? A sermon now is irksome; the offer of salvation, by the blood of

Jesus Christ, is now termed enthusiasm; but then you would give thousands of worlds, if in your power, for one tender of mercy, for one offer of grace, which now you so much despise.

Now, you are not weary of your diversions, nor are you heavy laden with the sins, with which they are accompanied; but then you will be weary of your punishment, and the aggravation which attends it. Your cards and dice, your hawks and hounds, and bowls, and your pleasant sports, will then be over. What mirth will you have in remembering your sports and diversions? I would not have you mistake me, and say, I am only preaching death and damnation to you; I am only showing you what will be the consequence of continuing in these sinful pleasures; and if the devil does not hurry you away with half a sermon, I shall show you how to avoid these dangers, which I now preach up as the effect of sin unrepented of. I mention this, lest you should be hurried away by the devil: but be not offended, if I point our unto you more of the terrors which will attend your following these polite and fashionable entertainments of the present age, and of not being weary and heavy laden with a sense of your sins.

They who delight in drinking wine to excess, and who are drunkards, what bitter draughts will they have instead of wine and ale? The heat of lust will be then also abated; they will no more sing the song of the drunkard; no more spend their time in courting their mistresses, in lascivious discourse, in amorous songs, in wanton dalliances, in brutish defilements: no, these are all over; and it will but prick each other to the heart to look one another in the face. Then they will wish, that instead of sinning together, they had prayed together; had frequented religious societies; had stirred up each other to love and holiness, and endeavored to convince each other of the evil of sin, and how obnoxious they are to the wrath of God; and the necessity of being weary and heavy laden with a sense thereof; that they might have escaped the punishment which they suffer, by their following the sinful an polite diversions of the age they fell into. But as it was against God himself they had sinned, so no less than God will punish them for their offenses: he hath prepared those torments for his enemies; his continual anger will still be devouring of them; his breath of indignation will kindle the flame; his wrath will be a continual burden to their souls. Woe be to him who falls under the stroke of the Almighty!

Thus they are not weary and heavy laden with their sins, who can follow the polite and fashionable entertainments of the age. But,

Secondly, I am to show you what it is to be weary and heavy laden with sins. And

1. You may be said, my brethren, to be weary and heavy laden, when your sins are grievous unto you, and it is with grief and trouble you commit them.

You, who are awakened unto a sense of your sins, who see how hateful they are to God, and how they lay you open to his wrath and indignation, and would willingly avoid them; who hate yourselves for committing them; when you are thus convinced of sin, when you see the terrors of the law, and are afraid of his judgments; then you may be said to be weary of your sins. And O how terrible do they appear when you are first awakened to a sense of them; when you see nothing but the wrath of God ready to fall upon you, and you are afraid of his judgments! O how heavy is your sin to you then! Then you feel the weight thereof, and that it is grievous to be born.

2. When you are obliged to cry out under the burden of your sins, and know not what to do for relief; when this is your case, you are weary of your sins. It does not consist in a weariness all of a sudden; no, it is the continual burden of your soul, it is your grief and concern that you cannot live without offending God, and sinning against him; and these sins are so many and so great, that you fear they will not be forgiven.

I come, *Secondly*, to show you what is meant by coming to Christ.

It is not, my brethren, coming with your own works: no, you must come in full dependence upon the Lord Jesus Christ, looking on him as the Lord who died to save sinners: Go to him, tell him you are lost, undone, miserable sinners, and that you deserve nothing but hell; and when you thus go to the Lord Jesus Christ out of yourself, in full dependence on the Lord Jesus Christ, you will find him an able and a willing savior; he is pleased to see sinners coming to him in a sense of their own unworthiness; and when their case seems to be most dangerous, most distressed, then the Lord in his mercy steps in and gives you his grace; he puts his Spirit within you, takes away your heart of stone, and gives you a heart of flesh. Stand not out then against this Lord, but go unto him, not in your own strength, but in the strength of Jesus Christ.

And this brings me, *Thirdly*, to consider the exhortation Christ gives unto all of you, high and low, rich and poor, one with another, to come unto him that you may have rest. And if Jesus Christ gives you rest, you may be sure it will be a rest indeed; it will be such a rest as your soul wants; it will be a rest which the world can neither give nor take away. O come all of ye this night, and you shall find rest: Jesus Christ hath promised it. Here is a gracious invitation, and do not let a little rain hurry you away from the hearing of it; do but consider what the devil and damned spirits would give to have the offer of mercy, and to accept of Christ, that they may be delivered from the torments they labor under, and must do so forever; or, how pleasing would this rain be to them to cool their parched tongues; but they are denied both, while you have mercy offered to you; free and rich mercy to come to Christ; here is food for your souls, and the rain is to bring forth the fruits of the earth, as food for you bodies. Here is mercy upon mercy.

Let me beseech you to come unto Christ, and he will give you rest; you shall find rest unto your souls. O you, my weary, burdened brethren, do but go to Christ in this manner, and though you go to him weary, you shall find rest before you come from him: let not anything short of the Lord Jesus Christ be your rest; for wherever you seek you will be disappointed; but if you do but seek unto the Lord Jesus Christ, there you will find a fullness of every thing which your weary soul wants. Go to him this night; here is an invitation to all you who are weary souls. He does not call you, O Pharisees; not, it is only you weary sinners; and sure you will not stay from him, but accept of his invitation; do not delay; one moment may be dangerous: death may take you off suddenly. You know not but that a fit of the apoplexy may hurry you from time into eternity; therefore, be not for staying till you have something to bring; come in all your rags, in all your filthiness, in all your distresses, and you will soon find

Jesus Christ ready to help, and to relieve you; he loves you as well in your rags, as in your best garments; he regards not your dress; no, do but come unto him, and you shall soon find rest for your souls.

What say you? Shall I tell my Master you will come unto him, and that you will accept him on his own terms. Let me, my brethren, beseech you to take Jesus without anything of your own righteousness: for if you expect to mix anything of yourself with Christ, you build upon a sandy foundation; but if you take Christ for your rest, he will be that unto you. Let me beseech you to build upon this rock of ages. O my brethren, think of the gracious invitation, "Come unto me," to Jesus Christ; it is he that calls you; And will you not go?

Come, come unto him. If your souls were not immortal, and you in danger of losing them, I would not thus speak unto you; but the love of your souls constrains me to speak: methinks this would constrain me to speak unto you forever. Come then by faith, and lay hold of the Lord Jesus; though he be in heaven, he now calleth thee. Come, all ye drunkards, swearers, Sabbath-breakers, adulterers, fornicators; come, all ye scoffers, harlots, thieves, and murderers, and Jesus Christ will save you; he will give you rest, if you are weary of your sins. O come lay hold upon him. Had I less love for your souls, I might speak less; but that love of God, which is shed abroad in my heart, will not permit me to leave you, till I see whether you will come to Christ or no. O for your life receive him, for fear he may never call you any more. Behold, the Bridegroom cometh; it may be this night the cry may be made. Now would you hear this, if you were sure to die before the morning light? God grant you may begin to live, that when the king of terrors shall come, you may have nothing to do but to commit your souls into the hands of a faithful Redeemer.

Now to God the Father, God the Son, and God the Holy Ghost, be all honor, praises, dominion, and power, henceforth and for evermore. Amen, Amen.

Chapter Sixteen

The Folly and Danger of Parting with Christ for the Pleasures and Profits of Life

Matthew 8:23–34 NKJV *"Now when He got into a boat, His disciples followed Him. And suddenly a great tempest arose on the sea, so that the boat was covered with the waves; but He was asleep. Then His disciples came to Him and awoke Him, saying, 'Lord, save us! We are perishing!' But He said to them, 'Why are you fearful, O you of little faith?' Then He arose and rebuked the winds and the sea, and there was a great calm. So the men marveled, saying, 'Who can this be, that even the winds and the sea obey Him?' When He had come to the other* *side, to the country of the Gergesenes, there met Him two demon-possessed men, coming out of the tombs, exceedingly fierce, so that no one could pass that way. And suddenly they cried out, saying, 'What have we to do with You, Jesus, You Son of God? Have You come here to torment us before the time?' Now a good way off from them there was a herd of many swine feeding. So the demons begged Him, saying, 'If You cast us out, permit us to go away into the herd of swine.' And He said to them, 'Go.' So when they had come out, they went into the herd of swine. And suddenly the whole herd of swine ran violently down the steep place into the sea, and perished in the water. Then those who kept them fled; and they went away into the city and told everything, including what had happened to the demon-possessed men. And behold, the whole city came out to meet Jesus. And when they saw Him, they begged Him to depart from their region."*

If we truly understood how necessary it is to be real Christians, we would never be satisfied with being Christians in name only. Yet many people have become comfortable with outward religion while lacking the inward life of Christ. They carry the name of Christian, but they do not truly know Christ. They may have been baptized, attend church, repeat prayers, and take part in religious customs, but their hearts remain far from God.

How strange it is that people can profess the name of Christ and yet speak so little of Him. The name of Jesus should be the joy of our conversation here on earth and the theme of our praise forever in heaven. There is no other name by which we must be saved. Yet many are taught to look within themselves for salvation. They are told there must first be some worthiness in them before God will give them grace.

But that is not the doctrine of Scripture. It is not the doctrine of Jesus. It is not the doctrine of the early Christians. It is not the doctrine of the Reformation. It is not the doctrine of grace. It makes Christ only half a Savior and sends sinners to Jesus in their own strength instead of in the strength of the Lord.

Unless you come to Christ depending only on Him, you cannot be saved. Unless Christ is your wisdom, your righteousness, your sanctification, and your redemption, He will not be your Savior at all. Salvation is the free gift of God. If any person is saved, it is because of the free love of God and the free grace of Jesus Christ.

Do not flatter yourself by thinking you are good enough because you live a moral life. Do not think that because you go to church, say prayers, or take communion, nothing more is needed. If that is all you have, you are deceiving your own soul. Unless God, in His free grace and mercy, shows you your error, outward religion may only lead you more quietly toward eternal ruin.

God must be exalted, and man must be humbled. You will never begin at the right place until you come to Jesus with nothing in your hands. You must not come trusting what you have done. You must come trusting what Christ has done and suffered.

This passage shows us how people can act like the Gergesenes, who begged Jesus to leave them. They had the Lord of glory in their region, yet they preferred their swine over the Savior. They were more troubled by the loss of their possessions than amazed by the deliverance of two tormented men. This is not only an ancient story. Many still do the same thing today.

The passage begins by telling us that Jesus entered a boat, and His disciples followed Him. Christ had been performing miracles and doing good. Now He was going to the country of the Gergesenes to deliver two men possessed by demons. His disciples followed Him.

No doubt, the disciples were often mocked for following Jesus. The scribes and Pharisees did not honor Him. Many treated Him as a deceiver, a babbler, or a troublemaker. Those who followed Him were likely ridiculed as well. They may have been called foolish, extreme, mad, or ignorant. But still they followed Him. They loved their Master too much to turn back because of a little reproach.

If you truly love the Lord Jesus Christ, you will follow Him even when people mock you. If you love Him above all, you will not turn away because of the opinions of the scribes and Pharisees of this generation. The love of Christ makes reproach bearable. A heart that truly knows Him would rather be mocked with Christ than praised without Him.

Then the Bible says that a great tempest arose on the sea. The presence of Christ in the boat did not keep the disciples from danger, fear, or trouble. Jesus was with them, and still the storm came. This teaches us that following Christ does not mean we will never face storms. Sometimes Christ allows storms to test our faith and show us what is truly in our hearts.

It is easy to follow Christ when everything is calm. It is easy to profess faith when there is no cost. But the sincerity of our love is often tested when trouble comes. If you had to lose your comfort, your reputation, your business, or even your life rather than deny Jesus, what would you do? True love for Christ is seen when following Him becomes costly.

The storm may look small at first, no bigger than a man's hand, but it can grow. Persecution, suffering, and testing may come. Such storms scatter hypocrites. They expose nominal Christians. They reveal who truly belongs to Christ and who only followed Him while it was easy.

When the storm grew fierce, the disciples came to Jesus and woke Him, saying, "Lord, save us! We are perishing!" Jesus answered, **Matthew 8:26 NKJV**, *"Why are you fearful, O you of little faith?"* Then He arose and rebuked the winds and the sea, and there was a great calm.

Here we see the compassion and power of Jesus Christ. As soon as the disciples cried out to Him, He helped them. He rebuked the winds and the sea, and everything became calm. What He did in the natural storm, He can also do in the soul. When Jesus speaks peace to a troubled heart, the storm within becomes calm.

Only God could command the winds and the sea. No wonder the men marveled and said, **Matthew 8:27 NKJV**, *"Who can this be, that even the winds and the sea obey Him?"* They saw His power and were amazed. The sea knew His voice. The wind obeyed His command. Creation bowed before its Creator.

When Jesus came to the other side, into the country of the Gergesenes, two demon-possessed men met Him. They came out of the tombs and were exceedingly fierce, so fierce that no one could pass that way. These men were tormented by the evil one. They frightened others, but when they saw Jesus, the demons in them were afraid.

They cried out, **Matthew 8:29 NKJV**, *"What have we to do with You, Jesus, You Son of God? Have You come here to torment us before the time?"* The demons knew who Jesus was. They knew He was the Son of God. They knew He had authority over them. They knew a day of judgment was coming. They feared that He had come to torment them before the appointed time.

This shows us that the devil is powerful, but he is not free. He is an enemy, but he is a chained enemy. He cannot do whatever he wants. He cannot even enter a herd of swine unless Christ permits him. The demons begged Jesus, saying, **Matthew 8:31 NKJV**, *"If You cast us out, permit us to go away into the herd of swine."*

Jesus simply said, "Go." When the demons came out, they entered the herd of swine, and the whole herd ran violently down the steep place into the sea and perished in the water. This shows the malice of the devil. He would destroy even animals if given permission. How much more would he destroy souls if Christ did not restrain him?

If Satan had his way, he would destroy every one of us. But Christ, by His power and grace, holds him back. Satan may desire to sift, tempt, terrify, and ruin, but he cannot go beyond the limits God sets.

Those who kept the swine ran into the city and told everything that had happened. Then the whole city came out to meet Jesus. But they did not come to worship Him. They did not come to thank Him for delivering the demon-possessed men. They came to beg Him to leave their region.

This is one of the saddest parts of the story. They preferred their swine to Christ. They cared more about the loss of earthly possessions than the presence of the Savior. They would rather have their business, their animals, and their profit than Jesus.

That is the danger this passage warns us about. Many people still part with Christ for the pleasures and profits of life. They would rather have entertainment than Christ. They would rather have worldly comfort than Christ. They would rather have money, reputation, pleasure, or self-righteous religion than Christ.

Now let us look at this story spiritually.

The disciples were in the storm, and the waves covered the boat while Jesus slept. Do we not often experience storms in this world? Do not waves of temptation beat against our souls? Do we not sometimes feel that we are about to be swallowed up? We fear that temptation will overcome us. We fear falling into the hands of the evil one. We fear that Christ is asleep and does not see.

But do not be afraid. Jesus may seem asleep to you, but He is not careless. He knows your storm. He knows your soul. He knows the raging of men, the attacks of Satan, and the fears within your heart. If you seek Him in your helplessness and unworthiness, you will find Him ready to pardon, ready to forgive, and ready to save.

Many people call God "Father" every day, but they have no right to call Him Father in a spiritual sense because they have not received the Spirit of adoption. God is the Creator of all, but He is spiritually Father only to those who are born again. Even animals owe their existence to God as Creator. But that does not mean they are His children by grace. In the same way, you must be born again. You must have an inward work of grace in your heart. This must be experienced. This must be real.

The Lord Jesus Christ sees every person. He knows why you come to hear His Word. He knows whether you come from curiosity, criticism, hunger, or faith. He knows the thoughts and intentions of every heart. Even if He seems silent for a time, as He seemed with the Syrophoenician woman, He sees. In due time, He can turn toward you with mercy and speak peace to your troubled soul.

When the storm rises, do not depend on yourself. Cry out as the disciples did: "Lord, save us! We are perishing!" Ask Him to be your guide and your salvation. Present yourself to Him. Bow your knees and your heart before Him.

Scripture says in **Ephesians 5:14 NKJV**, *"Awake, you who sleep, arise from the dead, and Christ will give you light."* Come to Christ, and you will be welcomed. Come despite your vileness. Come because without Him you will perish. Your good intentions cannot save you. Your good meanings cannot save you. Your religious habits cannot save you. Only Christ can save.

If Christ does not save you, you will perish in your sins. But if you come to Him, you will find mercy. There is salvation in no other. If the disciples could have saved themselves, they would not have cried out to Jesus. But they knew no one could save them except Him. So must you. If you are under conviction of sin and fear of judgment, do not run to your own works. Run to Christ.

There is no fitness in you by nature except a fitness for judgment. By nature, we are children of wrath, and our hearts are like Satan's stronghold. You may go to church, say prayers, take communion, and harm no one outwardly, and still have only a false peace. If that is the only peace you have, it will not stand. A self-created peace will perish.

But the door of mercy is not yet shut. There remains a sacrifice for sins for all who will receive Jesus Christ. He knows the deepest thoughts of your heart. He sees the first stirrings of grace in you. He welcomes poor sinners. The angels rejoice when sinners turn to God. Ministers of Christ rejoice to be instruments in turning people from darkness to light and from the power of Satan to God.

Jesus said to His disciples, **Matthew 8:26 NKJV**, *"Why are you fearful, O you of little faith?"* And the same question may be asked of you. Why are you afraid to leave your sins and turn to God? Why are you afraid to come to Christ? Come with the sense of your unworthiness. Tell Him how polluted and sinful you are. Do not be faithless, but believe.

Do not come in your own strength. If you come in your own strength, you have reason to fear. But if you come trusting Christ, you do not need to fear. Your sins will not keep Him from receiving you. Your unworthiness will not keep Him from receiving you. The only things that will keep you back are your own unbelief, your love of sin, or your trust in your own good works.

Christ loves to see poor sinners come to Him. He is pleased when they lie at His feet and plead His promises. If you come this way, He will not send you away empty. He will receive you and bless you.

Do not slight infinite love. What more would you have Christ do? Is it not enough that He came to save? He does not want only outward religion from you. He wants your heart. He says, in effect, "Give Me your heart." He does not ask this to make you miserable. He asks it to make you happy. He calls you away from sin so that you may sit down forever at the marriage supper of the Lamb.

When Jesus rebuked the winds and the sea, there was a great calm. Only Christ could do that. The disciples could have spoken to the storm forever, and nothing would have happened. But when Jesus spoke, the storm ceased.

So it is with preaching. A preacher may preach as long as he lives. He may speak until he has no strength left. But unless Christ applies the Word to the heart, it will not save. The power is not in the voice of man but in the command of Christ.

In all your troubles, look to Christ. Ask Him to rebuke the storm. If the Pharisees of this generation mock you, accuse you, and speak evil against you, do not answer with bitterness. Leave it to Christ. Your words alone cannot quiet the storm, but His word can.

Do not be discouraged if you suffer for following Him. Scripture says in **2 Timothy 3:12 NKJV**, *"Yes, and all who desire to live godly in Christ Jesus will suffer persecution."* There has always been enmity between the seed of the woman and the seed of the serpent. If you belonged to the world, the world would love its own. But because Christ has chosen His people out of the world, the world hates them.

Do not expect to follow Christ into glory without passing through trial here. Look beyond the suffering. Look into eternity. Christ is coming, and His reward is with Him. He will repay His people for every sorrow, temptation, and difficulty they endured for His sake.

The men marveled and said, **Matthew 8:27 NKJV**, *"Who can this be, that even the winds and the sea obey Him?"* We too should marvel. When troubles surround us from within and without, and Jesus speaks peace by the word of His power, there is peace indeed.

When God first awakens a soul to sin, there may be a great storm. The terrors of judgment rise. Satan fights hard to keep possession. He does not want the soul to close with Christ. But when Jesus comes, He breaks the false peace. He alarms the conscience. He brings fear, sorrow, and conviction until the soul yields to mercy and receives Him as Lord. Then Satan is cast out, the storm is rebuked, and true peace is established.

There can be no true peace in the soul while it remains at enmity with Christ. A person may harden himself. He may speak peace to himself. He may pretend all is well. But if Christ has not spoken peace, there is no peace. Either the proud heart will be broken here in mercy, or it will be broken hereafter in wrath and judgment.

If you are easy while still under the storm of sin, and you do not cry to Christ for salvation, you are in great danger. It is a wonder that a person who has not made peace with God can eat, drink, sleep, and live without fear. How can you lie down at night and not tremble that you may wake up in hell? But if Christ speaks peace to your soul, no one can speak lasting trouble. Not men. Not devils. Not the world.

Lie down at the feet of Christ whom you have resisted and say, "Lord, what do You want me to do?" He can rebuke the winds and seas of your troubled mind, and all will be calm.

Jesus went to the country of the Gergesenes because He knew He would meet two men possessed by demons. He went on purpose to relieve them. The devil is full of hatred and malice, but he is chained. He could terrify those men and those who passed by, but he could not do more than God allowed.

So it is with you. Satan will try to frighten you away from Christ. He will use every method to keep sick, weary sinners from coming to Jesus. If he can make you lose your soul, that is his goal.

How many people are kept from Christ by fear of reproach? Many would like to be with Christ in glory, but they are afraid of being laughed at now. They fear being called one of His followers. They fear losing business, reputation, friendships, or comfort. They fear being called extreme, foolish, or mad for Christ.

But what will such people say when Jesus appears in glory? If you want Him to confess you then, you must not be ashamed to confess Him now. Do not let the fierceness of the devil keep you from Christ. The day will show who was truly wise and who was truly mad.

Are you afraid to stand for Christ in the world? Are you afraid to be noticeably godly? Are you ashamed to be counted as belonging to Jesus? Do not let the temptations of the devil keep you from coming to Christ. Satan may be fierce, but if you resist him by looking to Christ, he must flee. Christ will dispossess him. Do not be afraid to meet Jesus. Tell Him everything your soul needs, and He will give it to you.

The demons cried out, **Matthew 8:29 NKJV**, *"What have we to do with You, Jesus, You Son of God? Have You come here to torment us before the time?"* Even the demons knew who Jesus was. They knew

He was the Son of God. They knew a day of judgment was coming. They knew He had power to condemn them.

This should correct all low and dishonoring thoughts of Christ. Jesus is not merely a good man. He is not merely a prophet. He is not less than God. He is God the Son, eternal with the Father, equal in power and glory. Scripture teaches that all things were made through Him. He is the Alpha and the Omega. He thought it not robbery to be equal with God.

Jesus had to be both God and man to save us. As man, He suffered. As God, He satisfied divine justice. He took our nature and offered Himself on the cross for the sins of those who come to Him. If He were not God, He could not have made full satisfaction for our sins.

The demons believe in His divine power and tremble. How serious it is when people deny what demons are forced to acknowledge. Those who deny the deity of Christ will one day feel the power of the One they refused to honor. May they repent before that day comes.

The demons begged Jesus, asking permission to enter the herd of swine. Jesus said, "Go." As soon as they had permission, they acted with violence and destruction. This shows what Satan does when he has power. He hurries souls from one temptation to another, from one sin to another. If he could, he would hurry every person into hell as violently as he drove the swine into the sea.

But Christ prevents him. Jesus died for souls, and the devil cannot do with them as he pleases. Satan has the will to destroy, but he does not have unlimited power.

When the devil or wicked men are given power, they harass Christians. If the laws allowed it, many would gladly persecute the people of God. But blessed be God, Christ has not said to them, "Go." He restrains them. He hedges up their way. They may desire to destroy, but they cannot move beyond His permission.

Therefore, do not be afraid of their wrath. Their anger may be fierce, and their words may be bitter arrows, but the shield of faith can preserve you. Christ is your protector.

When God preserves His people, it becomes a cause of joy in the Holy Spirit. Many mock the joy of the Holy Spirit as madness or emotionalism, but those who have tasted it know it is real. It carries its own evidence. Pray in the name of Jesus Christ. Continue wrestling with God until He blesses you and gives you the joy that the world does not know.

The devil may stir up trouble after trouble, but he cannot drag Christ's people into hell. The Lord Jesus will give His Spirit, and His Spirit will preserve them against the assaults of the enemy.

After the swine perished, those who kept them fled into the city and told everything. They told what had happened to the demon-possessed men. When God works in a soul, something similar happens. When you feel the power of God in your heart, you cannot remain silent. You will want to tell others what great things God has done for your soul.

You will speak of how God delivered you from Satan's power. You will remember how He touched you through His Word. You will talk about what He did in your heart. You will love to speak of Jesus. No conversation will be as sweet as conversation about the Lord Jesus Christ. Once you have tasted His love and felt the power of His grace, He will be altogether lovely to you.

But the Gergesenes responded differently. The whole city came out to meet Jesus, but not to worship Him. Not to thank Him. Not to rejoice over the two delivered men. They came to beg Him to leave.

They valued their swine more than the Savior. They would rather lose Christ than lose their possessions. This is still the condition of many who call themselves Christians. They would rather part with Christ than part with their pleasures. A play, a party, entertainment, sensual pleasure, comfort, reputation, or worldly profit is more desirable to them than the presence of Jesus.

If they can indulge the lust of the flesh, the lust of the eyes, and the pride of life, they are content, as though they will live here forever. But I hope none of you will be satisfied with such a life. I hope you love the company of Jesus too much to trade Him for a few passing pleasures.

There are also many who part with Christ for their own good works. They think they can go to heaven because they go to church, say prayers, and take communion. But they are deceived. If they build on anything short of Christ, they will fall short of salvation. Christ must be the chief cornerstone. Without Him, everything collapses.

Now let me make a personal appeal. Come to Jesus Christ. I invite every one of you to come to Him and receive Him as Lord and Savior. He is ready to receive you. If you are afraid to come because you are lost, remember that He came to save the lost. If you are weary and heavy laden under the weight of sin, He has promised to give you rest.

Jesus said in **Matthew 11:28 NKJV**, *"Come to Me, all you who labor and are heavy laden, and I will give you rest."* If you feel the burden of your sins and do not know how to be delivered, come to Christ. In the name of the Lord Jesus, I invite you to come and find rest for your soul.

If you come to Him, He will not reproach you. He will not shame you for not coming sooner. He will rejoice over you. He will say, as He said to others, **Matthew 9:2 NKJV**, *"Son, be of good cheer; your sins are forgiven you."* If you come to Him by faith in His blood, He is ready to speak the same mercy to you.

Jesus is the same today as He was then. Scripture says in **Hebrews 13:8 NKJV**, *"Jesus Christ is the same yesterday, today, and forever."* Though He suffered on the cross long ago, He is still the same in goodness, power, mercy, and grace.

He calls you through His Word and through His servants. Come to Him. Ask Him to break your stubborn heart and make you willing to be brought to Him in His own way. Ask Him to make you poor in spirit and give you an inheritance among those who are sanctified.

Come and drink of the water of life. You may buy without money and without price. Christ is calling you away from sin and Satan to Himself. Open the door of your heart, and the King of glory shall come in.

But if this doctrine is strange to you and seems foolish, or if you think you have enough goodness of your own to recommend you to God, you do not yet know the grace of Christ in truth. You may attend church. You may take communion. But if you do not know the new birth, if you do not know what it is to have your nature changed, you cannot enter the kingdom of God.

What more can be said? Is your soul of no value to you? Do you think it is not worth saving? Are your pleasures worth more than your soul? Would you rather have the passing diversions of this life than the eternal salvation of your soul?

If so, you cannot share in Christ's glory. But if you come to Him, He will give you a new nature. He will supply you with grace here and bring you to glory hereafter. Then you will sing praise and hallelujahs to the Lamb forever.

May this be the blessed end of all who hear this message. May the Lord guide you by His counsel until He brings you home to heaven and makes you partakers of His glory.

Amen.

Chapter Seventeen

Marks of True Conversion

Matthew 18:3 NKJV *"Assuredly, I say to you, unless you are converted and become as little children, you will by no means enter the kingdom of heaven."*

I suppose most people believe that every person must one day die. Most also believe that after death there will be judgment. Every soul will either be separated from God in darkness or welcomed into the presence of the blessed God forever. And whether people live like it or not, almost everyone hopes to go to heaven when they die.

My heart's desire and prayer is that every person would enter the kingdom of our heavenly Father. But though many hope to go to heaven when they die, the lives of many show that they are not walking on the road that leads there. Jesus told us that people are known by their fruits. If we judge by the fruit of many lives, it is clear that thousands who hope for heaven are not yet in the way of heaven.

Many call themselves Christians and would be offended if someone questioned whether they were Christians. Yet many who bear the name of Christ do not truly understand what Christianity is. If you ask some people why they believe they are going to heaven, they will say they belong to a certain church, denomination, or religious group. Others will say they were baptized as children and that their names are written in the church register. They may have fought against Christ with their lives ever since, but because they were baptized and outwardly connected to the church, they assume their names are written in the book of life.

Others do not build their hopes on baptism or church membership alone. They build on the fact that they are decent people. They say they do not harm anyone. They live honestly. They are kind from time to time. They give to the poor, attend church, take communion occasionally, and live outwardly sober lives. The world calls such a person a good Christian. We should be charitable in how we think of others, but we must not confuse outward morality with true conversion.

There are also many who go through a regular round of duties and religious performances and think this will take them to heaven. They may have Christ in their heads, but they do not have Christ in their hearts.

The Lord Jesus knew how deceitful the human heart is. He knew many would go very near the gates of heaven and still never enter. He knew many would knock at the door and hear the dreadful words, "I do not know you." Therefore, He plainly tells us what must happen before we can have any well-grounded hope of entering the kingdom of heaven.

Jesus told Nicodemus that unless a man is born again, he cannot see the kingdom of God. He said a man must be born of water and the Spirit. And in our text, He gives one of the most solemn declarations in Scripture: **Matthew 18:3 NKJV**, *"Assuredly, I say to you, unless you are converted and become as little children, you will by no means enter the kingdom of heaven."*

These words were first spoken to the disciples. The disciples had come to Jesus asking who was the greatest in the kingdom of heaven. In some sense, they had already tasted the grace of God, but there was still much pride, ambition, and corruption remaining in them. They needed a deeper work of humility. They needed to be more fully converted in their spirit and attitude. The kingdom of Christ was not to be built on outward greatness, pride, or worldly ambition. It was spiritual, humble, and holy.

Yet these words also apply to all people, both saints and sinners. They speak to those who already know Christ and need to grow in childlike humility, and they speak to those who have never been truly converted at all.

First, these words show us that before anyone can have a true hope of heaven, a great change must take place in the soul. Every adult knows that a great change has taken place in the body since childhood. You have the same basic body, but you are greatly changed from what you were as an infant. Someone who knew you only as a baby might not recognize you years later.

In the same way, before we enter heaven, a great change must take place in the soul. The soul remains the same soul, but the temper, desires, habits, affections, and direction of life must be changed. Those who knew us before conversion should be able to see that something real has happened. There should be such a difference that people may stand amazed at the change God has worked in us.

But we must also be careful not to misunderstand Jesus' words. Some people use this verse to deny original sin. They say that since Jesus tells us to become like little children, children must be completely innocent and pure. They argue that children come into the world like blank paper, without corruption.

But that is not what Jesus means. Scripture teaches plainly that we are born in sin. David said in **Psalm 51:5 NKJV**, *"Behold, I was brought forth in iniquity, and in sin my mother conceived me."* Jeremiah says in **Jeremiah 17:9 NKJV**, *"The heart is deceitful above all things, and desperately wicked; who can know it?"* Paul teaches that all have gone out of the way and that there is none righteous by nature, no, not one.

Parents can see this truth in their children. Very early, self-will appears. Resistance to correction appears. A desire to have one's own way appears. Children must be trained, taught, corrected, and prayed over because they are born with a sinful nature. Their hearts, like ours, need grace.

So when Jesus says we must become like little children, He is not saying children are sinless. He is speaking comparatively and spiritually. Little children are innocent in some ways compared with grown adults, but they still need the grace of God. Jesus is pointing to certain qualities of children that must be found in His people.

The disciples had asked, "Who then is greatest in the kingdom of heaven?" They were thinking in worldly terms. They imagined position, honor, rule, and greatness. So Jesus called a little child and set him in the midst of them. It was as though He said, "You are thinking too highly. You are dreaming of crowns, power, and position. But unless you become lowly and childlike, you are not even in the right spirit for My kingdom."

A little child has no real understanding of crowns, kingdoms, thrones, and worldly greatness. Give a little child something simple, and he is content. He is not trying to rule a kingdom. In this sense, we must become like little children. We must become loose from the world. We must not be ruled by ambition, pride, position, or earthly greatness.

This does not mean Christians must shut up their shops, leave their work, abandon their families, or live as hermits. Christianity is not an escape from all responsibilities. You cannot leave your sinful heart behind simply by leaving society. The problem is not only around us. It is within us.

The religion of Jesus is a social religion. Christ does not call us to abandon lawful work or neglect our children. We must provide, labor, serve, and fulfill our duties. But if we are truly converted, our hearts will be loose from the world. We may live in the world, work in the world, and serve in the world, but the world will not be our treasure.

To become like little children also means we become aware of our weakness. A little child knows he needs help. He must be led by the hand. He must be taught. He must be guided. If someone does not hold him, he may fall.

So it is with those who are truly converted. They no longer boast in their own strength. They no longer say, "I am rich and have need of nothing." Instead, they see that by nature they are poor, miserable, blind, and naked. They know they need God's help every hour.

As a little child gives his hand to a parent, the converted soul gives the heart, mind, will, and affections to be guided by God's Word, God's providence, and God's Spirit. Paul says in **Romans 8:14 NKJV**, *"For as many as are led by the Spirit of God, these are sons of God."*

Little children also know they must learn. They go to school. They receive instruction. They are not ashamed to be taught. In the same way, converted people become teachable. They know they do not know everything. They want to learn from Christ every day.

This is why John speaks to believers as little children. The flock of Christ is called a little flock, not only because it is small in number compared with the world, but because true believers are little in their own eyes. The greater a person grows in grace, the smaller he becomes in his own estimation.

Paul was a great apostle. He preached to multitudes. He planted churches. He suffered for Christ. Yet he said in **Ephesians 3:8 NKJV**, *"To me, who am less than the least of all the saints, this grace was given, that I should preach among the Gentiles the unsearchable riches of Christ."* Some may think Paul was exaggerating, but he was not. The closer a soul comes to God, the more deeply it feels its own unworthiness.

Young Christians are often like green corn that grows high but has little weight. Older, mature Christians are like ripe corn that bends lower because it is full. Young Christians may be like shallow streams that make much noise, while mature Christians are like deep rivers that move quietly toward the ocean.

To become like little children also means becoming sincere and without allowed guile. A little child is generally simple and open. He has not yet learned all the arts of deception. Jesus said of Nathanael in **John 1:47 NKJV**, *"Behold, an Israelite indeed, in whom is no deceit!"*

This does not mean Christians should be foolish or careless. We should pray for wisdom. We should not expose ourselves unnecessarily to harm or deception. Jesus told us to be wise as serpents and harmless as doves. But the Christian heart should not be marked by hypocrisy, manipulation, or deceit. A converted person may still have remaining sin, but he will not live in allowed dishonesty. He will desire truth in the inward parts.

Now let us bring this personally to our own hearts. Jesus introduced this truth with solemn words: **Matthew 18:3 NKJV**, *"Assuredly, I say to you."* What He said then, He still says now. Unless you are converted and become as little children, you will by no means enter the kingdom of heaven.

All of us hope to go to heaven. I pray that every one of us will be there. But we must ask honestly: Has this great change happened in us? Has God, by His Spirit, truly changed our hearts? I am not asking whether you have become perfect angels. That will never happen in this life. I am asking whether you have reason to believe God has made you a new creature in Christ Jesus.

Can you say that the main direction of your heart has changed? Can you say, "I have a family, a job, responsibilities, and business to attend to, but I want to do all for Christ. I love these blessings for God's sake. If God called me away, I could say, Lord, I am ready. Whom have I in heaven but You? And there is none upon earth I desire besides You."

Can you thank God for His earthly gifts and still say, "These are not my Christ"? Can you enjoy the blessings of life without making them your god?

Are you aware of your weakness? Do you know that by nature you are poor, blind, miserable, and naked? Have you given your heart, will, affections, and understanding to be guided by the Spirit of God, as a child gives his hand to be led by a parent? Are you little in your own eyes? Do you think humbly of yourself? Do you want to learn from Christ every day?

Some believers become discouraged because they do not feel the same emotional joy they once felt. They think because they are not always on the mountaintop, they must have no grace at all. But if Jesus is humbling you, emptying you, and teaching you that you are nothing without Him, then grace is at work. You may not be growing upward in visible excitement, but you may be growing downward in humility. And the heart that is being emptied may soon be more abundantly filled.

If you are converted and have become like a little child, then welcome into the family of God. Welcome, in the name of Jesus, into the company of God's children. The world may see nothing special in you. Outwardly, you may look like everyone else. But in the sight of God, you are a son or daughter of the King of kings.

Let this melt your heart. The great God could have judged you for secret sins that no one knew but Him and your own soul. He could have condemned you many times over. Yet He cast His mantle of love over you and said, "Live." He found a ransom. He showed mercy.

If an earthly king adopted one of your children, you would think it a great honor. Pharaoh's daughter showed great kindness when she took up Moses, a poor child in a basket, and raised him as her own. But what is that compared with the mercy of God? You were once a child of wrath, but by converting grace you have become a child of God.

If God is your Father, then obey Him. If God is your Father, serve Him. Love Him with all your heart, all your soul, all your mind, and all your strength. Flee from everything that displeases Him. Walk worthy of the God who has called you into His kingdom and glory.

If you are converted and have become like a little child, then act like a child of God. Newborn children desire milk. In the same way, Peter says in **1 Peter 2:2 NKJV**, *"As newborn babes, desire the pure milk of the word, that you may grow thereby."* If you are born again, desire the sincere milk of the Word. Do not be satisfied with empty religion or man-centered teaching. Feed on the doctrines of grace. Feed on Christ. Grow in grace and in the knowledge of the Lord Jesus Christ.

Parents grieve when their children do not grow. They worry and say, "My child is not growing as he should." How much more must it grieve the heart of Christ when His people remain spiritually small and do not grow? Will you always remain children? Will you always stay at the first principles and never press forward? Pray, "Lord Jesus, help me grow. Teach me to live so that my progress may be seen."

If you are God's child, then go to Him as children go to their parents. When children need something or when someone hurts them, they run to their father or mother. So if Satan troubles you, go tell your Father. If the world troubles you, go tell your Father. If your own family opposes you, go tell your Father.

You may say, "I cannot pray with fine words." But do parents require fine words from their children? If a child comes crying and can barely speak, the parent's heart is moved. How much more does your heavenly Father pity His children? **Psalm 103:13 NKJV** says, *"As a father pities his children, so the Lord pities those who fear Him."* Go boldly to your Father and say, "Abba, Father. Satan troubles me. The world troubles me. My own heart troubles me. Plead my cause." The Lord will speak for you in His own way.

If you are God's child, you should also expect your Father to correct you. Scripture says in **Hebrews 12:7–8 NKJV**, *"If you endure chastening, God deals with you as with sons; for what son is there whom a father does not chasten? But if you are without chastening, of which all have become partakers, then you are illegitimate and not sons."*

God loves His children too much to leave them alone in sin. He is not a foolish parent. He corrects those He loves. He corrected Miriam. He corrected Moses. Through all ages, He has corrected His dearest children.

Many believers pray for greater humility, greater faith, greater love, and greater grace. But often they do not realize that such prayers may bring trials. How will we know whether we have faith unless faith is tested? How will we know whether we have humility unless pride is exposed? How will we know whether we have love unless we are placed in situations where love is required?

When God allows trials, do not immediately think He has abandoned you. If He takes away a child, a possession, a friend, or a comfort, do not blame your heavenly Father. Say, "Lord, I am a stubborn child. You would not strike me unless I needed correction." God is loving and tender. In all the afflictions of His people, He is afflicted with them.

When God spoke to Moses from the burning bush, the bush burned with fire but was not consumed. This can remind us of God's people. They may burn with affliction, but God is with them in the fire. He is with them in the furnace. He is with them in the waters. The waters may rise, but they will not overflow them.

If you are God's child, you should also long to go home and see your Father. Blessed are those who have already gone home to glory. Blessed are those who have passed beyond this field of conflict. When we see coldness among God's people and feel the burdens of this life, how can we not desire to be with the Lord forever?

Yet do not become impatient. God will bring you home in His own time. Some of you may have little in this world. You may have narrow circumstances and hard trials. But God and the gospel with simple bread are great riches. In your Father's house there is bread enough and to spare. Though you may suffer now, you will be comforted soon. The angels will count it an honor to carry you to Abraham's bosom, even if you are a poor Lazarus here.

If you are converted and have become like little children, then be careful not to do what children often do: do not quarrel with one another. Love one another. Scripture says in **1 John 4:16 NKJV**, *"God is love, and he who abides in love abides in God, and God in him."*

Joseph knew his brothers might quarrel on the way, so he told them not to fall out along the way. You are all children of the same Father. You are all going to the same place. Why should you fight? The world already has enough against us. The devil has enough against us. We do not need to quarrel with one another.

Walk in love. If nothing else could be said, let this be said: Little children, love one another. Nothing grieves the heart more than division among God's people. May God hasten the day when we either go to heaven or never quarrel again.

But this comfort belongs to the children of God. It is children's bread. It belongs to those who have been converted and brought into God's family. If you are still graceless, Christless, and unconverted, do not take the comfort without the conversion. You must first come to Jesus Christ.

If you have never been converted, go to God with your stubborn heart. Do not wait until you get home. Begin now. Let the prayer of your heart be, "Lord, convert me. Lord, make me like a little child. Lord Jesus, do not let me be shut out of Your kingdom."

There is more implied in Jesus' words than first appears. When He says, **Matthew 18:3 NKJV**, *"You will by no means enter the kingdom of heaven,"* it also means that without conversion you will be shut out. You will be lost. You will be separated from God. You will go where the worm does not die and the fire is not quenched.

May God press this truth into every heart. May an arrow dipped in the blood of Christ reach every unconverted sinner. Only God can do this work. If you confess your sins, leave them, and lay hold of the Lord Jesus Christ, the Spirit of God will be given to you.

Go to God and say, "Turn me, O my God." You do not know how God may answer. If preaching alone could convert you, if arguments alone could bring you in, I would speak until midnight. But conversion is the work of God. Still, the gospel call is real. Come to Christ.

Precious souls, think what will become of you if you die without being converted. If you leave this world without the wedding garment, God will strike you speechless, and you will be banished from His presence forever. You cannot dwell with everlasting burnings.

But behold, there is a way of escape. Jesus is the way. Jesus is the truth. Jesus is the resurrection and the life. His Spirit must convert you. Come to Christ, and you shall receive mercy.

May God, for Christ's sake, give His Spirit to every soul. May He convert us, make us like little children, and bring us at last into His heavenly kingdom, where we will meet and never part again.

Amen.

Chapter Eighteen

The Wise and Foolish Virgins

Matthew 25:13 *"Watch therefore, for you know neither the day nor the hour in which the Son of Man is coming."*

There are few truths more serious than the truth that every person will one day stand before God. Life moves quickly. Years pass faster than we expect, and one day every one of us will step out of time and into eternity. The Bible tells us that it is appointed for man to die once, and after that comes judgment. A day is coming when the heavens and earth will pass away, and every person who has ever lived will stand before Jesus Christ to give an account of their life.

Most people do not like to think about judgment. They stay distracted with work, entertainment, money, pleasures, and daily responsibilities. Yet deep within the human heart is an awareness that life does not end at the grave. Even those who mock God often become fearful when death draws near. When a person realizes eternity is close, the soul suddenly understands that one day it must answer to God.

This reality should cause every person to examine their heart honestly. The question is not simply whether we attend church or call ourselves Christians. The question is whether we truly know Jesus Christ. There are many people who appear religious outwardly but have never truly surrendered their lives to God. They may know Scripture, practice religious routines, and look moral in the eyes of others, yet inwardly remain spiritually empty.

Jesus addressed this very issue in the parable of the ten virgins.

Matthew 25:1

"Then the kingdom of heaven shall be likened to ten virgins who took their lamps and went out to meet the bridegroom."

In the culture of Jesus' day, weddings were often held at night. Those waiting for the bridegroom would carry lamps as they went out to meet him. In this parable, the bridegroom represents Jesus Christ, and the virgins represent those who profess to follow Him. At first glance, all ten virgins appeared alike. All carried lamps. All were waiting for the bridegroom. All appeared prepared. Yet beneath the surface there was a difference that would eventually be revealed.

Matthew 25:2

"Now five of them were wise, and five were foolish."

The difference between them was not outward appearance, but inward reality.

Matthew 25:3–4

"Those who were foolish took their lamps and took no oil with them, but the wise took oil in their vessels with their lamps."

The foolish virgins carried lamps, but they had no oil. They had religion without spiritual life. They had appearance without transformation. They practiced outward forms of faith, but their hearts had never truly been changed by God.

These foolish virgins represent people who are satisfied with outward Christianity. They may attend church regularly, pray occasionally, and live respectable lives, but they have never experienced genuine repentance or true surrender to Jesus Christ. Their faith exists mostly on the surface. They know about God, but they do not truly know Him.

The wise virgins also carried lamps, but unlike the foolish virgins, they carried oil with them. The oil represents true salvation, genuine faith, and the presence of the Holy Spirit within the believer's life. The wise virgins did not merely practice religion outwardly. Their relationship with God was real. Their faith was alive. Their obedience came from love for Christ rather than mere obligation or routine.

Jesus then said that while the bridegroom delayed, all ten virgins became drowsy and slept.

Matthew 25:5

"But while the bridegroom was delayed, they all slumbered and slept."

This points to the reality of death. Every person, whether believer or unbeliever, eventually faces physical death. Yet death is very different for those who belong to Christ. For the believer, death is not the end. Jesus removed its sting through His resurrection. For those who know Him, death becomes the doorway into eternal life.

Then suddenly, at midnight, everything changed.

Matthew 25:6

"And at midnight a cry was heard: 'Behold, the bridegroom is coming; go out to meet him!'"

The cry came unexpectedly. The bridegroom had arrived. One day Jesus Christ will return just as He promised. He will not return as the suffering Savior hanging upon a cross. He will return in glory, power, and majesty. Every eye will see Him. Every knee will bow before Him.

In that moment the foolish virgins realized something terrifying. Their lamps were going out. Their outward religion could not sustain them. Their appearance of spirituality could not prepare them to meet the bridegroom. They had no real relationship with God.

In desperation they turned to the wise virgins and pleaded for help.

Matthew 25:8

"Give us some of your oil, for our lamps are going out."

But true salvation cannot be borrowed from someone else. No person can live on another person's faith. Every individual must personally come to Christ. Parents cannot save their children. A pastor cannot save his church members. A husband cannot save his wife. Every soul must personally repent and trust in Jesus Christ.

The wise virgins answered:

Matthew 25:9

"No, lest there should not be enough for us and you; but go rather to those who sell, and buy for yourselves."

While the foolish virgins went away searching, the bridegroom arrived.

Matthew 25:10

"And while they went to buy, the bridegroom came, and those who were ready went in with him to the wedding; and the door was shut."

Those final words are deeply sobering: *"and the door was shut."*

Right now the door of mercy remains open. Right now forgiveness is available through Jesus Christ. Right now people can repent, believe, and be saved. But the day is coming when the opportunity will end. There will come a moment when eternity is permanently settled.

Afterward the foolish virgins returned.

Matthew 25:11

"Afterward the other virgins came also, saying, 'Lord, Lord, open to us!'"

They called Him "Lord." They wanted entrance. They wanted heaven. But it was too late.

Jesus answered with some of the most heartbreaking words found in Scripture.

Matthew 25:12

"Assuredly, I say to you, I do not know you."

Notice carefully why they were rejected. They were not condemned because they lived openly immoral lives. They were condemned because they never truly knew Christ. Their religion was external, not internal. They had lamps without oil. They had profession without possession. They looked prepared outwardly, but inwardly they were spiritually empty.

This warning still speaks loudly today. It is possible to grow up in church and still not know God. It is possible to quote Scripture and still not belong to Christ. It is possible to appear spiritual while remaining unchanged within.

The greatest question every person must answer is this: Do I truly know Jesus Christ?

Not do I attend church.

Not do I call myself a Christian.

Not do others think I am religious.

But do I truly belong to Him?

Have I truly repented of my sin? Has my heart been changed by God? Has my faith become real and personal?

Jesus closed the parable with this warning:

Matthew 25:13

"Watch therefore, for you know neither the day nor the hour in which the Son of Man is coming."

No one knows when Christ will return. No one knows the day of their own death. Life is fragile and uncertain. Scripture says our life is like a vapor that appears for a little while and then disappears.

One day the final trumpet will sound. One day every person reading these words will stand before God. For those who truly know Christ, that day will be filled with joy beyond imagination. For those who only possessed outward religion, it will be a day of eternal regret.

Yet even now there is still hope.

Jesus Christ still saves sinners. No matter how broken, guilty, or far from God a person may be, forgiveness is available through the cross of Christ. Jesus died for sinners and rose again so that anyone who believes in Him can receive eternal life.

The invitation remains open today.

Come to Christ while the door is still open.

Do not settle for outward religion without inward transformation.

Do not be content with carrying a lamp while lacking oil.

Seek Jesus personally. Walk closely with Him daily. Live prepared for eternity.

And when the cry finally comes, *"Behold, the bridegroom is coming!"* may you be found ready to enter into His everlasting presence.

Chapter Nineteen

Blind Bartimeus

Mark 10:52 NKJV *"Then Jesus said to him, 'Go your way; your faith has made you well.' And immediately he received his sight and followed Jesus on the road."*

When the apostle Peter preached about Jesus of Nazareth, he gave one of the most beautiful descriptions of our Lord. He said that Jesus went about doing good. That was the life of Christ. He looked for opportunities to show mercy, heal the broken, teach the lost, and bring sinners back to God. Doing the will of the Father was His meat and drink. He lived to do the work of the One who sent Him.

Jesus is rightly called the Sun of Righteousness. As the sun in the sky gives light, warmth, and life to the world, so Jesus brings healing, mercy, and salvation wherever He shines. The prophet said He would arise with healing in His wings. Jesus proved Himself to be the promised Messiah by the miracles He performed. Moses had worked miracles under the old covenant, but many of those miracles were connected with judgment. The miracles of Jesus were full of mercy. He came to bear our sicknesses, heal our infirmities, and save our souls.

Sometimes the same person received mercy both in body and soul. One beautiful example is the poor blind beggar named Bartimaeus. Jesus healed his eyes, but He also touched his heart. The text says, **Mark 10:52 NKJV**, *"Then Jesus said to him, 'Go your way; your faith has made you well.' And immediately he received his sight and followed Jesus on the road."*

May Jesus bless this message so that every spiritually blind person may receive sight, and after the example of Bartimaeus, follow Jesus in the way.

To understand the story, we must go back to the beginning of the account. Jesus and His disciples came to Jericho. Jericho was once a city under the curse of God, yet even there Jesus showed mercy. Zacchaeus had been called there, and now Bartimaeus would also receive mercy there. This reminds us that God's grace can reach people in the most unlikely places. Good can come even out of Nazareth, because Christ Himself came from there. His grace is sovereign. It can reach the worst people in the worst places.

Jesus came to Jericho, and this teaches those who preach the gospel not to avoid places that seem unlikely to produce fruit. If providence points the way, ministers should go. There may be chosen vessels even in places that seem spiritually barren.

Jesus and His disciples were often on the move. They did not always stay long in one place. This does not mean that settled pastors are unnecessary, but it does show that traveling preaching has a place when people are properly called and equipped for it. When God brings a real revival of religion to a land, gospel preaching often spreads beyond ordinary boundaries.

As Jesus went out of Jericho with His disciples, a great multitude followed Him. The religious leaders of that generation often looked down on such crowds. They may have called them common people or rabble. But these were the kind of people who often followed Jesus. The poor received the gospel. The common people heard Him gladly.

Not everyone who followed Jesus was truly His disciple. Some followed Him for bread. Some followed Him out of curiosity. Some came to hear His words and were truly helped by them. Jesus knew the difference. He knew why people followed Him. But He still taught them with compassion. He saw them as sheep without a shepherd.

This gives gospel ministers a warrant to preach to all kinds of people who come to hear the Word, even if their motives are mixed. At the same time, people must be warned not to think they are Christians simply because they follow a preacher or enjoy hearing sermons. Many heard Jesus gladly and still did not follow Him to the end. Some who once followed Him may later have cried, "Crucify Him."

Popularity is not something to trust. It is like a morning cloud or early dew that passes away. Jesus was often surrounded by crowds, yet many did not truly believe. Those who serve publicly must remember this. A crowd can be encouraging, but it can also be dangerous.

Popularity is like a fiery furnace. Only Christ can preserve a minister from being harmed by it.

One thought should humble every preacher: How many hearers will go away without receiving saving benefit? How many may even have their judgment increased because they heard the truth but did not obey it? Jesus said that some will one day say that He taught in their streets, but He will answer, "I do not know you."

As Jesus passed by, blind Bartimaeus sat by the road begging. He was a poor man, blind and dependent on the mercy of others. Some believe his name may suggest he was the blind son of a blind father. If so, his condition was even more pitiful. Since he could not see, he could not work in the usual way, so he begged for his living.

We should not despise those who must beg when providence has brought them to such a low place. Pride often makes people ashamed to receive help from others. But Jesus Himself lived in humility. The women who followed Him ministered to Him from their substance. Bartimaeus was not able to dig, so he begged. And to do so, he sat by the road where people passed in and out of the city.

Though Bartimaeus had lost his sight, he still had his hearing. That was a mercy. When we lose one comfort or ability, we should thank God for the ones that remain. It was a blessing that Bartimaeus could hear, because by hearing he learned that Jesus was passing by.

When he heard the noise of the crowd, he likely asked what was happening. Someone told him that Jesus of Nazareth was passing by. Jesus was called "of Nazareth" because He had been raised there, but some used the name with contempt. Nazareth was not highly respected. Nathanael once asked whether anything good could come out of Nazareth. But Bartimaeus did not stumble over the name. He heard that Jesus was near, and he began to cry out.

The Bible says in **Mark 10:47 NKJV**, *"And when he heard that it was Jesus of Nazareth, he began to cry out and say, 'Jesus, Son of David, have mercy on me!'"*

This shows that although Bartimaeus was blind in body, the eyes of his soul had begun to open. He knew something about Jesus. He believed Jesus was able and willing to heal him. As soon as he heard Jesus was passing by, he cried out. His prayer did not come from cold lips. It came from need. He knew his misery. He knew he needed mercy. He cried loudly so Jesus could hear him above the noise of the crowd.

He also cried out immediately because he did not know whether he would ever have this opportunity again. Jesus was passing by. Bartimaeus did not say, "I will wait until tomorrow." He did not say, "I will call on Him another time." He cried now.

He did not merely say, "Jesus of Nazareth." He said, "Jesus, Son of David." By calling Jesus the Son of David, Bartimaeus was confessing that Jesus was the promised Messiah. The Scriptures had said the Messiah would come from David's line, and that when He came, the eyes of the blind would be opened. Bartimaeus believed this.

Then he prayed, "Have mercy on me." That is the true language of a soul lying at the feet of God. He did not claim healing as something he deserved. He did not bring his works, his prayers, his religion, or his suffering as a reason Jesus should help him. He did not say, "Lord, I am better than others." He simply cried, "Have mercy on me."

This is the prayer of a broken heart. It is the language of the publican who cried, "God, be merciful to me a sinner." Bartimaeus was saying, "Jesus, friend of sinners, Savior of the lost, Son of David, have mercy on a poor blind beggar."

You might think that such a cry would move the crowd to compassion. You might think they would help carry Bartimaeus to Jesus. But instead, many warned him to be quiet. They tried to silence him. They likely thought he was beneath the notice of Jesus. They may have thought Jesus had more important things to do.

This must have been discouraging. It is hard when opposition comes from people who seem to be following Christ. But true faith is not stopped by opposition. Instead of becoming silent, Bartimaeus cried out even more.

Mark 10:48 NKJV says, *"Then many warned him to be quiet; but he cried out all the more, 'Son of David, have mercy on me!'"*

This was not vain repetition. It was earnest prayer. Sometimes a person may repeat the same words and still be sincere. Jesus Himself prayed in Gethsemane and repeated the same request. Bartimaeus kept crying because his need was great and because he believed Jesus could help him.

How did Jesus respond? Did He join the crowd in silencing Bartimaeus? Did He ignore him because he was poor? No. **Mark 10:49 NKJV** says, *"So Jesus stood still and commanded him to be called."*

Jesus was on a journey, but He stopped for a blind beggar. It is never wasted time to stop and show mercy. By stopping, Jesus also corrected the misguided zeal of those who tried to silence Bartimaeus. He showed that the poor and needy are not beneath His attention.

Jesus commanded Bartimaeus to be called. Then the people said to him, **Mark 10:49 NKJV**, *"Be of good cheer. Rise, He is calling you."* Perhaps some of the same people who had told him to be quiet now encouraged him to come. This often happens. Some who once opposed the work of God may later become friends to it. When a person's ways please the Lord, He can make even his enemies be at peace with him.

This should teach us patience toward those who oppose awakened souls. Some people discourage others from seeking Christ because they are misinformed, prejudiced, or afraid. They may think their loved one is going too far or walking in error. Later, God may open their eyes, and they may become supporters of the very work they once resisted.

When Bartimaeus heard that Jesus was calling him, he cast away his garment, rose, and came to Jesus. He could have objected. He could have said, "Why are you telling me to come? I am blind. I cannot see the way. If Jesus wants me, He must come to me." But he did not reason that way. He used the strength he had and came.

This teaches an important lesson. Some people object to gospel preaching by saying, "Why do you call sinners to come to Christ if they cannot come without the Father drawing them?" But calling sinners to come does not mean sinners have power in themselves to come. When Jesus called Lazarus out of the tomb, Lazarus did not have power in himself to rise. But the command of Christ came with power.

In the same way, preachers call sinners to come to Jesus because Christ commands the gospel to be preached to every creature. We call, hoping and praying that the power of Christ will accompany the Word and raise dead souls to life. The call also shows sinners their inability, so they may cry out to God for faith.

Bartimaeus gives us an example. He did what he could. He cast away his garment, rose, and came to Jesus. That garment was likely a large cloak he used to protect himself from cold and rain. It was probably one of his most valuable possessions. But he threw it aside because it might slow him down. He believed that if Jesus healed him, he would not need to go back to his old life.

So it is with all who are serious about coming to Christ. They will lay aside every weight and the sin that so easily ensnares them. They will cut off the right hand and pluck out the right eye, if necessary. They will leave father, mother, wife, children, and even their own life rather than lose Christ. Anything that keeps them from Jesus must be cast away.

When Bartimaeus came, Jesus asked him, **Mark 10:51 NKJV**, *"What do you want Me to do for you?"* This may seem like a strange question, because Jesus already knew what he needed. But Jesus often makes us state our needs, not because He lacks knowledge, but because we need to confess our dependence on Him.

Bartimaeus answered, **Mark 10:51 NKJV**, *"Rabboni, that I may receive my sight."* He asked not for silver, gold, or earthly comfort. He asked for what only Jesus could give. He believed Jesus could open his eyes.

Immediately Jesus answered. **Mark 10:52 NKJV** says, *"Then Jesus said to him, 'Go your way; your faith has made you well.' And immediately he received his sight and followed Jesus on the road."*

With the word of Christ came power. The One who said at creation, "Let there be light," now commanded light into the eyes of this poor blind beggar. Bartimaeus received his sight immediately. And what was the first thing he saw? He saw Jesus. What a blessed sight. The first object before his newly opened eyes was the altogether lovely Savior.

Jesus told him to go his way, but Bartimaeus did not go back for his garment. He did not return to his old life. He followed Jesus in the way. With his physical sight, he received a deeper spiritual sight. Others may have seen no beauty in Jesus that they should desire Him, but Bartimaeus saw His glory by faith. He was drawn to his Savior. Like Ruth, he could have said, "Where You go, I will go. Your people shall be my people, and Your God, my God."

He followed Jesus in the way, the narrow way, the way of the cross. And I do not doubt that long ago he followed Jesus all the way into glory.

Now we must ask how this story should affect our hearts. Are we not ready to say, "Who is like You, O Lord, glorious in holiness, fearful in praises, doing wonders?" Marvelous are the works of Jesus. But we must not only admire what Jesus did for Bartimaeus. This story was written for our learning. We must make spiritual use of it.

A natural person may read this miracle only as an interesting story, the way someone reads about ancient battles or famous rulers. But we must not stop there. If you are still in your natural condition, you are as blind in your soul as Bartimaeus was in his body. You are a blind child of a blind father, Adam, who lost his spiritual sight when he lost his innocence. That blindness has passed to all his descendants.

Some people think they can see, but Scripture says fallen man is spiritually blind and spiritually dead. By nature, we no more know the way of salvation in Christ than blind Bartimaeus knew the colors of a rainbow.

Some of you may be beginning to feel this. You may feel concerned. You may feel sorrow. You may be asking, "What do I need?" And if I asked you, perhaps you would answer, "That I may receive my sight."

God forbid that I should tell you to hold your peace. No. If you feel your spiritual blindness and are crying after Jesus, this may be a sign that the Holy Spirit has begun to awaken you. Therefore I say to you what the people finally said to Bartimaeus: "Be of good cheer. Rise, He is calling you."

Follow the example of Bartimaeus. Cast away your garment. Lay aside every weight and the sin that so easily ensnares you. Rise and come to Jesus. He commands His servants to call you. He says in **Matthew 11:28 NKJV**, *"Come to Me, all you who labor and are heavy laden, and I will give you rest."*

Do not be afraid. You are seeking Jesus of Nazareth. Behold, He comes forth to meet you. You are on the highway side, and Jesus is passing by. Cry mightily to Him, because He is mighty to save. Lay yourself at the feet of sovereign grace and say, "Jesus, Son of David, have mercy on me."

Satan and unbelief will raise many objections. Your own flesh may join them. Carnal relatives may also tell you to be quiet. One may say your blindness is too deep to be cured. Another may say it is too late. Another may say Jesus can heal others, but He will not have mercy on such a poor, blind, sinful beggar as you.

But the more they tell you to be quiet, cry out all the more, "Jesus, Son of David, have mercy on me." Jesus is the Savior. He is the friend of sinners. Though He is David's Lord, He became David's Son according to the flesh, so that through Him we might become children of God.

No matter who you are, come to Him. If you are poor, do not think your condition is too low for Jesus. He came into the highways and hedges to call poor beggars in. If you are rich, do not think yourself too high to stoop to Jesus. He is the King of kings. You will never be truly rich until you are made rich in Christ.

Do not be afraid of losing worldly honor. One sight of Jesus will make up for everything. When you see Him by faith, you will find something so satisfying in the Lamb of God that earthly pleasures will lose their power over you. Former amusements will no longer hold your heart, just as Bartimaeus no longer cared about the garment he left behind.

There are many people gathered to hear the gospel. It is encouraging to see the fields white for harvest and to cast the gospel net among many. But hearing a preacher is not enough. Do not rest in following a minister. Follow Jesus. Believe on the Lamb of God who takes away the sin of the world.

I do not despair of anyone. Jesus called Zacchaeus in Jericho. Jesus called Bartimaeus as He passed through that same place. If He called sinners there, why can He not call sinners here? Is His arm shortened that He cannot save? Is He not as mighty and willing now as He was then? Yes, He is. He is able to save to the uttermost all who come to God through Him.

Jesus said in **John 6:37 NKJV**, *"The one who comes to Me I will by no means cast out."* What encouraging words. By no means will He cast out the one who comes. Sinners, do you believe this? Then arise. Be of good comfort. Jesus is calling you.

Some of you have already obeyed this call. You received a sight of Christ long ago. You know His mercy. You love Him. If He said to you, "Go your way," your heart would answer, "We love our Master and will not leave Him."

Let me encourage you, then, to show that you have truly seen Him by following Him in the way. Follow Him in the way of the cross. Follow Him in His ordinances. Follow Him in His holy commandments. The love of many has grown cold, and few follow Jesus as closely as they should. Many still have some idol clinging to them, some garment hanging around their feet, hindering them from running the race set before them.

Awake, then, sleepy believers. Awake, even if you are wise virgins. Put on strength. Shake yourself from the dust. Arise and follow Jesus more closely than ever before. Lift up the hands that hang down and strengthen the weak knees. Make straight paths for your feet, so that what is lame may not be turned out of the way, but rather healed.

The way is narrow, but it is not long. The gate is strait, but it opens into everlasting life. May you receive a fresh sight of Jesus today. That sight will be like oil to the wheels of grace. It will make the soul move more freely after God.

The reason you often go so heavily from day to day is that you lose sight of Christ. A fresh sight of Jesus is like the rising sun that drives away darkness and gloom from the soul. Therefore, take a fresh view of Him, believers. Do not rest until you are brought to see Him as He is and live with Him forever in the kingdom of heaven.

Even so, Lord Jesus.

Amen.

Chapter Twenty

The Extent and Reasonableness of Self-Denial

Luke 9:23 NKJV *"Then He said to them all, 'If anyone desires to come after Me, let him deny himself, and take up his cross daily, and follow Me.'"*

Whoever reads the gospel with an honest heart will quickly see that Jesus never promised His followers an easy, worldly life. He often reminded His disciples that His kingdom was not of this world. He did not call them to a life of pride, comfort, and earthly greatness. He called them to the cross. He called them to surrender. He called them to a life of self-denial.

Jesus made this clear in the words of our text. Just before this, Peter had confessed that Jesus was the Christ of God. This was a great revelation. But Jesus did not want His disciples to think that following the Christ would only bring honor, power, and outward success. So He told them that the Son of Man would suffer many things, be rejected, be killed, and rise again the third day. Then He turned to them all and said, **Luke 9:23 NKJV**, *"If anyone desires to come after Me, let him deny himself, and take up his cross daily, and follow Me."*

This means that anyone who wants to follow Jesus must share in His way of life. Christ suffered before He entered glory. His followers must also learn self-denial before they enter the fullness of His glory. The Christian life is not a life of pleasing self, serving self, and protecting self. It is a life of surrendering self to God.

To understand self-denial, we must first see where it reaches. Self-denial is not only about giving up outward pleasures. It reaches into the soul. It touches the understanding, the will, and the affections.

We must first deny ourselves in our understanding. This means we must not lean on our own wisdom as though we know better than God. We must not be wise in our own eyes or proud in our own reasoning. Our natural understanding is limited. It is short-sighted. There are mysteries in the Christian faith that are above our reason, though they are never against true reason. Therefore, if we are to be Christians, we must bring every proud thought under the authority of Christ.

Paul says in **2 Corinthians 10:5 NKJV**, *"Casting down arguments and every high thing that exalts itself against the knowledge of God, bringing every thought into captivity to the obedience of Christ."*

This is part of self-denial. We must be willing to humble our minds before God's Word. We must not believe only what we can fully explain. We must believe what God has revealed because God cannot lie.

In this sense, we must become like little children. We must be teachable. We must be willing to follow the Lamb wherever He leads us, even into truths that are deeper than our natural understanding. The proud mind says, "I will not believe unless I can understand everything." The humble mind says, "Lord, speak, and I will receive Your Word."

This is one reason unbelief is so dangerous. At its root, unbelief is often pride of the understanding. It is a refusal to bow before the truth of God. Many who claim to be wise become foolish because they reject the Lord who made them. They dispute the divinity of Christ, even though in Him they live and move and have their being. Unless they repent, such pride will bring destruction.

We must also deny ourselves in our will. This means that our own will must no longer be the ruling principle of our lives. We must not live merely to please ourselves. Paul says in **1 Corinthians 10:31 NKJV**, *"Therefore, whether you eat or drink, or whatever you do, do all to the glory of God."* That is the Christian rule. We may find joy in what we do, because wisdom's ways are pleasant, but pleasing ourselves must never be the main goal. Pleasing God must be first.

This is one of the great secrets of true Christianity. It is what separates a real Christian from a moral person or an outward religious person. Two people may do the same outward action, but one does it to be seen, praised, or satisfied in self, while the other does it for the glory of God. The heart makes the difference.

Jesus said in **Matthew 6:22 NKJV**, *"The lamp of the body is the eye. If therefore your eye is good, your whole body will be full of light."* When the eye is single, when the aim is truly to please God, the life is full of light. But when the intention is selfish or divided, even outwardly good actions become darkened by sin.

We must not only do the will of God. We must do it because it is His will. When we pray, "Your will be done on earth as it is in heaven," we are asking to obey like the angels obey. The angels do God's will cheerfully because it is God's will. If we want to live as we pray, we must do the same.

But we must not only deny our will in doing God's will. We must also deny our will in suffering God's will. Whatever God allows in our lives, we must learn to say with Eli, "It is the Lord. Let Him do what seems good to Him." Even more, we must learn to say with Jesus, **Luke 22:42 NKJV**, *"Nevertheless not My will, but Yours, be done."*

Jesus had an innocent will, yet He submitted it to the Father. How much more should we, whose wills are often sinful and stubborn, submit ourselves to God? When trouble, loss, disappointment, sickness, or sorrow comes, we must learn to say, "Father, not my will, but Yours be done."

We must also deny ourselves in our affections. Our loves, desires, and attachments must be brought under the lordship of Christ. This includes our affection for riches. Jesus said in **Luke 14:33 NKJV**, *"So likewise, whoever of you does not forsake all that he has cannot be My disciple."*

This does not mean every rich person must literally sell everything and give it all away immediately. If that were always required, they would no longer be able to help the poor in the future. But it does mean that every Christian must hold earthly possessions loosely. We must be willing to part with anything when God requires it. We must use the world as though we do not abuse it. We must live as stewards, not owners.

What God gives us should not be wasted on pride, luxury, vanity, and needless excess. We must first provide what is necessary for ourselves and our households. But beyond that, we should use what God has entrusted to us to feed the hungry, clothe the naked, relieve the distressed, and serve the disciples of Jesus Christ. This is part of what it means to forsake all in affection.

Some will find this hard because they are covetous or lovers of pleasure more than lovers of God. But the servant of Christ must speak the truth. We must not be like the false prophets who only say what people want to hear. We must faithfully declare the will of God, even when it cuts against our comfort.

We must also deny ourselves in our affection for family and earthly relationships when they stand in opposition to Christ. Jesus said in **Luke 14:26 NKJV**, *"If anyone comes to Me and does not hate his father and mother, wife and children, brothers and sisters, yes, and his own life also, he cannot be My disciple."*

These are strong words. Jesus is not telling us to hate our families in a sinful or cruel way. Scripture commands us to honor father and mother. The meaning is comparative. Jesus explains it in **Matthew 10:37 NKJV**, *"He who loves father or mother more than Me is not* *worthy of Me. And he who loves son or daughter more than Me is not worthy of Me."*

Our love for Christ must be supreme. If those closest to us try to pull us away from obedience to God, we must choose Christ. If friends or family urge us to spare ourselves, avoid the cross, and follow the easy way, we must answer as Jesus answered Peter: "Get behind Me." We must love our families deeply, but we must love Christ more.

We must also deny ourselves in things that may be lawful in themselves. Many people do not perish only through gross outward sins. Many are ruined by the excessive use of things that are not sinful in themselves. A wise Christian asks not only, "Is this lawful?" but also, "Is this helpful? Does this bring me closer to Christ? Does this strengthen my soul? Does this weaken my will or feed my flesh?"

There are many things that may not be openly sinful, but they may become weights. They may dull our spiritual life, waste our time, stir our pride, feed our appetites, or distract our hearts from God. Self-denial teaches us to choose what best helps us follow Christ, not merely what our flesh prefers.

Finally, we must deny ourselves in our own righteousness. This is one of the hardest forms of self-denial. Even if we gave all our goods to feed the poor and gave our bodies to be burned, if we trusted in those things to make us right with God, they would profit us nothing.

Christ alone is our righteousness. Paul says in **Romans 10:4 NKJV**, *"For Christ is the end of the law for righteousness to everyone who believes."* We are complete in Him, and in Him only. Our own righteousnesses are like filthy rags if we trust them for acceptance with God. We must count all things loss so that we may be found in Christ, not having our own righteousness, but the righteousness that comes from God through faith in Jesus Christ.

If this is true Christianity, then we must ask whether much of the Christian world is asleep. Why is there so much self-righteousness? Why is there so much self-indulgence? Why is there such a love of riches? Why is there such a hunger for sensual pleasure? Many live as though pleasure were their god. But Scripture says that those who live in pleasure are dead while they live.

Therefore, the Word of God says in **Ephesians 5:14 NKJV**, *"Awake, you who sleep, arise from the dead, and Christ will give you light."* But only God can raise the spiritually dead. Jesus called Lazarus from the grave by His almighty word. May He also speak to souls bound by sin and pleasure, and bring them to life.

Now we must consider whether this command to deny ourselves applies to all Christians. Some people try to escape the force of Christ's words by saying that these commands were only for the apostles or the first disciples. They say that self-denial, forsaking all, and taking up the cross belonged to those early Christians, not to us today.

But this is a serious mistake. Jesus said in **Luke 9:23 NKJV**, *"If anyone desires to come after Me, let him deny himself, and take up his cross daily, and follow Me."* The words are for anyone. In another place, Jesus spoke to the multitudes and gave the same command. His doctrine has not changed. Jesus Christ is the same yesterday, today, and forever. What He said to one generation, He says to all.

It is true that some commands about selling and forsaking all may not apply in the same outward way to every Christian in every age. The situation of the early church was unique in some respects. But the heart of the command remains the same. The same deadness to the world, the same willingness to part with goods for Christ's sake, the same heavenly-mindedness, and the same holiness are required of us now.

The outward condition of the church may change from age to age, but the inward purity of the church does not change. When Scripture tells us to put to death our members on the earth, to set our minds on things above, and not to be conformed to this world, it is calling us to the same self-denial Christ taught His first disciples.

Those who object to self-denial not only misunderstand Scripture, they also show that they do not understand the power of godliness in the heart. True religion is recovery from our fall in Adam through new birth in Christ. If we are alive to God, we must be dead to ourselves and to the world. If the life of the Spirit is growing in us, the old man must be dying in us.

We must mourn before we are comforted. We must know the spirit of bondage before we fully enjoy the Spirit of adoption. Then, with the assurance of faith, we can cry, "Abba, Father."

If we were still in the innocence of Adam before the fall, self-denial would not be necessary in the same way. But we are fallen, sick, disordered, and self-righteous creatures. Therefore, we must deny ourselves if we would follow Christ to glory.

To reject self-denial because it is difficult is like a sick child refusing medicine because it tastes unpleasant. If we saw Lazarus full of sores at the rich man's gate, or Job covered with painful boils, and we offered them medicine, we would think them foolish if they refused it simply because it hurt. But our souls by nature are in a far worse condition. Scripture says in **Isaiah 1:5–6 NKJV**, *"The whole head is sick, and the whole heart faints. From the sole of the foot even to the head, there is no soundness in it."*

If we are unwilling to deny ourselves and come after Jesus to be healed, it shows that we do not truly understand how sick we are.

When Naaman refused to wash in the Jordan River, his servants said, in effect, "If the prophet had told you to do some great thing, would you not have done it? How much more when he says, 'Wash and be clean'?" In the same way, if Jesus had commanded some far more difficult thing, should we not obey Him? How much more should we obey when He only tells us to deny what would destroy us and promises us a crown of life?

Another picture may help us. In Acts 12, Peter was in prison, sleeping between two soldiers and bound with chains. An angel came, struck Peter on the side, and told him to rise quickly. Then his chains fell off. But suppose Peter had hugged his chains and begged to keep them. Would we not say he loved slavery and deserved to remain bound?

That is what we do when we refuse self-denial. By nature, our souls are in a spiritual prison, bound by the world, the flesh, and the devil. Christ comes by the gospel, opens the prison door, and says, "Deny yourself and follow Me." If we refuse to rise and follow Him, we are choosing bondage over freedom.

To the natural person, this doctrine may seem foolish. To a young convert, it may seem hard. But Jesus said in **John 7:17 NKJV**, *"If anyone wills to do His will, he shall know concerning the doctrine, whether it is from God."* The best way to understand the reasonableness of self-denial is to begin obeying. Rise and follow Christ. As you do, He will remove the scales from your eyes and show you the wisdom, necessity, and blessing of this doctrine.

Now let us consider some motives that may help us practice self-denial.

First, meditate often on the life of Jesus Christ. Follow Him from the manger to the cross. See what a self-denying life He lived. Shall we not drink from the cup He drank? Shall we not be baptized with the baptism He was baptized with? Do we think Jesus suffered so that we would never have to suffer anything? No. Peter says in **1 Peter 2:21 NKJV**, *"Christ also suffered for us, leaving us an example, that you should follow His steps."*

If Jesus had placed heavy burdens on us while refusing to touch them Himself, we might have reason to complain. But He has commanded nothing that He did not first practice. Therefore, the disciple has no excuse for wanting to be above his self-denying Master. The servant is not faithful if he refuses to suffer with his Lord.

Second, think often about the lives of the apostles, prophets, and martyrs. They looked to Jesus, the Author and Finisher of their faith. They fought the good fight. They denied themselves. They endured suffering. They have gone before us to inherit the promises.

If self-denial was necessary for them, why should it not be necessary for us? Were they not people with the same nature as ours? Did they not live in the same kind of wicked world? Did they not need the same Holy Spirit? Did they not look forward to the same eternal inheritance?

If we have the same sinful nature to overcome, the same world to resist, the same Spirit to help us, and the same glory set before us, then why should we not live with the same spirit of self-denial? The church remembers the lives and deaths of the saints so that we may be stirred up to follow them as they followed Christ.

Third, think often on the pains of hell. Consider whether it is not better to cut off a right hand or pluck out a right eye, if it causes you to sin, than to be cast into hell, where the worm does not die and the fire is not quenched. Think of the many souls now reserved in darkness for the judgment of the great day. And remember that this will be our condition unless we are wise in time, deny ourselves, and follow Jesus Christ.

Do those who are lost now think Jesus was a hard Master? No. If they could return to life and take Christ's easy yoke upon them, they would give ten thousand worlds to do so. If we cannot bear the command, "Deny yourself and take up your cross," how will we bear the sentence, **Matthew 25:41 NKJV**, *"Depart from Me, you cursed, into the everlasting fire prepared for the devil and his angels"*?

But I hope we will not need to be driven only by terror. The love of Christ should draw us.

So lastly, meditate often on the joys of heaven. Think of the glory now surrounding those who denied themselves on earth and followed Christ. Lift your heart to the mansions of eternal joy. By faith, like Stephen, see heaven opened and the Son of Man standing in glory, surrounded by the saints who have gone before us.

Can you hear them singing their everlasting hallelujahs? Do you not long to join that heavenly choir? Does your heart not burn within you? As the deer pants for the water brooks, should not your soul long for the living God?

Behold, the ladder to heaven is set before you. Believe on the Lord Jesus Christ. Deny yourself. Follow Him. This is the path every saint has walked on the way to glory. And if we follow Christ, we too will one day be lifted into that blessed place, where we will enjoy eternal rest with the people of God and join them in songs of praise to the Father, the Son, and the Holy Spirit forever.

May God, in His infinite mercy, grant this through Jesus Christ our Lord.

Amen.

Chapter Twenty-One

What Do You Think of Christ?

Matthew 22:42 NKJV *"What do you think about the Christ?"*

When the eternal Son of God came into the world and lived among us, people had many different opinions about Him. Some thought He was Moses. Others thought He was Elijah, Jeremiah, or one of the old prophets. Very few truly understood who He was. Very few confessed Him as He really is, God blessed forever.

People also had different opinions about His teaching. The common people, who were often more open and less prejudiced, saw that His life was full of goodness. They heard Him gladly. Many said He was a good man. But the proud, religious, worldly-minded leaders of the Jewish church were offended by Him. They were jealous of His influence. They could not understand the purity and power of His teaching because they had never truly been taught by God.

Though Jesus spoke as no man ever spoke, and though He performed miracles that no man could do unless God was with Him, they accused Him of deceiving the people. Some even went so far as to say that He cast out demons by Beelzebub, the prince of demons. Even His own relatives, according to the flesh, were so blinded by unbelief that when He went out to teach the multitudes, they tried to take hold of Him, saying He was out of His mind.

This is how the King of glory was judged when He came in human flesh. Therefore, His ministers should not expect better treatment. If we come in the spirit and power of our Master, we must also be willing to share in His reproach. The same kinds of accusations that were thrown at Him will be thrown at those who faithfully preach Him.

Those who received Christ and His doctrine will receive those who preach His truth. The poor, by the grace of God, receive the gospel, and the common people still hear it gladly. But those who sit in religious places of honor, who love outward position, and who do not know the righteousness of God by faith in Jesus Christ, will often cry out against faithful ministers. Because they have never felt the power of God in their own hearts, they accuse gospel preachers of being mad, deceiving the people, or acting under evil influence.

But no man is worthy to be called a minister of the gospel if he is not willing to have his name cast out as evil for the sake of Christ. He must be willing, if necessary, even to die for the truths of the Lord Jesus. It is the mark of hirelings and false prophets, who do not truly care for the sheep, to seek the praise of all men. Jesus said His servants would be blessed when men spoke all kinds of evil against them falsely for His sake.

Such offenses must come. People often judge others by the principles that rule their own hearts. If they do not want to obey the doctrines being preached, they will attack the preacher in order to defend themselves. If they admitted the preacher spoke truth, they would have to answer the question the Pharisees feared concerning John: "Why then did you not believe him?"

In such cases, the servant of God must search his own heart. If his conscience bears witness before God that he acts with a single eye to God's glory, then he must go forward cheerfully in his work. He must not be overly concerned with what men or devils may say or do against him.

But let us return to the main point. There were many different opinions about Jesus while He was on earth. The same is still true now, even though He is exalted at the right hand of the Father. A stranger to Christianity might assume that since Christians profess one Lord, they all think and speak the same thing about Him. But sadly, though Christ is not divided, those who profess His name are deeply divided in their thoughts about Him. This division does not only concern small matters of religion. It often concerns essential truths that must be believed if we hope to inherit eternal salvation.

Some people call themselves Christians, yet rarely, if ever, seriously think about Jesus Christ at all. They can think about their shops, farms, business, entertainments, social gatherings, pleasures, and worldly amusements. They can think about things that easily push religion out of the heart. But as for Christ, the Author and Finisher of our faith, the Lord who bought sinners with His precious blood, the One who is most worthy of all our thoughts, He is barely in their minds.

O earthly-minded and fleshly professors, however little you think of Christ now, and however carefully you try to keep Him out of your thoughts by chasing pleasure, profit, status, and pride, there is a time coming when you will wish you had thought of Christ more and of your pleasures less. The rich must die. The fashionable must die. The successful must die. Everyone must leave behind their wealth, comforts, and vanities. And what will you think of Christ then?

But I must not stay too long on that reflection. My purpose is to ask what those who truly desire to worship God in spirit and truth ought to think concerning Jesus Christ, whom God has sent to be the end of the law for righteousness to everyone who believes.

I trust you will not think it too strict for me to try to regulate your thoughts about Christ. We will be judged not only by our words and actions, but also by our thoughts. We cannot believe in Christ rightly or worship Him rightly unless our principles agree with the truth revealed in Scripture.

Many deceivers have gone into the world. In many places, simple morality is preached instead of Jesus Christ. How can people think rightly of Christ if they hardly ever hear Him truly preached? Therefore, allow me to ask you several important questions concerning Jesus Christ. There is no other name under heaven given among men by which we must be saved.

First, what do you think about the person of Christ? Whose Son is He? This was the question Jesus asked the Pharisees after the words of our text. This question is still necessary today. Many who call themselves Christians openly deny that Jesus Christ is truly and properly God. Some even pretend to preach Him while denying His divine nature.

But no one who has truly received the Spirit of Christ will speak lightly of Him. If they are asked, as Peter was asked, "Who do you say that I am?" they will answer, "You are the Christ, the Son of the living God." The confession of Christ's divinity is the rock on which He builds His church. If this truth could be removed, the gates of hell would quickly prevail.

If Jesus Christ is not very God of very God, then I would never preach the gospel of Christ again. If He were not truly God, then the gospel would not truly be gospel. It would be only a system of morals. Seneca, Cicero, or any other philosopher could be as useful as Jesus of Nazareth if Jesus were not divine. But it is His divinity that gives infinite value to His death. It is His divinity that makes Him the High Priest we need, one who could offer a full, perfect, and sufficient sacrifice for sin.

Those who deny the true deity of Christ are not faithful ministers of God, whatever office they may hold. If a man uses the language of the church, benefits from the church, and yet denies the true divinity of Christ, he is not a true shepherd. He is a wolf in sheep's clothing.

Some may think this is too severe. But it is not unloving to say that those who deny Christ's divinity are not true Christians. Some say Jesus is only a created being. Others say He is only a good man.

Others deny that His death was an atonement for sin and claim He only died to confirm His teaching. But if Jesus were only a man and accepted worship, then He would not be good. He would be a blasphemer.

In **John 9:38 NKJV**, the man born blind said, *"Lord, I believe!" And he worshiped Him.* Jesus received that worship. If Christ is not God, our faith is useless and we are still in our sins. No created being, however great, could merit anything before God or take away the sin of the world. Only the divine Son of God could do that.

This is why John says of Christ in **John 1:1 NKJV**, *"In the beginning was the Word, and the Word was with God, and the Word was God."* Paul also says in **Colossians 2:9 NKJV**, *"For in Him dwells all the fullness of the Godhead bodily."* Jesus Himself took the divine name when He said in **John 8:58 NKJV**, *"Most assuredly, I say to you, before Abraham was, I AM."* He also said in **John 10:30 NKJV**, *"I and My Father are one."*

The Jews understood what Jesus meant. That is why they tried to stone Him for blasphemy. They knew He was making Himself equal with God. Therefore, we must think rightly of Christ. Even demons confessed that He was the Holy One of God. They believe and tremble. How terrible it is when men who call themselves Christians refuse to confess what demons are forced to acknowledge.

Second, what do you think about the manhood and incarnation of Jesus Christ? Christ was not only God. He was God and man in one Person. In the verses around our text, Jesus asked, "What do you think about the Christ? Whose Son is He?" The Pharisees answered, "The Son of David." Then Jesus asked how David, by the Spirit, could call Him Lord. This shows that Christ is both David's Son and David's Lord. He is perfect God and perfect man.

Jesus is called Christ, the Anointed One, because He was set apart by the Father and anointed by the Holy Spirit to be the Mediator between God and sinful man.

Why did the Son of God take our nature? He did so because of the fall of our first parents. No one should think that man made himself. God made us. And no one should think that God made us as sinful and broken as we now are. Scripture says that God made man in His own image. Man was made upright, holy, and good.

God placed man in the garden of Eden and entered into covenant with him. God promised life upon perfect obedience and warned of death if man disobeyed. But man ate the forbidden fruit. Since Adam acted as our representative, his sin brought guilt and death upon himself and upon us.

Yet here the mystery of godliness begins: God was manifested in the flesh. The eternal Father, foreseeing the fall, had already provided a way for the serpent's head to be crushed. Man was permitted to fall and become subject to death. But Jesus, the only begotten Son of God, begotten of the Father before all worlds, Light of Light, very God of very God, offered Himself to die, to make atonement for sin, and to fulfill all righteousness in man's place.

As God, He could not suffer and die. As man, He could. And because man had sinned, it was fitting that man should obey and suffer. Therefore, in the fullness of time, the eternal Son of God took on a true human body and soul. He became an infant. In that human nature He obeyed the law of God perfectly. He fulfilled the covenant of works in our place. Then He became obedient to death, even death on the cross.

As God, His suffering had infinite value. As man, He obeyed and suffered in our nature. Being God and man in one Person, He brought God and sinners together again.

Now, what do you think of the love of Christ? Is it not wondrously great? Consider that we were His enemies. He would have been infinitely blessed in Himself even if we had perished forever. Yet He came for us. The angels, who are not redeemed in the same way we are, desire to look into this mystery and will admire it forever. Why will sinners not think deeply on this love? Surely it should melt the hardest heart.

While I speak of this infinite and condescending love, it warms my own soul. I could dwell on it forever. But I must ask another question.

Third, what do you think about being justified by Christ? Many people think they can be counted righteous before God without Jesus Christ. But outside of Christ, God is a consuming fire. Others believe that Christ is God and man and that He came to save sinners in general, but they never seriously ask whether Christ has saved them personally.

Paul said in **Galatians 2:20 NKJV**, *"The life which I now live in the flesh I live by faith in the Son of God, who loved me and gave Himself for me."* Notice those words: "for me." It is not enough to say Christ died for sinners in general. The soul must receive Christ by faith and know Him personally.

Many say they believe they can only be justified through Christ, but they still make Him only part of a Savior. They try to do what they can, and then they think Christ will make up what is lacking. This is the heart of much modern religion. Many people may have depended on this idea for years. But it is not the gospel.

If you think this way, you are like the Jews who went about trying to establish their own righteousness and refused to submit to the righteousness of God by faith in Christ. You must think differently about justification.

We are justified freely through faith in Jesus Christ, without any regard to any work or fitness in us. Salvation is the free gift of God. The only fitness we have by nature is a fitness for judgment. Our righteousnesses are filthy rags in God's sight. Our holiness, if we have any, is not the cause of our justification. It is the effect of it.

We do not come to God like the proud Pharisee, bringing a list of our services. We come like the tax collector, beating our breast and saying, **Luke 18:13 NKJV**, *"God, be merciful to me a sinner!"* Jesus justifies the ungodly. He came not to call the righteous, but sinners to repentance. The poor in spirit, those who are willing to go outside themselves and rely wholly on the righteousness of another, are blessed members of His kingdom.

The whole righteousness of Jesus Christ must be imputed to us instead of our own. We are not under law as a covenant of salvation, but under grace. Boasting is completely excluded. If even one work of ours were added to the merit of Christ, we would still have room to boast. But salvation is all of God from beginning to end. It is not of works, lest anyone should boast.

Christ is made to us wisdom, righteousness, sanctification, and redemption. His active obedience and His suffering obedience must be applied to poor sinners. He fulfilled all righteousness in our place so that we might become the righteousness of God in Him. All we must do is lay hold of this righteousness by faith. The moment we receive Christ by living faith, we may know that His blood cleanses us from all sin.

This promise is for us, for our children, and for as many as the Lord our God shall call. If we believe, we shall be saved, just as the jailer and his household were saved. The righteousness of Jesus Christ is everlasting and perfect. It is as effective for believers now as it was for believers then, and it will remain so until time is no more.

Search the Scriptures like the Bereans to see whether these things are true. Read Romans and Galatians. There you will find this doctrine clearly taught. Unless a person refuses to see, it is plain.

This doctrine of free justification by faith in Christ is not a cold doctrine. It is full of comfort for all who are weary and heavy laden and want to find rest in Jesus Christ. This is gospel. This is glad tidings of great joy for all who feel themselves poor, lost, undone, and condemned sinners.

God says in **Isaiah 55:1 NKJV**, *"Ho! Everyone who thirsts, come to the waters; and you who have no money, come, buy and eat."* A fountain has been opened in the Savior's side for sin and uncleanness. Look to Him whom you have pierced. Look to Him by faith, and you shall be saved, even if you came only to mock, ridicule, or blaspheme and never truly thought of God before.

But do not think God saves you because of your faith, as though faith itself earned salvation. Faith is not a work that merits justification. Faith is the instrument by which the sinner receives and applies the redemption of Jesus Christ to the heart. Faith itself is the gift of God. When God gives such faith, the sinner may lift up his head. He has passed from death to life and shall not come into condemnation.

This is the gospel we preach. If any man or angel preaches another gospel than free justification through faith in Jesus Christ, the apostle gives us authority to call that message accursed.

Now, what do you think of this preaching? To those who have tasted the good Word of life and seen the riches of God's free grace in Christ, I know it is precious. But some may say, "This is a dangerous doctrine. It will encourage people to sin." That objection is not new. It is as old as the doctrine itself. Paul faced it in Romans. After he clearly taught justification by faith, someone asked, "Shall we continue in sin that grace may abound?" Paul answered, **Romans 6:2 NKJV**, *"Certainly not!"*

The faith we preach is not dead or empty. It is not merely agreement in the head. It is a living principle worked in the soul by the Spirit of the living God. It convinces the sinner of his lost condition. It enables him to lay hold of the perfect righteousness of Christ freely offered in the gospel. Then, out of love and gratitude, it stirs him up to abound in every good word and work.

This doctrine does not destroy good works. It teaches people how to do good works from the right principle. Works done before the grace of Christ and the inspiration of the Spirit do not please God because they do not spring from faith in Jesus Christ. Telling people to do good works before they have Christ is like telling someone to build a beautiful house without laying a foundation.

It is true that the doctrine of free justification can be abused by corrupt minds. But those who receive the truth in love will always show their faith by their works. Paul said in **Ephesians 2:8–9 NKJV**, *"For by grace you have been saved through faith, and that not of yourselves; it is the gift of God, not of works, lest anyone should boast."* Then he immediately adds in **Ephesians 2:10 NKJV**, *"For we are His workmanship, created in Christ Jesus for good works."*

Good works are the fruit of faith. They follow justification. They cannot remove our sins or endure the severity of God's judgment, but they are pleasing and acceptable to God in Christ because they spring from a true and living faith. A living faith can be known by its works just as a tree is known by its fruit.

This is important. Good works are the fruits of faith and follow after justification. Therefore, they cannot come before justification as the cause of it. Our persons must be justified before our works are accepted. God first had respect to Abel, and then to his offering. In the same way, the righteousness of Christ must first be imputed to us and received by faith before we can offer acceptable service to God. Outside of Christ, God is a consuming fire. Whatever is not of faith is sin.

People often misunderstand free justification because they do not rightly understand the difference between Paul and James. Paul says we are justified by faith apart from works. James says Abraham was justified by works. But they are not contradicting one another. Paul is speaking of our justification before God. James is speaking of the way our faith is shown before men.

Paul was writing against those who tried to be justified by the works of the law. He tells them to look only to the perfect righteousness of Christ received by faith. James was writing against those who abused grace and thought a bare profession of faith could save them. He shows that true faith must be proven by works.

So the truth can be summarized this way. Every saved person is justified in three ways. First, meritoriously, by the death of Jesus Christ. It is the blood of Christ alone that cleanses us from all sin. Second, instrumentally, by faith. Faith is the instrument by which the merits of Christ are applied to the sinner's heart. Third, declaratively, by good works. Good works declare and prove before the world that our faith is true and saving.

Consider Zacchaeus. There was no fitness for salvation in him when he climbed the tree to see Jesus. His motive may have been nothing more than curiosity. Yet Jesus called him by free grace and sweetly but powerfully inclined him to obey. Zacchaeus received Jesus joyfully into his house, and by faith he also received Him into his heart. He was freely justified before God. But immediately the fruit appeared. He said in **Luke 19:8 NKJV**, *"Look, Lord, I give half of my goods to the poor; and if I have taken anything from anyone by false accusation, I restore fourfold."*

So it will be with every believer. When God's Son is revealed in the heart by living faith, the soul will desire to show love and gratitude through obedience.

Consider Saul of Tarsus. There was no fitness for salvation in him. He was a persecutor, breathing threats and slaughter against the disciples of the Lord. Yet Jesus stopped him by grace, struck him down by a light from heaven, convicted him by the Spirit, and brought him to faith. Immediately Saul cried, **Acts 9:6 NKJV**, *"Lord, what do You want me to do?"* Every true believer will ask the same. Not to justify himself, but to show love and gratitude to the merciful High Priest who plucked him like a brand from the fire.

Some self-righteous people may think they are not as bad as Zacchaeus or Saul, and therefore have more fitness for salvation. But that is thinking too highly of yourself. By nature, we are all alike fallen short of the glory of God. We are all dead in trespasses and sins. The same almighty power that converted Zacchaeus and Saul is needed to convert the most moral and respectable person.

Search the Scriptures. Ask God to make you willing to be saved in the day of His power. Flesh and blood cannot reveal these things to you. Only the Spirit of Jesus Christ can.

Fourth and lastly, what do you think of Jesus Christ being formed within you? Those whom Christ justifies, He also sanctifies. He finds us unholy, but He does not leave us unholy. A true Christian does not merely live for himself. Christ lives in him. Those who are led by the Spirit of Christ are the true sons of God.

The faith we preach is not dead. It is living and active. It is worked in the soul by the Holy Spirit and brings a real change in the whole person. Unless Christ is in you, you are not in a state of salvation, no matter how orthodox your beliefs may be, no matter how many good desires you have, and no matter how often you attend the means of grace.

Paul says in **2 Corinthians 13:5 NKJV**, *"Examine yourselves as to whether you are in the faith. Test yourselves. Do you not know yourselves, that Jesus Christ is in you? unless indeed you are disqualified."*

Christ came not only to save us from the guilt of sin, but also from the power of sin. Until He has done this work in us, we have no well-grounded assurance that He has saved us. We know we are sealed for redemption when we receive His Spirit and feel Him bearing witness with our spirit that we are children of God.

This is a great mystery, but I speak of Christ and the new birth. Do not be surprised that I ask whether Christ has been formed within you. Either God must change His nature, or we must be changed. Since God does not change, we must be made new. As in Adam all spiritually died, so all who are truly saved by Christ must be spiritually made alive in Christ.

The purpose of Christ's death, resurrection, and intercession is to redeem us from the misery of our fallen nature and make us fit for the inheritance of the saints in light. Only those changed by His grace here will appear with Him in glory hereafter.

Therefore, examine yourselves. Do not be satisfied with saying in your creed, "I believe in Jesus Christ." Many say those words who do not truly believe and are still spiritually dead. You take God's name in vain when you call Him Father if you do not truly believe in Christ and have your life hidden with Christ in God. Branches receive life from the vine. So must you receive life from Christ.

Many in this generation deny that there is such a thing as feeling Christ within. But to deny spiritual feeling is to reduce Christianity to the condition of those who are past feeling. There is a spiritual feeling just as there is a physical feeling. It is not communicated to us in the same way outward things affect the body, but it is real. Those who are born again know it.

Did Naaman feel the difference when he was healed of leprosy? Did the woman with the issue of blood feel virtue go out from Jesus when she touched the hem of His garment? So surely may the believer know and feel when Jesus Christ dwells in the heart by faith. May God make every soul know and feel this before you depart.

My heart is enlarged toward you. I trust I feel something of the hidden but powerful presence of Christ while preaching to you. It is sweet. It is exceedingly comfortable. All the harm I wish to those who oppose me is that they would feel the same. Though it would be hell to my soul to return to a natural state, I would willingly change places with you for a little while if it would help you know what it is to have Christ dwelling in your heart by faith.

Do not turn away. Do not let the devil hurry you off. Do not be afraid of conviction. Do not think less of this doctrine because it is preached outside church walls. In the days of His flesh, Jesus preached on a mountain, in a boat, and in the field. Many have felt His presence outside ordinary places.

We speak what we know. Do not reject the kingdom of God against yourselves. Be wise and receive the witness. I cannot let you go without pleading with you. However lightly you may esteem your souls,

Jesus has placed unspeakable value on them. He counted them worth His precious blood.

Therefore, I beg you, sinners, be reconciled to God. Do not be afraid of being accepted in the Beloved. Behold, He calls you. He comes before you and follows you with mercy. He sends His servants into the highways and hedges to compel you to come in.

Remember that on this day, in this place, you were told what you ought to think concerning Jesus Christ. If you perish now, it will not be because you lacked knowledge. I am free from the blood of you all. I have not preached damnation without hope. I have not told you to make bricks without straw. I have not told you to make yourselves saints and then come to God. I have offered you salvation on the freest terms. I have offered you Christ's wisdom, Christ's righteousness, Christ's sanctification, and Christ's eternal redemption, if you will only believe on Him.

If you say you cannot believe, you speak correctly. Faith, like every blessing, is the gift of God. But then wait upon God. Who knows whether He may have mercy on you? Why do we not think more lovingly of Christ? Do you think He will have mercy on others and not on you? Are you not sinners? Did Jesus not come into the world to save sinners?

If you say you are the chief of sinners, I answer that this will not keep you from salvation if you lay hold of Christ by faith. Read the Gospels and see how kindly Jesus treated His disciples after they fled from Him and denied Him. After He rose from the dead, He said, "Go tell My brethren." He did not say, "Go tell those traitors." He called them brethren. He especially remembered poor Peter. Though

Peter had denied Him three times with oaths and curses, Jesus had died for his sins and risen for his justification.

This is the kindness of our merciful High Priest. Do you think He has changed now that He is exalted at the right hand of God? No. He is the same yesterday, today, and forever. He sits there to make intercession for sinners.

Come then, you who have sinned greatly. Come, publicans and harlots. Come, most abandoned sinners. Believe on Jesus Christ. Though the whole world may despise you and cast you out, He will not refuse to take you in. He will not be ashamed to call you His brethren. What amazing, condescending love.

How will you escape if you neglect such a great salvation? What would the damned spirits in hell give if Christ were now freely offered to them? And why are we not lifting up our eyes in torment? Does anyone here dare say he does not deserve damnation? If not, why are some of us still alive while others have been taken by death? This is God's free grace and a sign of His patience toward us. Let His goodness lead us to repentance.

O let there be joy in heaven over some sinners repenting. Though we are gathered in a field, I believe the angels of God are near. They long to rejoice over your conversion. Blessed be God, I hope their joy will be fulfilled. There is a solemn stillness among us. I hope the words spoken today have not fallen to the ground. Your tears and deep attention give hope that the Lord is truly among us.

Come and see, even in spite of opposition, the Lord Jesus is gaining the victory. I speak the truth in Christ. If only one soul is brought today to think savingly of Jesus Christ, I would not care if my enemies carried me to prison and put my feet in the stocks as soon as this sermon is finished.

My heart's desire and prayer to God is that you may be saved. For this reason, I follow my Master outside the camp. I do not care how much of His reproach I bear, so long as some of you are turned from the error of your ways. Let men and devils do their worst. The Lord who sent me will support me.

When Christ, who is our life, appears, I also, along with His despised little ones, shall appear with Him in glory. And then, what will you think of Christ? I know what you will think of Him then. You will think Him the fairest among ten thousand. But if you reject Him now, you will also know Him as a just and sin-avenging Judge.

Therefore, be persuaded to kiss the Son, lest He be angry and you perish from the way. I come to you as the angel came to Lot. Flee for your lives. Do not linger in your spiritual Sodom, or you will be destroyed. No doubt, some will treat this warning the way Lot's sons-in-law treated his. They thought he was joking. Some may think I am only mocking or exaggerating. But I speak the truth in Christ. As surely as fire and brimstone fell from heaven on Sodom and Gomorrah, so surely the wrath of God will fall on those who refuse the gospel of Christ.

I have warned you beforehand. May God cause all who forget Him to think seriously about these things before He plucks them away and there is none to deliver.

Now to God the Father, God the Son, and God the Holy Spirit be all honor, praise, glory, majesty, and dominion, now and forever.

Amen.

Chapter Twenty-Two

Christ's Transfiguration

Luke 9:28–36 NKJV *"Now it came to pass, about eight days after these sayings, that He took Peter, John, and James and went up on the mountain to pray. As He prayed, the appearance of His face was altered, and His robe became white and glistening. And behold, two men talked with Him, who were Moses and Elijah, who appeared in glory and spoke of His decease which He was about to accomplish at Jerusalem. But Peter and those with him were heavy with sleep, and when they were fully awake, they saw His glory and the two men who stood with Him. Then it happened, as they were parting from Him, that Peter said to Jesus, 'Master, it is good for us to be here, and let us make three tabernacles: one for You, one for Moses, and one for Elijah' not knowing what he said. While he was saying this, a cloud came and overshadowed them, and they were fearful as they entered the cloud. And a voice came out of the cloud, saying, 'This is My beloved Son.*

Hear Him!' When the voice had ceased, Jesus was found alone. But they kept quiet, and told no one in those days any of the things they had seen."

When the angel spoke to John in the book of Revelation, he said, "Come up here." John was being lifted higher so he could receive greater revelations from God. As we come to this passage about the transfiguration of Jesus, we should hear something similar in our own hearts. We should come up higher in our thoughts. We should leave earthly distractions for a while and lift our minds toward heaven.

This is especially fitting on the Lord's Day, when we should think more deeply about eternal things. We should pray that God would lift us, as it were, to the top of Pisgah, so that we may catch a glimpse of the promised land. It is true that eye has not seen, ear has not heard, nor has it entered into the heart of man all that God has prepared for those who love Him. We cannot fully understand the glory that waits for the people of God. Yet Jesus has graciously given us some glimpses of His glory while He walked on earth, so that we may form some faint idea of the happiness that awaits His people in heaven.

One of the clearest glimpses of that glory is found in the transfiguration of Christ. Here we see Jesus wonderfully changed before His disciples. We see Him owned and honored by the Father. We see Moses and Elijah appearing with Him in glory. We hear the voice from heaven saying, "This is My beloved Son. Hear Him."

This event likely happened soon after Jesus had spoken about the cost of discipleship and the glory that would follow. He had told His disciples that whoever was ashamed of Him and His words, of that person the Son of Man would be ashamed when He came in His own glory, and in the glory of His Father and the holy angels. Then He added that some standing there would not taste death until they saw the kingdom of God.

Some have thought this referred to the growth of the gospel church, when the kingdom of Satan would be pulled down and the kingdom of Christ would be built up. Others have thought it referred to John living long enough to see Christ come in judgment upon Jerusalem. But it seems best to understand it as referring to the transfiguration. Some of the disciples would see, before they died, a glimpse of Christ's kingdom glory. They would see a foretaste of that glory which one day will be fully revealed.

About eight days after these sayings, Jesus took Peter, John, and James and went up on the mountain to pray. He did not take all the disciples. He chose three. This reminds us that Christ is sovereign in the special comforts and experiences He gives to His people. He loved all His disciples, but He was pleased to give some of them particular privileges. John was especially called the disciple whom Jesus loved. Peter, James, and John were allowed to see things others did not see.

Jesus took three because the testimony of two or three witnesses was enough to establish a matter. These three would be able to bear witness to what they saw. He also took these three because they would later see Him in the garden of Gethsemane, sweating great drops of blood in agony. If they had not first seen His glory on the mountain, His agony in the garden might have overwhelmed their faith. But having seen His majesty, they could better understand that

His suffering was voluntary and that the One bowed down in sorrow was still the beloved Son of God.

Jesus went up on the mountain to pray. Mountains often served as places of retirement, quietness, and communion with God. Moses met with God on a mountain. Jesus often withdrew to lonely places to pray. When He desired to be alone with His Father, He chose places away from crowds and noise. This teaches us to seek places and times where our hearts can be free from distraction and lifted toward God.

And what did Jesus do there? He prayed. Jesus had no sins to confess. He had no corruption to mourn over. He had very few personal wants compared with us. Yet He was much in prayer. He rose early to pray. He spent whole nights in prayer. He went up into mountains to pray. If Jesus, the sinless Son of God, prayed so much, how much more should we pray, who have so many sins to confess, so many needs to bring, and so much weakness to overcome?

While Jesus prayed, the appearance of His face was changed, and His robe became white and glistening. Notice that this happened while He was praying. Prayer is often the place where the soul is transformed. If we want our hearts to be changed, we must spend time with God. The greatest spiritual influences are often received while we are seeking Him in prayer.

There was deep meaning in this. When Moses had been on the mountain with God, his face shone so brightly that the people could not look steadily at him. The shining of Moses' face proved that he had been with God. Moses had also told Israel that God would raise up a Prophet like him, and that the people were to hear Him.

Now, on another mountain, the Father gives testimony to His Son. But Jesus is shown to be far greater than Moses. Moses' face shone after speaking with God, but Jesus' own face shone like the sun. His clothing became white and glistening. The glory came from within Him, because He is the Lord of glory.

Then Moses and Elijah appeared and talked with Him. They appeared in glory, and they spoke of His decease, which He was about to accomplish at Jerusalem. Moses was the great lawgiver. Elijah was the great prophet and restorer of true worship. The law and the prophets came, as it were, to bear witness to Christ. They did not come to compete with Him. They came to honor Him.

Moses had died, and God had hidden his body. Elijah had been taken up into heaven without seeing death. Now both appear with Jesus in glory. They came to speak with Him about His coming death. This is remarkable. Even in a scene of glory, the subject was the cross. Heaven was interested in the death of Christ. Moses and Elijah spoke of His sufferings, the place of His sufferings, and the fact that those sufferings would be accomplished. They would have an appointed end. Jesus would suffer, but He would finish the work the Father had given Him to do.

Peter, James, and John were heavy with sleep. This likely does not mean ordinary sleep only, but that they were overwhelmed by the glory they saw. Like Daniel, who lost his strength when he saw a heavenly vision, these disciples were overcome. The brightness of Christ, the glory of Moses and Elijah, and the wonder of the moment were more than they could bear. But when they were fully awake, they saw His glory and the two men standing with Him.

How they must have gazed upon Jesus. How they must have looked at Moses and Elijah. Peter, always quick to speak, said, "Master, it is good for us to be here." We can understand that part. Who would not have felt the same? To see Christ in glory, to stand in the presence of Moses and Elijah, to be surrounded by such heavenly brightness, surely it was good to be there.

But then Peter said, "Let us make three tabernacles: one for You, one for Moses, and one for Elijah." The Scripture adds that he did not know what he said. Peter was overwhelmed. He had received a little taste of heaven and did not want to leave. But he was wrong to think of building tabernacles there. He wanted the crown before the cross. He wanted to stay on the mountain when there was still work to be done below.

Peter had once said, "Master, spare Yourself," when Jesus spoke of suffering. Something of that same spirit appears here. He wanted the glory without the suffering. He forgot the other disciples below. He forgot the needy souls who still needed Jesus' teaching and healing. He forgot that Christ had come not merely to reveal glory on a mountain, but to die for sinners in Jerusalem.

Peter was also wrong to place Moses and Elijah alongside Christ in this way. Christ and the prophets are not divided. Moses and Elijah pointed to Christ. They came to speak of His death. They did not come to be treated as equal with Him. The law and the prophets find their fulfillment in Jesus.

Yet even in Peter's mistake, we can see the sincerity of his heart. He did not worship Moses or Elijah. He did not pray to departed saints. He spoke directly to Jesus. He said, "Master." Even in confusion, he knew where to turn. He also did not presume to build without Christ's permission. He asked if they should build. And he did not ask for a tabernacle for himself. He was willing to stay in the cold night if only Christ and His heavenly visitors were honored.

This shows how mixed the best of our zeal can be. There may be love and ignorance, sincerity and confusion, grace and weakness, all together. Even when we are near the throne of grace, even when we have been on the mountain with God, we still need humility. Perfect wisdom and perfect holiness are found only among the spirits of just men made perfect in heaven.

While Peter was speaking, a cloud came and overshadowed them. Matthew tells us it was a bright cloud. This was not like the dark cloud on Mount Sinai, because the gospel brings a brighter revelation than the law. The cloud brought holy awe and, at the same time, shielded them from glory too bright for them to bear.

As they entered the cloud, they were afraid. Since the fall, there is such a consciousness of guilt in us that even when Jesus is near, the presence of divine glory makes us tremble. Peter had just said, "It is good for us to be here," but now he was silent. His strong mountain was quickly shaken. He and the others trembled in holy fear.

Then the Father's voice came from the cloud: **Luke 9:35 NKJV**, *"This is My beloved Son. Hear Him!"*

Matthew and Mark add, "in whom I am well pleased." This was the same testimony the Father gave at Jesus' baptism. Now it is repeated to strengthen Him as He moves toward His suffering and death. The voice likely came not with thunder and terror, but with divine majesty, love, and authority.

By this voice, the Father gives a solemn discharge to Moses and Elijah, as though the law and the prophets had now completed their testimony and must give way to Christ. The morning star fades when the Sun of Righteousness rises. The Father says, "This is My beloved Son. Hear Him."

The emphasis is powerful. This Jesus, whom you will soon see in agony, sweating blood, spit upon, mocked, scourged, and crucified, is My beloved Son. I am not ashamed to own Him. He is My only begotten Son, who was with Me before the foundations of the world. He is the One in whom My soul delights. I appoint Him as King, Priest, and Prophet of the church. Hear Him.

Do not look to Moses for salvation. Do not look to Elijah. Do not look to the works of the law. Hear Christ. Believe Him. Love Him. Serve Him. Obey Him. Follow Him. If necessary, die for Him. Hear His doctrine. Follow His example. Receive His gospel.

When the voice had ceased, Jesus was found alone. Moses and Elijah were gone. The cloud lifted. The voice was past. But Jesus remained. This is the point. The law and prophets bear witness, but Jesus stands alone as the Savior. The Father points all eyes and hearts to Him.

The disciples kept quiet and told no one in those days what they had seen. According to the other Gospels, Jesus commanded them to keep silent until after His resurrection. This was wise. If they had told the other disciples immediately, it might have stirred jealousy or confusion. If they told the crowds, many would not have believed them. They might have thought Peter, James, and John were simply excited or deluded. But after Christ rose from the dead, their testimony about His transfiguration would strengthen the evidence of His glory.

Now we must bring this passage home to our hearts.

First, we learn that those who receive special spiritual experiences must use wisdom in speaking of them. When God gives a person deep communion, strong comfort, or unusual manifestations of His love, that person may be tempted to tell everyone immediately. Young Christians especially are prone to this. They often have more honesty than wisdom. Like Joseph telling his brothers his dreams, they may speak true things at the wrong time, to the wrong people, or in the wrong way.

It is good to tell what God has done for your soul, but it is also good to know when to be silent. Some things are better kept close for a season. As believers mature, they learn that every spiritual experience does not need to be spoken everywhere. There is a time to speak and a time to be silent.

Second, we learn the duty of family prayer. Jesus took Peter, James, and John with Him into the mountain to pray. Are you a father, mother, master, mistress, or leader of a household? Then learn to take those under your care away from worldly distractions at appointed times, not only to pray for them, but to pray with them.

If Christ, who had no sin to confess and very few personal needs, loved prayer so much, how much more should we pray? I am not saying you must shut yourself away all day and neglect your work, family, or responsibilities. But you must redeem the time. If you are a child of God, you will often retire from the world and seek communion with your Father.

Third, we learn that prayer transforms the soul. Jesus was transfigured while He prayed. If we want to be made more like God, we must spend time with God. People often become like the company they keep. Those who walk with the wise become wise. Those who spend much time with God begin to reflect something of His character. Pray much, and your soul will receive more of His light.

Fourth, we learn comfort for aging and suffering believers. Moses and Elijah appeared in glory. This should encourage the saints of God, especially those whose bodies are weak and declining. Are you afraid of death? Are you carrying a body that weighs down your soul? Look beyond the grave. Your body will one day be fashioned like Christ's glorious body.

This poor body, subject to pain, weakness, disease, and weariness, will not always hinder you. It will be sown in corruption, but raised in incorruption. It will be sown in dishonor, but raised in glory. It will be sown in weakness, but raised in power. Therefore Paul could say in **1 Corinthians 15:55 NKJV**, *"O Death, where is your sting? O Hades, where is your victory?"*

The knees that have bowed in prayer, the tongue that has sung hymns to Christ, the hands that have worked for God, the feet that have run to His ordinances, will one day be changed. In a moment, in the twinkling of an eye, the people of God will be raised in glory. Believers, take heart. You may be weak now, but soon you will have a body full of strength, purity, and glory.

But while this comforts the saints, it warns sinners. If the bodies of believers will be glorified, what will become of those who die without Christ? What will outward beauty matter in the resurrection if the soul has never been reconciled to God? What will fine clothing, outward charm, or bodily strength profit those who neglected Christ and eternal life?

If people love their bodies, they should care even more for their souls. The body will rise again, either to glory or to shame. Therefore, seek Christ now.

Fifth, we learn that the saints will know one another in heaven. Peter seemed to know Moses and Elijah, though they had lived long before him. This suggests that the people of God will know each other in glory. Other passages point the same way. The rich man knew Lazarus. Adam knew Eve. Paul told the Philippians that they were his joy and crown in the day of the Lord.

What comfort this gives to spiritual fathers and mothers. In heaven, one may say, "Lord, this is the one who first pointed me to Christ." Another may say, "This is the one whose words struck my heart." Those who prayed together, wept together, fought spiritual battles together, and encouraged one another will be forever with the Lord and with one another.

We will see Abraham, Isaac, Jacob, the apostles, the prophets, the martyrs, and all the redeemed. We will know those whose names we have read in Scripture. We will know those we loved in Christ on earth. What a blessed prospect. Those who have lost believing fathers, mothers, spouses, children, or friends may take comfort. You are parted for a little while, but you will see them again. You will go to them, though they cannot return to you. Do not sorrow as those who have no hope.

But this same truth is dreadful for the lost. If glorified souls know one another in heaven, it is likely that lost souls will know one another in hell. The company of the blessed increases the joy of heaven, but the company of the damned will increase the torment of hell. The rich man in torment asked that someone warn his brothers, not because hell had made him kind, but because he knew that if they came there, they would increase his misery. They could say, "You helped lead us here. You taught us to drink, curse, swear, sin, and ignore God." The memory of sinful influence will become part of eternal torment.

Sixth, we learn that spiritual comforts in this life are often short. A cloud overshadowed the disciples. One moment they were on the mountain beholding glory. The next moment they were afraid in the cloud. This is often the experience of God's people. You may be on the mount one hour and in the valley of the shadow of death the next.

After a sweet season with God, a cloud may come. Sometimes we begin to say, "It is good to be here," and we start making a Christ out of our feelings, comforts, or experiences. Then the Lord sends a cloud to humble us and teach us to depend on Christ alone. But do not be afraid. God can speak to you out of the cloud. The cloud will pass. Soon enough, believers will be in the glory where no cloud can ever come.

Finally, we must hear the Father's command: **Luke 9:35 NKJV**, *"This is My beloved Son. Hear Him!"*

Let every heart echo that testimony and say, "This is my beloved Savior." God loved the world and sent His only begotten Son. His beloved Son came to preach to us, suffer for us, die for us, and save us. Therefore, hear Him.

If you have never heard Him before, hear Him now. Hear Him as your Prophet, Priest, and King. Hear Him as your God and your all. Hear Him today while it is called today. Young people, hear Him now before God cuts you off and you have no further invitation. Hear Him while He cries, "Come to Me." Hear Him while He opens His hand and His heart. Hear Him while He knocks at the door of your soul, lest one day you hear Him say, "Depart from Me, you cursed, into everlasting fire prepared for the devil and his angels."

Older people, hear Him. You who have gray hairs and one foot in the grave, hear Him. If you are dull of hearing, ask God to open the ears of your heart. If you are blind, ask Him to open your eyes. Beg Him for an enlarged and believing heart, so you may know what the Lord says concerning you.

God will avenge Himself on those who refuse to hear His beloved Son. Jesus came on a great errand. He came to shed His precious blood for sinners. He came to cleanse from all sin and save with an everlasting salvation.

And you who have already heard Him, hear Him again. Keep believing. Keep obeying. Keep following. Soon He will say to His faithful people, **Matthew 25:34 NKJV**, *"Come, you blessed of My Father, inherit the kingdom prepared for you from the foundation of the world."*

May God grant this to us all, for the sake of the Lord Jesus Christ.

Amen.

Chapter Twenty-Three

A Penitent Heart, the Best New Year's Gift

Luke 13:3 NKJV *"I tell you, no; but unless you repent you will all likewise perish."*

When we think about how serious our sins are in the sight of a just and holy God, we should be moved to turn away from evil. Sin brings guilt. Sin offends God. Sin places us under His righteous judgment. If we truly understood this, we would not treat sin lightly. We would not continue in it carelessly. We would seek repentance and mercy.

But man is often thoughtless about eternity. He gives little attention to the condition of his immortal soul. He sins as though he will never stand before God. Even when he does think about his behavior, his thoughts often do not lead him to true repentance. He may stop certain sins for a short time. He may make promises and resolutions.

But when temptation comes again with power, he is carried away by his desires. Then he breaks his promises almost as quickly as he made them.

This is highly offensive to God. It is like mocking Him. True repentance is more than a temporary resolution. When God gives us grace to truly repent, we turn wholly to Him. Therefore, I beg you to repent of your sins. The time is quickly coming when you will have no more opportunity to repent. There is no repentance in the grave, where we are all going.

But do not despair. God often receives the greatest sinners into mercy through the merits of Jesus Christ. This magnifies the riches of His free grace. It should encourage even great and notorious sinners to repent, because God will have mercy on those who return to Him through Christ.

Paul is a powerful example of this. He called himself the chief of sinners, yet God showed mercy to him. Christ loves to show mercy to sinners. If you repent and come to Him, He will have mercy on you.

But because the word repentance is often misunderstood, we must consider what true repentance is. First, we must understand the nature of repentance. Second, we must consider its parts and causes. Third, we must see why repentance is necessary for salvation. Fourth, we must urge every person, high and low, rich and poor, to seek true repentance.

Repentance, in its nature, is the changing of a carnal and corrupt heart into a renewed and sanctified heart. A person who has truly repented has truly been regenerated. These are different words describing the same great work of grace. The old mixture of beastlike desires and devilish corruption is taken away. A new creation is worked in the heart.

If your repentance is true, you are renewed in soul and body. Your understanding is enlightened with the knowledge of God and of the Lord Jesus Christ. Your will, which was once stubborn, rebellious, and opposed to what is good, becomes obedient and conformed to the will of God.

Some people say man has a free will to do good, love God, and repent whenever he chooses. But by nature, man's will is free only to sin. In his natural condition, man's will is so corrupt that, if possible, he would pull God from His throne. This may offend the self-righteous, but it is the truth. Every person, by nature, is opposed to God. But when he is turned to the Lord by true evangelical repentance, his will is changed.

Then the conscience, which was once hardened and numb, is awakened. The hard heart is melted. The unruly affections are crucified. The whole soul is changed. A person receives new inclinations, new desires, and new habits.

This shows how vile we are by nature. It takes a great change to recover us from our sinful condition. That should make us cry earnestly to God to change us. True repentance includes that kind of deep change.

Consider how hateful your ways are to God while you continue in sin. Consider how offensive you are to Him while you run after evil. You cannot truly be called a Christian while you hate Christ and His people. True repentance will change you. The direction of your soul will be turned. You will delight in God, in Christ, in His Word, and in His people.

Then you will believe that inward spiritual experience is real, even if now you think such language sounds like madness. You will not be ashamed to become a fool for Christ's sake. You will not be dismayed when others mock you, point at you, or call you one of His followers. Your soul will no longer love the ways of sin. The ways of Christ and His people will become your delight.

This is the nature of repentance. It brings the greatest change that can be made in the soul on this side of eternity. It includes hatred of evil and forsaking evil.

Now let us consider the parts of repentance. True repentance includes sorrow for sin, hatred of sin, and a full forsaking of sin.

Our sorrow for sin must not come merely from fear of punishment. If we are only sorry because we are afraid of wrath, then our sorrow springs from self-love, not love for God. If love for God is not the main motive in our repentance, then our repentance is not true.

Many people think repentance is simply saying, "God forgive me," "Lord have mercy on me," or "I am sorry." But they are mistaken. God does not accept lips that draw near while the heart remains far from Him. Repentance does not come in quick fits and starts. It is a continuing work in the life. Since we sin daily, we need daily repentance before God.

It is not enough to confess that you are a sinner. It is not enough to know that your condition is sad and dangerous while you continue in sin. Your heart must be deeply affected by it. You must feel that you are a lost and undone creature. Christ came to save those who are lost. If you are enabled to groan under the burden of your sins, then Christ will give you rest.

Until you are truly aware of your misery and lost condition, you remain a servant of sin and lust, under the bondage and command of Satan. You are under the curse of God and liable to judgment. Consider how dreadful your state will be at death and after the day of judgment if you die without repentance. The misery will be beyond what the ear has heard or the heart can imagine, and it will last forever.

But I hope better things for you, things that accompany salvation. Go to God in prayer. Be earnest with Him. Ask Him, by His Spirit, to convince you of your miserable condition by nature and make you truly sensible of it. Be humbled. Be humbled for your sins. You have spent many years sinning. Is it too much to spend time mourning over sin and humbling yourself before God?

Look back over your life. Bring your sins to mind as much as you can. Remember the sins of your youth and the sins of your later years. See how you have departed from a gracious Father and wandered in the way of wickedness. In that way, you have lost yourself, the favor of God, the comforts of His Spirit, and the peace of your conscience.

Then go and beg pardon from the Lord through the blood of the Lamb. Ask forgiveness for the evil you have committed and for the good you have failed to do. Consider also how serious and aggravated your sins are. Think about how you have abused the patience of God, which should have led you to repentance. When you find your heart hard, beg God to soften it. Cry mightily to Him, and He can take away your stony heart and give you a heart of flesh.

Resolve to leave all your sinful lusts and pleasures. Renounce, forsake, and hate your old sinful way of life. Serve God in holiness and righteousness for the rest of your days. If you mourn over past sins but do not forsake them, your repentance is empty. You are mocking God and deceiving your own soul. You must put off the old man with his deeds before you can put on the new man, Christ Jesus.

Therefore, those of you who have been swearers and cursers, those who have lived in sexual sin and drunkenness, those who have stolen or acted dishonestly, those who have followed the sinful pleasures and diversions of life, I beg you by the mercies of God in Christ Jesus: continue in these things no longer. Forsake your evil ways and turn to the Lord.

He waits to be gracious to you. He is ready and willing to pardon all your sins. But do not expect Christ to pardon you while you willingly run into sin and refuse to resist temptation. If you will turn from evil and choose what is good, if you will return to the Lord and repent of your wickedness, He has promised to pardon abundantly. He will heal your backslidings and love you freely.

Resolve this very day to be done with your sins forever. Let your old ways and you be separated. There can be no true repentance without a resolution to forsake sin. Resolve for Christ. Resolve against the devil and his works. Go forward fighting the Lord's battles against the devil and his servants. Attack him in his strongest holds. Fight as men. Fight as Christians. You will soon find that he is a coward. Resist him, and he will flee from you.

But do not base your resolutions on your own strength. Resolve in the strength of the Lord Jesus Christ. He is the way, the truth, and the life. Without His help, you can do nothing. Through His grace strengthening you, you can do all things. If Christ is for you, what can all the men of the world do against you? You will not fear what they say, because you will have the testimony of a good conscience.

Resolve to cast yourself at the feet of Christ in submission to Him. Throw yourself into His arms for salvation. Consider the many invitations He has given you to come to Him and be saved. **Isaiah 53:6 NKJV** says, *"And the Lord has laid on Him the iniquity of us all."*

Above all things, choose the Lord Jesus Christ. Resign yourself to Him. Take Him on His own terms. Whoever you are, and however great a sinner you have been, I offer Jesus Christ to you in the name of the great God. As you value your life and soul, do not refuse Him. Stir yourself up to receive the Lord Jesus. Take Him wholly as He is, because He will be received wholly or not at all.

Jesus Christ must be your whole wisdom. Jesus Christ must be your whole righteousness. Jesus Christ must be your whole sanctification. Jesus Christ must be your eternal redemption.

No matter how wicked and sinful you have been, if you abandon your sins and turn to the Lord Jesus Christ, He will be given to you, and all your sins will be freely forgiven. Why would you neglect the great work of repentance? Do not delay one more day. Today, even now, receive the Christ freely offered to you.

Now let us consider the causes of repentance. The first cause is God. He is the author of repentance. We are born of God. He is the One who works in us both to will and to do for His good pleasure.

Another cause is God's free grace. It is because of the riches of His free grace that we have not been sent to hell long ago. It is because the compassions of the Lord do not fail. They are new every morning and fresh every evening.

Sometimes God uses unlikely instruments. A poor, despised minister or ordinary member of Christ may be used by God to bring someone to true repentance. God does this to show that the power is not in man but entirely in His good pleasure. If any good has been done through the preaching of the Word, even if it was preached in a field, and even if the preacher was called a madman, a boy, or an enthusiast, then I rejoice and will continue to rejoice. Let enemies say what they will.

Now we must consider why repentance is necessary for salvation.

This is plainly revealed in the Word of God. The soul that does not repent and turn to the Lord will die in its sins, and its blood will be on its own head. Since we have sinned, we must repent. A holy God cannot admit anything unholy into His presence. Repentance is the beginning of grace in the soul. There must be a change in heart and life before a person can dwell with a holy God.

You cannot love sin and God at the same time. You cannot serve God and mammon. No unclean person can stand in God's presence. It is contrary to the holiness of His nature. There is a direct opposition between the holy nature of God and the unholy nature of unconverted men.

What fellowship can there be between a sinless God and creatures full of sin? What communion can there be between a pure God and impure creatures? If you were admitted into heaven with your present sinful heart, heaven itself would be like hell to you. The songs of angels would seem strange and unbearable. Therefore, your heart must be changed. You must be holy, as God is holy. He must be your God here, and you must be His people here, or you will never dwell with Him forever.

If you hate the ways of God and cannot spend even an hour in His service, how do you expect to be happy forever singing praises to Him who sits on the throne and to the Lamb?

This will be the eternal employment of those admitted into that glorious place where no sin and no sinner can enter. No scoffer can come there without repentance from evil ways, turning to God, and cleaving to Him. This must happen before anyone can enter the glorious mansions prepared for all who love the Lord Jesus Christ in sincerity and truth.

Repent, then, of all your sins. O my dear brethren, it makes my blood run cold to think that any of you might not be admitted into those glorious mansions above. If it were in my power, I would place all of you, even my scoffing brethren and the greatest enemy I have on earth, at the right hand of Jesus. But I cannot do that.

What I can do is advise and exhort you with love and tenderness to make Jesus your refuge. Flee to Him for relief. Jesus died to save sinners like you. He is full of compassion. If you go to Him as poor, lost, undone sinners, He will give you His Spirit. You shall live and reign with Him, love and live with Him, and live and love with Him for all eternity.

Now I exhort every one of you, high and low, rich and poor, to repent of all your sins and turn to the Lord.

Every person hearing this has either repented or has not. You are either a believer in Christ Jesus or an unbeliever.

First, let me speak plainly to those who have never truly repented of their sins and never truly forsaken their lusts. Do not be offended. It is love for your soul that makes me speak plainly. I must lay before you your danger and the misery to which you are exposed while you remain impenitent in sin. My prayer is that this warning will make you flee to Christ for pardon and forgiveness.

While your sins remain unrepented of, you are in danger of death. If you die in that condition, you will perish forever. There is no hope for those who live and die in their sins. They will dwell with devils and damned spirits forever. And how do you know that you will live much longer? You are not even sure you will return safely to your home tonight.

Why then are you at ease while your sins are not pardoned? As surely as the Word of God is true, if you die in that condition, you will be shut out from all hope and mercy forever and pass into endless misery.

What are all your pleasures and entertainments worth? They last only a moment. They are empty and short-lived. It is terrible foolishness to chase sinful pleasures that war against the soul, harden the heart, and keep you from coming to the Lord Jesus. These things destroy your peace here and, without repentance, will destroy your peace hereafter.

O the folly and madness of this sensual world. Even if there were nothing in sin but present slavery, that should be enough to keep an honest heart from it. But when people do the devil's work, they will receive the devil's wages, which is eternal death and condemnation.

Consider this, guilty sinners. You who think it is no crime to swear, commit sexual sin, get drunk, scoff, or mock the people of God, consider how your voice will change then. You who thought the lives of God's people were madness and without honor will one day howl and lament your own madness and folly for bringing yourself into such distress.

Then you will mourn your dreadful condition, but it will not help. The One who is now offered to you as a merciful Savior will then be your unchangeable Judge. Now He is easy to be entreated. Then your tears and prayers will be in vain. God has given every person a day of grace and a time of repentance. If that time is neglected and despised, that person cannot be saved.

Therefore, while you continue in sin and unrighteousness, think carefully about the consequences of wasting your precious time. Your soul is worth serious concern. Even if you enjoy every pleasure and diversion of life, at death you must leave them all. Death will put an end to all your worldly concerns.

How dreadful it will be to have enjoyed your good things here, all your earthly, sensual, devilish pleasures, and then lose eternal life for such trifles. That thought will gnaw at your soul.

Your wealth and greatness will not help you. You can carry none of it into the next world. Then your lack of charity toward the poor and the ways you gained your wealth will torment your conscience.

Now you have the means of grace. You have the preaching of the Word, prayer, and the ordinances of God. God has sent His ministers into the fields and highways to invite and persuade you to come in. But these things may seem tiresome to you. You may prefer your pleasures. Soon they will be over. You will no longer be troubled by sermons or calls to repentance. But then you would give ten thousand worlds for one moment of the time of mercy you now abuse.

Then you will cry for one drop of the precious blood you now trample under your feet. You will wish for one more offer of mercy, one more invitation to Christ and His free grace. But your crying will be in vain. If you would not repent in Christ's time, you will not be allowed to repent in your own.

What a dreadful condition that will be. What horror and astonishment will seize your soul. Then all your lies and oaths, your mockery of God's people, your filthy thoughts and actions, your wasted time in sinful entertainments, your worldliness, your covetousness, and your lack of love will be brought to your remembrance and charged against your guilty soul.

How can you bear the thought of these things? I am full of compassion toward you as I think this may be the portion of anyone hearing me. These are truths, though they are dreadful truths. They are the truths of the gospel. If there were no need to speak this way, I would gladly avoid it. This is not a pleasing subject to me, any more than it is to you. But it is my duty to show you the dreadful consequences of continuing in sin.

I am acting like a surgeon who searches a wound before he heals it. I show you your danger so that you may gladly receive deliverance.

However much you try to put the evil day far from you or hide your sins, at the day of judgment there will be a full discovery of everything. Hidden things will be brought to light. After your sins are revealed before all, you must depart into everlasting fire, which will not be quenched day or night. It will be without pause and without end.

What spiritual numbness has possessed your heart that you are not frightened from your sins? Fear of Nebuchadnezzar's fiery furnace made men do almost anything to avoid it. Shall not everlasting fire make you do anything to avoid it?

O that this would awaken you and cause you to humble yourself for your sins and beg pardon, so that you may find mercy in the Lord.

Do not go away. Do not let the devil hurry you away before the message is done. Stay, and you will hear Jesus offered to you, the One who has made full satisfaction for all your sins.

I beg you to cast away your transgressions, fight against sin, watch against it, and ask Christ for power and strength to restrain the lusts that hurry you along in sinful ways.

But if you will not do these things, if you are determined to continue in sin, then you must expect eternal death as the consequence. You must expect horror, trembling, and amazement when you hear the dreadful sentence of condemnation pronounced against you. Then you will call for the mountains to fall on you and hide you from the Lord and from the fierceness of His wrath.

If you now had a heart to turn from your sins to the living God by true repentance, and to pray for mercy through the merits of Jesus Christ, there would be hope. But at the day of judgment, your prayers and tears will be useless. The Judge will not be entreated then. Since you would not listen when He called, since you despised Him and His ministers and refused to leave your sins, He will not hear your cries on that day.

God says in **Proverbs 1:24–28 NKJV**, *"Because I have called and you refused, I have stretched out My hand and no one regarded, because you disdained all My counsel, and would have none of My rebuke, I also will laugh at your calamity; I will mock when your terror comes, when your terror comes like a storm, and your destruction comes like a whirlwind, when distress and anguish come upon you. Then they will call on Me, but I will not answer; they will seek Me diligently, but they will not find Me."*

Now you may call this madness or enthusiasm. But at that great day, if you do not repent here, you will discover by bitter experience that your own ways were madness indeed. But God forbid that you wait until then. Seek the Lord while He may be found. Call upon Him while He is near, and you shall find mercy. Repent this hour, and Christ will joyfully receive you.

What will you say? Must I go to my Master and tell Him that you will not come to Him and that you reject His counsel? No. Do not send me on such an unhappy errand. I cannot and will not tell Him that. Shall I not rather tell Him that you are willing to repent and be converted, to become new people and walk in a new life? This is the only wise resolution you can make.

Let me tell my Master that you will come to Him and wait upon Him. If you do not, it will be your ruin in time and eternity.

At death, you will wish you had lived the life of the righteous so that you could die the death of the righteous. Be advised, then. Consider what is before you: Christ and the world, holiness and sin, life and death. Choose now. Let your choice be made immediately, and let that choice be your dying choice.

If you would not choose to die in your sins, to die as drunkards, adulterers, swearers, scoffers, and rebels, then do not live another night in your present dreadful condition.

Some of you may say, "I have no power. I have no strength." But have you not failed in things that were within your power? Do you not have as much power to go hear a sermon as to go to a playhouse, ball, or sinful entertainment? Do you not have as much power to read the Bible as to read novels, romances, and useless things? Can you not associate with the godly as easily as with the wicked and profane?

This is only an idle excuse to continue in sin. If you place yourself in the means of grace, Christ has promised to give strength. While Peter was preaching, the Holy Spirit fell on those who heard the Word. Therefore, be found in the way of duty. Jesus Christ will give you strength. He will put His Spirit within you. He will be your wisdom, righteousness, sanctification, and redemption.

Try what a gracious, kind, and loving Master He is. He will help you in all your burdens. If the burden of sin is on your soul, go to Him as weary and heavy laden, and you will find rest.

Do not say your sins are too many or too great for mercy. No. Whether they are many or great, the blood of the Lord Jesus Christ cleanses from all sin. God's grace is free, rich, and sovereign.

Manasseh was a great sinner, yet he was pardoned. Zacchaeus was far from God and went to see Christ only from curiosity, yet Jesus met him and brought salvation to his house. Manasseh was an idolater and murderer, yet he received mercy. Zacchaeus was an oppressor and extortioner who had gained wealth by fraud and by grinding the faces of the poor, yet he received mercy. Matthew was also a tax collector, and he found mercy.

Have you been a blasphemer and persecutor of God's people? So was Paul, yet he received mercy. Have you been unclean and sinful? Mary Magdalene received mercy. Have you been a thief? The thief on the cross found mercy. I despair of none of you, however vile and sinful you have been, especially since God has had mercy on such a wretch as I am.

Remember the poor tax collector. He found favor with God while the proud, self-righteous Pharisee was rejected. If you go to Jesus as the tax collector did, under a sense of your own unworthiness, you will find mercy as he did. There is enough virtue in the blood of Jesus to pardon greater sinners than He has yet pardoned.

Do not be discouraged. Come to Jesus. You will find Him ready to help in all your distresses, to lead you into all truth, and to bring you from darkness to light and from the power of Satan to God.

Do not let the devil deceive you by saying that if you come to Christ all your delights and pleasures will be over. That is a lie. Coming to Christ does not remove joy. It opens the door to unspeakable delight, known only by those who are truly born again. The new birth is the beginning of a life of peace and comfort. The greatest joy is found in the ways of holiness.

Solomon had tasted every kind of earthly pleasure, yet he said of wisdom in **Proverbs 3:17 NKJV**, *"Her ways are ways of pleasantness, and all her paths are peace."* Do not let the devil deceive you. He wants to make religion look miserable, gloomy, and foolish. But he was a liar from the beginning and remains a liar.

What words can I use? What pleadings can I offer to make you come to the Lord Jesus Christ? The little love of Christ I have experienced since being brought from sin to God is so great that I would not return to my natural state for ten thousand worlds. And what I have felt is only a little compared with what I hope to feel. Yet even that little love is enough to carry me through all the storms of this world. Let men and devils do their worst, I rejoice in the Lord Jesus, and I will rejoice.

If you repent and come to Jesus, I will rejoice for you too, and we will rejoice together for all eternity when we pass beyond the grave. Come to Jesus. The arms of Jesus Christ will embrace you. He will wash away all your sins in His blood. He will love you freely.

Come, I beg you, come to Jesus Christ. O that my words would pierce your very soul. O that Jesus Christ would be formed in you. O that you would turn to the Lord Jesus Christ, that He might have mercy upon you. I would speak until midnight, yes, until I could speak no more, if it would bring you to Jesus.

Let the Lord Jesus enter your soul, and you will find peace that the world can neither give nor take away. There is mercy for the greatest sinner among you. Go to the Lord as sinners, helpless and undone without Him. Then you will find comfort in your souls and at last be admitted among those who sing praises to the Lord forever.

Now let me speak a word to those of you who have already been brought to the Lord Jesus, who are born again, who belong to God, who have been granted repentance, and who have been cleansed from guilt. Be thankful to God for His mercy toward you. Admire the grace of God and bless His name forever.

Are you made alive in Christ Jesus? Has the life of God begun in your soul? Do you have evidence of this work? Then be thankful for this unspeakable mercy. Never forget to speak of His mercy. Since your life was once devoted to sin and the pleasures of the world, let it now be spent wholly in the ways of God. Embrace every opportunity to do good and receive good. Whatever opportunity you have, do it earnestly and quickly. Do not delay.

If you see someone rushing toward destruction, do all you can to stop him. Show him his need for repentance and warn him that without it he is lost forever. Do not be discouraged if he despises you. Keep showing him his danger. If your friends mock and despise you, do not let that stop you. Hold on and hold out to the end. You will receive a crown that is incorruptible and does not fade away.

Let the love of Jesus keep you humble. Do not be high-minded. Stay close to the Lord. Follow the instructions Christ has given in His Word. Do not waste the lessons you are able to give others. Consider how much reason you have to thank the Lord Jesus Christ for giving you the repentance you needed, a repentance that works by love.

Now you find more pleasure in walking with God for one hour than in all your former carnal delights and sinful pleasures. O the joy you feel in your soul, which all the men of the world and all the devils in hell combined cannot destroy. Do not fear their wrath or malice. Through many tribulations we must enter into glory.

A few days, weeks, or years more, and you will be beyond their reach. You will be in the heavenly Jerusalem. There is harmony and love. There is joy and delight. There the weary soul is at rest.

Now we have many enemies, but at death they are all left behind. They cannot follow us beyond the grave. This should encourage us not to fear the scoffs and insults of this world.

Let the love of Jesus be continually in your thoughts. It was His death that brought you life. It was His crucifixion that satisfied divine justice for your sins. His death, burial, and resurrection completed the work. He is now in heaven, interceding for you at the right hand of the Father.

Can you do too much for the Lord Jesus Christ, who has done so much for you? His love for you is unfathomable. O the height, the depth, the length, and the breadth of this love, that brought the King of glory from His throne to die for rebels like us. We had acted unkindly toward Him and deserved nothing but eternal condemnation. Yet He came down, took our nature upon Himself, was put to death for us, and paid our ransom.

Surely this should make us rejoice in Him. Let us not crucify Jesus afresh by returning to sin. Let us do all we can to honor Him.

Come, all of you, and behold Him stretched out for you. See His hands and feet nailed to the cross. Come and nail your sins there. Come and see His side pierced. There is a fountain opened for sin and uncleanness. Wash and be clean. Come and see His head crowned with thorns, and all for you.

Can you think of a panting, bleeding, dying Jesus and not be moved? He endured all this for you. Come to Him by faith. Lay hold of Him. There is mercy for every soul who comes to Him. Do not delay. Fly to the arms of Jesus, and you shall be made clean in His blood.

What else shall I say to make you come to Jesus? I have shown you the dreadful consequence of not repenting of your sins. If after all this you are determined to continue in sin, your blood will be on your own head. But I hope better things of you, things that accompany salvation.

Pray earnestly for the grace of repentance. I may never see your faces again, but I will meet you at the day of judgment. There you will either bless God that you were moved to repentance, or this sermon will be a swift witness against you.

Repent, repent, therefore, my dear brethren, as John the Baptist preached and as our blessed Redeemer Himself preached. Turn from your evil ways, and the Lord will have mercy on you.

Father, show them where they have offended You. Make them see their own vileness and that they are lost and undone without true repentance. Give them repentance, we ask, that they may turn from sin to You, the living and true God.

Grant these things, and whatever else You see we need, because of what dear Jesus Christ has done and suffered. To Him, with Yourself and the Holy Spirit, three Persons and one God, be all power, glory, might, majesty, and dominion, now and forever.

Amen.

Chapter Twenty-Four

The Gospel Supper

Luke 14:22–24 NKJV *"And the servant said, 'Master, it is done as you commanded, and still there is room.' Then the master said to the servant, 'Go out into the highways and hedges, and compel them to come in, that my house may be filled. For I say to you that none of those men who were invited shall taste my supper.'"*

Though there is a large and serious gathering here, I believe all of you know that you will not live in this world forever. Even the most careless person among us likely believes, deep down, what Scripture plainly says: every person must die, and after death comes judgment. We must all appear before the judgment seat of Christ and give an account for the things done in the body, whether good or evil.

This may sound hard at first, but I am persuaded that many people will be condemned at the judgment not only for open and obvious sins, such as drunkenness, adultery, sexual immorality, or other gross sins, but also for pursuing lawful things in a wrong way, from a wrong heart, and with too much attachment. The world is sinful, but there are still many people who, because of religious upbringing, self-respect, or concern for reputation, avoid the worst outward sins. They may even look with disgust at those who openly practice them.

Yet while they avoid public scandal, their hearts may be deeply asleep toward God. They may be so eager in their pursuit of the things of this life that their souls become spiritually dull. Little by little, they become as dead to God and as deaf to the invitations of the gospel as the most reckless sinner.

This is why our Lord warned His disciples not only against drunkenness and overindulgence, but also against being weighed down by the cares of this life. The anxious concerns of this world can intoxicate the soul just as surely as strong drink can intoxicate the body. They distract the mind, burden the heart, and keep people from coming to Christ.

To warn us of this danger, Jesus spoke many parables. Few are more powerful than the parable connected to our text. In it, we see the freeness of the gospel invitation, the foolish excuses people make for rejecting it, and the dreadful judgment that follows those who refuse the call of God.

Jesus said that the master told his servant, "Go out into the highways and hedges, and compel them to come in, that my house may be filled." Then He added the solemn warning, "None of those men who were invited shall taste my supper."

To understand this parable clearly, we must look at the setting. At the beginning of Luke 14, Jesus entered the house of one of the chief Pharisees to eat bread on the Sabbath day. The Pharisees watched

Him closely. They were not watching because they loved Him. They were watching to find fault with Him. They wanted to accuse Him either for what He said or for what He did.

Yet Jesus accepted the invitation. He came eating and drinking. He was free, gracious, approachable, and willing to be with all kinds of people. Even though He knew the Pharisees were His enemies, He entered the house. This teaches us that much inward hatred toward Christ can be hidden beneath a great outward profession of religion.

Still, Jesus was more than a match for His enemies. By accepting this invitation, He gave His ministers and disciples an example. We may accept invitations and speak freely about the things of God, even when those who invite us may not have real religion in their hearts. Who knows whether something spoken in faith may benefit their souls? If they watch you, then watch unto prayer while you are with them. The same Jesus who entered the Pharisee's house and spoke faithfully there can enable you to do the same.

Jesus did not waste the opportunity with empty conversation. He did not behave like a careless guest, but like a faithful physician of souls. He noticed how the guests chose the best seats. The Lord Jesus observes our behavior even in ordinary settings. He sees how we act, even when we simply sit down to eat.

If Christians truly remembered this, religion would not be confined to church services or religious meetings. It would enter our homes, our tables, our conversations, and our daily behavior. Many unnecessary and unchristian forms of pride would be avoided. Sadly, many professors of religion still love the highest places in houses as well as in public gatherings.

Jesus saw this pride in the guests. He noticed how they chose the best rooms, or the most honored places. So He gave them a lesson in humility. He told them that when they were invited to a wedding feast, they should not sit in the highest place, in case someone more honorable had been invited. Then the host might come and say, "Give place to this man," and they would be ashamed. Instead, they should sit in the lowest place, so that when the host came, he might say, "Friend, go up higher."

This was a beautiful example of faithfulness and love. Ministers especially should follow the example of their Master. With humility, wisdom, and sincerity, they should be willing to correct sin when they see it, even if the people involved are above them in social position. Some say we should not reprove natural men, or that there is no need to correct those who are not converted. But that is not what Jesus did. These guests were likely natural men, yet our Lord corrected them.

Jesus did not stop there. He noticed that the host had invited only the rich, the powerful, and the respected. So He gave His host a word of instruction as well. The best return we can make for a friend's kindness is to be faithful to his soul. Jesus said that when he made a dinner or supper, he should not invite only friends, brothers, relatives, or rich neighbors, because they might invite him back and repay him. Instead, he should invite the poor, the maimed, the lame, and the blind, because they could not repay him. Then he would be repaid at the resurrection of the just.

This is how Jesus spoke at the table. His words were timely, faithful, and full of grace. If the followers of Christ would speak in this way when they are in company, bringing up useful conversation for their Master, they do not know how much good they might do. Their example might encourage others to speak for Christ as well.

This happened in the passage. One of those who sat at the table heard these things and said, "Blessed is he who shall eat bread in the kingdom of God." This was a fitting statement. They were sitting down to eat bread on earth, and his heart was lifted to the day when the righteous would eat bread in the kingdom of heaven. We should never sit down to eat without remembering and longing for that great feast above.

His words opened the way for Jesus to tell the parable. It was as though Jesus said, "You speak rightly. Blessed indeed are those who eat bread in the kingdom of God. But sadly, many people, especially the self-righteous, act as though they do not believe this." Then Jesus told of a certain man who made a great supper and invited many.

The man who made the supper represents God the Father. The supper represents the great provision God has made for perishing souls through the obedience and death of His beloved Son, Jesus Christ. The supper was a fitting picture because, among the ancients, supper was the great meal of the day.

Man could never have prepared this salvation for himself. Angels could not have prepared it for him. Salvation is entirely from God, from beginning to end. He made the supper. He prepared the provision. It is not our wisdom, but divine wisdom, that has made a way for sinners to become the people of God and the sheep of His pasture.

This provision is rightly called great. It is great because there is rich and full provision in the gospel for many souls. Christ's flock may seem little when scattered, but when all His people are gathered together, they will be a multitude no one can number. It is also great because it was purchased at a great price, the precious blood of Jesus Christ. When the apostle calls Christians to glorify God in body and spirit, he reminds them that they were bought with a price. He does not even need to explain the price, because there is no price like the blood of Christ.

The parable says that the man sent his servant at supper time to say to those who were invited, "Come, for all things are now ready." The invitation first points to the Jews. Under the Old Testament, God had invited them through types, shadows, prophecies, and promises to partake of the blessings of the gospel.

At supper time, in the fullness of time, God sent His servant. This servant is Christ, God's Son, called a servant because, as Mediator, He humbled Himself and took the place of obedience. Through Christ the message came to those who were invited: "Come." That means, "Repent and believe the gospel."

Nothing is required from man except to come and receive what God has provided. This is not the old covenant message, "Do and live." This is the gospel message: "Come, believe, and be saved." All things are ready. Nothing is lacking on God's side. The sacrifice is ready. The righteousness is ready. The pardon is ready. The Spirit is ready. The invitation is ready.

There is a special emphasis on the word now. "All things are now ready." This was a season of grace. God was making His great gospel call to lost man.

If the great God went to such expense to make a great supper for perishing creatures, and if He sent so great a Person as His own Son to invite them, one would think everyone who heard the invitation would gladly say, "Lord, I come." But instead, they all began to make excuses.

Their consciences likely told them they should come. They may even have had some weak desire to come. They did not seem to object to the one who prepared the supper. They did not seem to object to the servant who invited them. They did not seem to object to the supper itself. They may even have admitted that all was good and that the invitation was kind. But they were busy. They thought they had lawful reasons not to come. So they began to make excuses.

But their excuses only made their refusal more inexcusable.

The first man said that he had bought a piece of ground and needed to go see it. But who buys land and then goes to see it afterward? A wise man would look at the land before buying it. And even if he had bought it, why did he need to see it immediately? The land was his. It would still be there tomorrow. He could have accepted the invitation that day and seen the land later. Yet he said, "I ask you to have me excused."

The second excuse was even worse. Another man said he had bought five yoke of oxen and was going to test them. Again, this was foolish. A wise buyer would test the oxen before purchasing them. This shows us that people will often trust one another, and even trust the devil, more readily than they will trust God.

The third excuse was worst of all. One said, "I have married a wife, and therefore I cannot come." If he had said, "I will not come," he would have spoken more honestly. It is not usually a lack of ability that keeps people from the gospel feast, but a lack of will and desire.

Why could he not come? He had married a wife. But if he had married a wife, that was all the more reason to come. The supper was like a wedding feast, and there was plenty of provision. He could have brought his wife with him. If she was unwilling to come, he should have urged her to come. No greater kindness can a husband or wife do than to bring the other to the gospel feast. And if she still refused, he should have come without her. Those who have wives must live as though they had none when earthly affection would keep them from Christ. Adam paid dearly for listening to the voice of his wife when it led him into sin. Sometimes, unless we are willing to forsake even wife, houses, and lands for Christ, we cannot be His disciples.

The servant returned and reported these things to his master. He must have come with sorrow. Ministers must also report to the Lord what success their ministry has had. They must spread the case before Him in prayer now, and one day they will give account before the great assembly of the whole world.

How heartbreaking it is when ministers must cry before God, "My leanness, my leanness," and plead with Him about those to whom they would gladly have given not only the gospel but even their own lives. Yet this must be done. The servant came and told his lord these things.

The master of the house became angry. He was not angry with the servant. Faithful ministers will be rewarded whether people receive the gospel or not. They are a sweet aroma to God, whether their message becomes a fragrance of life to life or death to death.

The master was angry with the worldly-minded, pleasure-loving people who refused his gracious invitation. They probably went on to see their land, test their oxen, and attend to their marriage, assuming their excuses would be accepted because they were lawfully employed. And in one sense, their excuses were accepted. They asked to be excused, and they were excused. We do not hear that they were ever invited again. God took them at their word, though they would not take Him at His.

Let us therefore not harden our hearts. **2 Corinthians 6:2 NKJV** says, *"Behold, now is the accepted time; behold, now is the day of salvation."*

But would the feast have no guests? No. If those first invited would not come, others would. So the master told his servant to go quickly into the streets and lanes of the city and bring in the poor, the maimed, the lame, and the blind.

Every word carries urgency. Go quickly. Make no delay. Fear no danger. Bring them in. Do not merely call them, but bring them. The poor, the maimed, the lame, and the blind were to be brought to the supper.

This was fulfilled when the gospel, rejected by many Jews, was opened to Gentiles, publicans, harlots, and those despised by the self-righteous. While scribes and Pharisees rejected the kingdom of God, others pressed into it by holy violence. This was also a rebuke to the rich Pharisee whose table Jesus was sitting at. He had not invited the poor, the lame, the blind, or the maimed to his feast, but God would invite such people to His gospel supper.

The servant returned with a joyful report: "Master, it is done as you commanded, and still there is room." No one can fully understand the comfort ministers feel when God blesses their labors unless they have experienced it. Paul said to the believers, "Now we live, if you stand fast in the Lord." The salvation and steadfastness of souls are the joy and crown of faithful ministers.

The servant was glad that the poor, maimed, lame, and blind had been brought in. Yet he added, "Still there is room." This shows that he longed to be sent again. The more we do for God, the more we desire to do. Present success encourages future diligence. Christ delights to see His servants ready for more work and waiting for fresh orders.

Then the master said, **Luke 14:23 NKJV**, *"Go out into the highways and hedges, and compel them to come in, that my house may be filled."*

These were glad tidings for the publicans, harlots, and Gentiles, who had been rejected by proud religious leaders as strangers to the promises. This was fulfilled when Jesus sent His apostles not only into Jerusalem and Judea, but into all the world to preach the gospel to every creature, Jew and Gentile alike. He not only commanded them to go, but blessed their labor so powerfully that three thousand were converted in one day.

This parable was first spoken to the Jews on a particular occasion, but it still applies to us, to our children, and to all whom the Lord our God shall call. It gives support to preaching not only in churches, but also in fields and highways. It also shows, in a lively way, the kind of reception the gospel receives in every age.

Is it not plain that many professors in our generation have made light of the gospel offer? Again and again, the message has been preached: God has made a great supper. He has invited many. All things are ready. Believe on the Lord Jesus Christ, and you shall be saved. Yet many hear the message and continue too busy with their farms, businesses, marriages, possessions, and pleasures to come to the Lord of life.

We have told people that we do not want them to hide themselves from the world, but to learn how to live in the world without being of the world. Yet many still will not come. Some religious leaders also reject the kingdom of God against themselves, like the scribes and Pharisees of old. They deny the free preaching of justification by faith alone and oppose the invitation for sinners to come freely to the gospel feast without money and without price.

But the great Master of the house is not hindered. He sends His servants to the streets, lanes, highways, and hedges. He calls the poor, the maimed, the lame, the blind, the publicans, the harlots, the common cursers, swearers, Sabbath-breakers, adulterers, and those who perhaps have never entered a church or heard that Jesus Christ died for sinners like them.

By grace, His servants obey. They go out, even if they are despised for doing so. And blessed be God, their labor is not in vain in the Lord. Many have been made willing in the day of God's power. With humility, they can say, "Lord, it is done as You commanded, and still there is room."

Christ continues to send His servants. He sends them into the highways and hedges and gives them a commission to compel sinners to come in. This compelling is not by force, fire, or sword. It is not the violent compulsion of false religion. It is the earnest, loving, powerful persuasion of the gospel, made effective by the Spirit of God. If the Lord did not attend the Word with power and sweetly incline human wills to receive the gospel call, preaching would be like sounding brass or a clanging cymbal.

But Christ will do it. His house must be filled. Every soul for whom He shed His blood will finally be saved. **John 6:37 NKJV** says, *"All that the Father gives Me will come to Me, and the one who comes to Me I will by no means cast out."* This comforted our Lord when His gospel was rejected by many. Even when some despised His grace, His blood would not be shed in vain.

Supported by this truth, I am not ashamed to go into the highways and hedges and call poor, maimed, lame, blind, self-condemned, helpless sinners to the marriage supper of the Lamb. My cry is this: Come. Believe on the Lord Jesus. Throw yourselves at the footstool of His mercy, and you shall be saved. All things are now ready.

God the Father is ready. God the Son is ready. God the Holy Spirit is ready. The blessed angels above are ready. The saints below are ready to welcome you to the gospel feast.

A perfect and everlasting righteousness has been worked out by Jesus Christ. God can now, on honorable terms, pardon the guilty. God can be just and still justify the ungodly. **2 Corinthians 5:21 NKJV** says, *"For He made Him who knew no sin to be sin for us, that we might become the righteousness of God in Him."*

The fatted calf has been killed. Christ our Passover has been sacrificed for us. Come, sinners, and feed upon Him in your hearts by faith, with thanksgiving.

For Jesus Christ's sake, do not begin making excuses. Do not let land, oxen, marriage, family, business, or pleasure keep you from this great supper. These may be enjoyed as gifts from God and used for the glory of the Mediator, while still coming to the gospel feast. True religion does not take away the proper comforts of life. It increases them by putting them in their right place. Jesus did not pray that His people would be taken out of the world, but that they would be kept from its evil.

O that all of you would say with one heart, "Lord, we come." Be assured, there is enough provision. It is a great supper. In our Father's house there is bread enough and to spare. Though a great God makes the supper, He is as good and condescending as He is great. Though He is the high and lofty One who inhabits eternity, He dwells with the humble and contrite heart, with the one who trembles at His Word.

You cannot complain that there is no room, because still there is room. In our Father's house are many mansions. If it were not so, Jesus would have told us. The grace of Christ is as rich, free, and powerful as ever. **Hebrews 13:8 NKJV** says, *"Jesus Christ is the same yesterday, today, and forever."*

He is full of grace and truth. Out of His fullness, all who come to Him may receive grace upon grace. He gives generously and does not reproach. He does not desire the death of a sinner, but that sinners should believe and live.

Come then, all you poor, lame, maimed, and blind sinners. Take comfort. The Lord Jesus has sent His servant to call you. It is supper time. It is a day of uncommon grace. The day may be far spent. Hurry, then, and come to the supper of the Lamb.

If you do not come, the Master will be angry. And who can stand before Him when He is angry? Do not harden your hearts as in the day of rebellion. Do not provoke the Lord to say, "None of those who were invited shall taste My supper." Those are dreadful words. They mean more than they say. They are like the words in the Psalms, where God swore in His wrath that unbelieving people would not enter His rest. If you do not enter God's rest and do not taste Christ's supper, you must lift up your eyes in torment. There will be no rest there, and you will have your portion with the damned forever.

Knowing the terror of the Lord, we persuade you. Make haste and stop making empty excuses. There is no valid excuse against believing.

Perhaps you say, "You call the lame, maimed, blind, and poor. But if we are lame and maimed, how can we come? If we are blind, how can we see the way? If we are poor, how can we be admitted to so great a table?"

If you feel that you are lame and maimed, you are blessed to know your condition. If you are grieving over it, who knows whether God may send His Spirit with the Word even now and bring you home? Though you are blind, Jesus has eye salve to anoint your eyes. Though you are poor, you are welcome to this rich feast. It cost Jesus Christ a great price, but you may receive it freely. It was designed for sinners like you. **Matthew 5:3 NKJV** says, *"Blessed are the poor in spirit, for theirs is the kingdom of heaven."*

Rich, self-righteous, self-sufficient sinners will often scorn both the feast and the One who prepared it. Many have already done so. Therefore, the Lord sends His servants into the highways and hedges to bring poor souls in. Venture, then, dear friends. Honor God by taking Him at His Word. Come to the marriage feast. Believe me, you will partake of the richest provision.

Those of you who have already tasted that the Lord is gracious, will you not recommend this feast to others? Are you not ready to cry out, "Come, all of you outside. Obey the call. We have sat under the Redeemer's shadow with great delight, and His fruit has been sweet to our taste"? While this message is being preached, does not the fire kindle in your heart? Do you not long for others to come and be blessed too?

If you are true Christians, I know this is your desire. The language of your heart is, "Lord, while Your servant is calling, let Your Spirit compel them to come in." May the Lord say amen to that prayer.

Why should we doubt? Surely our Savior will not let His servant labor in vain. I seem to see many desiring to come. How shall I compel you to come forward? I will not use fire or sword. I will tell you of the love of God, the love of God in Christ. Surely that love should compel you. Surely that love should constrain you.

Sinners, my heart is enlarged toward you. I could fill my mouth with arguments. Consider the greatness of the God who makes the supper. Consider the greatness of the price by which it was purchased. Consider the greatness of the provision made for you. What more do you want? Consider God's infinite condescension in calling you now, when you might already have been in hell, where the worm does not die and the fire is not quenched.

So that you would be without excuse, He has sent His servant into the highways and hedges to invite you. O that you could taste what I taste now. If you did, you would not need arguments to come in. You would fly to the gospel feast like doves to their windows.

But poor souls, many of you may not be hungry. You do not feel yourselves lame, maimed, or blind. Therefore, you have no desire for this spiritual feast. Do not be angry with me for calling you. Do not be offended if I weep over you, because you do not know the day of your visitation.

If I must appear in judgment as a witness against you, I must. But the thought chills my blood. I can hardly bear it. I feel that I could lay down my life for you. I am not willing to go without you.

So I ask again: Will you taste Christ's supper, or will you not? You are all welcome. There is milk for babes and meat for strong men. There is provision for young and old, high and low, rich and poor. The Savior will receive you gladly.

Amazing condescension. Astonishing love. The thought of it overwhelms me. Believers, help me bless and praise Him.

And may this love stir all of us to come to Him afresh, as though we had never come before. Though we have often feasted on Christ, our souls will starve unless we renew our faith and continually throw ourselves at His feet as lost and undone sinners. Feeding on past experiences will not satisfy the soul any more than yesterday's meal will sustain the body today. Believers must look for fresh influences of divine grace and ask the Lord to water them every moment.

This parable speaks to saints as well as sinners. Come again to the marriage feast. You are as welcome now as ever. May God make your soul long for the day when we will sit down and eat bread in the kingdom of heaven. There we shall drink deeply of divine love and enjoy our glorious Immanuel forever.

Even so, Lord Jesus.

Amen.

Chapter Twenty-Five

The Conversion of Zacchaeus

Luke 19:9–10 NKJV *"And Jesus said to him, 'Today salvation has come to this house, because he also is a son of Abraham; for the Son of Man has come to seek and to save that which was lost.'"*

Salvation is described throughout Scripture as the free gift of God through Jesus Christ our Lord. It is free because God is sovereign and may give mercy as He pleases. It is also free because there is nothing in man that can move God to save him. No person deserves mercy. No person earns grace. No person has anything in himself that can make God accept him.

The righteousness of Jesus Christ is the only reason sinners can find favor in the sight of God. This righteousness is received by faith, and even that faith is the gift of God. When faith is true, it does not remain alone. It works by love. It produces fruit. It changes the life.

These truths are part of the glad tidings of the gospel. Next to the plain Word of God, the experience of those who have been saved is one of the clearest proofs of them. God has recorded many examples of His saving grace in Scripture so that we may see how He deals with sinners and understand how we ourselves must be saved.

The conversion of Zacchaeus is one of those examples. If we rightly consider his story, it will help us understand the way of salvation. Zacchaeus was the man to whom Jesus said, "Today salvation has come to this house." Jesus also declared him to be a son of Abraham.

Let us look carefully at his conversion, and then let us take encouragement from the words of Christ: **Luke 19:10 NKJV**, *"For the Son of Man has come to seek and to save that which was lost."*

Luke begins the story by saying that Jesus entered and passed through Jericho. The Lord Jesus made it His business to go about doing good. As the sun shines over the natural world, giving light, warmth, and life, so the Sun of Righteousness went through the world bringing healing, mercy, and salvation.

In the previous chapter, Jesus had healed blind Bartimaeus. That was a great miracle. But in this chapter, an even greater miracle is set before us. The healing of a blind man's eyes was wonderful, but the conversion of a sinner's heart is greater still.

Luke calls special attention to this story by saying, "Behold." He wants us to stop and consider it carefully. He says there was a man named Zacchaeus, who was chief among the tax collectors, and he was rich.

This is remarkable because, by human judgment, there were many obstacles in the way of Zacchaeus being saved. There was no natural fitness in him for salvation. He was a tax collector, and tax collectors were often notorious sinners. They collected taxes for Rome and were infamous for greed, dishonesty, and extortion. Their very name was hated. The Pharisees often criticized Jesus because He was a friend of tax collectors and sinners.

Zacchaeus was not only a tax collector. He was chief among the tax collectors. So if tax collectors were sinners, he was likely chief among sinners. And not only that, he was rich. Scripture says that not many mighty and not many noble are called. It also says that God has chosen the poor of this world to be rich in faith. Jesus Himself said it is easier for a camel to go through the eye of a needle than for a rich man to enter the kingdom of God.

Therefore, let no rich person glory in riches. Riches are not a sign of salvation. They can often become a snare to the soul.

Yet, rich as he was, Zacchaeus sought to see Jesus. That alone is a wonder. The common people heard Jesus gladly. The poor received the gospel. The crowds often followed Him on foot into the countryside and sometimes remained with Him for days to hear Him preach. But did many rich people believe in Him? Did many of the great and powerful attend Him? Not usually.

Jesus preached the doctrine of the cross. His preaching was too searching for proud hearts. Because of this, many rich and respectable people treated Him as an enemy. They persecuted Him and spoke evil against Him falsely.

Therefore, ministers of Christ should not be surprised if they receive similar treatment from the rich and powerful in this present age. It should not be considered a disgrace if mostly the poor attend the preaching of the gospel. Their souls are as precious to Jesus Christ as the souls of the greatest people on earth. The poor followed Him in the days of His flesh. God has chosen many of them to be rich in faith and great in the kingdom of heaven.

If the rich and worldly always speak well of a preacher, that may be a dangerous sign. It may mean he is only preaching smooth things and saying, "Peace, peace," when there is no peace. God forbid that we should despise the poor. To despise them would be to reproach their Maker. The poor are dear to the heart of Christ. Blessed are those poor who receive the gospel and are transformed by it, for theirs is the kingdom of heaven.

But let us return to Zacchaeus. The Scripture says he sought to see Jesus. I wish I could say that he did this from a holy motive. But without violating charity, we may say that it seems curiosity first drew him. He did not come, as far as we are told, to hear Christ's teaching. He came to see who Jesus was.

The fame of Jesus had spread throughout Jerusalem and the surrounding region. Some said He was a good man. Others said He deceived the people. Zacchaeus had heard these different reports, and curiosity drew him out to see this Jesus for himself.

But he could not see Jesus because of the crowd, and because he was short. Many people are kept from seeing Christ because of the crowd. I do not mean only a physical crowd. Many are kept from Christ by the crowd of fashionable friends, worldly acquaintances, and social pressure. They are ashamed to be serious about God. They are afraid to stand alone. They follow the multitude to do evil because they cannot bear the thought of being mocked, rejected, or thought strange.

This fear of man is a deadly snare. It has ruined many souls. Many people are convinced that the gospel is true, but because they cannot bear contempt, they refuse to act on their convictions. They do not want to be thought too religious, too serious, or too different.

Happy are those who, like Zacchaeus, are resolved to overcome every obstacle that keeps them from seeing Christ. Zacchaeus did not give up because of the crowd or because he was short. He did not say, "It is useless. I cannot see Him." Instead, he ran ahead of the crowd and climbed into a sycamore tree, because Jesus was going to pass that way.

There is no seeing Christ in glory unless we are willing to run ahead of the crowd in holy seriousness. The broad way, where so many walk, can never be the narrow way that leads to life. Christ's flock has always been comparatively small. Unless we are willing to be among the despised few, unless we are willing to be counted fools for Christ's sake, we will never see Jesus with comfort when He appears in glory.

Zacchaeus also teaches us that those who desire to see Christ must be willing to endure difficulty. Climbing that tree was not easy, especially for a rich and respected man. No doubt people laughed at him. Some may have mocked him and said, "Look at rich Zacchaeus, forgetting his dignity, running with the crowd and climbing a tree just to see this preacher."

But Zacchaeus did not care. His curiosity was strong enough that he was willing to endure the shame. If he could only see Jesus, he was not concerned with what people said.

So it will be, and even more, with those who truly desire to see Jesus in heaven. They will go from strength to strength. They will break through difficulties. They will not be stopped by what men or devils say or do. May the Lord make us all like that, for His dear Son's sake.

At last, after taking pains and likely enduring contempt, Zacchaeus climbed the tree. There he sat, perhaps hidden among the leaves, waiting to see Jesus pass by.

But sing, O heavens, and rejoice, O earth. Praise and adore sovereign, electing, free, preventing love. Jesus, the everlasting God and Prince of Peace, who saw Nathanael under the fig tree and had known Zacchaeus from eternity, now saw him in the sycamore tree and called him in time.

Luke 19:5 NKJV says, *"And when Jesus came to the place, He looked up and saw him, and said to him, 'Zacchaeus, make haste and come down, for today I must stay at your house.'"*

Amazing love. No wonder Luke began the story with "Behold." It deserves our highest admiration. Zacchaeus was not expecting this. He did not think Jesus knew him. Yet Jesus looked up, saw him, and called him by name. Then Jesus did something we do not read of Him doing before or after in quite the same way. He invited Himself to Zacchaeus's house.

He did not say, "Please let Me stay at your house." He said, "Today I must stay at your house." He called him by name because He knew him. Zacchaeus's name was written in the book of life. He was one of those whom the Father had given to the Son from eternity. Therefore, Jesus said, "I must stay at your house." As Scripture teaches, those whom God predestines, He also calls.

Here we see the doctrine of free grace clearly displayed. There was no spiritual fitness in Zacchaeus. He was a tax collector, chief among tax collectors, rich, and he came to see Jesus only from curiosity. But sovereign grace triumphed over everything.

If God has truly worked in us, we must admit that there was no more fitness in us than there was in Zacchaeus. If Christ had not first called us, we would have remained dead in trespasses and sins, separated from the life of God like everyone else.

Now consider what Zacchaeus must have felt when Jesus spoke to him. Surely he was surprised. He may have thought, "Am I dreaming? How does He know me? I have never met Him before. And if I receive Him into my house, I will be mocked even more."

But Scripture says that in the day of God's power, His people are made willing. Along with the outward call of Jesus, there was an inward power from God that sweetly overcame Zacchaeus's natural will. So **Luke 19:6 NKJV** says, *"So he made haste and came down, and received Him joyfully."*

He received Jesus not only into his house, but also into his heart.

This is how God brings His children home. He calls them by name through His Word or providence. Then He speaks to them by His Spirit. Their hearts are opened, and they are made willing to receive the King of glory.

Because of Zacchaeus, we should not completely condemn people who come to hear the Word from no better motive than curiosity.

Who knows whether God may call them? It is good to be where the Lord is passing by. May every person who came only from curiosity hear the voice of the Son of God speaking to the soul and live.

This does not mean people should be encouraged to come from curiosity. Many came to see Christ from curiosity and were never savingly called. But this gives encouragement to the servants of God and to Christians who may be too harsh toward those who attend for imperfect reasons. Let them come. Pray for them. A few words from Christ, applied by the Spirit, can save their souls.

Zacchaeus came down and received Jesus joyfully. Scripture often tells us that people rejoice when they believe in Christ. The Ethiopian eunuch went on his way rejoicing. The jailer rejoiced with his whole household. Zacchaeus received Christ joyfully.

And well may those rejoice who receive Jesus Christ. With Him they receive righteousness, sanctification, and eternal redemption. Some people give religion a bad name and try to persuade others that it will make them miserable or gloomy. But this is false. Joy is part of the kingdom of God in the heart. **Romans 14:17 NKJV** says, *"For the kingdom of God is not eating and drinking, but righteousness and peace and joy in the Holy Spirit."*

To rejoice in the Lord is a gospel duty. Scripture says in **Philippians 4:4 NKJV**, *"Rejoice in the Lord always. Again I will say, rejoice!"* Who has more reason to rejoice than those who know their pardon is sealed before they leave this world?

The ungodly may laugh, but their laughter is hollow. In the middle of it there is heaviness. Their joy is like thorns crackling under a pot. It makes a quick blaze and then goes out. But the joy of the godly is solid and lasting. It is a joy that strangers do not understand and that no man can take away. It is joy in God, joy unspeakable and full of glory.

It seems that Zacchaeus may not have remained long in soul distress. Perhaps it lasted only a short time. Sometimes the Lord Jesus delights to deliver quickly. God is sovereign in the way He calls His children. Spiritual birth, like natural birth, does not come with the same experience for everyone. Not all believers have the same degree of conviction or the same length of struggle. But all true believers have Christ formed in their hearts.

Those who have fewer trials at first may have greater conflicts later, though they never return again to the spirit of bondage once they have received the Spirit of adoption. Paul says in **Romans 8:15 NKJV**, *"For you did not receive the spirit of bondage again to fear, but you received the Spirit of adoption."*

We do not know what Zacchaeus experienced before he died. But we know this: he believed in Christ and was justified, though he had been chief among tax collectors only moments before. So it is with all who receive Jesus Christ by faith into their hearts. The moment they rest in Him, they are freely justified from all things from which they could not be justified by the law of Moses. **Ephesians 2:8 NKJV** says, *"For by grace you have been saved through faith, and that not of yourselves; it is the gift of God."*

Do not say this is a loose or lawless doctrine. True faith works by love and produces the fruits of holiness. Zacchaeus is proof. As soon as he received Jesus Christ by faith, he showed it by his works.

Luke 19:8 NKJV says, *"Then Zacchaeus stood and said to the Lord, 'Look, Lord, I give half of my goods to the poor; and if I have taken anything from anyone by false accusation, I restore fourfold.'"*

Having believed in Jesus with his heart, Zacchaeus now confessed Him with his mouth. He stood openly before others. He was not ashamed. True faith casts out sinful fear of man.

He said, "Look, Lord." It is striking how quickly people in Scripture confessed the divine glory of Christ after conversion. The woman at Jacob's well said, "Could this be the Christ?" The man born blind said, "Lord, I believe," and worshiped Him. Zacchaeus said, "Look, Lord." This is strong evidence that those who truly feel the power of Christ will not speak lightly of Him. They will not deny His eternal power and Godhead.

Then Zacchaeus said that he would give half of his goods to the poor. This was noble fruit from a living faith. He did not offer a tiny portion. He gave half. He did not give what belonged to someone else. He gave his own goods. He did not say, "I will give when I die." He said, "I give." He became his own executor. While he had time, he would do good.

And to whom did he give? Not to the rich, not to those who could repay him, but to the poor. He gave to those who could not recompense him until the resurrection of the just.

But Zacchaeus also knew he must be just before he could be charitable. He was conscious that in his office he had wronged many. So he added, "If I have taken anything from anyone by false accusation, I restore fourfold."

Let every dishonest person hear this. If God gives you true faith, you will not rest until, as far as you are able, you have made restitution to those you have wronged. Before his conversion, Zacchaeus may have thought it was no great harm to cheat others. He may even have been pleased that he became rich that way. But now his heart was grieved. He confessed his injustice before men and promised full restitution.

If a person refuses to make restitution where he can, the Lord Jesus will one day make him confess his sins before men and angels and condemn him for them when He comes in the glory of His Father to judge.

After this, Jesus had good reason to say, **Luke 19:9 NKJV**, *"Today salvation has come to this house, because he also is a son of Abraham."* Zacchaeus was not merely a son of Abraham by natural descent. He was a son of Abraham spiritually. He had received the same precious faith. Like Abraham, he believed God, and it was accounted to him for righteousness. Like Abraham, his faith worked by love. I do not doubt that he has long since been resting with Abraham in glory.

Now, are you not ashamed if you speak against the doctrines of grace, especially the doctrine of justification by faith alone, as though it leads to careless living? What could be more unjust than such an accusation? Is not Zacchaeus enough proof to the contrary?

I affirm that we are saved by grace and justified by faith alone. But I also affirm that true faith will show itself by good works when there is opportunity to perform them.

What has been said about Zacchaeus may help us judge whether our faith is real. You say you have faith. But how do you prove it?

Have you ever heard the Lord Jesus call you by name? Have you been made willing to obey His call? Have you received Jesus Christ joyfully into your heart? Does your faith move you to confess the Lord Jesus before men? Have you been humbled for your past offenses? Does your faith work by love? Do you give according to how God has prospered you for the support of the poor? Have you made restitution to those you have wronged?

If so, happy are you. Salvation has come to your soul. You are sons and daughters of Abraham, and you will be forever blessed with faithful Abraham.

But if this is not your heart, do not deceive yourself. Though you may talk about justification by faith like an angel, it will do you no good. It will only increase your condemnation. If you hold the truth in unrighteousness, your faith is dead. You have the devil, not Abraham, for your father. Unless you receive a faith of the heart, a faith working by love, you will dwell with devils and lost spirits forever.

Now let us consider the latter part of the text: **Luke 19:10 NKJV**, *"For the Son of Man has come to seek and to save that which was lost."*

Jesus spoke these words in answer to self-righteous Pharisees. Instead of rejoicing with the angels in heaven over the conversion of a sinner, they murmured because Jesus had gone to be a guest with a sinful man. To defend His action, Jesus explained that this was exactly why He came: to seek and save the lost.

He could have called Himself the Son of God. But see the wonderful humility of our Redeemer. He delights to call Himself the Son of Man. He came not only to save, but to seek and to save that which was lost. He came to Jericho to seek and save Zacchaeus. If Christ had not sought him, Zacchaeus would never have been saved.

From where did Christ come? He came from heaven, His dwelling place, to this lower world, this valley of tears. He came to seek and save the lost. He came for all who feel themselves lost and are willing, like Zacchaeus, to receive Him into their hearts.

And what a salvation He gives. He saves from the guilt of sin and from the power of sin. He makes sinners heirs of God and joint heirs with Himself. He makes them partakers of the glory He had with the Father before the world began.

This is why the Son of Man came. He became man so that He might save the lost. He had no other purpose in leaving His Father's throne, obeying the moral law, and hanging on the cross. He did it all to satisfy divine justice and provide righteousness for poor, lost, undone sinners, without respect of persons.

He came to save the lost of every nation and language who feel and mourn over their lost condition and truly desire deliverance from it. He is mighty to save. He is also willing to save to the uttermost all who come to God through Him. He will by no means cast out those who come. He is the same today as He was yesterday.

He comes to sinners now as surely as He came to sinners then. I hope He has sent this message today to seek and bring home some lost sheep.

What will you say? Shall I go home rejoicing, saying that many who had gone astray have believed on Jesus Christ and returned to the Shepherd and Overseer of their souls? If the Lord would be pleased to bless this work, I would not care how many legalists and self-righteous Pharisees murmur against me for offering salvation to the worst sinners. I know the Son of Man came to seek and save them.

The Lord Jesus will be a guest to the worst tax collector and the vilest sinner among you, if you will believe on Him. Make haste, then, sinners. Make haste and come by faith to Christ. This day, this hour, this very moment, if you believe, Jesus Christ will come and make His eternal home in your heart.

Which of you is willing to receive the King of glory? Which of you will obey His call as Zacchaeus did? Why do you stand still? How do you know whether Jesus Christ will ever call you again?

Come, poor guilty sinners. Come, poor lost and undone souls. Make haste and come to Jesus Christ. The Lord condescends to invite Himself under the filthy roof of your soul. Do not be afraid to receive Him. He will fill you with peace and joy in believing.

Do not be ashamed to run ahead of the crowd. Do not be ashamed if people speak evil against you falsely for His sake. One sight of Christ will make up for all of it. Zacchaeus was likely laughed at, and all who live godly in Christ Jesus will suffer persecution. But what of that? Zacchaeus is now crowned in glory, and so will you be if you believe on Christ and are reproached for His sake.

Do not put me off with empty excuses. There is no excuse for not coming to Christ. You are lost and undone without Him. If He is not glorified in your salvation, He will be glorified in your destruction. If He does not come and make His home in your heart, you must make your eternal home with the devil and his angels.

O that the Lord would pass by some of you at this time. O that He would call you by His Spirit and make you a willing people in this day of His power. My call will not be enough unless He, by His effective grace, compels you to come in.

O that you once felt what it is to receive Jesus Christ into your heart. You would soon, like Zacchaeus, give Him everything.

You do not love Christ because you do not know Him. You do not come to Him because you do not feel your need of Him. You think you are whole and not brokenhearted. You are sick, but you do not feel your sickness. Therefore, you do not apply to Jesus Christ, the great and almighty Physician.

You do not feel lost, and therefore you do not seek to be found in Christ. O that God would wound you with the sword of His Spirit and send arrows of conviction deep into your heart. O that He would shine divine light into your soul. If you do not feel yourself lost without Christ, you are most miserable. Your soul is dead. You are not only an image of hell, but in some sense you carry hell within you, and you do not know it.

O that I could see some of you becoming aware of this and hear you cry, "Lord, break this hard heart. Lord, deliver me from this body of death. Draw me. Make me willing to come after You. I am lost. Lord, save me, or I perish."

If this were your cry, how quickly the Lord would stretch out His almighty hand and say, "Be of good cheer. It is I. Do not be afraid." What a wonderful calm would then fill your troubled soul. Your fellowship would be with the Father and with His Son. Your life would be hidden with Christ in God.

Some of you, I hope, have experienced this. You can say, "I was lost, but now I am found. I was dead, but now I am alive again. The Son of Man came and sought me in the day of His power, and He saved my sinful soul."

Do you regret coming to Christ? Has He not been a good Master? Is not His presence sweet to your soul? Has He not been faithful to His promise? Have you not found that even in doing and suffering for Him, there is a great present reward? I am persuaded you will answer yes.

Then, saints of God, recommend the love of Christ to others. Speak of Him. Tell others what great things the Lord has done for you. This may encourage them to come to Him. Who knows whether the Lord may make you fishers of men?

The story of Zacchaeus was recorded for this very purpose. No truly convicted soul should despair after seeing such an example of divine grace. What if you are a tax collector type of sinner? Zacchaeus was a tax collector. What if you are chief among sinners? Zacchaeus was chief among tax collectors. What if you are rich? Zacchaeus was rich too. Yet almighty grace made him more than conqueror over all these hindrances.

All things are possible with Jesus Christ. Nothing is too hard for Him. He is the Lord Almighty. Our mountains of sin must all fall before Him. On Him, God the Father has laid the iniquities of all who believe. In His own body, He bore them on the tree.

There, by faith, mourners in Zion may see the Savior hanging with arms stretched out. Hear Him speaking, as it were, to your soul: "Behold how I have loved you. Behold My hands and My feet. Look into My wounded side and see a heart flaming with love, love stronger than death. Come into My arms, sinners. Come wash your stained souls in My blood. Here is a fountain opened for all sin and uncleanness. See, guilty souls, the wrath of God abiding on you. Come quickly and hide yourselves in the wounds of Christ. I was wounded for your transgressions. I am dying that you may live forever. As Moses lifted up the serpent in the wilderness, so I am lifted up on a tree. I became a curse for you. The chastisement for your peace is upon Me. I was scourged, wounded, and crucified so that by My stripes you may be healed. Look to Me, trembling sinners, even to the ends of the earth. Look to Me by faith, and you shall be saved. I came to be obedient unto death so that I might save that which was lost."

What do you say to this, sinners? Suppose you saw the King of glory dying and speaking this way to you. Would you believe on Him? No, you would not, unless you believe on Him now. Though He died, He still speaks in the Scriptures. In effect, He says all of this in the words of the text: **Luke 19:10 NKJV**, *"For the Son of Man has come to seek and to save that which was lost."*

Do not keep crucifying the Lord of glory. Bring those rebels, your sins, which refuse to have Him reign over them, and bring them out to Him. Though you cannot slay them yourself, He will slay them for you. The power of His death and resurrection is as great now as it ever was.

Make haste, therefore. Make haste, publicans and sinners, and give the dear Lord Jesus your hearts, your whole hearts. If you refuse to listen to His call, remember that your condemnation will be just. I am free from the blood of you all. You must acquit both my Master and me at the terrible day of judgment.

O that you may know the things that belong to your everlasting peace before they are hidden from your eyes forever.

Let all who love the Lord Jesus Christ in sincerity say, Amen.

Chapter Twenty-Six

The Marriage at Cana

John 2:11 NKJV *"This beginning of signs Jesus did in Cana of Galilee, and manifested His glory; and His disciples believed in Him."*

The apostle John wrote his Gospel with a clear purpose. He wanted to show that Jesus Christ is truly the Son of God. Jesus is not merely a good teacher, a prophet, or a holy man. He is the eternal Word who was with God from the beginning and who is Himself God. John shows this through the words Jesus spoke, the works Jesus performed, and the glory Jesus revealed.

John is especially careful to record the miracles of Christ. These miracles were not done by power borrowed from another, as the prophets did miracles by the power of God. Jesus performed miracles by His own divine authority. His works revealed who He truly was.

The verse before us speaks of the first public miracle Jesus performed. At a wedding in Cana of Galilee, He turned water into wine.

By this miracle, He manifested His glory, and His disciples believed in Him.

With God's help, let us consider the circumstances of this miracle, the certainty of it, and the spiritual lessons it teaches. May the same Jesus who revealed His glory at Cana reveal His glory in our hearts, so that we, like His disciples, may believe in Him.

John begins by telling us that on the third day there was a wedding in Cana of Galilee, and the mother of Jesus was there. Jesus and His disciples were also invited to the wedding.

From this we learn that feasting on special occasions is not in itself sinful. Jesus attended a wedding feast. However, we must be very careful about the way we attend such gatherings. We should not go merely for eating, drinking, pleasure, or vain conversation. We should go with a desire to honor God, encourage others, and do good. If we eat and drink without any regard for the glory of God, then even lawful things become sinful to us.

The Son of Man came eating and drinking. When a Pharisee invited Him to his house, Jesus went and sat down with him. But when Jesus was in such settings, His conversation was always useful and edifying. He did not waste His words. He spoke truth. He instructed. He corrected. He used ordinary moments for spiritual good. We may go and do likewise.

We also learn from Jesus' presence at the wedding that marriage is honorable. To forbid marriage to certain people as though it were unholy is a false and dangerous teaching. Scripture says in **Hebrews 13:4 NKJV**, *"Marriage is honorable among all."* Marriage was instituted by God in paradise before sin entered the world. Jesus honored marriage by attending a wedding and performing His first miracle there.

This also helps us understand why there are so many unhappy marriages in the world. Many people do not invite Christ into their marriage. They do not seek Him in prayer. They do not ask wisdom from His Word. They do not seek godly counsel from true disciples of Jesus. Instead, Christ and religion are often the last things considered.

Many marriages are made only because of outward beauty, money, status, attraction, or selfish desire. No wonder such marriages often become painful and burdensome. If a marriage is formed without regard to Christ, it should not surprise us when it lacks the peace, grace, and blessing that only Christ can give.

This is especially important for young Christians. The devil lays a great snare before them when he tempts them to be unequally yoked with unbelievers. An unbeliever is not simply someone with no religion at all, but anyone who has not been born again by the Spirit of God.

This was one of the great sins before the flood. The sons of God saw that the daughters of men were beautiful, and they took wives for themselves according to their own desire, not according to the will of God. Soon the world was filled with corruption, and judgment came. In the same way, Esau showed rebellion when he married women from the Canaanites, strangers to the covenant promises.

Therefore, whenever you enter marriage, imitate the people of Cana. Call Christ to the wedding. Seek His will. Ask Him to guide your choice. He knows what is best. His choice will always be better than yours. He can give you a spouse who will be a true help in the work of salvation, and He can enable you to serve Him without distraction, walking in His commandments and ordinances.

We are not told exactly who the bride and groom were. Some have thought they were related to Mary, since she was there and seemed concerned about the needs of the feast. Whoever they were, it seems they were not wealthy. They ran out of wine, which suggests they did not have enough provision for such a gathering.

When the wine failed, the mother of Jesus said to Him, "They have no wine." It seems Mary had already seen enough of Jesus in His private life to know something of His miraculous power. She simply told Him the need. She knew He was as ready to give as she was to ask.

At first, Mary's request may seem innocent. But Jesus' answer shows that there was something in it He needed to correct. He said in **John 2:4 NKJV**, *"Woman, what does your concern have to do with Me? My hour has not yet come."*

Notice that He called her "Woman," not "Mother." He did this to show that although she was His mother according to His human nature, she was still His creature according to His divine nature. She had no authority over Him as the Son of God. He was not bound to perform miracles at her command.

This also shows how wrong it is to treat Mary as though she can command her Son to show mercy. If Jesus would not turn water into wine merely at her command while He was on earth, how wrong it is to pray to her as though she could command Him from heaven. Christ alone is the Mediator. We come to the Father through Him.

Yet even though Mary needed correction, she gives us an example in another way. She noticed the need of others and brought it to Jesus. Those who are rich should learn from her. Go into the homes of the poor. See their needs. Your Lord was not above entering humble places. Why should you be? When you see that they lack what is necessary, do not shut up your heart against them. Thank God that He has given you enough and more than enough, and use what you have to help those in need.

Such visits would do your soul good. They would make you more thankful for the blessings God has given you. And every small gift given to feed the hungry and clothe the naked disciples of Jesus will bring you more comfort at death and at judgment than all the money wasted on vain entertainments.

Those who are poor and cannot give much in material help can still learn from Mary. You may pray for one another. Mary could not turn the water into wine, but she could bring the need to Christ. So can you. Pray for your fellow believers. Pray for the poor. Pray for the needy. Pray for ministers of the gospel. God has chosen many of the poor of this world to be rich in faith. Your prayers may draw down many blessings.

Though Jesus corrected Mary, He did not reject the need. He said, "My hour has not yet come." In other words, the wine was almost gone, but not quite. When the people came to the point of need, when they truly felt their lack, then He would reveal His glory.

This is often how the Lord deals with His people. Sometimes His presence seems hidden. Sometimes His comforts seem almost gone. We go to Him and say, "Lord, I have no fresh token of Your love. I do not feel Your nearness as before." At times He may seem silent. It may feel as though He says, "What does your concern have to do with Me?" Then we walk sorrowing, foolish and slow to believe.

Yet He loves us still. He loved Lazarus even though He waited two days after hearing he was sick. When our hour of extremity comes, when our will is broken and our need is clear, He often lifts up the light of His countenance again. He reveals His glory. He turns our water into wine. He makes us ashamed that we ever doubted Him.

Do not be discouraged, then, if the Lord does not immediately seem to answer your prayer. Mary was not discouraged. She believed His time was best. So she said to the servants in **John 2:5 NKJV**, *"Whatever He says to you, do it."*

That is advice for every believer. Whatever Jesus says, do it. Do not argue. Do not delay. Do not adjust His command to fit your comfort. Obey Him.

Now the hour had come for the eternal Son of God to reveal His glory. There were six waterpots of stone nearby, used for the Jewish custom of purification. Each could hold a large amount of water. The Jews had many washing customs. They washed their hands often before eating and after coming from the marketplace. Much of this had become superstitious. Yet we may learn a spiritual lesson from it. Whenever we return from being among the people of the world, we should examine our hearts and pray to be cleansed. It is difficult to pass through the world and remain unspotted by it.

Jesus told the servants, "Fill the waterpots with water." They obeyed and filled them to the brim. Then He said, "Draw some out now, and take it to the master of the feast." They took it.

We are not told exactly how Jesus turned the water into wine. We do not need to know. We should not try to be wise beyond what is written. It is enough to know that He did it. The miracle itself is the proof of His divine power.

When the master of the feast tasted the water that had been made wine, he did not know where it came from, though the servants knew. He called the bridegroom and said in **John 2:10 NKJV**, *"Every man at the beginning sets out the good wine, and when the guests have well drunk, then the inferior. You have kept the good wine until now!"*

In those days, it was customary at public feasts to appoint a governor or master of the feast. His job was to oversee the meal and make sure everything was done decently and in order. The servants brought the wine to him, and his words show how excellent it was.

Here, then, we see the outward miracle. Jesus turned water into wine. He did this publicly enough for the servants to know it, and clearly enough for the master of the feast to testify that the wine was good. By this, He manifested His glory, and His disciples believed in Him.

But we must not stop at the outward miracle. There are deeper spiritual lessons here. If we only look at the outside of this miracle, we have seen only the outer court. If God removes the veil from our eyes, we will see truths here that can make our hearts rejoice and our mouths praise Him forever.

Before we move further, however, we must reject a wrong use of this miracle. Some have used this passage to justify excess, indulgence, and worldly pleasure. They argue that because Jesus made wine at a wedding, even after the guests had already been drinking, He must have approved of pleasure and indulgence beyond what is necessary.

This is a dangerous and dishonoring thought. It is true that Jesus came eating and drinking. It is true that He attended a wedding. It is true that He made wine. But it is not true that the guests had been drinking to excess. The master of the feast spoke generally about what men commonly do at feasts. He did not say these particular guests were drunk or overindulging.

Can we imagine the holy Lamb of God, who came to destroy the works of the devil, encouraging drunkenness or excess? Can we imagine Jesus, who told His disciples to deny themselves and take up their cross daily, making more wine so that people could continue in indulgence? Can we imagine Jesus, who warned against hearts being weighed down with drunkenness, helping people become more sinful?

To suggest this is to make Christ a minister of sin. It is to treat Him like the Pharisees did when they called Him a glutton and a winebibber. God forbid that we think this way of our Lord. Jesus had a far higher purpose in this miracle.

First, He did this miracle to show His glory. John says plainly in **John 2:11 NKJV**, *"This beginning of signs Jesus did in Cana of Galilee, and manifested His glory; and His disciples believed in Him."*

There may be an allusion here to the glory of God appearing in the tabernacle. John had already said in his Gospel that the Word became flesh and dwelt, or tabernacled, among us. Jesus, though very God of very God, veiled His glory in human flesh when He came to make His soul an offering for sin. But through His miracles, He gave glimpses of that glory so people might believe in Him as Savior.

Second, Jesus may have performed this miracle to reward those who invited Him and His disciples to the wedding. Jesus will never be behindhand with those who receive Him or His followers for His name's sake. Those who honor Him, He will honor. Even a cup of cold water given in the name of a disciple will not lose its reward.

Those who give to the poor and serve Christ's people out of faith and love may seem to cast their bread upon the waters, but they will find it again after many days. Those who give to the poor lend to the Lord, and He will repay. Even in this life, God often returns blessing in good measure, pressed down and running over.

The same is true spiritually. To the one who has and faithfully uses what he has for Christ, more will be given. Those willing to spend and be spent for Christ and His disciples will find that He enriches their souls. The Lord often feeds the soul of the one who feeds others with the bread of life.

Third, the turning of water into wine may point to the abundant pouring out of the Holy Spirit into the hearts of believers. In Scripture, the Spirit is sometimes compared to wine because He fills, strengthens, and gladdens the soul. The prophet calls thirsty souls to buy wine and milk without money and without price. Paul says in **Ephesians 5:18 NKJV**, *"And do not be drunk with wine, in which is dissipation; but be filled with the Spirit."*

Natural people do not understand this language. Spiritual truths are spiritually discerned. But those who are justified by faith and know the work of the Spirit in their hearts understand. They know what it means to be filled, as it were, with new wine by the inspiration of the Holy Spirit.

Yet even what believers experience now is only a foretaste. Christ keeps the best wine until the last. He will give more. He will not leave His people until they are filled to the brim. Do not be narrow in your own heart, because Christ is not narrow in His. Open your heart wide by faith, and the Spirit of the Lord will fill it.

Our hearts are like empty vessels. As long as we bring them to Christ by faith, the oil of gladness, the love of God through Christ, will continue to be poured in. Believers are to be filled with all the fullness of God.

Fourth, the turning of water into wine and the keeping of the best wine until last may point to the future glory of Christ's church. God has already done great things, and many saints have rejoiced in them. God is doing great things now. But we shall yet see greater things than these.

Many righteous people desired to see what we see and hear what we hear but did not. Still, greater days are coming. Scripture speaks glorious things of the time when the earth will be filled with the knowledge of the Lord as the waters cover the sea. There is a holy expectation among God's people for the day when the dividing wall between Jew and Gentile will be fully broken down and all Israel will be saved.

Happy are those who live to see such days. Then Satan will fall like lightning from heaven. Then the people of God will not weep as the Jews did when they saw the second temple, but will rejoice with exceeding great joy. The former glory of the Christian church will seem small compared with the glory that shall be revealed. Then the people of God will say with the master of the feast, "You have kept the good wine until now."

Fifth, this miracle points us to the blessed state when all the redeemed will sit together at the marriage supper of the Lamb and drink the new wine in Christ's eternal kingdom.

The rewards Christ gives His faithful servants and the comforts of His love on earth are often so great that, if He had not promised more, it would almost seem presumptuous to hope for greater blessings hereafter. But all the manifestations of God we enjoy here are only a drop compared with the boundless ocean of glory to come.

Christ often fills His saints even to the brim. Yet our corruptible bodies still weigh down our souls and make us cry out with Paul, "Who will deliver me from this body of death?" These earthly tabernacles cannot hold the fullness of glory. But blessed be God, these earthly tabernacles will one day be dissolved. This corruptible will put on incorruption. This mortal will put on immortality.

Then, when God causes His glory to pass before us, we will say, "Lord, You have kept the good wine until now." We have tasted Your Spirit. We have heard glorious things about Your city. But now we see that not even the thousandth part had been told us.

Eye has not seen, ear has not heard, nor has it entered into the heart of man what Christ will reveal there. Paul was caught up into the third heaven and heard things too wonderful for human speech. No wonder he could give us so little description of it. He saw and heard things that a person in flesh and blood cannot fully express.

Even speaking of these things can almost carry the heart beyond itself. It gives a foretaste of that new wine which the saints will drink with Christ forever in His heavenly kingdom.

Why have I spoken these things? Some may say it is to show my own pride. But it is a small thing to be judged by man's judgment. The Lord is the One who judges me. He knows that I speak of this miracle for the same purpose for which Jesus first performed it: to show forth His glory, so that you may believe in Him.

If I came to preach myself rather than Christ Jesus the Lord, I would come with enticing words of human wisdom. If my desire were to please natural men, I would not need to preach plainly or in uncomfortable places. My aim is to do what every true gospel minister should do: point you to the God-man, Christ Jesus.

Behold, then, by faith, the Lamb of God who takes away the sin of the world. Look to Him and be saved. You have heard how He manifested His glory and how He will yet manifest His glory to true believers. Why then, sinners, will you not believe in Him?

Now I speak to sinners. May God give you hearing ears and obedient hearts.

The Lord Jesus, who showed His glory at Cana, has made a marriage feast. He offers to unite sinners to Himself. He is willing to make them flesh of His flesh and bone of His bone. He is willing to join them to Himself by one Spirit.

In every age, in different ways and at different times, He has sent His servants to invite many. Yet still there is room. The Lord has sent His servants to compel poor sinners by the cords of love to come in.

His house must and shall be filled. He will not shed His precious blood in vain.

Come, then. Come to the marriage. Let this be the day of your union with Jesus Christ. He is willing to receive you, even though other lords have ruled over you. Come to the marriage. The oxen and fatted cattle are prepared. All things are ready. May I hear you say, as Rebekah said when asked whether she would go to Isaac, "I will go."

You will not regret it. The Lord will turn your water into wine. He will fill your soul with richness and joy, and cause you to praise Him with joyful lips.

Do not say, "I am miserable, poor, blind, and naked, and therefore I am ashamed to come." That is no reason to stay away. In fact, the invitation is sent to such people. The rich, busy, self-righteous people of this generation have already been invited, but many have rejected the counsel of God against themselves. One goes to his country house. Another to his business. Another is married to the pleasures and vanities of this wicked world. With one consent, they make excuses.

But do not follow them. Since the Lord condescends to call first, because if left to yourself you would never call after Him, answer Him as He answered for you when divine justice called Him to die for your sins: "Behold, I come to do Your will, O God."

What if you are miserable, poor, blind, and naked? That is no excuse. Faith is the only wedding garment Christ requires. He does not call you because you are already saints. He calls you because He intends to make you saints. He pities your nakedness. He wants to cover you with His righteousness.

In short, He desires to show His glory, the glory of His free love, through your faith in Him. He will be glorified whether you believe or not. His free love remains infinitely glorious either way. But He will not always send His servants to call you in vain. The time will come when He will say that those who were invited and would not come shall not taste His supper.

The Lord is a God of justice as well as love. If sinners will not take hold of His golden scepter, He will bruise them with His iron rod. It is for your sake, sinners, not His own, that He condescends to invite you. Let Him show forth His glory in you, even the glory of the exceeding riches of His grace, by believing on Him.

We are saved by grace through faith. It was grace, free grace, that moved the Father to love the world and give His only begotten Son, that whoever believes in Him should not perish but have everlasting life. It was grace that made the Son come down and die. It was grace that moved the Holy Spirit to sanctify the elect people of God. It was grace that moved the Lord Jesus to send His ministers to call poor sinners.

Do not let this invitation come to nothing. Why will you not believe in Him? Will the devil do for you what Christ will do? No. The devil may give you a little sinful pleasure at first, but what will he give you at the end? A cup of fury and trembling. A never-dying worm. A self-condemning conscience. The bitter pains of eternal death.

But Christ does not deal this way with His servants. He keeps the best wine until last. Though He may lead you through affliction on the way to heaven, He sweetens the cup with a sense of His goodness and makes even suffering useful to the soul.

I appeal to every saint here: Has Christ not been faithful since you were joined to Him? Has He not shown His glory since you first believed on Him?

And now, sinners, what objection do you have? If you will not be drawn by the cords of infinite and everlasting love, what will draw you? I could speak to you of the terrors of the Lord. But if the love of Jesus Christ will not constrain you, your case is desperate.

Remember this day: you were invited, even the worst of sinners, to be joined to the Lord Jesus. If you perish, you will not perish because no invitation was given. You yourselves will stand forth at the last day, and I summon you now to meet me at the judgment seat of Christ and clear both my Master and me.

If tears would prevail with you, I could wish my head were waters and my eyes fountains of tears, so I might weep out every argument and melt you into love. If anything I could do or suffer would influence your hearts, I think I could bear to lose my eyes or even lay down my life for your sake. If persistence alone could prevail, I could continue pleading until midnight and wrestle with you until morning as Jacob wrestled with the angel.

But this power belongs only to the Lord. I can invite. He alone can work in you both to will and to do according to His good pleasure. He alone can take away the heart of stone and give you a heart of flesh. His Spirit must convince you of unbelief and of the everlasting righteousness of His dear Son. He alone must give you faith to apply that righteousness to your heart. He alone can give you the wedding garment and bring you to sit down and drink new wine in His kingdom.

Spiritually, we are dead. We have no more power to turn ourselves to God than Lazarus had to raise himself after four days in the grave. If you could breathe on dry bones and make them live, or divide a river with your mantle as Elijah did, then perhaps you could claim power to turn to God by yourself. But as you must despair of those things, so you must despair of turning yourself to God without Christ's quickening grace.

Your only help is in Him. Fly to Him by faith. Say to Him as the leper did, "Lord, if You are willing, You can make me clean." Say, "Lord, if You are willing, You can make me willing." He will stretch forth the right hand of His power to help and relieve you. He will guide you by His wisdom on earth and afterward receive you into His glory in heaven.

To His mercy and almighty protection, I now earnestly, humbly, and affectionately commit you. May the Lord bless you and keep you. May the Lord lift up the light of His blessed countenance upon you and give you all peace and joy in believing, now and forever.

Amen.

Chapter Twenty-Seven

Persecution: Every Christian's Lot

When our Lord took upon Himself the form of a servant and went about preaching the kingdom of God, He often warned His disciples not to seek great things for themselves. He also warned them ahead of time that they should expect many troubles, afflictions, and persecutions for His name's sake.

The apostle Paul followed the steps of his blessed Master in this, as he did in all things. In this letter, he warned young Timothy about the difficulties he would face in the work of ministry. Paul told him that in the last days perilous times would come. People would be lovers of themselves, covetous, proud, blasphemers, disobedient to parents, unthankful, unholy, without natural affection, unforgiving, false accusers, without self-control, fierce, despisers of good, traitors, headstrong, high-minded, and lovers of pleasure rather than lovers of God. They would have a form of godliness, but deny its power. From such people, Timothy was to turn away.

Paul said these kinds of people would creep into houses and lead captive foolish people who were weighed down with sins and carried away by different lusts. They would always be learning, but never able to come to the knowledge of the truth. Then Paul compared them to Jannes and Jambres, the Egyptian magicians who resisted Moses. In the same way, these false teachers resisted the truth. Though they kept an outward form of religion, they were corrupt in mind and rejected concerning the faith.

But Paul did not want Timothy to sink under their opposition. So he reminded him that God may allow false teachers to oppose the truth for a season, but they will not succeed forever. Their folly will be made clear to all, just as the folly of the magicians was made clear when they could not stand before Moses.

Then, to encourage Timothy even more, Paul pointed to his own example. Timothy had fully known Paul's doctrine, manner of life, purpose, faith, patience, love, perseverance, persecutions, and afflictions. He knew what happened to Paul at Antioch, Iconium, and Lystra. He knew what persecutions Paul endured, and how the Lord delivered him out of them all. But Paul did not want Timothy to think this was only Paul's particular case. So he added the words of the text: **2 Timothy 3:12 NKJV**, *"Yes, and all who desire to live godly in Christ Jesus will suffer persecution."*

These words contain an important truth: persecution is the common lot of every godly person. This is a hard saying, and few are willing to receive it. But with God's help, we will consider it carefully. First, we will look at what it means to live godly in Christ Jesus. Second, we will consider the different kinds of persecution that godly people face. Third, we will see why godly people must expect persecution. Then we will apply the whole matter to our own hearts.

To live godly in Christ Jesus means first that we have been made the righteousness of God in Christ. It means we have been born again. It means we are one with Christ by a living faith and a vital union, even as Jesus Christ and the Father are one. Unless we are converted and transformed by the renewing of our minds, we cannot properly be said to be in Christ. Much less can we be said to live godly in Him.

To be in Christ merely by baptism and outward profession is not to be in Him in the fullest and strictest sense. Scripture says in **2 Corinthians 5:17 NKJV**, *"Therefore, if anyone is in Christ, he is a new creation."* Those who are truly in Christ are new creatures. Old things have passed away. All things have become new in their hearts.

Their life is hidden with Christ in God. Their souls daily feed on the invisible realities of another world. To live godly in Christ means to make the will of God, and not our own will, the ruling principle of all our thoughts, words, and actions. It means that whether we eat or drink, or whatever we do, we do all to the glory of God.

Those who live godly in Christ may not so much be said to live as Christ lives in them. He is their Alpha and Omega, their first and last, their beginning and end. They are led by His Spirit as a child is led by the hand of his father. They are willing to follow the Lamb wherever He leads them. They hear, know, and obey His voice. Their affections are set on things above. Their hopes are full of immortality. Their citizenship is in heaven.

Because they are born again of God, they habitually live to God and walk daily with God. They are pure in heart. From a principle of faith in Christ, they seek to be holy in all manner of conduct and godliness.

This is what it means to live godly in Christ Jesus. From this, we may easily understand why so few suffer persecution. It is because so few truly live godly in Christ Jesus. You may live formally in Christ, attending outward duties. You may live morally in Christ, doing no one harm, as people say, and still avoid persecution. But those who will live godly in Christ Jesus shall suffer persecution.

Now let us consider what persecution means and the different kinds of persecution there are.

The word persecution means to pursue, and it usually means pursuing or opposing a person because of his goodness or because of God's favor upon him.

The first kind of persecution is persecution in the heart. We have an early example of this in wicked Cain. Because the Lord accepted Abel and his offering, but did not accept Cain and his offering, Cain became angry. His countenance fell, and at last he cruelly murdered his brother.

In the same way, the Pharisees hated and persecuted our Lord in their hearts long before they laid hands on Him. Jesus also mentioned being hated by men as one kind of persecution His disciples would suffer.

This inward hatred is the root of all other persecution. In some measure, it is found in every unregenerate heart. Many people are guilty of this kind of persecution even though they never have the power or opportunity to persecute in any other way. In fact, many would practice every other kind of persecution if persecution had not become hateful in the eyes of mankind, and if they were not afraid of losing their reputation.

How many people will be exposed at the great day, though we do not know them now. It will be revealed that throughout their lives they secretly held evil will against Zion. They may hide it before men now, but God sees the enmity of their hearts, and He will judge them as persecutors at the great and terrible day of judgment.

The second kind of persecution is persecution of the tongue. Jesus said that out of the abundance of the heart the mouth speaks. Many people think it is no great harm to shoot arrows, even bitter words, against the disciples of the Lord. They scatter their firebrands, arrows, and death, and then say, "Are we not joking?" But however lightly they think of it, evil speaking is, in God's account, a serious form of persecution.

Ishmael's mocking of Isaac is called persecution. Jesus said in **Matthew 5:11 NKJV**, *"Blessed are you when they revile and persecute you, and say all kinds of evil against you falsely for My sake."* From this, we may gather that reviling and speaking evil of Christ's people for His sake is a high degree of persecution.

A good name, Scripture says, is better than precious ointment. To many people, it is dearer than life itself. Slandering anyone is a great breach of God's commandment. But to slander the disciples of Christ merely because they are His disciples is especially provoking in the sight of God.

Those who are guilty of such speech, unless they repent, will find that Jesus Christ will call them to account. He will punish them for all their ungodly and harsh speeches, and their portion will be the lake of fire and brimstone.

The third and last kind of persecution is persecution by actions. This includes when wicked people separate the children of God from their company. Jesus said in **Luke 6:22 NKJV**, *"Blessed are you when men hate you, and when they exclude you."*

It also includes when people expose believers to religious censure. Jesus said His followers would be put out of the synagogues. It includes threatening believers and forbidding them to openly profess Christ or worship Him. It includes forbidding ministers to preach the Word, just as the high priests threatened the apostles and commanded them not to speak any more in the name of Jesus. It includes calling believers before courts, fining them, imprisoning them, confiscating their goods, scourging them, and even putting them to death.

It would be impossible to list all the shapes persecution has taken. It is a many-headed monster, cruel as the grave and insatiable as hell. What makes it worse is that it often appears under the cloak of religion. But however cruel, insatiable, and horrible it is, those who live godly in Christ Jesus must expect to face it in its various forms.

Now we must ask why godly people must expect to suffer persecution.

First, this is clear from the whole teaching of our Lord.

In the Sermon on the Mount, Jesus said in **Matthew 5:10 NKJV**, *"Blessed are those who are persecuted for righteousness' sake, for theirs is the kingdom of heaven."* If our Lord spoke truth, then we are not so blessed as to have an interest in the kingdom of heaven unless we are, or have been, persecuted for righteousness' sake.

It is remarkable that our Lord used several verses for this beatitude, while He used only one for most of the others. He did this not only because people are naturally unwilling to believe this truth, but also because persecution is a necessary consequence of being a Christian.

This is also clear from the passages where Jesus tells us that He did not come to bring peace on earth, but a sword. He said that family members would be divided against one another, and that a man's enemies would be those of his own household. Some false prophets try to confine these words only to the first age of the church. But I am persuaded that they will be verified in the experience of true Christians in every age.

It would take too long to recount all the places where Jesus warned His disciples that they would be brought before rulers, cast out of synagogues, and that the time would come when men would think they were serving God by killing them. For this reason, Jesus often declared that unless a person forsakes all he has, and even hates his own life in comparison with Christ, he cannot be His disciple.

It is also worth noticing that when Jesus gave that remarkable promise to those who leave all for Him, He carefully included persecution. He said in **Mark 10:29–30 NKJV**, *"There is no one who has left house or brothers or sisters or father or mother or wife or children or lands, for My sake and the gospel's, who shall not receive a hundredfold now in this time... with persecutions, and in the age to come, eternal life."*

He that has ears to hear, let him hear what Christ says in all these passages. Then let him confess that all who live godly in Christ Jesus shall suffer persecution.

This truth is also evident from our Lord's life. Follow Him from the manger to the cross, and see whether any persecution was like what the Son of God, the Lord of glory, suffered while He was on earth. How He was hated by wicked men. How often their hatred would have made them seize Him, if they had not feared the people. How He was reviled. He was called a blasphemer, a winebibber, a Samaritan, and even possessed by a devil. In one word, all kinds of evil were spoken against Him falsely.

What contradiction of sinners He endured against Himself. How people separated themselves from His company and were ashamed to walk openly with Him. At one point, He even said to His own disciples, **John 6:67 NKJV**, *"Do you also want to go away?"*

He was threatened with stones. He was pushed out of synagogues. He was accused of deceiving the people, of being seditious, of being an enemy of Caesar. He was scourged, blindfolded, spit upon, condemned, and nailed to an accursed tree.

Thus the Master was persecuted. Thus the Lord suffered. The servant is not above his Master, nor the disciple above his Lord. Jesus said in **John 15:20 NKJV**, *"If they persecuted Me, they will also persecute you."* In all these things, our Lord has set us an example, that we should follow His steps. Therefore, far be it from anyone who lives godly in Christ Jesus to expect to escape persecution.

Not only the example of Christ, but the example of all the saints also proves Paul's words. How soon was Abel made a martyr for his faith? How was Isaac mocked by the son of the bondwoman? What a large catalogue of suffering Old Testament saints is recorded in Hebrews 11.

Read the book of Acts and see how the first Christians were threatened, stoned, imprisoned, scourged, and persecuted even to death. Examine church history after the apostles, and you will find that Herod's murder of the innocent children was only an early sign of the innocent blood that would later be shed for the sake of Jesus. Examine the experience of saints now living on earth. And if it were possible to speak with the spirits of just men made perfect, I am persuaded they would all agree with the apostle: **2 Timothy 3:12 NKJV**, *"Yes, and all who desire to live godly in Christ Jesus will suffer persecution."*

How could it be otherwise? Since the fall, there has been irreconcilable enmity between the seed of the woman and the seed of the serpent. Wicked men hate God, and therefore they cannot help hating those who are like Him. They hate to be reformed, and therefore they hate and persecute those whose opposite behavior testifies that their deeds are evil.

Pride of heart also leads men to persecute the servants of Jesus Christ. If they commend godly people, they fear being asked, "Why do you not follow them?" And because they dare not imitate them, even when they are forced to approve their way, pride and envy make them turn persecutors.

So it was before, so it is now, and so it will be until the end of time. He who is born according to the flesh will persecute him who is born according to the Spirit. Because Christians are not of the world, but

Christ has chosen them out of the world, therefore the world will hate them.

Some may object and say that we now live in a Christian world, and therefore should not expect persecution as in former days. I answer that not all are Christians who are called Christians. Until the heart is changed, enmity against God remains. And because that enmity is the root of all persecution, false Christians will persecute true Christians just as others do.

I said earlier that Paul especially warned Timothy about those who had a form of religion. As our Lord and His apostles were mostly persecuted by their own countrymen, the Jews, so we must expect similar treatment from the formalists of our own nation, the Pharisees who appear religious.

The most horrible and barbarous persecutions have often been carried out by those who called themselves Christians. Think of the days of Queen Mary. Think of the fines, banishments, and imprisonments of the children of God in the last century. Think also of the bitter and irreconcilable hatred that appears in many who call themselves Christians even in our own day.

Those who argue against this doctrine are not aware enough of the bitter enmity in every unregenerate heart against God. For my own part, I am so far from wondering that Christians are persecuted that I wonder our streets do not run with the blood of the saints. If men had power equal to their wills, such a horrible sight would soon appear.

Persecution is also necessary for the godly themselves. If we never have all kinds of evil spoken against us, how can we know whether we seek only the honor that comes from above? If we have no persecutors, how can our passive graces be exercised? How can many Christian commands be practiced? How can we love, pray for, and do good to those who mistreat us? How can we overcome evil with good? In short, how can we know that we love God better than life itself?

Paul understood all this. Therefore he speaks positively and clearly: **2 Timothy 3:12 NKJV**, *"Yes, and all who desire to live godly in Christ Jesus will suffer persecution."*

This does not mean all Christians are persecuted to the same degree. That would be contrary to Scripture and experience. Not all Christians are actually called to suffer every kind of persecution. Yet all Christians are liable to it. Some may live in more peaceful times of the church than others. Still, Christians in every age will find by experience that, whether they act in private or public, they must in some degree suffer persecution.

Now let us apply this truth.

First, every person should stop and examine himself. From what has been said, you have one mark by which you may judge whether you are truly a Christian. Have you ever been persecuted for righteousness' sake? If not, you have not yet lived godly in Christ our Lord. Whatever you may say to the contrary, the inspired apostle plainly says that all who live godly in Christ Jesus shall suffer persecution.

This does not mean that everyone who is persecuted is a true Christian. Some suffer for reasons other than righteousness. The real question is this: Have you ever been persecuted for living godly?

You may boast of your prudence and wisdom, and indeed prudence and wisdom are excellent things. You may glory that you have not gone too far, that you have not made yourself so unusual, or exposed yourself to contempt like others have. But alas, this is not necessarily a mark of Christianity. It may be a mark of a Laodicean spirit, neither hot nor cold, fit only to be spit out of the mouth of God.

What you call prudence may often be cowardice, hypocrisy, and pride of heart. You may dread contempt. You may be afraid to give up your reputation for God. You may be ashamed of Christ and His gospel. And if Christ were to appear again on earth, you might deny Him in words as well as works.

Awake, therefore, all of you who live only formally in Christ Jesus. No longer seek the honor that comes from man. I do not wish to flatter you. I urge you to live godly and not fear contempt for the sake of Jesus Christ. Ask God to give you His Holy Spirit so that you may see through the hidden hypocrisy of your hearts and no longer deceive your own souls.

Remember, you cannot reconcile God and mammon. You cannot join the friendship of the world with the favor of God. Scripture says in **James 4:4 NKJV**, *"Do you not know that friendship with the world is enmity with God?"* If you are in friendship with the world, despite all your religious appearances, you are at enmity with God. You are heart-hypocrites. And what is the hope of the hypocrite when God takes away his soul?

Let the words of the text sound like an alarm in your ears. Let them sink deep into your hearts: **2 Timothy 3:12 NKJV**, *"Yes, and all who desire to live godly in Christ Jesus will suffer persecution."*

Second, these words speak to those who are preparing to enlist under the banner of Christ's cross.

What do you say? Are you resolved to live godly in Christ Jesus, even though the result will be persecution? You are beginning to build, but have you taken our Lord's advice to sit down first and count the cost?

Have you seriously considered His weighty declaration in **Matthew 10:37 NKJV**, *"He who loves father or mother more than Me is not worthy of Me"*? Have you weighed His words in **Luke 14:33 NKJV**, *"Whoever of you does not forsake all that he has cannot be My disciple"*?

Perhaps some of you have great possessions. Will you go away sorrowful if Christ requires you to sell all that you have? Others may be related to or dependent upon powerful people who oppose the church of Christ. What do you say? Will you, with Moses, choose rather to suffer affliction with the people of God than enjoy the passing pleasures of sin?

Perhaps you say, "My friends will not oppose me." That is more than you know. In all probability, your chief enemies may be those of your own household. If they oppose you, are you willing to follow a naked Christ with nothing of your own? Are you willing to wander in sheepskins and goatskins, in dens and caves of the earth, afflicted, destitute, and tormented, rather than cease to be Christ's disciple?

You may now follow with zeal, as Ruth and Orpah followed Naomi, and you may weep under the Word. But are your tears real, or are they crocodile tears? When difficulties come, will you go back from following the Lord, as Orpah went back from following Naomi? Do you truly have the root of grace in your heart, or are you only stony-ground hearers? You receive the Word with joy, but when persecution arises because of the Word, will you immediately stumble?

Do not be angry with me for asking these questions. I am jealous over you with a godly jealousy. How many have put their hands to the plow and then shamefully looked back? I am only dealing with you as our Lord dealt with the man who said, "Lord, I will follow You wherever You go." Jesus answered in **Matthew 8:20 NKJV**, *"Foxes have holes and birds of the air have nests, but the Son of Man has nowhere to lay His head."*

What do you say? Are you willing to endure hardship and prove yourselves good soldiers of Jesus Christ? You now walk from towns and villages to hear the Word and receive me as a messenger of God. But will you later cry, "Away with him, away with him. It is not fit for such a man to live on the earth"?

Perhaps some of you, like Hazael, may say, "Are we dogs, that we should do this?" But sadly, I have met many unhappy souls who have drawn back to destruction and afterward counted me their enemy because I dealt faithfully with them. Once, if it had been possible, they would have plucked out their own eyes and given them to me.

Therefore, sit down, I beg you, and seriously count the cost. Ask yourselves again and again whether you count all things as rubbish and are willing to suffer the loss of all things so that you may gain

Christ and be found in Him. Be assured, the apostle has not spoken in vain: **2 Timothy 3:12 NKJV**, *"Yes, and all who desire to live godly in Christ Jesus will suffer persecution."*

Third, this text speaks to those who are patiently suffering for the truth's sake.

Rejoice and be exceedingly glad, for great is your reward in heaven. To you it has been given not only to believe, but also to suffer, and perhaps to suffer in a remarkable way, for the sake of Jesus. This is a mark of your discipleship. It is evidence that you do live godly in Christ Jesus.

Do not fear, and do not be dismayed. Do not grow weary or faint in your minds. Jesus, your Lord and your life, is coming, and His reward is with Him. Though all men forsake you, He will not. The Spirit of Christ and of glory shall rest upon you.

Therefore, possess your souls in patience. Sanctify the Lord God in your hearts. Do not be terrified by your adversaries. On their part, Christ is spoken against. On your part, He is glorified. Do not be ashamed of your glory, since others are not ashamed to glory in their shame.

Do not think it strange concerning the fiery trial by which you are or may be tested. The devil rages because he knows his time is short. He and his agents have no more power than what is given them from above. God sets their boundaries, and they cannot pass them. Even the hairs of your head are all numbered.

Fear not. No one can set upon you to hurt you without your heavenly Father's knowledge. Do your earthly friends and parents forsake you? Are you cast out of the synagogues? The Lord will reveal

Himself to you, as He did to the man born blind. Jesus Christ will take you up.

If they carry you to prison and load you with chains, so that the iron enters your soul, Christ can send an angel from heaven to strengthen you. He can enable you, like Paul and Silas, to sing praises at midnight.

Are you threatened with a den of lions or a burning fiery furnace because you will not bow down and worship the beast? Fear not. The God whom you serve is able to deliver you. Or if He allows the flames to consume your body, they will only become fiery chariots to carry your soul to God.

So it was with the martyrs of old. One martyr, while burning, cried out, "Come, you Papists, if you want a miracle, behold one here. This bed of flames is to me a bed of down." So it was with many who suffered in former times. Though Jesus withdrew the comfort of His own divinity from Himself in His suffering, He has often lifted up the light of His countenance upon the souls of His suffering saints.

Therefore, Jesus said in **Matthew 10:28 NKJV**, *"Do not fear those who kill the body but cannot kill the soul. But rather fear Him who is able to destroy both soul and body in hell."* Dare, dare to live godly in Christ Jesus, even though you suffer all kinds of persecution.

Fourth, are there any true ministers of Jesus Christ here? You will not be offended if I tell you that the words of the text apply especially to you.

Paul wrote them to Timothy. Of all people who live godly in Christ Jesus, ministers must expect to suffer the severest persecution. Satan will try to bruise our heels, whoever else escapes. It has often been

God's providence in times of persecution to allow the shepherds to be struck first before the sheep are scattered.

Let us not show ourselves to be hirelings who do not care for the sheep. Let us instead imitate the great Shepherd and Bishop of souls, and be ready to lay down our lives for the sheep. While others boast of their great positions and promotions, let us rather glory in our afflictions and persecutions for Christ's sake.

Paul rejoiced that he suffered afflictions and persecutions at Iconium and Lystra. Out of them all, the Lord delivered him. Out of them all, the Lord will deliver us too, and He will cause us hereafter to sit down with Him on thrones when He comes to judge the twelve tribes of Israel.

I could continue, but in this part of my discourse I know I must speak especially to myself. I know that Satan has desired to have me, that he may sift me as wheat. Without any spirit of prophecy, we may easily discern the signs of the times. Persecution is even at the door. The tabernacle of the Lord has already been driven into the wilderness. The ark of the Lord has fallen into the unhallowed hands of uncircumcised Philistines.

They have long since put us out of their synagogues. High priests have been calling on civil rulers to use their authority against the disciples of the Lord. Men in power have been breathing threats. We may easily guess what will follow: imprisonment and slaughter. The storm has been gathering for some time. It must break soon. Perhaps it may fall on me first.

Therefore, brethren, whether you are in ministry or not, I beg you to pray for me. Pray that I may never suffer justly as an evildoer, but only for righteousness' sake. Pray that I may not deny my Lord in any way, but that I may joyfully follow Him both to prison and to death, if He calls me to seal His truths with my blood.

Do not be ashamed of Christ or His gospel, even if I become a prisoner of the Lord. Though I may be bound, the Word of God will not be bound. No. An open and effective door is opened for the preaching of the everlasting gospel, and men or devils shall never prevail against it. Only pray that whether in life or death, Christ may be glorified in me. Then I shall rejoice, yes, and I will rejoice.

And now, to whom shall I speak next?

Fifth, I speak to those who persecute their neighbors for living godly in Christ Jesus.

What shall I say to you? Weep and howl for the miseries that shall come upon you. For a little while, the Lord permits you to ride over the heads of His people. But soon death will arrest you, judgment will find you, and Jesus Christ will ask you a question that will strike you speechless: "Why did you persecute Me?"

You may plead your laws and your religious rules. You may pretend that what you do is out of zeal for God. But God will expose the cursed hypocrisy and serpent-like enmity of your hearts, and He will give you over to the tormentors.

It is a mercy if God does not put some mark upon you in this life. He pleaded the cause of Naboth when Naboth was falsely condemned for blaspheming God and the king. Our Lord sent forth His armies and destroyed the city of those who killed the prophets and stoned those sent to them.

Therefore, if you are determined to fill up the measure of your sins, go on. Persecute and despise the disciples of the Lord. But know this: for all these things, God will bring you into judgment. Those whom you now persecute will in part be your judges. They will sit at the right hand of the Majesty on high, while you are dragged by infernal spirits into the lake that burns with fire and brimstone, and the smoke of your torment will ascend forever and ever.

Lay down your arms, therefore, you rebels against the Most High God. No longer persecute those who live godly in Christ Jesus. The Lord will plead their cause. The Lord will avenge their cause. You may be permitted to bruise their heels, but in the end they shall bruise your accursed heads.

I do not speak this because I am afraid of you. I know in whom I have believed. I warn you out of pure love, because I do not know whether Jesus Christ may make some of you vessels of mercy and snatch even you persecutors like brands from the fire.

Jesus Christ came into the world to save sinners, even persecutors, the worst of sinners. His righteousness is sufficient for them. His Spirit is able to purify and change their hearts. He once converted Saul. May that same God magnify His power by converting all those who are causing the godly in Christ Jesus to suffer persecution.

The Lord be with you all.

Amen.

Chapter Twenty-Eight

On Regeneration

The doctrine of regeneration, or the new birth in Christ Jesus, is one of the most important teachings of the Christian faith. It is plainly taught throughout Scripture. It is so clear that anyone who reads the Bible honestly can see it. In fact, the salvation of every soul depends on it. All sincere Christians, no matter their denomination, agree that a person must be born again. Yet this doctrine is often neglected and poorly understood by many who call themselves Christians.

If we judged this doctrine by the experience of many religious people today, we might think they had never even heard that there is such a thing as regeneration. Many people are orthodox in the basic articles of their faith. They believe there is one God. They believe there is one Mediator between God and man, the man Christ Jesus. They believe there is no other name under heaven by which we must be saved.

But when they are told that they must be regenerated, that they must be born again, that their hearts and minds must be renewed by the Spirit of God before they can truly call Christ "Lord," they are confused. They are ready to ask, like Nicodemus, "How can these things be?" Or like the Athenians, they may say, "What is this man talking about? He seems to be bringing strange teaching." Yet what we are preaching is not strange. We are preaching Christ and the new birth.

Many people make a deadly mistake. They separate what God has joined together. They think they can be justified by Christ and have their sins forgiven, while their hearts remain unchanged and unholy. They imagine that Christ's righteousness can be counted to them while their nature remains the same. But Scripture teaches that those whom Christ justifies, He also sanctifies. Those who are truly in Christ become new creatures.

The apostle says in **2 Corinthians 5:17 NKJV**, *"Therefore, if anyone is in Christ, he is a new creation; old things have passed away; behold, all things have become new."*

Let us consider this truth carefully. First, we must understand what it means to be "in Christ." Second, we must understand what it means to be a new creature. Third, we must consider arguments that prove this doctrine. Fourth, we must draw some practical lessons and end with an exhortation.

A person may be said to be in Christ in two ways.

First, a person may be in Christ by outward profession only. In this sense, everyone who is called a Christian or baptized into the visible church may be said to be in Christ. But this cannot be the full meaning of Paul's words. If it were, then everyone who bears the name Christian or has been baptized would automatically be a new creature. But that is plainly not true.

Many are born of water who are not born of the Spirit. Many are baptized with water who have never been baptized with the Holy Spirit. Therefore, being in Christ must mean more than outward profession or being called by His name.

Just as Paul said that not all who are descended from Israel are truly Israel, so not all who are called Christians are true Christians. Our Lord Himself said that many who preached in His name, cast out demons in His name, and did many wonderful works in His name will hear Him say at the last day, "Depart from Me, I never knew you, you workers of lawlessness."

Therefore, to be in Christ in the true and full sense means something deeper. It means to partake of the benefits of His sufferings. It means to be united to Him, not merely by outward profession, but by an inward change of heart. It means to have the Holy Spirit dwelling within. It means to be joined to Christ by a true and living faith, receiving spiritual life from Him, as members of the body receive life from the head, and as branches receive life from the vine.

This is what Paul meant when he spoke of knowing a man "in Christ." This is also what he desired for himself when he said he wanted to be found in Christ. A true Christian is not merely one outwardly. True baptism is not merely outward washing with water. A true Christian is one inwardly. His baptism is of the heart, by the Spirit. His praise is not from man, but from God.

Paul says elsewhere that neither circumcision nor uncircumcision avails anything in itself, but a new creation. This agrees with the text: if any man is truly in Christ, he is a new creature.

Now we must ask what it means to be a new creature.

This does not mean that our physical bodies must be destroyed and created again. It does not mean, as Nicodemus mistakenly thought, that a man must enter a second time into his mother's womb and be born again physically. If that were possible, it would not make a person spiritually new. That which is born of the flesh is still flesh. We would still be the same carnal people, born from sinful parents, carrying the same seeds of sin and corruption.

To be a new creature means that the qualities, desires, affections, and direction of the soul are changed. It means the person is so altered in heart and mind that he becomes, in a spiritual sense, a new person.

A piece of gold may remain the same gold, but after it is taken from the ore, cleansed, purified, and polished, it may be called new. A glass covered with filth remains the same glass, but when it is cleaned and made clear, it may be called new. Naaman was still Naaman after he was healed of leprosy, but when his flesh became like the flesh of a little child, he could be called a new man.

So it is with the soul. The soul remains the same soul, but by the blessed work of the Holy Spirit, it is cleansed from its natural filth, corruption, and spiritual leprosy. It is renewed and made new.

How this great change takes place cannot be fully explained. No one knows the deep workings of the Spirit except the Spirit of God. But this should not make us deny the doctrine. Jesus Himself told Nicodemus in **John 3:8 NKJV**, *"The wind blows where it wishes, and you hear the sound of it, but cannot tell where it comes from and where it goes."* If we cannot fully explain natural things, we should not be surprised if we cannot fully explain the invisible work of the Holy Spirit.

The doctrine of regeneration is difficult for the natural man to understand. But that there is such a thing, and that every one of us must be born again, is plainly taught in Scripture.

First, God Himself has told us so in His Word. Many passages in the Old Testament teach this. David prayed for God to create in him a clean heart and renew a right spirit within him. The prophets called people to receive a new heart and a new spirit and to turn to the Lord their God.

But the doctrine is even more plainly taught in the New Testament. Jesus Himself said in **John 3:3 NKJV**, *"Most assuredly, I say to you, unless one is born again, he cannot see the kingdom of God."* He also said in **John 3:5 NKJV**, *"Most assuredly, I say to you, unless one is born of water and the Spirit, he cannot enter the kingdom of God."*

Notice how strongly Jesus speaks. He does not say this as a suggestion. He speaks with divine certainty. Unless a person is born again, he cannot enter the kingdom of God.

The apostles teach the same truth. We are commanded to be renewed in the spirit of our minds. We are told to put off the old man, which is corrupt, and put on the new man, created according to God in righteousness and true holiness. We are told that old things must pass away and all things must become new. We are told that salvation includes the washing of regeneration and renewing of the Holy Spirit.

Even if we had no other passage than **2 Corinthians 5:17 NKJV**, it would be enough: *"Therefore, if anyone is in Christ, he is a new creation."*

Second, this doctrine is proven by the purity of God and the corrupt condition of man.

God is described in Scripture as a Spirit. He is infinitely holy. He is of purer eyes than to behold evil. Even the heavens are not clean in His sight, and He charges His angels with folly. God is pure, holy, and righteous beyond our full understanding.

Man, on the other hand, is described as conceived and born in sin. By nature, no good thing dwells in us. We are carnal, sold under sin. The natural mind is at enmity with God.

How then can a filthy, corrupted, polluted sinner dwell with an infinitely pure and holy God unless he is changed and made, in some measure, like Him? Can God, who is of purer eyes than to behold evil, dwell with uncleanness? Can light have fellowship with darkness? Can Christ have agreement with Belial? No. There must be a real change in the soul.

Third, this doctrine is proven by the nature of the happiness God has prepared for those who love Him.

We cannot fully describe heaven. Scripture says that eye has not seen, ear has not heard, nor has it entered into the heart of man the things God has prepared for those who love Him. If that is true of the blessings God gives even in this life, how much more true is it of the glory to come?

Yet we may say this: because God is Spirit, the happiness He has prepared for His people is spiritual. Therefore, unless our carnal minds are changed and made spiritual, we can never be fit to enjoy that inheritance with the saints in light.

This is why Scripture says that without holiness no one will see the Lord. Jesus did not merely say that unless a person is born again, he shall not enter the kingdom of God. He said he cannot enter. This is rooted in the nature of things.

A person cannot enjoy something unless he has a nature suited to it. What pleasure can music give to a deaf man? What joy can a beautiful painting give to a blind man? What delight can rich food give to someone with no taste? What pleasure would a pig have in a fine garden of flowers? None, because there is no inward ability to enjoy those things.

So it is with the soul. Death does not change the nature of the soul. It only enlarges its capacity for joy or misery. If a soul delighted in communion with God on earth, it will be filled with joy in seeing His glory in heaven. If it loved the fellowship of the saints on earth, it will rejoice infinitely more in the fellowship of angels and the spirits of just men made perfect.

But if a person had no delight in God here, no love for holiness here, and no desire for spiritual fellowship here, then heaven itself would not be happiness to him. Even if God were to admit such a soul into heaven, which He will not, it would not enjoy heaven. The heart must be changed.

Fourth, Christ's redemption would not be complete in us unless we are made new creatures.

The first and chief purpose of Christ's coming was to be a propitiation for our sins, to give His life as a ransom for many. But if Christ's death only purchased forgiveness and did nothing to change our nature, we would still be unfit for heaven.

Imagine a condemned criminal who receives a pardon but is still dying from a terrible disease. He may have been pardoned by the judge, but he still needs healing. So it is with us. There is a legal obstacle to our happiness because we have broken God's law. But there is also a moral impurity in our nature that makes us unable to enjoy heaven unless a mighty change is worked in us.

Therefore, for Christ's redemption to be complete, God must give us the Holy Spirit to change our nature and prepare us for the happiness Christ purchased by His blood.

Scripture tells us that those whom Christ justifies, He also sanctifies. Those whose sins He forgives and to whom He imputes His righteousness are also purified, cleansed, and changed in their nature. Christ becomes to His people wisdom, righteousness, sanctification, and redemption.

Now let us draw some practical lessons from this doctrine.

First, if anyone in Christ is a new creature, then this rebukes those who rest in outward religious duties without any inward change of heart.

Many people are careful to pray publicly and privately. They receive communion. They may occasionally fast. But the problem is that they rest in the outward duties themselves. They think their religion is complete because they have performed these practices.

But prayer, fasting, hearing the Word, reading Scripture, receiving communion, and other means of grace are useful only as they make us inwardly better and carry on spiritual life in the soul. They are means. They are not the whole of religion.

If outward duties alone made a person righteous, who would have been more religious than the Pharisee? He fasted twice a week and gave tithes of all he possessed, yet Jesus tells us he was not justified before God.

You may fast often. You may make long prayers. You may hear sermons gladly, as Herod did. But if you remain vain, worldly, immoral, proud, or unchanged, what good is it? If the only difference between you and your neighbor is that you attend church or perform certain religious duties, you are not better. In some ways, you may be worse, because by using holy things without being changed by them, you may lead others to think there is no power in religion.

Second, if anyone in Christ is a new creature, then this rebukes those who rest in moral behavior and think they are good Christians because they are honest, moderate, and harmless.

If morality alone made someone a Christian, then many heathens of old could be called Christians. Some of them were known for justice, self-control, and outward virtue. Paul himself, before his conversion, lived in all good conscience according to his understanding. Yet after he met Christ, he renounced all confidence in himself and desired only to be found in Christ and to know the power of His resurrection.

Christianity includes morality, just as grace includes reason. But if we are only moral people and have not been inwardly changed by the Holy Spirit, then however much we call ourselves Christians, we will be found spiritually naked at the great day. We will not have Christ's righteousness imputed to us for justification, nor holiness in our souls as the fruit of that justification.

Third, this doctrine rebukes those who rest in partial improvement without a true inward change of heart.

There are many who once lived openly sinful lives. Then, seeing the bad consequences of their sins, they become more civilized. They stop some scandalous practices. They are not as openly wicked as they once were. Because of this, they think they have become religious.

But often such people still keep some secret beloved sin. They may have a hidden lust they refuse to mortify, some darling sin they will not give up, some sinful habit they refuse to root out. They have changed in part, but not in heart.

What does the Lord require? Nothing less than a true and thorough conversion. It is not enough to turn from open profanity to outward civility. You must turn from mere civility to godliness. Not some things, but all things must become new in the soul. It will profit you little to do many things if one thing still rules your heart against Christ. You must not be almost a new creature. You must be altogether a new creature, or your claim to be a Christian is empty.

Fourth, this doctrine gives every person a rule by which to examine himself.

This is the only solid foundation for real assurance of pardon, peace, and happiness. We may rest on outward profession. We may think we are safe because we live sober, honest, moral lives. We may depend on church attendance, private prayer, or religious habits. But unless these things lead to a changed heart and a reformed life, Christianity will profit us nothing.

Therefore, let each of us seriously ask our own heart: Have I received the Holy Spirit since I believed? Am I a new creature in Christ or not? If I am not yet, is it my daily desire and pursuit to become one? Do I seriously and faithfully use the means of grace? Do I watch, pray, and fast? Do I merely seek lazily, or do I strive to enter through the narrow gate? Do I renounce my own righteousness, take up my cross, and follow Christ?

If so, then we are in the narrow way that leads to life. The good seed has been sown in our hearts, and if it is watered and nourished by persevering use of God's means, it will grow up to eternal life.

But if we have only heard about the Holy Spirit and do not know His work by experience, if we are strangers to prayer, watchfulness, spiritual discipline, and devotion, if we are content to walk in the broad way simply because most people are walking there, if we are enemies to the cross of Christ by worldly-mindedness and sensual living, then Christ has so far died in vain for us. We are still under the guilt of sin and strangers to true conversion.

But beloved, I hope better things for you, things that accompany salvation. I hope you are persuaded that whoever does not have the Spirit of Christ does not belong to Him. I hope you know that unless the Spirit who raised Jesus from the dead dwells in you here, your mortal bodies will not be raised by that same Spirit to dwell with Him hereafter.

Therefore, I earnestly exhort you in the name of our Lord Jesus Christ: live as Christians who have been commanded in Scripture to put off the old man and put on the new man, created according to God in righteousness and true holiness.

This is a great and difficult work. But blessed be God, it is not impossible. Many thousands of souls have been helped by divine power to experience this change. Why should we despair? Is God's hand shortened that it cannot save? Was He the God of our fathers only? Is He not also the God of their children? Yes, without doubt, He is.

This work will cost us pain. It may require us to part with some lust, break with some sinful friend, or put to death some beloved passion that seems as dear to us as a right hand or right eye. But what of that? Will it not be worth it to become a real living member of Christ, a child of God, and an inheritor of the kingdom of heaven? Surely it will.

This work may also expose us to ridicule. Thoughtless people will wonder why we no longer run with them into the same excess of sin. Because we deny our sinful appetites and refuse to conform to the world, they may call our lives foolish and our end without honor. But being numbered among the saints and shining like the stars forever will more than repay all ridicule, slander, and reproach we may suffer here.

Even if there were no reward except the peace of God that follows true conversion, we would still have reason to rejoice. That peace passes all understanding even in this life. But that peace is only the beginning. It is only the first taste of an eternal succession of joys.

For the unconverted sinner, death is dreadful. But for the one who is born again, the day of death will be like the first day of a new birth into everlasting happiness and comfort. Those who are regenerated and born again have a real title to the promises of the gospel. They are certain to be made as happy, both here and hereafter, as an all-wise, all-gracious, all-powerful God can make them.

Therefore, anyone who has even the smallest concern for the salvation of his precious and immortal soul should not stop watching, praying, and striving until he knows that a real, inward, saving change has been worked in his heart. Then he will know that he dwells in Christ and Christ in him. He will know that he is a new creature, a child of God, and an heir of the kingdom of heaven.

May God, in His infinite mercy, grant this to us all through Jesus Christ our Lord.

Amen.

Chapter Twenty-Nine

Christians, Temples of the Living God

Isaiah spoke of the glory of gospel days when he said in **Isaiah 64:4 NKJV**, *"For since the beginning of the world men have not heard nor perceived by the ear, nor has the eye seen any God besides You, who acts for the one who waits for Him."* If a world lying in wickedness could truly be convinced of this, people would need no other motive to deny themselves, take up their cross, and follow Jesus Christ. And if believers always kept this truth deeply impressed upon their souls, they would abstain from every evil, continually pursue every good, and diligently walk worthy of the One who has called them to His kingdom and glory.

This, I believe, is what the apostle Paul intended when he said, **2 Corinthians 6:16 NKJV**, *"For you are the temple of the living God."* These words were originally written to the church at Corinth, but they also belong to us, to our children, and to as many as the Lord our God shall call. My purpose is to explain their meaning and then apply them to our lives.

Christians are the temple of the living God, Father, Son, and Holy Spirit. The same blessed Trinity who took counsel in the creation of man is also involved in the redemption of man. The Father creates, the Son redeems, and the Holy Spirit sanctifies all the elect people of God. Those who were loved from eternity are effectually called in time. They are chosen out of the world, not merely by an outward dedication in baptism or at the Lord's Supper, but by a free, willing, and sincere offering of themselves to God. They devote spirit, soul, and body to the service of Him who loved them and gave Himself for them.

This is true and undefiled religion before God our heavenly Father. This is the Christian's reasonable service. It requires nothing less than a total renunciation of the world. It turns the Christian's whole life into one continual sacrifice of love to God, so that, whether he eats or drinks, he does all to the glory of God.

This does not mean that Christians must become hermits or shut themselves away in monasteries, convents, or secluded places. God forbid that we should think so. The religion taught in the Bible is a social religion. It is a religion that can be lived by high and low, rich and poor. It requires us to faithfully fulfill the duties of our relationships and callings, wherever God has placed us.

It is true that in every age some sincere people have separated themselves from the world, hoping to save their souls and reach higher levels of holiness through solitude. I do not doubt their sincerity. But such zeal is not according to knowledge. Private Christians, as well as ministers, are called the salt of the earth and the light of the world. Jesus commanded His people in **Matthew 5:16 NKJV**, *"Let your* *light so shine before men."* But how can our light shine before men if we shut ourselves away from all conversation and contact with the world?

Even if we could fly to the most distant and lonely place on earth, what would it profit us if our wicked hearts and the tempter followed us there? We would not find the ease and comfort we expected. A hermit once told me that a tree standing alone is most exposed to the strongest winds. There is much truth in that. When our Savior was tempted by the devil, He was led by the Spirit into the wilderness. How contrary this is to those who go into the wilderness to avoid temptation.

Surely such people forget the prayer of Jesus for His disciples in **John 17:15 NKJV**, *"I do not pray that You should take them out of the world, but that You should keep them from the evil one."* This is true Christianity: to be in the world, but not of the world. Our hands may be employed in the duties of earth according to our calling, while our hearts are fixed on things above.

Then, indeed, we are temples of the living God. Then we can say with humble boldness that we are the same in the parlor as we are in the closet. Then at night we can cast off our cares as we cast off our clothes. Being at peace with the world, with ourselves, and with God, we can be content whether we sleep or die.

The Jewish temple was also a house of prayer. God said in **Isaiah 56:7 NKJV**, *"My house shall be called a house of prayer for all nations."* This teaches us that the hearts of true believers are to be seats of prayer. The temple was built and furnished for this purpose. When Solomon dedicated the temple, he prayed that God would hear the prayers of His servant and His people when they prayed toward that place.

This is why Daniel, even in captivity, prayed three times a day with his face toward Jerusalem. And what was said of the first temple, our Lord applied to the second temple: **Matthew 21:13 NKJV**, *"My house shall be called a house of prayer."*

In this way also, true believers are the temple of the living God. Because they are wholly devoted to God in Christ, their hearts become houses of prayer. From these living altars, a continual sacrifice of prayer and praise rises to the Father of mercies and the God of all comfort. Those who worship God in the temple of their hearts are truly priests unto God. They are a royal priesthood. They alone may truly be called the temple of the living God, because they pray to Him in their hearts and worship Him in spirit and truth.

Let no one say this kind of devotion is impossible, or that it can only be practiced by a few people who have nothing to do with ordinary life. This is the common duty and privilege of all true Christians. The commands to pray without ceasing and to rejoice in the Lord always are binding on all who name the name of Christ.

It is true that those who are deeply involved in worldly business often find it hard to serve the Lord without distraction. It is also true that the lamp of devotion, even in the best saints, sometimes burns dimly. But those who are temples of the living God find prayer to be their very element. When people come to love prayer as much as some unhappy people love swearing, they will find no more difficulty in praying and praising God than those people find in cursing and swearing.

What I am describing is not a life reserved only for those who retire from the world. The love of God is the great thing. When the soul possesses the love of God, as it must if it is truly the temple of the living God, then meditation, prayer, praise, and other spiritual exercises become habitual and delightful.

When once the soul is touched by this divine magnet, it feels a holy attraction and continually turns toward its center, which is God. If it is drawn away by sudden or violent temptation, yet when that obstruction is removed, it returns again to its rest, its center, its God, its all.

The Jewish temple was also the place where the great Jehovah was pleased to dwell in a special way. He put His name there. He was said to dwell between the cherubim. When Solomon dedicated the temple, the house was filled with a cloud, so that the priests could not continue ministering because the glory of the Lord filled the house.

Why did God give this amazing display of glory? It was to show that the high and lofty One who inhabits eternity would one day make believers' hearts His living temple. He would dwell with and make His home in those who tremble at His Word.

This is what Paul means when he says in **2 Corinthians 6:16 NKJV**, *"For you are the temple of the living God. As God has said: 'I will dwell in them and walk among them. I will be their God, and they shall be My people.'"* These are strong and wonderful words. But every true temple of the living God must experience the reality behind them.

Believers are called a holy habitation through the Spirit. They are said to dwell in God, and God in them. They have the witness within themselves. The Spirit of God bears witness with their spirit that they are the children of God. All of this means what Jesus prayed for shortly before His suffering: **John 17:21 NKJV**, *"That they all may be one, as You, Father, are in Me, and I in You."* And again, **John 17:23 NKJV**, *"I in them, and You in Me; that they may be made perfect in one."*

This glorious truth is not only for apostles. It is the privilege of every true believer. Those who truly receive Christ dwell in Christ, and Christ dwells in them. They are one with Christ, and Christ is one with them. This is the inspiration of the Holy Spirit we pray for. This is the fellowship of the Holy Spirit we ask God to be with us forever.

Time would fail to mention every Scripture, every prayer, and every confession that speaks of this inestimable blessing: the indwelling of the blessed Spirit, by which believers become the temples of the living God. If you have eyes to see and ears to hear, you may find this truth throughout the living Word of God.

Therefore, when we teach this doctrine, we are not speaking the imaginations of a disordered mind. We are not inventing new doctrines. We are not promoting the private opinion of one group of Christians. We are speaking words of truth and soberness. We are showing the old and good way in which all sincere Christians, despite other differences, agree.

This doctrine may rightly be called one of the great marks of true Christianity. Ignatius, one of the early fathers of the church, called himself a bearer of God and called Christians bearers of God. Because of this, he was brought before Emperor Trajan, who demanded,

"Where is this man who says he carries God about with him?" Ignatius answered with humble boldness, "I am he," and then quoted the passage: **2 Corinthians 6:16 NKJV**, *"For you are the temple of the living God."* For this confession, he was condemned to be devoured by lions.

Blessed be God, we are not presently in danger of being brought before such persecuting rulers. In our time, the worst that is legally used against us is usually the scourge of the tongue. But if greater suffering were permitted, we need not be ashamed of this good confession. Grace for suffering will be given in suffering times. And if we are truly bearers of God, we also shall be enabled to say, as Ignatius did when led to the lions, "Now I begin to be a disciple of Christ."

Now let us make practical use of what has been said.

You have heard in what sense true Christians are the temple of the living God. Do you believe these things? I know some of you do believe them, not merely because I have said them, but because you have experienced them.

I congratulate you from my heart. May your hearts be tuned today to magnify the Lord, and may your spirits rejoice in God your Savior. Like the Virgin Mary, you are highly favored, and from this time forward the generations of God's people will call you blessed.

You can call Christ Lord by the Holy Spirit. You have not only outward evidence, but inward evidence of the divinity of His person and His holy Word. You can prove by experience that the Scriptures contain the perfect and acceptable will of God. You have found the second Adam to be a life-giving Spirit. He has raised you from death to life.

Being taught and born of God, even if you are unlearned in other ways, you can say, "Is not this the Christ?" What an unspeakable blessing. What an unimaginable privilege. God's Spirit bears witness with your spirit that you are the children of God.

When you think of this, are you not ready to cry out with the beloved disciple in **1 John 3:1 NKJV**, *"Behold what manner of love the Father has bestowed on us, that we should be called children of God!"* I believe John was almost overwhelmed with holy wonder when he wrote those words. Though he has now been in heaven so long, his astonishment is still only beginning and will continue through all eternity.

So it shall be with all of you whom the high and lofty One, who inhabits eternity, has made His living temples. He has sealed you for the day of redemption and given you the earnest of your future inheritance. His eyes and His heart will be upon you continually. In spite of all opposition from men and devils, the top stone of this spiritual building will be brought forth, and you will shout, "Grace, grace to it."

Your bodies will be fashioned like the glorious body of the Redeemer. Your souls, in which He now graciously delights to dwell, will be filled with all the fullness of God. You will go out no more. You will no longer need the light of the sun or moon, for the Lord Himself will be your temple, and the Lamb will be your glory.

Dearly beloved in the Lord, what do you say to these things? Do not your hearts burn within you while you think of these deep and glorious truths of God? As I think and speak of them, a fire kindles even in my own cold heart.

What shall we render to the Lord for all these mercies? Surely He has done great things for us. How great is His goodness and His bounty. O the height, depth, length, and breadth of the love of God. It passes knowledge.

O for humility. O for a soul-abasing and God-exalting sense of these things. When Mary visited Elizabeth, Elizabeth cried out with amazement, "Why is this granted to me, that the mother of my Lord should come to me?" When the Lord filled the temple with His glory, Solomon cried out, "But will God indeed dwell with men on the earth?"

How much more should we say, "Will the Lord Himself truly come to us? Will the high and lofty One who inhabits eternity dwell in our earthly hearts and make them His living temples?" My brethren, why has this happened? Was it because of any fitness in us that God foresaw? No. I know you reject such a thought. Was it because we improved our own free will? No. I am persuaded you will not dishonor the riches of free grace that way.

Are you not ready to say, "Not unto us, not unto us, but unto Your free, unmerited, sovereign, distinguishing love and mercy, O Lord, be all the glory"? This alone has made the difference between us and others. We have nothing except what has been freely given from above. If we love God, it is because God first loved us.

Let us look to the rock from which we were hewn and the pit from which we were dug. If there is any consolation in Christ, any comfort of love, any fellowship of the Spirit, any compassion and mercy, let us strive to walk as those who have been made temples of the living God, a holy temple unto the Lord.

What kind of people ought we to be in all holy conduct and godliness? How pure and holy should our lives be. Paul asks in **2 Corinthians 6:14–15 NKJV**, *"For what fellowship has righteousness with lawlessness? And what communion has light with darkness? And what accord has Christ with Belial?"* Shall those who are temples of the living God become dens of thieves or cages of unclean birds? Shall vain and impure thoughts be allowed to dwell there? Much less should anything impure be conceived or acted upon by us. Shall we provoke the Lord to jealousy? God forbid.

We all know with what holy zeal Jesus cleansed the earthly temple. Zeal for His Father's house consumed Him. With holy force, He overturned the tables of the money changers and drove out the buyers and sellers. Why? Because they had made His Father's house a house of merchandise. They had turned the house of prayer into a den of thieves.

O my brethren, how often have you and I been guilty of this evil? How often have the lust of the flesh, the lust of the eyes, and the pride of life secretly stolen our hearts away from God? Once our hearts were houses of prayer. Faith, hope, love, peace, joy, and all the other fruits of the Spirit dwelt there. But now, perhaps, thieves and robbers have entered.

This is why God sometimes hides His face. This is why we experience dryness, deadness, barrenness of soul, and weary nights and days. Many of us have groaned under these things. This is why we cry, "O that I knew where I might find Him. O that it were with me as in days past, when the candle of the Lord shone brightly on my soul."

This may also explain domestic trials, personal losses, disappointments, and even public rebukes. They may all be like small cords in the loving Redeemer's hands, used to drive the buyers and sellers out of the temple of our hearts.

O that we may know the rod and Him who has appointed it. He has chastised us with whips. May we become wise and walk more carefully so that He does not need to chastise us in time to come with scorpions. But who is sufficient for these things? None but You, O Lord, to whom all hearts are open, all desires known, and from whom no secrets are hidden. Cleanse the thoughts of our hearts by the inspiration of Your Holy Spirit, that from now on we may more perfectly love You and more worthily magnify Your holy name.

But perhaps some of you are ready to object. You may fear that the Lord has forgotten to be gracious, that He has shut up His lovingkindness in displeasure, and that He will no longer hear you. The psalmist once thought this when God's heavy hand was on him because of his backsliding. But he confessed that this was his weakness. Whether you realize it or not, this is your weakness too.

O dejected, discouraged, distrustful souls, hear the word of the Lord. Remember His wonderful declarations to His people. He says in **Isaiah 43:25 NKJV**, *"I, even I, am He who blots out your transgressions for My own sake."* He says in **Isaiah 54:7–8 NKJV**, *"For a mere moment I have forsaken you, but with great mercies I will gather you. With a little wrath I hid My face from you for a moment; but with everlasting kindness I will have mercy on you."*

Can a woman forget her nursing child? Yes, she may, but the Lord will not forget His people. O you of little faith, remember

Psalm 103:13 NKJV, *"As a father pities his children, so the Lord pities those who fear Him."* And remember God's words in **Hosea 11:8–9 NKJV**, *"How can I give you up, Ephraim? How can I hand you over, Israel? How can I make you like Admah? How can I set you like Zeboiim? My heart churns within Me; My sympathy is stirred. I will not execute the fierceness of My anger."*

All these gracious words speak like Joseph spoke to his guilty and troubled brothers: "Come near to me." O that it may be said of you as it was said of them, "And they came near."

Then you would find by blessed experience that the Lord God is merciful and gracious, slow to anger, and full of kindness. Who knows but He may come down this very day, this very hour, even this very moment, and suddenly revisit the temple of your hearts? Who knows but He may revive His work in your precious souls, restore you to your first love, help you do your first works, exceed your hopes, and cause the glory of this second visitation to surpass even the glory that filled your hearts on that blessed day when He first made you His living temples?

Even so, Father, let it be good in Your sight.

But the application must not end here. So far, I have been giving bread to the children, and it is my meat and drink to do so. But must nothing be said to those who are outside? I mean those who cannot yet say that they are the temple of the living God.

How great your number may be. In all probability, you may be the largest part of this audience. Do not say I am uncharitable. The God of truth has said in **Matthew 7:14 NKJV**, *"Narrow is the gate and difficult is the way which leads to life, and there are few who find it."*

Let me speak plainly to you, my brethren. You have heard what has been said about the text and what must be worked in us before we can truly say we are the temple of the living God. Is this true of you? Are you separated from the world and worldly tempers? Have your hearts become houses of prayer? Does the Spirit of God dwell in your souls? Whether you eat or drink, or whatever you do, is the habitual aim of your heart to do all to the glory of God?

These are short questions, but they are plain and very important. What answer can you give? Do not say, "Go away for now. At a more convenient time I will think about this." I will not, I must not, allow you to put this off so easily. I ask for an answer in the name of the Lord of hosts.

What do you say? Perhaps I hear you answer, "We were dedicated to God in baptism. We go to church or meeting. We say our prayers. We repeat the creed. We have subscribed to articles and confessions of faith. We are orthodox and are friends of the doctrines of grace. We do no one any harm. We are honest moral people. We are church members. We keep up family prayer and regularly come to the Lord's Table."

All these things are good in their proper place. But you may go this far, and much farther, and still be far from the kingdom of God. The unprofitable servant did no one any harm. The foolish virgins had lamps of outward profession and went all the way to heaven's gate, calling Christ, "Lord, Lord."

These things may make you whitewashed tombs, but they do not make you temples of the living God. Alas, one thing you still lack: the chief thing without which all else is nothing. I mean the indwelling of God's blessed Spirit. Without Him, you can never become temples of the living God.

Awake, therefore, deceived formalists. Awake, you who are puffed up with outward performance and cry, "The temple of the Lord, the temple of the Lord, the temple of the Lord are we." Awake, you outward-court worshipers. You are building on a sandy foundation. Take heed, lest you go to hell by the very door of heaven. Remember, I have warned you.

And as for those of you who do not even have outward religion, who have in effect renounced your baptism, who proclaim your sin like Sodom, and who willingly and boldly live without God in the world, I ask you: how shall you escape if you neglect so great a salvation?

I would utterly despair of your ever becoming temples of the living God if I had not heard of thousands who, by the grace of God, have been brought from the same darkness into His marvelous light. Paul wrote to the Corinthians and said that some of them had once been drunkards, immoral people, adulterers, and such like. But then he says in **1 Corinthians 6:11 NKJV**, *"And such were some of you. But you were washed, but you were sanctified, but you were justified in the name of the Lord Jesus and by the Spirit of our God."*

O that the same blessed Spirit would come today and pluck you as brands from the burning. Behold, I warn you to flee from the wrath to come. Go home and think seriously about these things. Ask yourself whether it is not infinitely better, even here in this life, to be temples of the living God than to be slaves to brutish lusts and led captive by the devil at his will.

The Lord Jesus can set your soul free. And if you flee to Him for refuge, He will. He has led captivity captive. He has ascended on high to receive the gift of the blessed Spirit for men, even for the rebellious, so that He might dwell in your hearts by faith here and prepare you to dwell with Him and all the heavenly host in His kingdom hereafter.

May this be the happy portion of you all. May God, in His infinite mercy, grant it for the sake of His dear Son, Jesus Christ our Lord. To Him, with the Father and the blessed Spirit, three Persons and one God, be all power, might, majesty, and dominion, now and forevermore.

Amen and Amen.

Chapter Thirty

Intercession: Every Christian's Duty

If we ask why there is so little love among Christians, and why the very mark by which all people should know we are disciples of the holy Jesus is almost missing from much of the Christian world, we will find one major reason. Many Christians have neglected, or only lightly practiced, that excellent part of prayer called intercession. Intercession is praying for others and asking God to show them grace and mercy.

Some forget to pray for others because they rarely pray for themselves. Even those who regularly pray to their Father in heaven are often selfish in their prayers. They do not enlarge their petitions for the spiritual and practical good of other Christians as they should. Because of this, they fall short of that Christian love, that sincere love for the brethren, which our holy profession requires. Without this love, even if we gave all our goods to feed the poor and gave our bodies to be burned, it would profit us nothing.

Since this is true, I want to show three things. First, it is every Christian's duty to pray for others as well as for himself. Second, we must consider whom we should pray for and how we should pray for them. Third, I will give some motives to stir all Christians to abound in this great duty of intercession.

First, it is every Christian's duty to pray for others as well as for himself.

Prayer is a duty founded even in natural religion. Even the heathen did not entirely neglect it, though many who call themselves Christians do. Prayer is so essential to Christianity that you might as reasonably expect to find a living man without breath as a true Christian without the spirit of prayer and supplication.

As soon as Paul was converted, the Lord said of him, "Behold, he is praying." So it will be with every child of God as soon as he becomes one. Prayer has rightly been called the natural cry of the newborn soul.

In the heart of every true believer there is a heavenly tendency, a divine attraction, that draws him to speak with God as surely as a magnet draws the needle. A deep sense of his own weakness and of Christ's fullness, a strong conviction of his natural corruption and his need for renewing grace, will not allow him to stop crying day and night to his almighty Redeemer. He prays that the divine image, which was lost in Adam, may be begun, continued, and perfected in both his soul and body through Christ's mediation and the sanctifying work of the Holy Spirit.

All sincere Christians are earnest in praying for themselves. But because they often do not feel the needs of their Christian brethren as deeply as they feel their own, they are often too weak and careless in praying for others.

If the love of God were truly shed abroad in our hearts, and if we loved our neighbor the way the Son of God loved us, according to His command and example, then we would be as earnest for the spiritual and temporal welfare of others as we are for our own. We would deeply desire that others share in the benefits of the death and suffering of Jesus Christ just as we desire those blessings for ourselves.

No one should think this is some uncommon level of love or a height of perfection that ordinary Christians cannot reach. We are all commanded to love our neighbor as ourselves. We are even called to lay down our lives for the brethren. If this is true, then it is the duty of every Christian to pray for others as much as for himself. By every possible act and expression of love, we should show that we are ready even to lay down our lives for them, if God ever calls us to do so.

Our blessed Savior has set us an example in everything, and especially in this. In His divine and perfect prayer recorded in **John 17**, which He prayed just before His suffering, we find only a few petitions for Himself, but many petitions for His disciples. And in the perfect pattern of prayer He gave us, He did not teach us to say "My Father," but **Matthew 6:9 NKJV**, *"Our Father in heaven."* By this He reminds us that whenever we come to the throne of grace, we ought not to pray for ourselves alone, but also for all our brethren in Christ.

Intercession, then, is certainly a duty that belongs to all Christians.

Second, we must consider whom we should intercede for and how this duty should be performed.

First, our intercession must be universal. Paul says in **1 Timothy 2:1 NKJV**, *"Therefore I exhort first of all that supplications, prayers, intercessions, and giving of thanks be made for all men."* As God's mercy is over all His works, and as Jesus Christ died to redeem a people out of every nation and language, so we should pray that all people may come to the knowledge of the truth and be saved.

Many precious promises are given in Scripture that the gospel will be preached throughout the world and that the earth will be filled with the knowledge of the Lord as the waters cover the sea. Therefore, we must not limit our prayers to our own nation. We should pray for all nations that now sit in darkness and in the shadow of death, that the glorious light of the gospel may shine upon them also.

You do not need any man to teach you this, because Jesus Himself has taught you to pray, **Matthew 6:10 NKJV**, *"Your kingdom come."* Part of the meaning of this petition is that God's ways may be known on earth and His salvation among all nations.

Next, after praying for all people, we should pray for kings and all those in authority, as Paul teaches. We should pray for our rulers and for all who govern under them, that we may lead quiet and peaceful lives in all godliness and honesty.

When we consider how heavy the burden of government is, and how much the welfare of a people depends on the wisdom, zeal, and godly character of those who rule over them, we should not only pity them, but pray for them. They face many dangers and difficulties because of their position. They are constantly tempted toward luxury, pride, self-indulgence, and worldly influence. Therefore, we should ask God, who preserved Esther, David, and Josiah unspotted from the world in the midst of courtly grandeur, to preserve our leaders holy and blameless and to prosper the work of their hands.

Third, we ought especially to pray for those whom the Holy Spirit has made overseers over us. Paul asked for this again and again from the churches to whom he wrote. He said, "Brethren, pray for us." He also wrote in **Ephesians 6:18–19 NKJV**, *"Praying always with all prayer and supplication in the Spirit... and for me, that utterance may be given to me."* In another place, to show how earnestly he desired their prayers, he urged the church to strive together with him in prayer.

If the great apostle Paul, that chosen vessel and favorite of heaven, needed the earnest prayers of his converts, how much more do ordinary ministers of the gospel need the intercession of their people.

I must especially press this part of your duty because it is so important. No doubt much good is often withheld from many people because they neglect to pray for their ministers. They might have received more spiritual benefit if they had prayed for them as they ought.

People often complain that there are not enough diligent and faithful pastors. But how do they deserve good pastors if they will not earnestly pray to God for them? If we will not pray to the Lord of the harvest, can we expect Him to send laborers into His harvest?

It is also great ingratitude not to pray for your ministers. They watch over you and labor in the Word and doctrine for your salvation. Should you not pray for them in return? If someone helps your body, you think it right to pray for him. Should you not remember those who feed and nourish your soul?

Praying for your ministers also proves that you believe that though Paul may plant and Apollos may water, God alone gives the increase. You will also find that it is one of the best ways to promote your own spiritual welfare. In answer to your prayers, God may give your ministers a double portion of His Holy Spirit, making them better able to feed you with spiritual knowledge and divide the Word of truth rightly.

If people would constantly observe this duty, we would see a greater blessing on preaching. When ministers pray in the name of the people, the people should humbly ask God to perform those petitions. When ministers speak in God's name to the people, the people should pray that the Holy Spirit would fall upon all who hear the Word. Then we would see more visible fruit from the doctrine preached and greater love between ministers and their people. The hands of ministers would be strengthened by the intercessions of the people, and the people would not dare to slander or despise those for whom they regularly pray.

Fourth, after our ministers, our friends should have a place in our intercessions. But we should not be satisfied with praying for them only in general terms. We should fit our prayers to their particular circumstances.

When Miriam was struck with leprosy, Moses cried out, **Numbers 12:13 NKJV**, *"Please heal her, O God, I pray!"* When the nobleman came to Jesus on behalf of his child, he said in **John 4:49 NKJV**, *"Sir, come down before my child dies!"*

In the same way, when our friends are in affliction, we should pray for them with their specific situation in mind. Is a friend sick? We should pray that, if it is God's will, the sickness will not end in death. But if God has appointed otherwise, we should pray that the person will receive grace to bear the trial and, after this painful life is over, dwell with God in everlasting life.

Is a friend in doubt about an important matter? We should bring the case before God, as Moses brought the case of the daughters of Zelophehad before the Lord. We should pray that the Holy Spirit would lead that person into all truth and give timely direction.

Is a friend in need? We should pray that his faith will not fail and that, in God's time, relief will come. In every case, we should not pray for our friends only in broad generalities, but shape our prayers according to their specific sufferings and needs. Otherwise, we may never ask for the very things they most need.

It is true that this kind of prayer may require some people to move beyond the forms they are used to. But if we practice it, and if we have a deep sense of what we are asking, even the least educated believer will find words enough to express himself.

Scripture gives us many noble examples of successful particular intercession. One remarkable example is Abraham's servant in Genesis. When he was sent to find a wife for Isaac, he prayed in a very specific way. The rest of the story shows how clearly God answered his prayer. If Christians today prayed for their friends in the same particular way and with the same faith, they would no doubt often receive clear answers and have great reason to bless God for them.

Fifth, as we ought to intercede for our friends, we must also pray for our enemies. Jesus said in **Matthew 5:44 NKJV**, *"Bless those who curse you, do good to those who hate you, and pray for those who spitefully use you and persecute you."* He gave the strongest possible example of this in His own life. In the pains of death, He prayed even for His murderers, saying in **Luke 23:34 NKJV**, *"Father, forgive them, for they do not know what they do."*

This is certainly a difficult duty, but it is not impossible for those who have renounced the things of this present life. Most enmity comes from an improper love of the world. Those who understand the terrible warnings spoken against those who offend Christ's little ones can pray for their enemies out of real pity and a sense of their danger.

Lastly, we should intercede for all who are afflicted in mind, body, or estate. We should pray for all who desire and need our prayers, and for all who do not pray for themselves.

O that everyone who hears me would set apart some time every day for the proper practice of this necessary duty.

Now, third, let us consider some advantages and motives to stir us to daily intercession.

First, intercession will fill your hearts with love for one another. A person who daily and sincerely intercedes at the throne of grace for all mankind cannot remain without love and charity. The frequent exercise of love in prayer will gradually enlarge his heart and make him a partaker of the abundant love that is in Christ Jesus our Lord.

Envy, malice, revenge, and other hellish tempers cannot long remain in the heart of a gracious intercessor. Instead, he will be filled with joy, peace, meekness, patience, and the other graces of the Holy Spirit. By frequently laying his neighbor's needs before God, he will gain a fellow-feeling for them. He will rejoice with those who rejoice and weep with those who weep. Every blessing given to another will not stir envy in him. Instead, he will see it as an answer to his prayers and be filled with joy unspeakable and full of glory.

Therefore, abound in general and particular intercession. When you hear of your neighbor's faults, do not spread them before others. Lay them secretly before God, and ask Him to correct and amend them. When you hear of a notorious sinner, instead of thinking you are right to be angry, beg Jesus Christ to convert him and make him a monument of His free grace. You cannot imagine what a blessed change this practice will make in your heart, or how much you will grow day by day in love and meekness toward all people.

Second, consider the many examples in Scripture that show the power and effectiveness of intercession. Great and excellent things are recorded as the results of this divine work. Intercession has stopped plagues. It has opened and shut heaven. It has often turned away God's wrath from His people.

Abimelech's house was healed after Abraham interceded for him. When Phinehas stood up and prayed, the plague stopped. When Daniel humbled himself and interceded for the Lord's people, an angel was quickly sent to tell him his prayer had been heard. And when Moses interceded for idolatrous Israel, God spoke as though He were overcome by Moses' pleading and said, "Let Me alone."

This shows the great power of intercession. We may, like Jacob, wrestle with God and by holy earnestness prevail for ourselves and others. No doubt it is because of the secret and prevailing intercessions of the few righteous people still among us that God has spared this sinful nation. If there were not some faithful ones like Moses standing in the gap, we would soon be destroyed like Sodom and reduced to ashes like Gomorrah.

Third, consider that intercession is very likely the frequent employment of the glorified saints. They are delivered from the burden of the flesh and restored to the glorious liberty of the sons of God. Yet their happiness will not be fully complete until the resurrection of the last day, when all their brethren will be glorified with them. Therefore, it is reasonable to think they often plead with our heavenly Father to complete the number of His elect and hasten His kingdom.

Should we not join, even while on earth, in this divine work with the glorious company of the spirits of just men made perfect? Since our future happiness will include the communion of saints in the church triumphant above, should we not often intercede for the church militant here below? Should we not earnestly pray that we may all be one, as Jesus and His Father are one, and that we may be made perfect in one?

Fourth, remember that intercession is the never-ceasing work of the holy and highly exalted Jesus Himself. He sits at the right hand of God to hear our prayers and to make continual intercession for us. Therefore, whoever is constantly interceding for others is doing on earth what the eternal Son of God is always doing in heaven.

When you lift holy hands in prayer for one another, imagine by faith that you see the heavens opened and the Son of God in all His glory as the great High Priest of your salvation. See Him pleading before the throne of His Father the all-sufficient merit of His sacrifice. Join your intercessions with His, and ask that through Him your prayers may rise like incense and be received as a sweet-smelling offering, acceptable in the sight of God.

This thought will strengthen your faith, stir holy earnestness in your prayers, and make you wrestle with God as Jacob did when he saw God face to face and his life was preserved. It will make you plead like Abraham for Sodom and pray like Jesus Christ Himself, who, being in agony, prayed more earnestly the night before His bitter suffering.

What more can I say? Jesus Christ Himself has taught you to abound in love and in this good work of praying for one another. Even if you are poor and lowly, even if you are as poor as Lazarus, by intercession you may become a benefactor to all mankind. Thousands, and tens of thousands, may be blessed for your sake.

After spending a few years in this divine exercise on earth, you will be taken to that happy place where you have so often prayed that others might go. You will be exalted to sit with our all-powerful and all-prevailing Intercessor in the kingdom of His heavenly Father.

I must press this duty upon you in a special way now, because in all probability many of you among whom I have been preaching may see me no more. I am now going from you, I trust under the guidance of God's most Holy Spirit, not knowing what will happen to me. Therefore, I need your most earnest intercessions, that nothing may move me from my duty and that I may not count my life dear to myself, so that I may finish my course with joy and the ministry I have received from the Lord Jesus, to testify to the gospel of the grace of God.

While I have been here, to the best of my knowledge, I have not failed to declare to you the whole counsel of God. Though my preaching may have been a savor of death leading to death for some, I trust it has also been a savor of life leading to life for others. Therefore, I earnestly hope that those who have been helped will not fail to remember me in their prayers.

As for me, the many undeserved kindnesses I have received from you will not allow me to forget you. Out of the depths, I trust my cry will come to God. While the winds and storms are blowing over me, I will make supplication to the Lord for you.

It is only a little while, and we must all appear before the judgment seat of Christ. There I must give a strict account of the doctrine I have preached, and you must give account of how you improved under it. O that I may never be called as a swift witness against any of those whose salvation I have sincerely, though too faintly, longed and labored for.

It is true that some have judged me as acting from selfish motives. But it is a small thing for me to be judged by man's judgment. I hope my eye is single. But I beseech you, brethren, by the mercies of God in Christ Jesus, pray that it may be even more so. Pray that I may increase with the increase of grace in the knowledge and love of God through Jesus Christ our Lord.

And now, brethren, what more shall I say? I could wish to continue much longer, because I can never fully express the desire of my soul toward you. Finally, brethren, whatever things are holy, whatever things are pure, whatever things are honest, whatever things are of good report, if there is any consolation in Christ, if there is any fellowship of the Spirit, if there is any hope that we may appear with comfort before one another at the solemn judgment seat of Jesus Christ, think on the things you have heard. Think also on the things your pastors have declared and will continue to declare to you.

Continue under their ministry to work out your own salvation with fear and trembling. Then, whether I never see you again, or whether God is pleased to bring me back at another time, I may always have the satisfaction of knowing that your conduct is worthy of the gospel of Christ.

I almost persuade myself that I could willingly suffer all things if it would in any way promote the salvation of your precious and immortal souls. As my last request, I beseech you: obey those who rule over you in the Lord, and always be ready to attend their ministry, as it is your duty.

Do not think that I desire to exalt myself at the expense of another man's character. Rather, do not admire any man's person too much. Esteem all your ministers highly in love for their work's sake, as they justly deserve.

And now, brethren, I commend you to God and to the word of His grace, which is able to build you up and give you an inheritance among all who are sanctified. May God reward you for all your works of faith and labors of love. May He make you abound more and more in every good word and work toward all people.

May He truly convert all who have been convicted. May He awaken all who are dead in trespasses and sins. May He confirm all who are wavering. May you all go on from one degree of grace to another until you arrive at the measure of the stature of the fullness of Christ. May you be made ready to stand before that God in whose presence is fullness of joy and at whose right hand are pleasures forevermore.

Amen and Amen.

Chapter Thirty-One

Satan's Devices

The occasion for this sermon comes from the church at Corinth. There was a man in that church who had committed a terrible sin, a kind of incest that was not even commonly named among the Gentiles. He had taken his father's wife. Yet, perhaps because of his wealth, influence, power, or some other reason, the church had not dealt with him as it should have.

The apostle Paul strongly corrected the Corinthians in his first letter because they had failed to practice proper church discipline. He commanded them, in the name of the Lord Jesus Christ, when they were gathered together, to deliver such a person to Satan for the destruction of the flesh, so that his spirit might be saved in the day of the Lord. In other words, they were to solemnly remove him from the fellowship of the church. In those days, this kind of discipline was sometimes accompanied by bodily affliction.

The Corinthians obeyed Paul's correction. They submitted to his instruction and put the offending man out of the church. But while they were trying to correct one error, they fell into another. Before, they had been too mild and too careless. Now they became too severe and resentful. So Paul corrected them again. He told them that the punishment given by many was sufficient. The man had suffered enough. Since he had shown signs of repentance, they should forgive him, comfort him, confirm their love toward him, and restore him in a spirit of meekness.

Paul was concerned that the man might be swallowed up with too much sorrow. He did not want Satan to take advantage of the situation by driving the man to despair. If the church acted in a cruel and merciless way, Satan could use that to bring reproach on the name of Christ. This is why Paul said in **2 Corinthians 2:11 NKJV**, *"Lest Satan should take advantage of us; for we are not ignorant of his devices."*

These words show us that Satan has many devices. He does not only tempt people to despair. His quiver is full of poisonous arrows. He has many subtle ways of drawing people aside and deceiving those who are careless and unguarded.

Let us first consider who Satan is. Then we will look at some of the chief devices he uses to draw converts away from Christ and consider remedies against them.

The word Satan means adversary. In Scripture, it is commonly used for the chief of the devils. He is the one who, through pride, sought to be like God and was cast down from heaven. He is now permitted, along with other evil spirits, to walk about seeking whom he may devour.

We hear of him soon after creation. In the form of a serpent, he lay in wait to deceive our first parents. He is called Satan in the book of Job, where we are told that when the sons of God came to present themselves before the Lord, Satan also came among them. Scripture also says that Satan moved David to number the people.

In the New Testament, Satan is called by several names. He is called the evil one because he is evil in himself and tempts others to evil. He is called the prince of the power of the air. He is called the spirit who now works in the children of disobedience. Those who are not born of God are said to lie under his influence.

Satan is an enemy of God and of all goodness. He hates truth. This is why he slandered God in the garden and told Eve, "You will not surely die." This is why he offered Jesus all the kingdoms of the world and their glory if only Jesus would fall down and worship him.

Satan is full of malice, envy, and revenge. Why else would he attack innocent man in paradise? Why else would he continue restlessly trying to destroy people who have done him no wrong?

Satan is also a being of great power. He was able to work on the imagination of our blessed Lord and show Him all the kingdoms of the world in a moment of time. He carried the sacred body of Jesus to the pinnacle of the temple. He drove a herd of swine violently into the sea. His strength is great. If God allowed him to use his full power, he could do terrible things in the earth.

But Satan is especially known for his subtlety. Since God has not allowed him to take us by force, he waits for opportunities to betray us and catch us by deception. This is why he used the serpent, the most cunning creature in the field, to tempt Adam and Eve. The New Testament says he lies in wait to deceive. Paul says, **2 Corinthians 2:11 NKJV**, *"For we are not ignorant of his devices."* This teaches us that we are often in more danger from his strategy than from his strength.

From this description of Satan, we may understand whose children they are who love lies, slander their neighbors, speak evil of others, and have hearts full of pride, malice, envy, revenge, subtlety, and unkindness. Surely such people show the family likeness of Satan. They know his temper and do his works. If they could see themselves and Satan as they truly are, they would be terrified by the resemblance and would humble themselves in dust and ashes.

Yet God is just in allowing His people to be tempted. We are in a state of spiritual warfare. God has promised that He will not allow us to be tempted beyond what we are able to bear. He has also promised that the one who overcomes will receive a crown of life.

Even the holy angels seem to have been tested. Adam was tempted in paradise. Jesus Christ, the second Adam, though He was the Son of God, was led by the Spirit into the wilderness to be tempted by the devil as our representative. There is not one saint in glory, not one prophet, apostle, martyr, or righteous soul made perfect, who was not assaulted on earth by the fiery darts of the wicked one.

What has been the common experience of God's children, of angels, and even of the eternal Son of God Himself, we should not expect to escape. It is enough if we are made perfect through temptations as they were. Therefore, since we cannot avoid being tempted unless we could cease being human, we should not complain about our condition. Instead, we should ask when Satan most violently attacks us and what devices he commonly uses to gain an advantage over us.

As to the time of life when Satan tempts us, we must expect temptation in some measure throughout our whole lives. This life is a continual warfare. We should never expect complete rest from our spiritual enemy, the devil, until, like our blessed Master, we bow our heads and give up the spirit.

But the time of conversion, when a person first enters the spiritual life, is often the most critical time. Satan knows that if he can prevent a person from truly setting out, he can continue to lead that person captive at his will. Scripture warns us that when we begin to serve the Lord, we should prepare our souls for temptation.

Now let us consider some of the devices Satan commonly uses at the beginning of conversion to gain an advantage over us. What follows is especially for those who have truly entered the divine life. It is not mainly for carnal, almost Christians, who have the form of godliness but have never felt its power in their hearts.

The first device Satan uses is to drive new converts to despair.

When God the Father awakens a sinner by the terrors of the law, and when the Holy Spirit convinces him of sin in order to lead him to Christ and show him his need of a Redeemer, Satan often comes in and tries to increase those convictions in a wrong way. He tries to make the sinner doubt whether mercy can be found through the Mediator.

This was part of his method when he tempted the Lord Jesus. He kept saying, "If You are the Son of God," do this or that. His goal was to make Jesus question His Sonship. No doubt Satan filled Paul with many dark and despairing thoughts during the three days after his conversion, when he neither ate nor drank. Paul spoke from experience when he said he was not ignorant of Satan's devices.

But do not let Satan drive you to despair of finding mercy. It is not the greatness or number of our sins that will ruin us, but impenitence and unbelief. Even if our sins were more numerous than the hairs of our head and darker than scarlet, the merits of the death of Jesus Christ are infinitely greater. Faith in His blood can make them white as snow.

Therefore, answer Satan's despairing suggestions the way Jesus answered him: with "It is written." Tell him that your Redeemer lives and always makes intercession for you. Tell him that the Lord has received full satisfaction from Christ for all your sins. Tell him that though you have sinned much, that is not a reason to despair, but a reason to love much because you have been forgiven much.

A second device Satan uses against young converts is to tempt them to presumption and pride. He tempts them to think more highly of themselves than they ought to think.

When a person has tasted the good Word of life and felt the powers of the world to come, he is often filled with great joy because of the change he sees in himself. In one sense, this joy is right. But Satan will try to use that joy to puff him up with pride, as though he were something great. He may tempt him to look down on other believers as if he were holier than they are.

Therefore, beware of this device of our spiritual enemy. Before honor comes humility, but a proud spirit goes before a fall. When we are lifted up with pride, God may send a humbling trial or permit us to fall, as He permitted Peter to fall into grievous sin, so that we may learn not to be high-minded.

To resist spiritual pride, remember that we did not take hold of Christ first. Christ took hold of us. We have nothing that we did not receive. Free grace alone has made the difference between us and others. If God left us to the deceitfulness of our own hearts for even one moment, we would become as weak and wicked as anyone else.

We should also remember that being proud of grace is one of the quickest ways to lose the comfort and strength of grace. God resists the proud and gives grace to the humble. Even if we had the perfections of angels, pride in those perfections would only make us more accomplished devils. Above all, we should pray earnestly that God would teach us to learn from Jesus, who is meek and lowly in heart. We should ask that grace itself would not become poison to us through the subtlety of Satan, but that we would always think soberly of ourselves.

A third device Satan uses is to tempt us to uneasiness and hard thoughts of God when we feel dead and barren in prayer.

The natural man does not understand this language. But those who have passed through the new birth know what it means to experience deadness and dryness in prayer. Many of God's people experience seasons when prayer feels cold, difficult, and lifeless.

When people are first awakened to spiritual life, because grace is still weak and nature is strong, God often gives them special comforts and illuminations of His Spirit. But as they grow, He sometimes seems to leave them to themselves. He may permit a dreadful deadness or heaviness to come upon them. At such times, Satan works hard to tempt them to impatience and hard thoughts of God.

But do not be afraid. Your blessed Redeemer went through something like this before you. Think of His agony in the garden, when His soul was exceedingly sorrowful, even unto death. He sweat great drops of blood falling to the ground. A sense of divine comfort was withdrawn from Him, and Satan was likely permitted to set his terrors before Him.

Therefore, rejoice when you fall into similar inward trials, knowing that you are partaking in some measure of the sufferings of Jesus Christ. Such trials are necessary to wean us from an excessive love of emotional comfort and teach us to follow Christ not merely for spiritual sweetness, but from love and obedience.

Possess your soul in patience. Do not be terrified by Satan's suggestions. Continue seeking Jesus in the means of grace, even if you seek Him sorrowing. Though your soul feels barren and you go mourning all the day, remember that the Bridegroom may be with you behind the curtain, as Jesus was near Mary at the tomb though she did not recognize Him.

Christ may withdraw for a little while so that His next visit will be more welcome. He may seem to frown on you, as He did with the Syrophoenician woman. Yet if you cry out all the more earnestly, like her, or like blind Bartimaeus, "Jesus, Son of David, have mercy on me," He will make Himself known to you again, whether in the temple, in the breaking of bread, or in some other way.

A fourth device of Satan is one of the most painful and successful. He troubles believers with blasphemous, profane, and unbelieving thoughts, sometimes to such a degree that they feel like torture.

Some people attribute all such thoughts to bodily disorder. There may be times when bodily weakness plays a part. But those who know the spiritual life can tell you that often these thoughts come from the wicked one. No doubt Satan still has permission from above at times to trouble the body, as he did Job's, so that he may more secretly and successfully disturb and torment the soul.

Those who have felt these fiery darts know this is true. You know how often Satan has tried to make you think, "Curse God and die." You know how he has shot a thousand blasphemous suggestions into your mind, even during your most secret and solemn times of prayer. When you look back on it, your heart trembles.

I appeal to your own conscience. Have some of you not been lifting holy hands in prayer when suddenly your mind was filled with horrible thoughts? Have you not been tempted to rise from your knees because you began to think your prayers were an abomination to the Lord? Have you not come to the Lord's Table, taken the symbols of Christ's body and blood, and instead of enjoying sweet remembrance of His death, found yourself fighting off evil thoughts, like Abraham driving away the birds from his sacrifice? Have you not feared that you were eating and drinking judgment to yourself?

Do not think some strange thing has happened to you. This has been the common experience of many of God's children. In Job's time, when the sons of God came to present themselves before the Lord, Satan also came among them to disturb their worship.

Do not think God is angry with you for thoughts that are unwanted and resisted, no matter how blasphemous they may be. God knows that these thoughts are not from your renewed heart, but from Satan working against you. He will punish Satan for them, but He will pity and reward you in the battle. It may be hard for you to believe this, but I do not doubt that you may be especially acceptable to God when you continue your holy duties in the midst of involuntary distractions. At such times, you are both doing and suffering the will of God.

You are like Nehemiah's servants while rebuilding the wall. They held a tool in one hand and a weapon in the other. So you are trying to pray while fighting. Do not allow these abominable suggestions to drive you away from the ordinances of God. If you leave the means of grace, Satan gets the very advantage he desires. His purpose in sending such thoughts is to make you fall out with prayer, communion, Scripture, and worship. He wants you to believe that because you do not please yourself, you do not please God.

Instead, persevere in the use of Holy Communion and all the other means of grace. When these temptations have produced the humility and surrender for which God allowed them, He will visit you with fresh tokens of His love, as He met Abraham after the battle with the kings. He will send strength from heaven, as He sent an angel to strengthen His own Son.

So far, we have considered devices Satan uses more directly. But a fifth device is also very common. Satan tempts us through carnal friends and relatives.

This is one of his most frequent and artful devices against young converts. When he cannot prevail by himself, he tries to work through the influence of others.

He tempted Eve so that she would tempt Adam. He stirred up Job's wife to say, "Curse God and die." He used Peter's tongue to persuade Jesus to spare Himself and avoid the sufferings by which alone we could be saved from eternal fire. In the same way, he often uses close friends, relatives, and loved ones to dissuade believers from walking in the narrow way that leads to life.

But our Lord has given us the answer to such temptations. We must say, "Get behind me, adversary." Otherwise, such people may become an offense to us. The reason they give such counsel is that they do not savor the things of God, but the things of men.

Therefore, anyone who is resolved to serve the Lord should prepare for such temptations. These offenses must come to test our sincerity, teach us to cease from man, and reveal whether we are willing to forsake all to follow Christ.

Modern teachers may try to persuade us that the strong demands of the gospel belonged only to the first Christians. They may say there is no longer any need to love Christ more than father and mother, or to suffer persecution for Christ and His gospel. But such people do not know the Scriptures or the power of godliness in the heart.

Whoever receives the love of God in truth will find that Christ still sends not peace but a sword. Family division for the sake of Christ still happens today, as it did in the early church. If we will live godly in Christ Jesus, we must expect persecution even from carnal friends and relatives.

A sixth device of Satan is very dangerous. Sometimes he does not seem to tempt us at all. Or rather, he withdraws for a while so that he may come again at an hour when we do not expect him.

Scripture says that Satan left Jesus only for a season. Our Lord has commanded us to watch and pray always so that we do not enter into temptation. This means that whether we are aware of it or not, Satan is always seeking how he may devour us.

If we want to behave like good soldiers of Jesus Christ, we must always be on guard. We must never lay down our spiritual weapons of prayer and watchfulness until our warfare is finished by death. If we do, our spiritual enemy will quickly gain an advantage.

What if Satan has left us for a time? It is only for a season. Soon enough, like a roaring lion, he may return with double fury. Though Satan is a coward, he rarely leaves us permanently after the first attack. As he followed our Lord with one temptation after another, so he will treat the servants of Christ. Sometimes he does not renew his attacks because God knows we are too weak to bear them at that moment. At other times, Satan waits for a more convenient season.

Therefore, Christian, watch carefully over your heart. Whenever you feel yourself falling into spiritual sleep, speak to your soul as Christ spoke to His disciples: "Arise, my soul. Why are you sleeping?" Awake. Put on strength. Watch and pray, or else the enemy will come upon you and lead you where you do not want to go.

Is this life a time to lie down and sleep? Arise and call upon your God. Your spiritual enemy is not dead. He is hiding in some secret place, seeking the right opportunity to betray you. If you stop striving against him, you stop acting like a friend of God. You stop walking in the narrow way that leads to life.

These are some of the devices Satan commonly uses to gain an advantage over us. No doubt there are many more. Because of my youth and limited experience, I cannot warn you of all of them. Those who have served Christ for many years and have fought long under His banner against our spiritual enemy can discern more of Satan's strategies. Because they have been tempted in many ways like their brethren, they are better able to advise and help those who are tempted.

In the meantime, let me exhort my young fellow soldiers, who, like me, are just entering the field. Do not be discouraged by the fiery trial through which you must pass if you would be found faithful servants of Jesus Christ.

You have heard that the way through the wilderness of this world to the heavenly Canaan is filled with thorns. You have heard that there are giants to fight before you possess the promised land. But do not let these things, like false spies, discourage you from going up to fight the Lord's battles. Rather say with Caleb and Joshua, "We are well able to overcome."

Jesus Christ, the great Captain of our salvation, has already defeated the great enemy of mankind in our place and as our representative. Our duty is to fight courageously under His banner and go forward from conquering to conquer.

Our glory is not that we are free from temptations, but that we endure them. Scripture says in **James 1:12 NKJV**, *"Blessed is the* *man who endures temptation."* It also says in **James 1:2 NKJV**, *"My brethren, count it all joy when you fall into various trials."* In the prayer our Lord taught us, we are not told to pray that we will never be tempted, but that we will be delivered from evil.

While we are on this side of eternity, temptations must come. No doubt Satan has desired to have all of us, that he might sift us as wheat. But why should we fear? The One who is for us is far more powerful than all who are against us. Jesus Christ, our great High Priest, is exalted to the right hand of God, where He ever lives to make intercession for us, that our faith may not fail.

Since Christ is praying for us, whom should we fear? Since He has promised to make us more than conquerors, of whom should we be afraid? Even if a whole army of devils rises against us, let us not be afraid. Even if the hottest persecution breaks out against us, let us put our trust in God.

Satan and his fallen spirits are powerful compared with us. But compared with the Almighty, they are weaker than the smallest worm. God has reserved them in chains of darkness for the judgment of the great day. They can go only as far as God permits, and no farther. Wherever God chooses, their proud and malicious plans must stop.

In the Gospel, a legion of demons possessed one man, yet they could not destroy him. They could not even enter a herd of swine without permission from above. It is true that we are often wounded when they attack us. But let us be strong and very courageous. Though they bruise our heel, we shall in the end bruise their head.

Yet a little while, and He who is coming will come. Then we shall see all our spiritual enemies put under our feet. What if they come against us like great Goliaths? If we go forward like young David in the name and strength of the Lord of hosts, we may say, "O Satan, where is your power? O fallen spirits, where is your victory?"

Therefore, let us be strong and very courageous. Let us put on the whole armor of God, so that we may stand against the fiery darts of the wicked one. Let us renounce ourselves and the world. Then we will take away the armor in which Satan trusts, and he will find nothing in us for his temptations to work upon.

Let us have our loins girded with truth. Let us put on the helmet of the hope of salvation. Let us pray always with all kinds of prayer and supplication. Above all, let us take the shield of faith and the sword of the Spirit, which is the Word of God. Let us look continually to Jesus, the author and finisher of our faith, who for the joy set before Him endured the cross, despised the shame, and now sits at the right hand of God.

May God, in His infinite mercy, bring us all to that blessed place through our Lord Jesus Christ. To Him, with the Father and the Holy Spirit, three Persons and one eternal God, be all honor and glory, now and forevermore.

Amen.

Chapter Thirty-Two

Marks of Having Received the Holy Ghost

Acts 19:2 NKJV *"Did you receive the Holy Spirit when you believed?"*

There have been different views about the meaning of these words. Some believe Paul was asking the disciples at Ephesus whether they had received the Holy Spirit through the laying on of hands, as in confirmation. Others believe these disciples had already received John's baptism, but had not yet been baptized in the name of Jesus Christ, and therefore had not yet received the fuller blessing of the Holy Spirit connected with faith in Christ.

Which interpretation is exactly right is not easy to decide, nor is it necessary for our present purpose. The question itself is deeply important: **Acts 19:2 NKJV**, *"Did you receive the Holy Spirit when you believed?"* From these words, I want to consider three things. First, who the Holy Spirit is, and why we must all receive Him before we can truly be called believers. Second, the scriptural marks by which we may know whether we have received Him. Third, I will apply this truth to several kinds of people.

First, we must understand who the Holy Spirit is. By the Holy Spirit, Scripture means the third Person of the blessed Trinity. He is one in substance and eternal with the Father and the Son. He proceeds from the Father and the Son, yet He is equal with them both. He is called holy because He is infinitely holy in Himself, and because He is the author and finisher of all holiness in us.

This blessed Spirit once moved upon the face of the waters. He overshadowed the Virgin Mary before the holy child Jesus was born of her. He descended in bodily form like a dove upon our blessed Lord when He came up from the waters of baptism. Later, on the Day of Pentecost, He came down in tongues of fire upon the apostles. This same Holy Spirit must move upon our souls. The power of the Most High must come upon us. We must be baptized with His baptism and refining fire before we can truly be called members of Christ's mystical body.

Paul says in **2 Corinthians 13:5 NKJV**, *"Do you not know yourselves, that Jesus Christ is in you? unless indeed you are disqualified."* Christ is in His people by His Spirit. Paul also says in **Romans 8:9 NKJV**, *"Now if anyone does not have the Spirit of Christ, he is not His."* John says in **1 John 3:24 NKJV**, *"And by this we know that He abides in us, by the Spirit whom He has given us."*

It is not necessary that the Spirit be given to us now in the same miraculous way He was first given to the apostles, with outward signs and wonders. But it is absolutely necessary that we receive the Holy Spirit in His sanctifying graces as truly as they did. This will remain necessary until the end of the world.

Here is the condition of man before God. In the beginning, God made man upright. Scripture says that man was made in the image of God. This means that man's soul reflected the divine nature. The God who spoke the world into existence breathed into man the breath of spiritual life. Man's soul was adorned with a likeness of God's own perfections.

This was the finishing touch of creation, the glory of both the moral and visible world. Man resembled his Maker so closely that God looked upon His creation and said it was very good.

How happy man must have been when he was a partaker of the divine nature. And he could have remained happy if he had remained holy. But God placed him in a state of testing. He gave him freedom to eat of every tree in the garden except the tree of the knowledge of good and evil. In the day he ate of it, he would surely die. This death included not only physical death, but spiritual death. He would lose the divine image, the spiritual life God had breathed into him. That spiritual life was both his happiness and his glory.

These were easy conditions for a creature's happiness. But man, unhappy man, was deceived by the devil. Desiring, like the devil, to be equal with his Maker, he ate the forbidden fruit. By doing so, he became subject to the curse that the eternal God, who cannot lie, had warned would follow disobedience.

After Adam fell, he complained that he was naked. He was not only physically exposed. He was spiritually naked, stripped of those divine graces that had once beautified his soul. The disorder that entered the visible creation, the thorns and thistles that sprang up from the ground, were only faint pictures of the deeper disorder that entered the soul of man. Confusion, rebellion, lusts, and sinful passions rose up in him and overwhelmed him.

Man was no longer the image of the invisible God as he had been before. Since he had imitated the devil's sin, he became in a sense a partaker of the devil's nature. Instead of union with God, he fell into a state of enmity against God.

This is the dreadful and disordered condition in which all of us are born. As the root is, so are the branches. Scripture says that Adam begot a son in his own likeness. That means Adam passed on the corrupt nature he had after the fall. Scripture and experience both prove that we are born in sin and corruption. In that condition, we are unable to have communion with God. Light cannot have communion with darkness, and God cannot have communion with polluted sons of Belial.

Here we see why Christ came in the flesh. He came to put an end to these disorders and restore us to the dignity in which we were first created. He shed His precious blood to satisfy His Father's justice for our sins. He also obtained for us the Holy Spirit, who restores the divine image to our hearts and makes us able to live with and enjoy the blessed God.

This was the great purpose of Christ's coming into the world. In fact, this is one reason the world is still being preserved. When the full number of God's people has been sanctified out of it, the heavens will be rolled up like a scroll, the elements will melt with fervent heat, and the earth and all its works will be burned up.

This sanctifying work of the Spirit is the new birth Jesus spoke of to Nicodemus. Without it, we cannot see the kingdom of God. This is what Paul calls being renewed in the spirit of our minds. It is the fountain of that holiness without which no one will see the Lord.

Therefore, it is undeniable that we must receive the Holy Spirit before we can truly be called members of Christ's mystical body.

Now let us consider some scriptural marks by which we may know whether we have received the Holy Spirit.

The first mark is having received a spirit of prayer and supplication. The spirit of grace always comes with the spirit of prayer. As soon as Paul was converted, it was said of him, "Behold, he is praying." This was used as evidence to Ananias that Paul had truly been changed. God's elect are also described as those who cry out to Him day and night.

One great work of the Holy Spirit is to convince us of sin and set us seeking pardon and renewing grace through the all-sufficient merits of a crucified Redeemer. Whoever has felt the power of the world to come awakening him from spiritual sleep cannot help crying, "Lord, what do You want me to do?" Or, like blind Bartimaeus, "Jesus, Son of David, have mercy on me."

Jesus received the Holy Spirit without measure, and He showed this in His frequent prayers to the Father. We read that He was often alone on the mountain praying. He rose long before day to pray. He even spent whole nights in prayer. Whoever partakes of the same

Spirit that was in holy Jesus will share this same mind. He will delight in drawing near to God and lifting holy hands and holy hearts in frequent and earnest prayer.

It is true that even those who have received the Holy Spirit may, for a time, feel as though the spirit of prayer has been lost or has grown weak. Through spiritual dryness and barrenness of soul, they may feel listless and reluctant in prayer. But they view this as their cross. They still continue seeking Jesus, even if they seek Him with sorrow. Their hearts remain fixed upon God, even when their affections are not as lively as usual because spiritual deadness has benumbed their souls for a season.

But it is different with the formal believer. He either does not pray at all, or when he enters his closet, he does it reluctantly, from habit, or merely to quiet his conscience. The true believer can no more live without prayer than he can live without daily food. He finds that his soul is truly fed by prayer just as his body is nourished by bread.

A second scriptural mark of having received the Holy Spirit is not committing sin as a settled practice. John says in **1 John 3:9 NKJV**, *"Whoever has been born of God does not sin, for His seed remains in him; and he cannot sin, because he has been born of God."*

This does not mean that a Christian can never fall into sin at all. Scripture says in **James 3:2 NKJV**, *"For we all stumble in many things."* John's meaning is that a person truly born of God does not willfully and habitually live in sin. How can someone who has died to sin continue living in it?

A person born again may, through surprise or the violence of temptation, fall into a sinful act. David fell into adultery. Peter denied his Master. But like them, the true believer quickly rises again. He goes out and weeps bitterly. He washes away the guilt of sin by sincere repentance joined with faith in the blood of Jesus Christ. He becomes more watchful over his ways and seeks to perfect holiness in the fear of God.

This can be illustrated by a covetous man. A generous and lavish spirit is completely contrary to his natural inclination. If, on some sudden occasion, he spends too freely, he quickly regrets it and returns with greater care to his usual stinginess. In a similar way, sin is contrary to the habitual direction of a born-again heart. If he is drawn into sin, he quickly repents and returns to duty with renewed zeal, bringing forth fruits worthy of repentance.

But the unconverted sinner is dead in trespasses and sins. Even if he avoids some outward sins for selfish or worldly reasons, there is still some right eye he will not pluck out, some right hand he will not cut off, some beloved Agag he will not sacrifice for God. This proves that he is like Saul, not truly obedient from the heart. Whatever claims he makes, he has not yet received the Holy Spirit.

A third mark of having received the Holy Spirit is conquest over the world. John says in **1 John 5:4 NKJV**, *"For whatever is born of God overcomes the world."*

By the world, we mean what John describes as the lust of the flesh, the lust of the eyes, and the pride of life. To overcome the world means to renounce these things so that we are not ruled or led by them. Whoever is born from above sets his affection on things above. He feels a divine attraction drawing his mind toward heaven. As the deer pants for the water brooks, so his soul longs for the enjoyment of God.

This does not mean that the spiritual person neglects the duties of this life. No true spiritual man dares to stand idle. He works faithfully in his calling. But while he labors for food that perishes, he is careful first to seek the food that endures to everlasting life. If God has raised him to a place of influence, he remains like Moses, Joseph, and Daniel, seeing himself as a stranger and pilgrim on the earth.

Because he has received a principle of new life, he walks by faith and not by sight. His hope is full of immortality. He can look on everything below as vanity and vexation of spirit compared with God. In short, though he is in the world, he is not of the world. Since he was made for the enjoyment of God, nothing but God can satisfy his soul.

Jesus is the perfect example of overcoming the world. Though He went about doing good and lived in the middle of crowds, His conversation always pointed heavenward. In the same way, the person joined to the Lord in one spirit will order his thoughts, words, and actions so that others can see his citizenship is in heaven.

The unconverted man is different. Being of the earth, he is earthly. Having no spiritual eye to discern spiritual things, he always seeks happiness in this life, where it never has been and never can be found. Because he is not born from above, he is bowed down by a spirit of natural weakness. The serpent's curse becomes his choice, and he feeds on the dust of the earth all his life.

A fourth scriptural mark of having received the Holy Spirit is loving one another. John says in **1 John 3:14 NKJV**, *"We know that* *we have passed from death to life, because we love the brethren."* Jesus Himself said in **John 13:35 NKJV**, *"By this all will know that you are My disciples, if you have love for one another."*

Love fulfills the gospel as well as the law. Scripture says in **1 John 4:16 NKJV**, *"God is love, and he who abides in love abides in God, and God in him."*

But this love is not merely natural softness, human kindness, or affection based on worldly reasons. A natural person may have that kind of tenderness. Christian love flows from love toward God. It loves all people in general because of their relationship to God as His creatures. It especially loves godly people because of the grace seen in them and because they love the Lord Jesus in sincerity.

This is Christian charity. This is the new commandment Christ gave His disciples. It is new, not because love had never been commanded before, but because it is now rooted in the motive and example of Jesus Christ. The early Christians were known for this love, so much so that others said, "See how these Christians love one another." Without this love, even if we gave all our goods to feed the poor and gave our bodies to be burned, it would profit us nothing.

This love is not limited to one group, party, or denomination. It is impartial and universal. It embraces the image of God wherever it sees it. It delights in nothing more than the coming of Christ's kingdom.

This is the love with which Jesus loved mankind. He loved all, even the worst of men, as seen when He wept over those who were stubborn and rebellious. But wherever He saw even the smallest appearance of divine likeness, He loved that soul in a special way. When the rich young ruler said he had kept the commandments from his youth, Jesus loved him for what was good in him. When Jesus saw great faith in a centurion or a Syrophoenician woman, even though they were outside Israel, He marveled, rejoiced, spoke of it, and commended it.

So every spiritual disciple of Jesus Christ will sincerely embrace all who worship God in spirit and truth, even if they differ in secondary matters of religion that are not essential to salvation.

It is true that the heart of a natural man is not enlarged in this way all at once. A person may truly have received the Holy Spirit and still not yet be fully mature in this love, as Peter had received the Spirit and yet was hesitant to go to Cornelius. But where a person is truly in Christ, narrowness of spirit decreases day by day. The wall of bigotry and party spirit is broken down more and more. The nearer he comes to heaven, the more his heart is enlarged with the kind of love that will fill heaven, where people of every nation, language, and people will sing with one heart and one voice to Him who sits on the throne forever.

A fifth mark of having received the Holy Spirit is loving our enemies. Jesus said in **Matthew 5:44 NKJV**, *"Love your enemies, bless those who curse you, do good to those who hate you, and pray for those who spitefully use you and persecute you."*

This duty is so necessary that without it, our righteousness does not exceed the righteousness of the scribes and Pharisees, or even of tax collectors and sinners. Jesus said in **Matthew 5:46 NKJV**, *"For if you love those who love you, what reward have you? Do not even the tax collectors do the same?"*

Jesus confirmed this command by His own example. He wept over Jerusalem, even though it was a rebellious and bloody city. He allowed Himself to be led like a sheep to the slaughter. He spoke gently even to Judas, saying, **Luke 22:48 NKJV**, *"Judas, are you betraying the Son of Man with a kiss?"* Most of all, while suffering the agony of death, He prayed for His murderers in **Luke 23:34 NKJV**, *"Father, forgive them, for they do not know what they do."*

This is difficult for the natural man. But whoever partakes of the promised Spirit will find it possible and, by grace, even delightful. If we are born of God, we must become like Him. Therefore, we will desire to be complete in this duty, doing good even to our worst enemies, in the same manner, though not in the same degree, as God does. He sends rain on the evil and the good. He makes His sun rise on the just and the unjust. And above all, He showed His love toward us in that while we were enemies, He sent His Son, born of a woman and made under the law, to become a curse for us.

Many other marks are found throughout Scripture by which we may know whether we have received the Holy Spirit. Scripture says in **Romans 8:6 NKJV**, *"For to be carnally minded is death, but to be spiritually minded is life and peace."* Paul also writes in **Galatians 5:22–23 NKJV**, *"But the fruit of the Spirit is love, joy, peace, longsuffering, kindness, goodness, faithfulness, gentleness, self-control."* Many more verses teach the same truth.

But most, if not all, of these marks are included in the ones already given. I dare say that whoever, after honest examination, finds these marks in his soul may be as certain of his pardon as if an angel came from heaven to tell him it was sealed.

For my own part, I would rather see these divine graces and this heavenly temper stamped upon my soul than hear an angel say to me, "Son, be of good cheer, your sins are forgiven." These graces are reliable witnesses. They are Emmanuel, God with us and in us. They make up the white stone that no one knows except the one who receives it. They are the firstfruits of the heavenly inheritance in our hearts. They are glory begun in the soul. They are that good thing, that better part, which, if we continue to stir up the gift of God, neither men nor devils will be able to take from us.

Now let us apply this doctrine to several different kinds of people.

First, I speak to those who are dead in trespasses and sins. O how I could weep over you as our Lord wept over Jerusalem. How far you must be from God. What a great work must be done in you. Instead of praying day and night, some of you rarely, if ever, pray at all. Instead of being born again so that you do not live in sin, you are so deeply sunk into the nature of devils that you mock sin and treat it lightly. Instead of overcoming the world, you are constantly making provision for the flesh to fulfill its lusts. Instead of being filled with the godlike disposition of loving all people, even your enemies, your hearts are full of hatred, malice, revenge, and you mock the sincere followers of the humble Jesus.

Do you think God will admit polluted people into His presence? And even if He did, do you think you could take any pleasure in Him? No. Heaven itself would not be heaven to you. The devilish dispositions in your hearts would make all the spiritual joys of heaven unable to make you happy. To enjoy the inheritance of the saints in light, you must be made fit for it. Seeking that fitness should be the chief business of your life.

It is true that, in one sense, you will see God. All must appear before the judgment seat of Christ. But if you remain in this condition, you will see Him once, only to be banished from Him forever. Since you carry the devil's image, you must dwell with devils. Being of the same nature, you must share the same doom. Therefore, repent and be converted, that your sins may be blotted out. See to it that you receive the Holy Spirit before you leave this world. Otherwise, how will you escape the damnation of hell?

Second, I speak to those who deceive themselves with false hopes of salvation. Some, through good upbringing or other restraints of providence, have not run into the same open excess as others. Because of this, they think they have no need to receive the Holy Spirit. They flatter themselves that they are already born again.

But do you prove it by bearing the fruits of the Spirit? Do you pray without ceasing? Do you refuse to live in sin? Have you overcome the world? Do you love your enemies and all mankind as Jesus Christ loved them?

If these things are in you and abound, then you may have confidence toward God. But if not, then although you may be civilized, you are not converted. You are still in your sins. The nature of the first Adam still reigns in your soul. Unless the nature of the second Adam is grafted in its place, you can never see God.

Do not dress yourself in the ornaments of good nature and civil education and say, like Agag, "Surely the bitterness of death is past." God's justice will still deal with you. However highly you may be esteemed by people, in the sight of God you are like the apples of Sodom, beautiful on the outside but rotten within. You are like snow-covered dung heaps, like whitewashed tombs that appear clean outwardly but are full of corruption and uncleanness within. Unless you are truly changed, you will hear Christ say at the last day, "I never knew you."

But the Word of God is useful for comfort as well as correction.

Third, I speak to those who are under the drawing of the Father and are experiencing the spirit of bondage. You do not yet find the marks I have described, and you cry out, "Who will deliver me from this body of death?"

Fear not, little flock. Though you are now in an infant state of grace, it is your Father's good pleasure to give you the kingdom. The grace of God through Jesus Christ will deliver you and give you what you thirst after. He has promised, and He will do it.

You shall receive the Spirit of adoption, the promise of the Father, if you do not faint. Persevere in seeking Him. Determine not to be at rest in your soul until you know and feel that you are born again from above, and until God's Spirit bears witness with your spirit that you are a child of God.

Fourth and lastly, I speak to those who have received the Holy Spirit in His sanctifying graces and are almost ripe for glory.

Hail, happy saints. Your heaven has already begun on earth. You have received the firstfruits of the Spirit and are patiently waiting for the blessed change when your harvest will be complete. I see and admire you, though, sadly, from a great distance. Your life is hidden with Christ in God. You have comforts and spiritual food that a sinful, carnal, mocking world knows nothing about.

Christ's yoke has become easy to you, and His burden light. You have passed through the pains of the new birth and now rejoice that Christ Jesus has been spiritually formed in your hearts. You know what it means to dwell in Christ and Christ in you. Like Jacob's ladder, your bodies are still on earth, but your souls and hearts are in heaven. By faith and continual recollection, like the blessed angels, you behold the face of your Father who is in heaven.

I hardly need to exhort you to press forward, because you already know that in walking in the Spirit there is great reward. Rather, I exhort you to possess your souls in patience a little while longer. Soon Jesus Christ will deliver you from the burden of the flesh. Then an abundant entrance will be given to you into the eternal joy and uninterrupted happiness of His heavenly kingdom.

May God, in His infinite mercy, grant this through Jesus Christ our Lord. To Him, with the Father and the Holy Spirit, three Persons and one God, be all honor, power, and glory forever and ever.

Amen.

Chapter Thirty-Three

The Almost Christian

Acts 26:28 NKJV *"You almost persuade me to become a Christian."*

The chapter where this text is found gives us a powerful account of Paul's conversion from Judaism to Christianity. Paul was brought before Festus, a Gentile governor, and King Agrippa, and there he gave his defense. Our Lord had already told His disciples that they would be brought before kings and rulers for His name's sake, as a testimony to them. God's wisdom was clearly seen in this. Christianity was, from the beginning, a doctrine of the cross. The rulers of the earth often thought themselves too high to be taught by humble messengers and too comfortable to be disturbed by unwelcome truths. Therefore, they would have remained strangers to Jesus Christ and Him crucified if the apostles had not been brought before them and given the opportunity to preach Jesus and the resurrection.

Paul understood this. He knew that his Master had allowed his enemies to bring him before this public court so that he might testify of Christ. Therefore, he did not think it enough merely to defend himself. He also tried to convert his judges.

He spoke with such power and evidence of the Spirit that Festus, unwilling to be convinced, cried out loudly, "Paul, you are beside yourself. Much learning is driving you mad." But Paul, like a true follower of the meek and holy Jesus, answered with gentleness, "I am not mad, most noble Festus, but speak the words of truth and reason."

Paul likely saw that King Agrippa was more affected by his words and seemed more open to the truth. So he turned more directly to him and said that the king knew these things, and that none of them were hidden from him. Then, hoping to complete the work of persuasion, Paul asked with great boldness and wisdom, "King Agrippa, do you believe the prophets? I know that you believe."

At this, Agrippa's emotions began to stir so strongly that he openly confessed how deeply Paul's preaching had affected him. He said, **Acts 26:28 NKJV**, *"You almost persuade me to become a Christian."*

These words, together with the context, give us a vivid picture of the different ways people still respond to the preaching of Christ's ministers. When ministers come in the spirit and power of Paul, they speak words of truth and reason. Their enemies may not be able to honestly refute them. Yet many, like Festus, are too proud to be taught, too sensual, too careless, or too worldly-minded to obey the doctrine. So they excuse themselves by saying that too much learning, too much study, or even too much religion has made these ministers mad.

Blessed be God, not everyone rejects the report in this way. Many gladly receive the Word and admit that the message is true and sober. Yet among those who gladly hear, there are still very few who rise beyond the condition of Agrippa. Many are persuaded only to be almost Christians.

Because of this, it is necessary to warn people of the danger of such a state. From the words of the text, let us consider three things. First, what is meant by an almost Christian. Second, the main reasons why so many are no more than almost Christians. Third, the uselessness, danger, foolishness, and unrest that belong to those who are only almost Christians. Then we will end with an exhortation to strive to be not only almost, but altogether Christians.

An almost Christian, in regard to his duty toward God, is a person who stops between two opinions. He wavers between Christ and the world. He tries to reconcile God and mammon, light and darkness, Christ and Belial. He has some inclination toward religion, but he is very careful not to go too far. His false heart is always saying, "Spare yourself. Do yourself no harm."

He may pray, "Your will be done on earth as it is in heaven," yet he is partial in his obedience. He hopes God will not be too strict in noticing the things he willingly does wrong, even though Scripture teaches that whoever offends in one point is guilty of all.

Most of all, the almost Christian depends heavily on outward ordinances. Because of this, he looks upon himself as righteous and despises others. Yet at the same time, he is a stranger to the divine life. In short, he loves the form of godliness but has never experienced its power in his heart. Year after year, he attends the means of grace, but like Pharaoh's lean cows, he is never better for them. In fact, he may become worse.

In regard to his neighbor, the almost Christian may be strictly just and fair. But this does not come from love to God or true love for man. It comes from self-love. He knows dishonesty would hurt his reputation and could hinder his success in the world. So he is honest because it serves his own interests.

He depends greatly on being negatively good. He comforts himself by saying he has done no one any harm. But he forgets that the unprofitable servant was cast into outer darkness, and the barren fig tree was cursed and dried up from the roots, not because it bore bad fruit, but because it bore no fruit.

The almost Christian is not against public charitable giving, as long as it is not urged too often. But he is unfamiliar with the private acts of mercy that true religion requires, such as visiting the sick and imprisoned, clothing the naked, and feeding the hungry. He may think these things belong only to ministers, though his own heart tells him that pride keeps him from such humble acts.

Jesus, in **Matthew 25:34–36 NKJV**, said, *"Come, you blessed of My Father, inherit the kingdom prepared for you from the foundation of the world: for I was hungry and you gave Me food; I was thirsty and you gave Me drink; I was a stranger and you took Me in; I was naked and you clothed Me; I was sick and you visited Me; I was in prison and you came to Me."* But to those on His left, He will say in **Matthew 25:41–43 NKJV**, *"Depart from Me, you cursed, into the everlasting fire prepared for the devil and his angels: for I was hungry and you gave Me no food; I was thirsty and you gave Me no drink; I was a stranger* *and you did not take Me in; naked and you did not clothe Me; sick and in prison and you did not visit Me."* Then He explains in **Matthew 25:45–46 NKJV**, *"Assuredly, I say to you, inasmuch as you did not do it to one of the least of these, you did not do it to Me. And these will go away into everlasting punishment, but the righteous into eternal life."*

This passage must be taken seriously because our Savior places great weight upon it. Yet it is so little regarded that if we judged by the practice of many who call themselves Christians, we might think these verses were not even in the Bible.

Now consider the almost Christian in regard to himself. As he may be outwardly honest toward his neighbor, so he may also be outwardly sober in himself. But both his honesty and sobriety come from the same false principle of self-love. It is true, he does not run into the same excess as other people. But this is not because of obedience to God. It may be because his body cannot handle intemperance, or because he is careful not to lose his reputation or make himself unfit for business.

Though he avoids drunkenness and excess, he still goes as far as he can in what he thinks is lawful. He is not a drunkard, but he has no Christian self-denial. He cannot imagine that the Savior is so strict as to deny him certain indulgences. In this way, he may be as destitute of true religion as if he lived openly in scandalous sin.

When it comes to forming his principles and conduct, he is guided more by the world than by the Word of God. He cannot believe the way to heaven is as narrow as some say. So he does not ask first what Scripture requires. Instead, he asks what certain respectable people do, or what best suits his own corrupt desires.

Because of this, he is cautious himself and also becomes a hindrance to young converts whose faces are set toward heaven. He is always doing the devil's work by telling them to spare themselves, even when they are doing no more than Scripture commands. The result is that he does not enter the kingdom of God himself, and he hinders those who are entering.

This is how the almost Christian lives. I have not fully described him, but I have given enough of his character that, if your conscience is awake and applies these things to your own heart, some of you may see features of his picture in yourselves. And if you do, I hope you will join the apostle in the words following the text and desire to be not only almost, but altogether Christians.

Now let us consider the reasons why so many are no more than almost Christians.

The first reason is that many begin with false ideas of religion. Though they live in a Christian country, they do not truly know what Christianity is. This may sound hard, but experience sadly proves it true. Some think religion consists in belonging to this or that church. Others place it in morality. Most place it in a round of duties and outward performances. But few understand religion as it truly is: a thorough inward change of nature, a divine life, a living participation in Jesus Christ, and a union of the soul with God.

Paul describes this in **1 Corinthians 6:17 NKJV**, *"But he who is joined to the Lord is one spirit with Him."*

Because so many do not understand the essence, life, and soul of religion, they are ignorant of the new birth in Christ Jesus. Like Nicodemus, they ask, "How can these things be?" No wonder so many are only almost Christians when so many do not know what Christianity truly is. No wonder so many are satisfied with the form when they are strangers to the power of godliness. No wonder they settle for the shadow when they know so little of the substance.

A second reason so many are no more than almost Christians is a slavish fear of man. Many have been awakened to a sense of divine life. They have tasted something of the powers of the world to come. Yet because they fear being thought strange, mocked, or despised by men, they allow those good impressions to fade away.

They have some respect for Jesus Christ, but like Nicodemus, they want to come to Him only by night. They are willing to serve Him, but only secretly, for fear of others. They want to see Jesus, but they cannot come to Him because of the crowd and because they fear being laughed at by the people with whom they once sat and ate.

Jesus said in **John 5:44 NKJV**, *"How can you believe, who receive honor from one another, and do not seek the honor that comes from the only God?"* Have such people never read that friendship with the world is enmity with God? Have they never heard the warning of Christ in **Mark 8:38 NKJV**, *"For whoever is ashamed of Me and My words in this adulterous and sinful generation, of him the Son of Man also will be ashamed when He comes in the glory of His Father with the holy angels"*?

No wonder many are no more than almost Christians when so many love the praise of men more than the honor that comes from God.

A third reason so many are no more than almost Christians is a ruling love of money. This was the sad case of the eager young man in the Gospel who came running to Jesus, knelt before Him, and asked what he must do to inherit eternal life. Jesus reminded him of the commandments. The young man replied that he had kept them from his youth. But when Jesus told him that he lacked one thing and must sell what he had, give to the poor, and follow Him, the young man went away sorrowful because he had great possessions.

Poor young man. He had a desire to be a Christian and inherit eternal life, but he thought the price too high if it required parting with his estate.

So it is with many today, young and old. They come running to worship Christ publicly and kneel before Him privately. They ask from His Gospel what they must do to inherit eternal life. But when they discover that they must renounce selfish enjoyment of riches and forsake all in affection to follow Him, they say, "Lord, excuse us in this matter."

But is heaven such a small thing that it is not worth giving up a little glittering earth? Is eternal life so cheap in people's eyes that it is not worth the temporary renunciation of a few passing riches? Surely this is madness. Yet the inordinate love of money is one common and deadly reason why many are no more than almost Christians.

A fourth reason is the love of pleasure. There are thousands who despise riches and would gladly be disciples of Jesus if merely parting with money would make them so. But when they hear that Jesus said whoever comes after Him must deny himself, they go away sorrowful because they love sensual pleasures too much.

They may send for ministers as Herod sent for John and hear them gladly. But touch their Herodias, tell them they must part with a darling pleasure, and they cry out like Ahab, "Have you found me, O my enemy?" Tell them of the necessity of self-denial and mortification, and they find it as hard to hear as if you told them to cut off a right hand or pluck out a right eye.

They cannot believe that Christ requires so much, though an inspired apostle commands us to put to death our members which are on the earth. Paul himself, even after converting thousands and nearing the end of his race, still said he disciplined his body and brought it into subjection, lest after preaching to others he himself should be disqualified.

But some people think they are wiser than Paul. They try to draw an easier path to heaven. They flatter people by telling them they may go to heaven without doing violence to their sinful appetites and may enter the narrow gate without striving against carnal desires. This is another reason so many are almost, but not altogether Christians.

The fifth and last reason I will mention is fickleness and instability of character. Many ministers and sincere Christians have had to weep over promising converts who seemed to begin in the Spirit but later ended in the flesh. This did not happen because they lacked right ideas about religion, nor because they feared man, loved money, or loved pleasure. It happened because they were unstable.

They took up religion as something new and interesting. It pleased them for a while. But after their curiosity was satisfied, they laid it aside again. Like the young man who followed Jesus with a linen cloth around his body and then fled naked when danger came, they followed Christ for a season, but when temptation seized them, they lacked resolution and fled.

At first, they seemed like trees planted by the water, growing and flourishing. But because they had no root in themselves, no inward principle of holiness, they dried up and withered like Jonah's gourd. Their good intentions were like the violent movements of a body just after death. They were strong for a moment, but not lasting.

In short, they began well on the journey to heaven. But when they found the way narrower or longer than expected, their unstable hearts caused them to stop. They returned like a dog to its vomit and like a washed sow to wallowing in the mire.

I tremble to speak of the end of such unstable professors. They put their hands to the plow, but because they lacked resolution, they shamefully looked back. Scripture says in **Hebrews 10:38 NKJV**, *"If anyone draws back, My soul has no pleasure in him."* It also says in **Hebrews 6:4–6 NKJV**, *"For it is impossible for those who were once enlightened, and have tasted the heavenly gift, and have become partakers of the Holy Spirit, and have tasted the good word of God and the powers of the age to come, if they fall away, to renew them again to repentance."*

Though the Gospel is severe against apostates, many who began well have, through instability of character, turned back to destruction. O may none of us be among them. This is the fifth and final reason I give for why so many are only almost, and not altogether Christians.

Now let us consider the folly of being only an almost Christian.

First, being almost a Christian is useless for salvation. It is true that such people are almost good. But almost hitting the mark is still missing it. God requires us to love Him with all our heart, all our soul, and all our strength. He loves us too much to allow any rival in our hearts, because whatever part of our hearts is empty of God must be unhappy.

The devil, like the false mother before Solomon, would gladly have our hearts divided. But God, like the true mother, will have all or none. His call is, “My son, give Me your heart.” Not half the heart, but the whole heart. If this is not done, we cannot expect mercy.

People may pretend before men, but at the great day God will expose them. Just as Ananias and Sapphira were struck down for pretending to offer everything while secretly keeping back part, so God will judge those who pretend to give Him all while keeping most of their hearts for themselves.

Such people may deceive others for a time. But the God who enabled the prophet to recognize Jeroboam’s wife when she came in disguise will also discover every hypocrite beneath his most careful disguise. If their hearts are not wholly with Him, He will appoint them their portion with hypocrites and unbelievers.

Second, halfway religion is not only insufficient for our own salvation, but also very harmful to others. An almost Christian is one of the most dangerous creatures in the world. He is a wolf in sheep’s clothing. He is like one of those false prophets our Lord warned us about in the Sermon on the Mount. He persuades people that the way to heaven is broader than it really is. In doing so, he does not enter the kingdom himself, and he hinders those who are trying to enter.

These are the people who spread a lukewarm Laodicean spirit through the world. They hang out false lights and cause unthinking, spiritually darkened souls to shipwreck on their voyage to eternity. They are greater enemies to the cross of Christ than outright unbelievers. People are usually on guard against unbelievers, but an almost Christian, by subtle hypocrisy, draws many after him. Therefore, he must expect the greater condemnation.

Third, being only an almost Christian is great ingratitude toward our Lord and Master, Jesus Christ. Did He come down from heaven and shed His precious blood to purchase our hearts, only for us to give Him half of them? How can we say we love Him when our hearts are not wholly His? How can we call Him Savior if we do not sincerely seek to please Him and let Him see the travail of His soul and be satisfied?

Imagine that one of us bought a slave at great cost. Suppose that slave had been in terrible misery and would have remained there forever if we had not shown compassion. If that slave later became rebellious or refused to give us more than half his service, how strongly would we condemn such ingratitude?

Yet that ungrateful slave is you, O man, if you confess that you have been redeemed from infinite and unavoidable misery by the death of Jesus Christ, and yet refuse to give yourself wholly to Him. Shall we treat God our Maker in a way we would not want to be treated by another person? God forbid.

Therefore, let me exhort you to become not only almost, but altogether Christians.

Let us despise all treacherous treatment of our King, our Savior, our God, and our Creator. Let us not take some pains all our lives to go to heaven, only to plunge ourselves into hell at last. Let us give

God our whole hearts and no longer halt between two opinions. If the world is God, serve the world. If pleasure is God, serve pleasure. But if the Lord is God, then let us serve Him alone.

Why should we stand back any longer? Why should we love slavery so much that we refuse to renounce the world, the flesh, and the devil, which are spiritual chains that bind our souls and keep them from rising to God?

What are we afraid of? Is God not able to reward full obedience? If He is, and even the almost Christian admits this by serving Him in part, then why not serve Him entirely? For the same reason we do so much, why not do more?

Do you think being half religious will make you happy, but going farther will make you miserable and uneasy? This is deception. It is this half-hearted religion, this wavering between God and the world, that makes so many seemingly good people strangers to the comforts of religion. They choose just enough religion to disturb them in their lusts, and follow their lusts just enough to rob themselves of the comforts of religion.

But if they sincerely left all in affection and gave their hearts wholly to God, then and only then would they experience the unspeakable pleasure of a mind at peace with itself. Then they would enjoy the peace of God, which passes all understanding. Before this, they were strangers to that peace.

It is true that if we give ourselves entirely to God, we must expect contempt. But that contempt is needed to heal our pride. We must renounce some sensual pleasures, but those pleasures unfit us for spiritual joys, which are infinitely better. We must renounce the love of the world, but only so that we may be filled with the love of God.

When the love of God enlarges our hearts, then like Jacob serving for Rachel, we will think nothing too difficult and no hardship too long because of our love for our dear Redeemer.

The ways of God will become easy and delightful even in this life. But when we finally put off these bodies and our souls are filled with all the fullness of God, what heart can imagine, and what tongue can express, the unspeakable joy and comfort we will have as we look back on our sincere service to Him?

Do you think we will regret having done too much for God? Or will we not rather be ashamed that we did so little? Will we not blush that we were so slow to give up all to God, when He intended to give us Himself?

Therefore, my dear hearers, keep before you the unspeakable happiness of enjoying God. Remember that every degree of holiness you neglect and every act of godliness you omit is like a jewel taken from your crown and a degree of blessedness lost in the vision of God.

Think and live this way, and you will no longer try to make peace between God and the world. Instead, you will daily seek to give yourself more and more to Him. You will be always watching, always praying, always reaching after greater purity and love, and always preparing yourself for a fuller sight and enjoyment of the God in whose presence is fullness of joy and at whose right hand are pleasures forevermore.

Amen and Amen.

Chapter Thirty-Four

The Holy Spirit Convincing the World of Sin, Righteousness, and Judgment

John 16:8 NKJV *"And when He has come, He will convict the world of sin, and of righteousness, and of judgment."*

These words are part of a gracious promise that Jesus gave to His sorrowful disciples. The time was drawing near when the Son of Man would first be lifted up on the cross, and afterward lifted up into heaven. During the time Jesus walked with His disciples on earth, He had been kind and merciful to them. He had compassion on their weaknesses. He answered for them when their enemies attacked them. He corrected them when they were wrong in their thinking or behavior. He did not treat them merely as servants, but as friends. He revealed His secrets to them. He opened their understanding so they could understand the Scriptures. He explained the mysteries of the kingdom of God to them, while He spoke to others in parables. He even became the servant of them all and humbled Himself to wash their feet.

Because Jesus had been such a loving Master, the thought of being separated from Him deeply troubled them. On one occasion, when He planned to be away from them for only one night, He had to compel them to leave Him. How much more sorrowful they must have been when He told them He was going away entirely. He also told them that in His absence, the religious leaders would put them out of the synagogues. They would be excommunicated. The time would come when whoever killed them would think he was serving God. No wonder Jesus said in **John 16:6 NKJV**, *"But because I have said these things to you, sorrow has filled your heart."*

Their hearts were full of grief. They were almost ready to break under the weight of it. So Jesus, in His compassion, explained why it was necessary for Him to go away. He said in **John 16:7 NKJV**, *"Nevertheless I tell you the truth. It is to your advantage that I go away."* It was as though He said, "My dear disciples, do not think I am leaving you because I am angry with you. I am going away for your good. If I do not go away, if I do not die on the cross for your sins, rise again for your justification, ascend into heaven, make intercession, and plead My merits before My Father's throne, then the Comforter, the Holy Spirit, will not come to you. But if I depart, I will send Him to you."

Then Jesus told them what the Holy Spirit would do when He came: **John 16:8 NKJV**, *"And when He has come, He will convict the world of sin, and of righteousness, and of judgment."*

The person spoken of in this verse is plainly the Comforter, the Holy Spirit. This promise was first given to the apostles. It was fulfilled in a powerful and visible way on the Day of Pentecost, when the Holy Spirit came like a rushing mighty wind. It was also fulfilled when three thousand people were pierced to the heart through Peter's preaching. But since the apostles represented the whole body of believers, this promise also belongs to us, to our children, and to as many as the Lord our God shall call.

My purpose is to explain the way the Holy Spirit generally works in the hearts of those who, by grace, are made vessels of mercy and are brought out of the kingdom of darkness into the kingdom of God's dear Son.

I say generally because God is sovereign. His Spirit blows where He wills, when He wills, and how He wills. We must not limit the Almighty to one exact method or say that every person experiences the same degree of conviction. There is a holy variety in the way God calls His people home. But this much we may say with certainty: wherever there is a true work of conviction and conversion in a sinner's heart, the Holy Spirit does what Jesus said He would do. He convicts of sin, righteousness, and judgment.

If any of you mock inward religion, or think there is no such thing as feeling or receiving the Holy Spirit, then this sermon may sound foolish to you. You may understand me no more than if I were speaking in an unknown language. But since the promise in the text concerns the world, and since I know it will continue to be fulfilled until time is no more, I will explain the general way the Holy Spirit works in every converted sinner's heart. And I pray that while I speak, the Lord will fulfill this promise in many of your hearts.

The word translated "convict" means more than simply to rebuke. It means to convince by strong argument and powerful demonstration. Many scoffers today ask those who speak of the Spirit how they feel the Spirit or how they know the Spirit. They might as well ask how someone knows or feels the sun when it shines on his body. The Spirit of God works on the soul with convincing power and demonstration.

First, the Holy Spirit convicts of sin.

He often begins by convicting a person of some great actual sin, perhaps the worst sin the person ever committed. When Jesus spoke with the Samaritan woman, He first convicted her of her adultery. He said in **John 4:16 NKJV**, *"Go, call your husband, and come here."* When she answered that she had no husband, Jesus told her that she had spoken truly, because she had had five husbands, and the man she was now living with was not her husband. With that conviction came a powerful awareness of her other sins. Soon she left her waterpot, went into the city, and said to the men in **John 4:29 NKJV**, *"Come, see a Man who told me all things that I ever did. Could this be the Christ?"*

Jesus also dealt this way with Saul the persecutor. He first convicted him of the terrible sin of persecution, saying in **Acts 9:4**

NKJV, *"Saul, Saul, why are you persecuting Me?"* At the same time, Saul likely became aware of many other sins. He died to all his false confidence and was thrown into such agony of soul that for three days he neither ate nor drank.

This is often how the Spirit of God deals with sinners. He first convicts them of some serious actual sin, and at the same time He brings their other sins to remembrance. He sets them in order before them like an army in battle array.

Has this ever happened to you? I must ask you this as I go, because I want to preach not only to your heads, but to your hearts. Has the Spirit of God ever brought your sins to your remembrance in this way? Has He ever made you cry out to God as though bitter things were written against you? Have your actual sins ever appeared before you as though they were drawn out clearly on a map? If not, unless you were sanctified from the womb, you have reason to question whether you have ever been truly convicted, much less converted. The promise of this text may never have been fulfilled in your heart.

But when the Comforter comes into a sinner's heart, He does not stop with actual sins. He leads the sinner to see and mourn over original sin, the fountain from which all polluted streams flow.

Everything around us and within us proves the truth that in Adam all died. Yet many people are hardened by the deceitfulness of sin. They may agree in their minds that original sin is a doctrine of Scripture, but they have never felt the truth of it in their hearts. Some even deny it openly, though their works plainly prove that they are sinful children of a sinful father.

But when the Comforter, the Spirit of God, arrests a sinner and convicts him of sin, all carnal arguments against original corruption are thrown down. Every proud thought that rises against this doctrine is brought low. The sinner is made to cry with Paul in **Romans 7:24 NKJV**, *"O wretched man that I am! Who will deliver me from this body of death?"*

Now he sees that sinful desire itself is sin. He does not only mourn over the sins he has committed. He mourns over the inward perverseness of his heart. He sees that his heart is not merely an enemy of God, but enmity itself against God.

Has the Comforter ever come with such convincing power into your heart? Have you ever been made to see and feel that in your flesh dwells no good thing? Have you ever felt that you were conceived and born in sin, and that by nature you are a child of wrath? Have you ever felt that God would be just to condemn you, even if you had never committed one outward sinful act in your life?

You may have often been to church. You may have often received communion. But have you ever truly confessed that there is no spiritual health in you apart from grace? Have you ever felt that the remembrance of your original and actual sins was grievous and that the burden of them was intolerable? If not, then you have only been offering vain religious service to God. You have never truly prayed in your life. The Comforter has never yet come effectually into your soul. Therefore, you are not truly in the faith. You are presently in a state of spiritual death and condemnation.

Again, when the Comforter effectually works on a sinner, He not only convicts him of the sin of his nature and the sins of his life, but also of the sin of his duties.

By nature, we are all legalists. We think we can be justified by works of the law. When we are somewhat awakened by the terrors of the Lord, we immediately begin, like the Pharisees, to establish our own righteousness. We think God will accept us if we seek Him with enough tears. Finding ourselves condemned by nature and by our actual sins, we then try to recommend ourselves to God by our religious duties. We hope that by doing this or that, we may inherit eternal life.

But when the Comforter comes into the heart, He convinces the soul that these are false resting places. He makes the sinner see that all his righteousnesses are like filthy rags. He shows him that even for his most impressive religious services, he deserves no better end than that of the unprofitable servant, to be cast into outer darkness where there is weeping and gnashing of teeth.

Has this kind of conviction ever been worked in your soul? Has the Comforter ever made you sick of your duties as well as your sins? Have you ever, with Paul, been made to reject your own righteousness that comes from the law? Have you ever acknowledged that you deserve condemnation even if you gave all your goods to feed the poor? Have you ever felt that your repentance itself needs to be repented of? Have you seen that everything in yourself is only loss and rubbish when compared with Christ?

Have you ever been made to lie at the feet of sovereign grace and say, "Lord, if You are willing, You may save me. If not, You may justly condemn me. I have nothing to plead. I cannot justify myself in Your sight. My best works would condemn me. All I can depend on is Your free grace"?

What do you say? Has this ever been the language of your heart? Is it the language of your heart now? You may have often gone to the temple, but have you ever gone in the spirit of the poor tax collector? After you have done all, have you ever acknowledged that you have done nothing? Have you ever, with a real sense of your own unworthiness and sinfulness, beaten your breast and cried, **Luke 18:13 NKJV**, *"God, be merciful to me a sinner!"*

If you have never been brought to this place, the Comforter has never effectually come into your soul. You are outside of Christ. If God required your soul in that condition, He would be to you a consuming fire.

There is also a fourth sin of which the Comforter convicts the soul. This is the only sin Jesus specifically mentions in this passage, as though it were the chief sin to be named. And truly, it is the root of all other sins. It is the reigning and condemning sin of the world. What is this sin? It is the cursed sin of unbelief. Jesus said in **John 16:9 NKJV**, *"Of sin, because they do not believe in Me."*

Does the Christian world need the Holy Spirit to convict people of unbelief? Do any of you need that conviction? Are there unbelievers here? Yes, I fear there are many. I do not only mean those who openly deny the Lord who bought them, though there are too many such people. I mean those who have no more true faith than the devils have.

Perhaps you think you believe because you repeat the creed, subscribe to a confession of faith, attend church or meetings, receive communion, and are accepted as a member. These are great privileges, but all of them may be done without true saving faith.

One way to expose false faith is to ask this question: How long have you believed? Many would answer, "As long as I can remember. I have never disbelieved." But if that is your answer, it may be a sure sign that you have no true faith at all, not even as much as a grain of mustard seed. If you believe now, unless you were sanctified from infancy, you must know that there was once a time when you did not believe on the Lord Jesus Christ. If you have received the Holy Spirit, He has convinced you of this.

None of us believe by nature. After the Holy Spirit has convicted us of the sin of our nature, the sin of our lives, and the sin of our duties, He also convicts us that we have no faith. He does this so we will see our utter inability to save ourselves and understand that we must depend on God for everything, even for faith itself. Without faith, it is impossible to please God or be saved by Christ.

The great question the Holy Spirit puts to the soul is this: "Do you believe on the Son of God?" At the same time, He works so powerfully that the soul sees and is forced to confess, "I have no faith."

This is something many people who call themselves believers have never considered. They think they are Christians because they live in a Christian country. If they had been born in another religion, they might have believed that religion in the same outward way. What many people call faith is nothing more than outward agreement with the religion around them.

Do not deceive yourselves. True faith is something entirely different. Ask yourself whether the Holy Spirit has ever powerfully convicted you of the sin of unbelief. Perhaps you have a list of sins that you confess formally when you come to communion. But among all your sins, have you ever confessed and mourned over the condemning sin of unbelief? Have you ever cried, "Lord, give me faith. Lord, help me believe in You. O that I had faith. O that I could believe"?

If you have never been distressed over your unbelief, if you have never seen and felt that you had no faith, it is a sure sign that the Holy Spirit, the Comforter, has never come and worked savingly in your soul.

But some may ask, "Is it not strange that the Holy Spirit should be called the Comforter when His work of conviction is often attended with deep inward conflict and soul trouble?" The answer is no. He may rightly be called the Comforter even in this work because conviction is the only path to true and lasting comfort. Blessed are those who are convicted by Him, for they shall be comforted. Even in the middle of these convictions, there is a hidden comfort. The soul secretly rejoices that it now sees its own misery. It blesses God for bringing it out of darkness into light and looks forward with hope for future deliverance, knowing that though sorrow may endure for a night, joy comes in the morning.

This is how the Holy Spirit convicts the soul of sin. If this is true, then those are sadly mistaken who confuse the light of the Spirit with the light of natural conscience. Some say that Christ enlightens every person who comes into the world, and that this light, if improved, will bring people to Jesus Christ. But if that were true, then the promise in this text would be unnecessary. The apostles already had the light of conscience. The world that was to be convicted already had the light of conscience. If that light were sufficient to bring people to Christ, why was it necessary for Christ to go to heaven and send down the Holy Spirit to do this work?

No, not everyone has the Spirit in this saving way. He is the special gift of God. Without this special gift, we can never come to Christ.

The light of conscience may accuse or convict us of ordinary sins, but natural conscience never has, never will, and never can convict a person of unbelief. If it could, why did none of the heathen, even those who greatly improved the light of nature, ever become convicted of unbelief? No, this is the special work of the Holy Spirit, the Comforter. When He comes, He convicts the world of sin, righteousness, and judgment.

Now we come to the second thing: the righteousness of which the Comforter convinces the world.

In some places in Scripture, righteousness means the justice we should practice toward others. For example, Paul reasoned with Felix about righteousness and self-control. But here, righteousness means the active and passive obedience of the Lord Jesus Christ. It refers to that perfect, personal, all-sufficient righteousness that He worked out for the world that the Spirit is to convict.

Jesus said in **John 16:10 NKJV**, *"Of righteousness, because I go to My Father and you see Me no more."* This is one argument the Holy Spirit uses to prove Christ's righteousness. Christ went to the Father, and we see Him no more. If He had not worked out a sufficient righteousness, the Father would have sent Him back as one who had not completed His work.

O the righteousness of Christ. It comforts my soul so much that I must be excused if I mention it in nearly every sermon. I would not willingly preach a single sermon without it. Whatever unbelievers may object, and whatever others may argue against imputed righteousness, those who truly know themselves and God must confess that Jesus Christ is the end of the law for righteousness to everyone who believes, and that we are made the righteousness of God in Him.

This righteousness, and this righteousness alone, is the sure anchor of hope for a poor sinner. Whatever other foundation people may try to lay, I can see no other foundation for salvation than the rock of Christ's personal righteousness imputed to the soul.

Many may agree with this in their minds. They may have a rational conviction of it. But rational conviction alone, if we rest there, is not enough. There must be a spiritual and experiential conviction of the truth. Therefore, Jesus says that when the Holy Spirit comes in power, He convinces the soul of this righteousness. He convinces the sinner of its reality, completeness, and sufficiency to save.

We have seen how the Holy Spirit convicts the sinner of the sin of his nature, the sin of his life, the sin of his duties, and the sin of unbelief. What, then, must the poor soul do? If there is no hope outside himself, he must completely despair.

But when the Spirit has hunted the sinner out of all his false refuges and hiding places, when He has taken away the fig leaves of his own works and driven him out from behind the trees of his outward reforms, when He sets him naked before the bar of a sovereign, holy, just, and sin-avenging God, then the Holy Spirit gives a sweet display of Christ's righteousness to the soul.

This is where the Spirit begins more directly to act as the Comforter. He convinces the soul so powerfully of the reality and sufficiency of Christ's righteousness that the soul begins to hunger and thirst for it. Now the sinner sees that though he has destroyed himself, his help is in Christ. He sees that though he has no righteousness of his own to recommend him, there is fullness of grace, fullness of truth, and fullness of righteousness in the dear Lord Jesus. If that righteousness is imputed to him, he will be happy forever.

Only those who have experienced this can tell with what power and demonstration this conviction comes. O how lovely and all-sufficient Jesus appears at that moment. With what new eyes the soul now sees the Lord our righteousness. It is beyond words.

If you have never been convinced of Christ's righteousness in your own soul, then even if you believe it doctrinally, it will not profit you savingly. If the Comforter has never come savingly into your soul, then you are comfortless indeed.

But what will this righteousness profit us if the soul does not possess it?

This brings us to the third thing. When the Comforter comes, He convinces the soul of judgment.

By judgment, I understand that well-grounded peace, that settled judgment which the soul forms about itself when the Spirit enables it to lay hold of Christ's righteousness. I believe this always happens when a person is truly convinced in the way already described.

Jesus said in **John 16:11 NKJV**, *"Of judgment, because the ruler of this world is judged."* When the soul is enabled by living faith to lay hold of Christ's perfect righteousness, the Holy Spirit works in that soul a conviction that the ruler of this world is judged. The soul, being justified by faith, has peace with God through our Lord Jesus Christ. It can triumphantly say, "It is Christ who justifies me. Who is he who condemns me?"

The strong man armed is now cast out. The soul is brought into true peace. The prince of this world may come and accuse, but he has no rightful claim anymore. The blessed Spirit received by the believer enables him to apply Christ's righteousness to his soul and powerfully convinces him of this. Why should he fear? Of what should he be afraid, since God's Spirit bears witness with his spirit that he is a child of God?

The Lord has ascended on high. He has led captivity captive. He has received the Holy Spirit, the Comforter, that best of gifts for men. And this Comforter has come into the believer's heart. He who promised is faithful. The soul can now say, "I, even I, have been powerfully, rationally, and spiritually convinced of sin, righteousness, and judgment. By this I know the ruler of this world is judged."

This is how the soul may triumph when the promise of the text is fulfilled in it. At the beginning, I said that many have never experienced anything like this, and therefore this preaching must seem foolish to them. But I do not doubt that there are some happy souls who, by grace, have been able to follow this step by step. The Holy Spirit may not have worked in exactly the same order as I have described. You may not be able to name the precise time when it happened. But you have a well-grounded confidence that the work has been done, and that you have truly been convinced of sin, righteousness, and judgment in some way and at some time.

What shall I say to you? Thank God. Thank the Lord Jesus. Thank the ever-blessed Trinity for this unspeakable gift. You would never have been so highly favored if the God who first commanded light to shine out of darkness had not loved you with an everlasting love and enlightened you by His Holy Spirit. And He did this not because of any good thing foreseen in you, but for His own name's sake.

Be humble, then, O believers. Be humble. Look to the rock from which you were hewn. Praise free grace. Admire electing love, which alone has made you differ from others. Has God brought you into light? Then walk as children of light. Do not provoke the Holy Spirit to depart from you. Though He has sealed you for the day of redemption, and though you know the ruler of this world is judged, yet if you backslide, grow lukewarm, or forget your first love, the Lord will visit your offenses with the rod and your sins with spiritual correction.

Do not be high-minded, but fear. Rejoice, but rejoice with trembling. As the elect of God, put on not only humility, but also compassion. Pray for your unconverted brothers and sisters. Help me now, children of God. Hold up my hands as Aaron and Hur held up the hands of Moses. Pray while I am preaching that the Lord may enable me to say, "This day the promise in the text has been fulfilled in some poor sinner's heart."

Cry mightily to God. With holy earnestness, pull down blessings on your neighbors' heads. Christ still lives and reigns in heaven. The fullness of the Spirit is still in His hand, and a plentiful outpouring of the Spirit has been promised in the latter days of the church. O that the Holy Spirit, the blessed Comforter, would now come down and convince those among you who are without Christ of sin, righteousness, and judgment. O that you would be made willing to be convinced.

But perhaps some of you would rather be filled with wine than with the Spirit. Perhaps you are daily driving the Holy Spirit away from your souls. What shall I say to God for you? "Father, forgive them, for they do not know what they do." What shall I say from God to you? I will tell you this: **2 Corinthians 5:19 NKJV**, *"God was in Christ reconciling the world to Himself."* Therefore, I plead with you as though in Christ's place: be reconciled to God.

Do not go away contradicting and blaspheming. I know Satan would like you to leave. Many of you may be uneasy and ready to say, "What a weariness this is." But I will not let you go easily. I have wrestled with God for my hearers in private, and now I must wrestle with you in public.

Of myself I can do nothing. And by your own power, you can no more come to Christ and believe on Him than Lazarus could come out of the grave by his own strength. But who knows whether God may bring some of you to new life through what the world calls the foolishness of preaching? Who knows whether some of you may be among those whom the Comforter is to convince of sin, righteousness, and judgment?

Poor Christless souls, do you know what condition you are in? You are lying under the power of the wicked one, the devil. He rules in you, walks in you, and dwells in you, unless you dwell in Christ and the Comforter has come into your hearts. Will you remain content under the power of that wicked one? What wages will he give you? Eternal death.

O that you would come to Christ. The free gift of God through Him is eternal life. He will receive you even now if you believe in Him. The Comforter may yet come into your hearts, even yours. All who are now living temples of God were once lying in the wicked one, just as you are. This blessed gift, the Holy Spirit, was received by Jesus even for the rebellious.

I see many of you affected. But are your emotions only stirred for a little while, or are your souls truly touched with a living sense of the greatness of your sins, your lack of faith, and the preciousness of the righteousness of Jesus Christ? If so, I hope the Lord has been gracious and that the Comforter is coming into your hearts.

Do not smother these convictions. Do not go away and immediately forget what kind of doctrine you have heard. If you do, you will show that these were only passing convictions floating on the surface of your hearts. Beg God to make you sincere, for He alone can do it. Ask Him to fulfill the promise of this text in your soul.

Who knows whether the Lord may be gracious? Remember, you have no plea except sovereign mercy. But for your encouragement, remember also that it is the world, people just like you, whom the Comforter comes to convince.

Wait, therefore, at the gates of wisdom. The smallest possibility of having a door of mercy opened should be enough to keep you striving. Christ Jesus came into the world to save sinners, even the chief of them. You do not know that He may have come to save you.

Do not argue with God's decrees and say, "If I am rejected, I will be damned. If I am elected, I will be saved. Therefore, I will do nothing." What do you have to do with God's secret decrees? Secret things belong to Him. Your business is to give all diligence to make your calling and election sure. If only few find the way that leads to life, then strive to be among those few. You do not know but that you may be one of them, and that your striving may be the very means God intends to bless to bring you in.

If you do not act this way, you are not sincere. But if you do, who knows whether you may find mercy? Though after all you can do, God may justly cut you off, yet no one was ever condemned who truly did all he could.

Therefore, though your hands are withered, stretch them out. Though you are powerless, sick, and lame, come and lie by the pool. Who knows whether the Lord Jesus may have compassion on you and send the Comforter to convince you of sin, righteousness, and judgment? He is a God full of compassion and longsuffering. Otherwise, you and I would have long ago lifted up our eyes in torment. But He is still patient with us.

O Christless sinners, you are still alive. Who knows whether God intends to bring you to repentance? If my prayers or tears could bring it about, you would have volleys of the one and floods of the other. My heart is touched with a sense of your condition. May our merciful High Priest now send down the Comforter and make you sensible of it too.

O the love of Christ. It constrains me again to plead with you to come to Him. What do you reject if you reject Christ, the Lord of glory? Sinners, give the dear Redeemer a lodging in your souls. Do not send Him away. Give Christ your hearts, your whole hearts. He is worthy. He made you, and not you yourselves. You are not your own. Give Christ your bodies and souls, for they belong to Him.

Is it not enough to melt your heart to think that the high and lofty One who inhabits eternity would humble Himself to invite you through His ministers? How quickly He could frown you into hell. How do you know that He may not do so this very moment if you refuse His voice? Did anyone ever harden his heart against Christ and prosper?

Come, then. Do not send me away sorrowful. Do not give me reason to cry, "O my leanness, my leanness." Do not make me go weeping into my closet and say, "Lord, they will not believe my report. Lord, I called them, and they would not answer. I was to them like a pleasant song and like one who plays skillfully on an instrument, but their hearts were running after the lust of the eyes, the lust of the flesh, and the pride of life."

Would you be willing for me to give such an account of you before God? Yet I must not only do so here, but I must also appear as a witness against you at the judgment, unless you come to Christ.

Once more, then, I plead with you to come. What objections do you have? Behold, I stand here in the name of God to answer all that you can say. But I know that no one can come unless the Father draws him. Therefore, I will now turn to my God and intercede with Him to send the Comforter into your hearts.

O blessed Jesus, God of unfailing compassion, in whom all the promises are Yes and Amen, You who sit enthroned between the cherubim, show Yourself among us. Let us see Your mighty works. Let us taste and see that You are gracious. Reveal Your almighty arm. Gain the victory in these poor sinners' hearts. Do not let the word spoken be like water spilled on the ground. Send down, send down, O great High Priest, the Holy Spirit, to convince the world of sin, righteousness, and judgment.

Then we will give thanks and praise to You, O Father, to You, O Son, and to You, O blessed Spirit. To You, three Persons and one God, be ascribed by angels and archangels, by cherubim and seraphim, and by all the heavenly host, all power, might, majesty, and dominion, now and forevermore.

Amen, Amen, and Amen.

Chapter Thirty-Five

The Good Shepherd: A Farewell Sermon

John 10:27–28 NKJV *"My sheep hear My voice, and I know them, and they follow Me. And I give them eternal life, and they shall never perish. Neither shall anyone snatch them out of My hand."*

There is a common saying, and I believe it is generally true, that bad manners often lead to good laws. Whether this is always true in the affairs of this world, I am persuaded it is often true in the things of God. Bad manners, bad treatment, and bad words have often been overruled by the sovereign grace of God to produce some of the best sermons ever preached by the God-man, Christ Jesus.

One would think that when Jesus came clothed with divine power, with divine credentials, and spoke as no man ever spoke, no one would have been able to resist the wisdom with which He taught.

One would think people would have been so struck by the demonstration of the Spirit that they would all agree He was the Prophet God had promised to raise up like Moses. But we seldom find our Lord preaching a sermon without someone criticizing or opposing what He said. Often their hatred broke through all proper manners. They interrupted Him while He was preaching. This showed the enmity in their hearts long before God allowed them to shed His innocent blood.

If we look only at this chapter, where Jesus presents Himself as the Good Shepherd, the One who lays down His life for the sheep, we see how people responded. The best response many gave Him was to say He was possessed or mad. There was a division among the Jews because of His sayings. Many of them said, “He has a demon and is mad. Why do you listen to Him?” If the Master of the house was treated this way, what should His servants expect?

Others, who were more sober-minded, said, “These are not the words of one who has a demon. Can a demon open the eyes of the blind?” Even among the crowd, He had some who spoke more fairly of Him. But none of this discouraged our Lord. He continued His work. And we will never continue faithfully in the work of God until, like our Master, we are willing to go through both good report and evil report. We must let the devil see that we are not so easily stopped by his barking as we go along.

We are told that our Lord was at Jerusalem during the Feast of Dedication, and it was winter. The Feast of Dedication was held in remembrance of the restoration of the temple and altar after they had been profaned by Antiochus. This feast was a human institution. It did not have the same divine command attached to it as the feasts appointed in the law. Yet I do not find that Jesus spent His time preaching against it. His heart was too full of greater things.

I believe that when we are filled with the Holy Spirit, we will not spend our time entertaining people with endless disputes about rites and ceremonies. We will preach the essentials of the gospel. When that happens, rites and ceremonies will be seen with proper moderation. Jesus did not refuse to go to the feast. He went, not so much to keep the feast, but to use the opportunity to spread the gospel net. That should be our method too. We should not be consumed with disputing. It is to the glory of the Methodists that for many years, our preachers have not filled the world with pamphlets about the nonessentials of religion.

Jesus always made the best use of every opportunity. We are told that He walked in the temple, in Solomon's porch. One might think the scribes and Pharisees would have placed Him in one of their seats and invited Him to preach. But no, they left Him to walk in Solomon's porch. Some think He walked there alone because no one wanted to keep company with Him.

I can almost see Him walking there, looking at the temple and foreseeing how soon it would be destroyed. He walked thoughtfully, seeing the dreadful calamities that would come upon the land because it did not know the time of its visitation. He also walked publicly to show that He was not afraid to appear before them. It was as though He was saying, "Do any of you have anything to ask Me? I am ready." Even though they had treated Him badly, He was still willing to preach salvation to them.

Then the Jews gathered around Him and said, **John 10:24 NKJV**, *"How long do You keep us in doubt? If You are the Christ, tell us plainly."* They surrounded Him when they saw Him walking in Solomon's porch. It was as though they said, "Now we have Him. Now we will attack Him." In this, the words of the Psalms were fulfilled: they surrounded Him like bees, or perhaps more like wasps, ready to sting.

Their question seemed reasonable on the surface. "How long will You keep us in doubt?" Some have understood it to mean, "How long do You intend to steal away our hearts?" They wanted to portray Him as a designing man, like Absalom, winning the people to Himself so He could set Himself up as Messiah. Carnal minds are always ready to misinterpret the actions of good men.

But the meaning seems to be that they were uncertain about Christ and wanted to blame Him for their uncertainty. Doubting people often think it is God's fault that they doubt, but God knows it is their own fault. They said, in effect, "We wish You would speak more plainly. We do not want any more parables. Tell us who You are from Your own mouth. If You are the Christ, tell us plainly."

No doubt they put on a religious face and appeared very sincere. But they were trying to catch Him. If He refused to say He was the Christ, they would accuse Him of being ashamed of His own cause. If He openly said He was the Christ, they would report Him to the governor and accuse Him of claiming to be a political Messiah who would challenge Caesar.

The devil has always tried to make people believe that God's people, who are actually the most loyal people in the world, are rebels against the government under which they live.

Jesus did not keep them waiting long. Honesty can answer quickly. He said in **John 10:25 NKJV**, *"I told you, and you do not believe. The works that I do in My Father's name, they bear witness of Me."* If Jesus had simply said, "I am the Messiah," they would have seized Him. He knew this. Therefore, He joined the wisdom of the serpent with the innocence of the dove. He appealed to His works and His doctrine. If they would not infer from those that He was the Messiah, He had no further argument for them.

Then He added in **John 10:26 NKJV**, *"But you do not believe, because you are not of My sheep."* Their unbelief grieved His heart. He complains of it twice. Then He speaks the words of our text: **John 10:27–28 NKJV**, *"My sheep hear My voice, and I know them, and they follow Me. And I give them eternal life, and they shall never perish. Neither shall anyone snatch them out of My hand."*

Jesus was saying, "You think your questions will puzzle Me. You think your conduct will trouble Me. But you are mistaken. You do not believe because you are not My sheep."

It is remarkable that Scripture divides people into only two classes. It does not divide the world first into Baptists and Independents, Methodists and Presbyterians. Jesus divides the whole world into sheep and goats. May the Lord help us see which class we belong to.

It is also worth noticing that believers are compared to things that are good and useful, while unbelievers are described by things that are harmful, unclean, or of little value.

Why are Christ's people called sheep? First, sheep generally love to be together. We speak of a flock of sheep. Sheep are little creatures, and Christ's people are often little in the eyes of the world, and even smaller in their own eyes.

Some people think the church would do far better if only the great people of the earth were on our side. They think, "If kings, nobles, and rulers were all true believers, how well the work of God would go." But would it really? If it became fashionable to be religious at court and fashionable to be a Methodist in public, many would carry a Bible or hymn book instead of a novel. But religion does not thrive best under too much sunshine. Paul says in **1 Corinthians 1:26–27 NKJV**, *"Not many wise according to the flesh, not many mighty, not many noble, are called. But God has chosen the foolish things of the world to put to shame the wise."*

Sheep are also among the most harmless and quiet creatures God has made. May God, in His infinite mercy, show us that we are His sheep by giving us this blessed temper through the Holy Spirit. Jesus said in **Matthew 11:29 NKJV**, *"Learn from Me, for I am gentle and lowly in heart."* He did not say, "Learn from Me to work miracles," but "Learn from Me to be meek."

A good man once said that if there was any temper he desired more than another, it was the grace of meekness: to bear bad treatment quietly, to forgive and forget, and even while knowing he had been wronged, not to be overcome by evil, but to overcome evil with good. Moses is honored in Scripture as the meekest man on the earth. Meekness is especially necessary for those in authority. A passionate and unforgiving man is dangerous. A man of an unrelenting spirit is no more fit for government than a reckless man is fit to drive the chariot of the sun. He only sets the world on fire.

Sheep are also very prone to wander and get lost. Christ's people may rightly be compared to sheep in this way. In our confession we say, "We have erred and strayed from Your ways like lost sheep." A horse or a dog may often find its way home, but a sheep wanders around helplessly. It bleats here and there as if saying, "Dear stranger, show me the way home again."

So Christ's sheep are too prone to wander from the fold. When they take their eyes off the great Shepherd, they go into this field and that field, over this hedge and that hedge, and often return home with the loss of their wool.

Yet sheep are also among the most useful creatures in the world. They enrich the land and help prepare it for seed. They clothe our bodies with wool. There is hardly any part of a sheep that is not useful. O my brethren, may God grant that you and I may answer the character of sheep in this way.

The world says that because we preach faith, we deny good works. This is the usual objection against the doctrine of imputed righteousness. But it is a slander, a bold and shameless slander. It was said in the time of the Reformers that though some preached good works loudly, you had to go to the Calvinists to find them practiced. Christ's sheep seek to be useful. They labor with their hands so that they may have something to give to those in need.

Believers also consider Christ's ownership of them. Jesus says, "My sheep." Blessed be God for that little, dear, great word "My." Believers are His by eternal election. Jesus speaks of "the sheep whom You have given Me." They were given by God the Father to Christ Jesus in the covenant made between the Father and the Son from all eternity. Those who do not see this, I wish better understanding. Yet I believe some who oppose this truth may still have better hearts than heads. The Lord help us bear with one another where there is an honest heart.

Christ also calls them "My sheep" because they are His by purchase. O sinner, you have come this morning to hear a poor creature take his last farewell. But I want you to forget the creature who is preaching. I want to lead you beyond the tabernacle. Where do I want to lead you? To Mount Calvary. There you may see the price of blood by which Christ purchased those He calls His own. He redeemed them with His own blood. They are His not only by eternal election, but also by actual redemption in time. The Father gave them to Him on the condition that He would redeem them by His heart's blood. It was a hard bargain, but Christ was willing to make it so that you and I might not be damned forever.

They are also His because they are enabled, in the day of God's power, willingly to give themselves to Him. Jesus says of these sheep that they hear His voice and follow Him.

Here Jesus uses the picture of a shepherd. In some places in Scripture, the shepherd is represented as going after his sheep. In England, that is what shepherds often do. But in Eastern countries, the shepherds usually went before the sheep. They held up their staff and had a particular call that the sheep understood.

Jesus says, "My sheep hear My voice." God the Father says in **Matthew 17:5 NKJV**, *"This is My beloved Son, in whom I am well* *pleased. Hear Him!"* Jesus also says in **John 5:25 NKJV**, *"The dead will hear the voice of the Son of God; and those who hear will live."*

What does it mean to hear Christ's voice?

First, we hear the voice of Moses. We hear the voice of the law. There is no going to Mount Zion except by the way of Mount Sinai. That is the straight road. Some people say they do not know when they were converted. I believe such cases are very few. Generally, God works otherwise. Some are called earlier than others, but before people see the glory of God, they usually hear the voice of the law.

The law makes a man cling more tightly to his corruptions, just as a person holds his cloak tighter in a storm. But when the gospel of the Son of God shines into the soul, then the sinner throws off the corruptions he once hugged so closely. He hears Christ's voice saying, "Son, daughter, be of good cheer. Your sins, which are many, are all forgiven you."

Christ's sheep hear His voice. This describes the settled habit of their hearts. The wicked hear the voice of the devil, the lust of the flesh, the lust of the eyes, and the pride of life. Christ's sheep also listened to those voices before conversion. But when they are called by God, they hear the voice of the Redeemer's blood speaking peace to them. They hear the voice of His Word and His Spirit.

The result and proof of hearing His voice is that they follow Him. Jesus said in **Luke 9:23 NKJV**, *"If anyone desires to come after Me, let him deny himself, and take up his cross daily, and follow Me."* In glory, the saints are described as those who follow the Lamb wherever He goes.

Wherever the Shepherd turns His staff, and wherever the sheep hear His voice, they follow Him. Sometimes, in their eagerness, they tread on and hurt one another in the way. But following Christ means following Him through life, following Him in thought, word, and deed, and following Him from one place and season to another.

Peter once said, "Lord, command me to come to You on the water." If we are commanded to go over the water for Christ, may God in His mercy go with us. But we must first be sure that the great Shepherd is pointing His staff for us. This is the character of a true servant of Christ: he endeavors to follow Christ in thought, word, and work.

Now, my brethren, before we go further, since this may be the last opportunity I have to speak to you for several months, let me urge you to examine yourselves. Some of you do not usually rise as early as you did this morning. I hope the world did not get into your hearts before you left your beds. Now that you are here, let me ask you to consider whether you belong to Christ's sheep.

Man, woman, sinner, put your hand to your heart and answer me. Have you ever heard Christ's voice so as to follow Him? Have you given yourself to Him without reserve?

I truly believe, from the depths of my soul, and this comforts me as I prepare to leave you, that I am preaching to a great multitude of dear and precious souls who, if it were proper for you to speak, would say, "Thanks be to God, we can follow Jesus in the character of sheep, though we are ashamed to think how often we wander from Him and how little fruit we bring to Him."

If that is the language of your heart, I wish you joy. Welcome, dear soul, to Christ. Blessed be God for His rich grace, His distinguishing, sovereign, electing love, by which He has distinguished you and me. If He has allowed you to hear His voice through the ministry of a poor, miserable sinner, a poor but happy pilgrim, may the Lord Jesus Christ have all the glory.

If you belong to Jesus Christ, He is speaking of you when He says, "I know them." What does that mean? It means He knows their number. He knows their names. He knows every one for whom He died. If even one were missing for whom Christ died, God the Father would send Him down from heaven again to fetch that one. Jesus said in **John 17:12 NKJV**, *"Those whom You gave Me I have kept; and none of them is lost."*

Christ knows His sheep. He not only knows their number, but He takes special notice of each one. He cares for each of them as if there were only one sheep in the whole world. To the hypocrite He says, "I never knew you." But He knows His saints. He knows their sorrows, trials, and temptations. He bottles up all their tears. He knows their family trials. He knows their inward corruptions. He knows all their wanderings, and He takes care to bring them back again.

I once heard a good preacher say that God has a great dog to fetch His sheep back. You know that when sheep wander, a shepherd may send a dog after them to bring them back. So when Christ's sheep wander, He may allow the devil to bark at them. But instead of driving them farther away, the devil's barking is overruled to bring them back to Christ's fold.

There is precious comfort in the words, “I know them.” Take notice of them. They can comfort you under all your trials. Sometimes we think Christ does not hear our prayers. We fear He does not know us. We suspect He has forgotten to be gracious. But what mercy it is that He does know us.

We accuse one another. We sometimes become like devils to one another, accusing the brethren. What will support God’s people when they are judged by others? This: “Lord, You know my integrity. You know how matters truly are with me.”

But there is even better news in the text. Jesus says, **John 10:28 NKJV**, *“And I give them eternal life, and they shall never perish. Neither shall anyone snatch them out of My hand.”*

O that these words may come to your hearts with as much warmth and power as they came to mine many years ago. I never prayed against any corruption in my life as much as I prayed against entering the ministry too soon, though my friends were urging me to do so. A bishop showed me great kindness and offered me preferment. My friends wanted me to begin quickly. But God knows what deep concern entering the ministry and preaching gave me.

I prayed many times, until sweat dropped from my face like rain, that God would not let me enter the church before He called me and thrust me forth into His work. I remember being in Gloucester, in a certain room. I still know the window, the bedside, and the floor where I lay prostrate before God. I said, “Lord, I cannot go. I will be puffed up with pride and fall into the condemnation of the devil. Lord, do not let me go yet.” I pleaded to remain at Oxford two or three more years. I intended to prepare many sermons and thought I would enter the work with a good stock in trade.

But while I was praying, wrestling, and striving with God, I said, "I am undone. I am unfit to preach in Your great name. Do not send me yet." I wrote to my friends in town and country, asking them to pray against the bishop's pressing me forward. Yet they insisted I should enter orders before I was twenty-two.

After all these struggles, these words came into my mind: **John 10:27–28 NKJV**, *"My sheep hear My voice, and I know them, and they follow Me. And I give them eternal life, and they shall never perish. Neither shall anyone snatch them out of My hand."*

O may these words be blessed to you, dear friends, as they were to me. When they came warmly upon my heart, then, and not until then, I said, "Lord, I will go. Send me when You will."

I remember once, when I was in a place near Georgia, we were delayed by bad winds. I had a large household to maintain and not a single farthing to do it with, in one of the most expensive parts of the king's dominions. I told a minister of Christ, who is now in heaven, that I had once received these words: "Nothing shall pluck you out of My hand." He told me to take comfort from them, because God would be as good as His word, even if He never told me so again.

Our Lord knew His poor sheep would often doubt whether they would ever reach heaven. Therefore He said, "I give them eternal life, and they shall never perish."

There are three blessed declarations or promises in this text.

First, Jesus says, "I know them."

Second, He says, "They shall never perish." Though they often fear they will perish by the hand of their lusts and corruptions, though they fear they will perish through the deceitfulness of their hearts, Christ says, "They shall never perish." It is as though He says, "I brought them out of the world to Myself. Do you think I will let them go to hell after that?"

Third, He says, "I give them eternal life." Notice that He does not say, "I will give," but "I give." Some speak as if we are only justified at the day of judgment. That is nonsense. If we are not justified here, we will not be justified there. He gives eternal life now in the form of its earnest, pledge, and assurance. The indwelling Spirit of God here is the earnest of glory hereafter.

Then He adds, "Neither shall anyone snatch them out of My hand." He holds them in His hand, that is, by His power. No one can pluck them out. Something is always pulling at Christ's sheep: the devil, the lust of the flesh, the lust of the eyes, and the pride of life. And, sadly, we often help all three try to pull us out of the hand of Jesus. But Christ says, "No one shall snatch them out of My hand." He gives them eternal life. He is going to heaven to prepare a place for them, and there they shall be.

O my brethren, if it would not keep you too long or exhaust my strength too much, I could call upon you to leap for joy. There is no more blessed text to support the final perseverance of the saints. I am amazed that any sincere souls can fight against this doctrine. Some may say, "But people may abuse it and persevere in wickedness." That is an abuse of the doctrine. Shall we never eat good food because some people spoil it? On this text, I can leave all my cares, all my friends, and all Christ's sheep to the protection of Christ Jesus and His never-failing love.

This morning, as I rode here from the other end of town, it felt to me like coming to a public execution. When the carriage turned near the walk and I saw you running here, I thought it was like a person coming to the very place where he was to be executed. When I went to put on my gown, I felt as though I were dressing myself to be made a public spectacle and to shed my blood for Christ.

I call heaven and earth, God and the holy angels, to witness: though I had preferment offered to me, though a bishop took me in his arms and offered me parishes before I was twenty-two, and though he often took me to his table, yet God knows that when the bishop laid his hand on my head, I looked for no other preferment than publicly to suffer for the Lamb of God. In this spirit I came out. In this spirit I came to this city.

When I read of Jacob crossing the brook with only a staff, I thought that I could not even say I had a staff. I came without a friend. I went to Oxford without a friend. I had no servant and no person to introduce me. But God, by His Holy Spirit, raised me up to preach for His great name's sake. Through His divine Spirit I continue to this day, and my affections are as strong as ever toward the work and the people of the living God.

The congregations at both ends of the town are dear to me. God has honored me to build this place and the other. Blessed be His name, when He first called me to Georgia, I left all London affairs to His care. At that time most of the churches in London were open to me. There were so many crowds that twelve or fourteen constables were sometimes needed to keep the doors. I had offers of money to settle in London. Yet I gave it all up to become a pilgrim for God and go to a foreign land. I hope I am going now with the same single intention.

Now I come to the hardest part. I feared when I left home that I could not bear the shock. But I hope the Lord Jesus Christ will help me bear it, and help you give me up to God. Let Him do with me what He wills.

This is the thirteenth time I am crossing the mighty waters. It is a little difficult at this stage of life. Though my strength has improved in some measure, weakness is still the best of my strength. But I am clear as light in my call, and God fills me with a peace that cannot be spoken, a peace with which a stranger cannot interfere. Into His hands I commend my spirit. And I ask that this may be the language of your hearts: "Lord, keep him. Let nothing pluck him out of Your hands."

I expect many trials while I am on board, for Satan always meets me there. But the God who has kept me, I believe, will keep me still. I thank God that I leave everything peaceful and well at both ends of town. My dear hearers, my prayers to God shall be that nothing may pluck you out of Christ's hands.

Bear witness against me if I have ever tried to set up a party for myself. Did any minister ever say that I spoke against anyone going to hear another dear minister? I thank God that He has enabled me to strengthen the hands of all, though some have afterward been ashamed to own me. I declare to you that I believe God will be with me and strengthen me. I believe it is in answer to your prayers that

God is pleased to revive my spirit. May the Lord help you to keep praying.

If I am drowned in the waves, I will say while drowning, "Lord, take care of my London friends. Take care of my English friends. Let nothing pluck them out of Your hands."

And since Christ has given us eternal life, some of you, I do not doubt, will be gone to Him before I return. But never mind that. We will part, but it will be to meet again forever. I dare not meet you personally now. I cannot bear your coming to me to part from me. It cuts me to the heart and overcomes me. But before long, all parting will be over, and all tears shall be wiped away from our eyes.

God grant that none who weep now at my parting may weep at our meeting at the day of judgment. And if you have never been among Christ's sheep before, may Christ Jesus bring you now.

O come, come and see what it is to have eternal life. Do not refuse it. Hurry, sinner, hurry away to Christ. May the great and good Shepherd draw your soul. If you have never heard His voice before, may God grant that you hear it now. Then I may have this comfort when I am gone, as I had the last time I left you, that some souls were awakened at the parting sermon.

O that this may be a farewell sermon to you in the best sense. May it be the means of your saying farewell to the world, farewell to the lust of the flesh, farewell to the lust of the eyes, and farewell to the pride of life. Come, come, come to the Lord Jesus Christ. To Him I leave you.

And you, dear sheep, who are already in His hands, may God keep you from wandering. May God keep you near Christ's feet. I do not care what shepherds keep you, so long as you are kept near the great Shepherd and Bishop of souls.

The Lord God keep you. May He lift up the light of His countenance upon you and give you peace.

Amen.

About the author

Tom Flores

Tom Flores is an author, speaker, and pastor of Elevate Life Church in California. He holds a master's degree in Biblical Studies. For over 40 years Tom Flores has studied the lives of influential men and women of God and the spiritual movements that shaped Christianity throughout the centuries. He is especially passionate about preserving powerful Christian voices from the past and helping a new generation connect with timeless biblical truths.

For speaking engagements or other resources please visit :

www.tomflores.com

www.ingramcontent.com/pod-product-compliance
Lightning Source LLC
Chambersburg PA
CBHW052002110726
47973CB00041B/270/J

9798994282892